Problems
of International
Justice

Problems of International Justice

EDITED BY

Steven Luper-Foy

WESTVIEW PRESS
Boulder and London

Copyright © 1988 by Westview Press, Inc.

Published in 1988 in the United States of America by Westview Press, Inc., 5500 Central Avenue, Boulder, Colorado 80301

Library of Congress Cataloging-in-Publication Data
Problems of international justice.
    Includes index.
    1. International relations.   2. International
organization.   3. Justice.   I. Luper-Foy, Steven.
JX1391.P76   1988   327.1'1   87-13570
ISBN 0-8133-0392-3
ISBN 0-8133-0393-1 (pbk.)

Printed and bound in the United States of America

∞   The paper used in this publication meets the requirements of the American National
    Standard for Permanence of Paper for Printed Library Materials Z39.48-1984.

10   9   8   7   6   5   4   3   2   1

For Susann

Contents

Preface

That kings should philosophize or philosophers become kings is not to be expected. Nor is it to be wished, since the possession of power inevitably corrupts the untrammeled judgment of reason. But kings or kinglike peoples which rule themselves under laws of equality should not suffer the class of philosophers to disappear or to be silent, but should let them speak openly. This is indispensable to the enlightenment of the business of government.
—Immanuel Kant, *Perpetual Peace*

Reflection on the requirements of justice among the various national communities is rudimentary and unsophisticated as compared with thought about justice within states. Little has been written on the former topic until recent years, aside from an occasional attempt to defend just statecraft as a way to end the brutality among nation-states, such as in 1795 when Immanuel Kant published *Perpetual Peace*. The attitude toward international affairs has changed little since the Peloponnesian Wars. As Thucydides records in *The Melian Debate*, the Athenians, in attempting to persuade a Spartan colony called Melos to submit to Athenian rule, said,

We will not go out of our way to prove at length that we have a right to rule . . . or that we attack you now because we are suffering any injury at your hands. . . . We both alike know that into the discussion of human affairs the question of justice only enters where there is equal power to enforce it, and that the powerful exact what they can, and the weak grant what they must.

Here the claim is that politicians do not care whether their foreign policy is just. Centuries later, Niccolò Machiavelli maintained in *The Prince* that the politician's contempt for justice is based on a prudent self-concern: "The fact is that a man who wants to act virtuously in every way necessarily comes to grief among so many who are not virtuous. Therefore if a prince wants to maintain his rule he must learn how not to be virtuous."

When the topic of international justice did arise, discussion rarely got beyond recommendations about how nations could avoid war, as well as suggestions about when a declaration of war was morally justifiable and what sorts of methods might be used in the course of a justifiable war—the topics of so-called just-war theory. Such is no longer the case.

To be sure, just-war theory is reaching greater states of sophistication, much of it focused around Michael Walzer's book *Just and Unjust Wars*. Excerpts from Walzer's book appear here, in Part Two, along with a set of newly written chapters that deal with issues arising from the use of violence among nations. The topics of these chapters are foreign interventionism and states' rights, deterrence and the threat of nuclear reprisal, and terrorism. But issues of international justice other than just-war theory have been discussed by an an ever-increasing group of twentieth-century scholars. These issues deal with what might be called (for lack of a better term) distributive justice, which concerns the distribution of the world's natural resources and the goods produced by laborers across the world, as well as the duties, rights, and liberties possessed by individuals. How such items ought to be distributed within nation-states has been discussed extensively by social and political philosophers. Only in recent years has any attention been paid to the proper distribution of goods internationally. The chapters in Part One all do so. With one exception, all of these chapters are written for this volume. The exception is an excerpt from Charles Beitz's book *Political Theory and International Relations*, Part Three of which is reproduced here almost in its entirety. The other chapters in this part are devoted to the topics of justice and the distribution of the world's resources, the obligation to assist the needy, the responsibilities of international corporations, and justice and the global environment.

In a sense, none of the preceding topics is as important as that of Part Three, which is the question of what sort of international political order there should be. A powerful centralized world government, supposing that such could be created given the present division of power among nations, might have the capacity to quickly bring about a just world order, but it would also have the ability to tyrannize on a global scale. A weak governmental order, such as a U.N.-style court of world opinion with little or no executive power, could not tyrannize, but on the other hand its capacity to effect just change might be very limited.

Half of the chapters here are critical responses to the others; this format should help readers form their own conclusions about the issues at hand. The brief introductory comments that precede each essay also might be of help. For a general introduction to the topic of just-war theory, I refer the reader to Chapter 9. In my introduction I offer a discussion of distributive justice across the globe.

Steven Luper-Foy

Acknowledgments

Several of the chapters included here were part of a symposium at Trinity University on the general topic of international justice. I am indebted to the organizations that funded the symposium—namely, the Matchette Foundation and the Texas Committee for the Humanities, a branch of the National Endowment for the Humanities. I also thank Trinity University for hosting the event, and several organizations for cosponsoring it: the National Organization of Women, the Bexar County Women's Bar Association, St. Mary's University School of Law, the Bexar County Women's Political Caucus, the San Antonio Bar Association, and the Mexican American Unity Council, Inc. Let me say finally how grateful I am to Spencer Carr for his support in this project and to Michele Junio for her skillful and patient work on the manuscript.

S. L-F.

Introduction:
Global Distributive Justice

STEVEN LUPER-FOY

Many people believe that issues of international distributive justice either do not arise or should not be allowed to arise. Anyone who takes seriously an issue such as whether justice demands that the world's goods be distributed more equitably is deluded about political realities, such as the sheer brutality of international relations, given which moral progress is simply out of the question. Niccolò Machiavelli is commonly associated with the view that politicians should focus on realpolitik, but Thomas Hobbes gave us the most interesting argument. After a word about the nature of distributive justice and its place in moral theory, I shall briefly review and reject Hobbes's argument. With the topic of international justice thus vindicated, I turn to a discussion of what distributive justice across the world demands. My method will be to outline a handful of the fairly sophisticated theories of justice that have been mapped out for societies, then tease out the implications of these theories for the world as a whole and assess the plausibility of these views. The theories I discuss (aside from Hobbes's) are those of John Rawls, Immanuel Kant, utilitarianism, and libertarianism. My assessment will then point the way toward a new conception of international justice, one that is a synthesis of previous theories. I begin, then, with a word about the place of the theory of distributive justice in moral philosophy.

MORAL THEORY AND THEORY OF JUSTICE

We all will grant that individuals and the associations they form ought to be given a great deal of freedom. People ought to be free to adopt from others or to devise for themselves values, a view of the world, and a life plan, and people ought to have as much freedom as possible to achieve their plans. Likewise, people should be free to come together to pursue goals that are (more easily) achievable through a joint effort. However, we also think that the freedom of individuals and associations ought to be limited in certain ways. Freedom is constrained by obligations.

As for what these obligations are, we might say as an approximation that people must not interfere with the actions of others who are meeting their own obligations. But this formulation is unhelpful, not only because it presupposes an independent specification of people's obligations, but also because people cannot possibly be expected to restrict themselves to ways of acting that are consistent with the plans of others who are meeting their own obligations. The problem is not just that this demand is impractical, although it is. There are too few resources and too many people with too many projects for us ever to succeed in avoiding interference. We must interfere with the pursuits of others if we are to live, just as others must interfere with ours. Even when we can avoid interference, it often is unreasonable to expect us to do so. Some people's plans are too burdensome for others to put up with, such as plans that include exorbitant expectations (for example, people might base their plans on the expectation that someone who prefers to remain single will join them in marriage).

Nor can we be expected to avoid interfering with all of those plans that do not include expectations for others. We all recognize that people's projects can impose unreasonable demands on limited natural resources (resources that are not produced by anybody). Suppose that Christopher Columbus had been the first person to set foot in (or even suggest the existence of) the New World, and suppose he claimed ownership of it along with the right to transfer ownership to his descendants (and they to theirs) through inheritance, so that he and his children could occupy the New World and use it in total isolation from everyone else. Certainly everyone else could have avoided interfering with his plan; those who were persecuted for their religious beliefs could have endured persecution rather than begin afresh in the New World, and victims of famine (such as the potato famine in Ireland) could have starved instead of seeking better land in the territory claimed by Columbus. But clearly Columbus would have been at fault, not the people he would have excluded, and they would have been above criticism if they had occupied the New World and thwarted Columbus's plans.

Once we acknowledge that interference must be tolerated, then we need an account of *legitimate* interference. One component of it would tell us how we may interfere with the lives of others in cases of conflicting life-styles. Another would deal with the distribution of the natural resources to which people make competing claims. Still another would specify legitimate ways for dealing with those who have interfered with *our* lives in impermissible ways. It would specify when and how we may resist, punish, and extract compensation from aggressors. A further component would cover our relationship to future generations. The desires of posterity have an important feature: One way to avoid interfering with the desires and needs of future generations is to avoid creating future people in the first place. Bringing them into existence creates people whose interests conflict with ours and thus subjects us to the requirement to avoid illegitimate interference with their lifestyles and their access to natural resources (by not destroying the environment, for example). Thus, our obligations toward posterity are conditional: *If we create future people,* we must not interfere illegitimately with their desires and needs.

After we provide ourselves a complete account of legitimate interference, we can say that everyone is obligated to avoid all but legitimate interference in the projects of others. However, our obligations would not end there. People also have obligations that arise from the fact that when they pursue goals as a joint effort, each voluntarily making a contribution in the expectation that the others will do so as well, they owe each other in ways they otherwise would not. They are obligated to treat their comrades-in-effort in ways they are not bound to treat those with whom they are not cooperating. Thus, in addition to an account of legitimate interference we need an account of legitimate cooperation that would specify the ingredients of legitimate schemes of cooperation, including the proper distribution of the benefits and burdens involved. We can then say that everyone is obligated to avoid all but legitimate cooperation with others.

Thus, a complete theory of morality would have two or three parts, depending on how we count. By one count there is an analysis of our obligations and an account of our freedoms, the latter resulting from the former in the sense that we are free to do anything so long as we meet our obligations. By another count, there are three parts: an account of legitimate interference, an analysis of legitimate cooperation, and an account of freedom, where again the account of freedom is fallout—so long as we restrict ourselves to legitimate interference and legitimate cooperation with others, we are free to do as we please. This schema makes it plain that we are unconditionally required to cooperate with others to the extent of avoiding interfering with their projects except in legitimate ways and that our further obligations are conditional; although we are not required to join with others in additional cooperative projects, if we choose to do so (as we will out of prudence) we must restrict ourselves to legitimate cooperation. The foregoing schema also clearly shows that our obligations limit our freedom and vice versa. Theorists who differ in how wide a scope they allow the one versus the other will defend very different theories of morality. Among the main theories of morality, utilitarianism allows the least scope to liberty while libertarianism allows the most. Just the opposite is true of the scope these two theories allow to our obligations.

The relationship between the theory of morality and the theory of justice is this: The latter is a component of the former, but exactly where the one ends and the other begins is unclear. The most helpful way to make the distinction is to say that an account of justice is that part of the theory of morality that deals with the legitimate structure of institutions. The institutions of a just nation, for example, are designed to enforce some of people's obligations on the one hand and to protect people's freedom on the other. The theory of justice details the features of these institutions. It also details the features of international or global institutions enforcing obligations and protecting freedom. The chapters of this volume are focused on international institutions, but unavoidably the authors sometimes consider institutions of nation-states as well. Indeed, theories that deal with the justness of institutions of nation-states are the most fruitful sources of ideas about the justness of global institutions. We shall investigate the implications of some of these theories as soon as we put behind us Hobbes's challenge to the very idea of international justice among hostile states.

HOBBES ON JUSTICE

Theories about the scope and nature of requirements of morality and justice range from the nihilistic contention (also called moral skepticism) that no such obligations whatever exist to the view that everyone has substantial obligations toward people even in distant countries, and even toward nonliving things such as beautiful desert tableaux. Thomas Hobbes is no skeptic, but he is notorious for defending the view that the requirements of justice are extremely limited. He maintained that these requirements extended no farther than those communities whose members find it advantageous for everyone in the group to submit to certain rules and who voluntarily take certain steps that make this conformity a requirement of justice. Those who think that the requirements of justice are minimal will want to update Hobbes's rather thin argument. Those who believe that the requirements are extensive will want to refute Hobbes's position and any updated versions of it.

An absolute sovereign is necessary if people (thought of as rational egoists) are to avoid war, according to Hobbes. For by threatening to punish severely individuals who do not honor mutually beneficial rules of conduct, the sovereign makes it irrational for anyone to break the rules. The sovereign has absolute impunity in deciding which mutually beneficial rules to make, how to construe them, and how to enforce them, but individuals nonetheless find it advantageous to abide by the sovereign's dictates because the only alternative is the horror of the state of war, in which "the life of man [is] solitary, poor, nasty, brutish and short." Moreover, the sovereign brings about a regime in which considerations of justice apply for the first time. In Hobbes's view,[1] justice consists in keeping agreements we have made with others, so long as it is rational to do so. The most important of these is our agreement to abide by the mutually beneficial rules laid down by the sovereign. Injustice consists in violating these agreements. Hence, although we have no *obligation* to subject ourselves to a sovereign—ironically, it is by consent, by a democratic process that we put ourselves into the yoke of the sovereign—it is rational to do so, and so as rational egoists we will.

The Hobbesian conception of a legitimate international regime is similar. His view here would be that people have no obligation to submit to the authority of a global sovereign, but if not doing so would bring about such strife that their lives would be "solitary, poor, nasty, brutish and short," then it would be rational to submit. If everyone joined together in submission to a sovereign, they would no longer be in a state of war among themselves and would have requirements of justice among themselves. But among nations that have not submitted to a sovereign, questions of justice do not arise.

Hobbes's conception of a legitimate regime, whether national or inter-national, is unacceptable for reasons that do not need rehearsing. However, it is tempting to view the present international situation as a Hobbesian state of war given that nations compete for scarce natural resources and that many nations strive to impose on other nations ideological principles that are incompatible with the latter's ideologies. But even if such contests amount to a kind of warfare, we would be mistaken if we concluded, Hobbes-style, that in such circumstances questions of justice are moot and that the only escape is an international absolute sovereignty. Even while we compete we must still ask whether competition for resources could be converted into sharing of resources on just terms. We also must ask whether ideological warfare—which already appeals to international justice because supporters of opposed ideologies fight in the name of worldwide justice—could be eliminated by setting up a body with the power to justly adjudicate disputes rooted in conflicting ideologies. If these questions receive affirmative answers, we then are obligated (we have what Rawls would call a "natural duty") to begin building the global order suggested by those answers.

Those who are interested in international justice ought to work out a conception of a just international order, so that any high-minded politicians who happen to come along will have an idea for which to strive. Meanwhile, it is important to avoid the mistaken Hobbesian assumption that any world government must resemble an absolute sovereignty capable of global tyranny, which is more worrisome (as Kant pointed out[2]) than tyrannies on the state level because no one could escape the reach of the global sort. It is easy to imagine a world regime with checks and balances that ensure that no governmental body has unlimited authority.

RAWLS ON JUSTICE

In addition to a Hobbesian assessment of the international order as a state of war, there is another route to the conclusion that requirements of justice within communities are much stronger than those across communities. Surprisingly, it derives from Rawls. Unfortunately, it is difficult to pin down his thoughts in this regard, and in later writings he makes it even more difficult. In one recent article he says that his concern has been to provide a conception of justice for a modern constitutional democracy only and that he wishes to leave open the question of whether justice as fairness can be extended to other forms of regime.[3] Does this entail leaving open the question of whether justice as fairness can provide a conception of international justice? A clue is provided by the importance Rawls attributes to the fact that justice as fairness originated within the traditions of a democracy and is justified as "acceptable" or "reasonable" (as opposed to "true," which, according to Rawls, carries divisive metaphysical baggage) to the extent that it is reached (or reachable) through an "overlapping consensus" of all opposing religious and philosophical traditions in society. This clue suggests that Rawls would refrain from extending his conception to societies in which a consensus failed to develop in favor of justice as fairness, such as societies with very different religious traditions. The clue suggests that he would not extend it to international affairs unless a universal consensus would uphold it. Presumably, the relevant consensus would involve the achievement of a reflective equilibrium between worldwide considered convictions and Rawls's conception. But if such a consensus really is requisite, then we must conclude that no conception of justice aside from a very weak one can be extended across any but the most homogeneous societies and that only an extremely weak conception could possibly be extended across the globe. Even Rawls's own conception of justice as fairness cannot be extended across democracies such as that in the United States where (given sixteen years of criticism of *A Theory of Justice*) it is clear that the requisite consensus is not forthcoming.

But let us leave aside such speculations and examine what Rawls says in *A Theory of Justice*. In this book he seems to suggest that requirements of justice exist only among people who are cooperating together. Like Hobbes, Rawls claims that a society is a "cooperative venture for mutual advantage" and (what is again in the spirit of Hobbes) that the role of principles of justice is to "define the appropriate distribution of the benefits and burdens of social cooperation."[4] This conception suggests that justice has no place where social cooperation does not exist, that among people who have not decided to enter into a cooperative arrangement, there is no such thing as injustice.

It is hard to believe that Rawls intended to defend such a peculiar view. The claim that requirements of justice hold only among cooperators glosses over the important distinction we made earlier between the obligations of legitimate interference and legitimate cooperation. Once this distinction is made, it is plain that whereas everyone must meet both sorts of obligation, the impact of the one sort is quite distinct from that of the other. Cooperation with others to the extent of avoiding illegitimate interference with their plans is not optional, but all other forms of legitimate cooperation are. Although one of the roles of principles of justice is to specify the appropriate distribution of the benefits and burdens of optional cooperation, this is not the only role, for there remains the specification of legitimate interference.

Consider also that it is Rawls's view that everyone is bound by what he calls the natural duties, which "apply to us without regard to our voluntary acts."[5] Natural duties "obtain between all as equal moral persons"[6] and include the duty to assist the needy, the duty to avoid harming others and causing unnecessary suffering, and "the duty of justice," which requires us "to support and to comply with just institutions that exist and apply to us. . . . It also constrains us to further just arrangements not yet established."[7]

Obviously, Rawls thinks that myriad moral requirements link us to those outside our cooperative groups. So presumably he also must think that only a subset of moral constraints hold strictly among co-members of cooperating groups, such as requirements concerning the distribution among themselves of the fruits and burdens of their particular cooperative scheme. Accordingly, (internally just) groups may keep the fruits of their labors for themselves even if they have far more than others. However, we are never told why some requirements but not others are limited to cooperators. Why, for instance, should we think that distributional requirements are restricted to cooperators? Moreover, the combination of intra- and intergroup requirements seems to have implications Rawls does not notice. For as we just saw, Rawls implies that we are required to help *set up* just cooperative schemes with others, which implies that any requirements of distributive justice that hold only among co-members of existing cooperative schemes will come to hold more widely as these groups are melded into more global cooperative arrangements. Our natural duties force us to bring about a more global order in which all of the requirements of distributive justice would take hold.[8]

However, further difficulties arise in understanding Rawls's position vis-à-vis international justice. His defense of his principles of natural duty and intrasocietal justice is quite distinct from the defense he suggests for principles of international justice, and there is very little by way of explanation for this difference. Given the importance of the difference, Rawls's failure to explain himself is most unfortunate.

Consider Rawls's method for selecting the most just way of arranging the main social and political institutions of a society whose citizens are willing and able to act justly. The method consists in (a) assigning each citizen in society a representative in the hypothetical situation Rawls calls the original position and (b) working out the selection those representatives would make. The preferable conception of justice from the standpoint of the original position, according to Rawls, consists of the following two principles, the first of which must be fully implemented before the second:

1. Each person is to have an equal right to the most extensive total system of liberty for all (the liberty principle).
2. Social and economic inequalities are to be arranged so that they are (a) to the greatest benefit of the least advantaged (the difference principle) and (b) are attached to offices and positions open to all under conditions of fair equality of opportunity.[9]

Rawls's main concern is intrasocietal, not intersocietal, justice. Nonetheless, in the course of an inquiry into conscientious refusal,[10] he discusses the requirements of justice for the law of nations and suggests a rather different procedure for working these out. In considering conceptions of justice for nation-states, Rawls considers the best to be the one chosen in the original position by citizens' representatives. But in selecting the best conception on the international level, he suggests that entire societies rather than individual citizens be represented in the original position. Given this method of choice, the best alternative conception of international justice, according to Rawls, includes a principle of equality stating that nations have certain equal rights; a principle of self-determination stating that nations have a right to determine their affairs without outside intervention; a principle specifying that each nation has the right of self-defense; and a principle stating that treaties must be honored that are consistent with the other principles of international justice. Finally, there are various principles limiting the means to which a nation may resort in the course of defending itself. (For doubts about Rawls's list, see Charles Beitz's discussion in the first chapter of this book.) A striking fact about this vision of international justice is that it does not call for substantial redistributions of goods from one nation to another, yet within particular nations a substantial equality of goods must be achieved in order to meet the demands of the difference principle. Thus, a fully just international order is entirely consistent with great inequalities across nations. The least well-off in one nation in a just order may be worse off than those in another nation, for Rawls's conception of international justice lacks a principle of equality such as the difference principle.

Rawls's proposed theories of national and international justice are subject to various sorts of criticism. One problem with Rawls's method of selecting principles of justice for society is that once again it glosses over the distinction between the obligation to avoid illegitimate interference, which dictates that everyone across the world must join into some sort of fairly minimal cooperative association, and the obligation to limit ourselves to legitimate forms of cooperation, which does not. It is reasonable to adopt a limited version of "justice as fairness" and say that the obligation to avoid illegitimate interference amounts to the obligation to limit ourselves to a fair scheme of interference identified using the apparatus of the original position. Our freedom should be restricted to that extent. Unfortunately, representatives in the original position will restrict our freedom far too much if, like Rawls, we turn over to them the task of deciding on the principles of legitimate cooperation for the basic structure of society. They clearly will require citizens to make contributions that benefit the worst-off, as indeed the difference principle does,[11] thus taking away the freedom to opt instead for a scheme of cooperation that does not benefit the worst-off but that nonetheless is initiated and continued by people who are fully informed about its workings and who freely choose to participate. Given that we are constrained morally to cooperate according to a scheme of legitimate interference, the original-position apparatus is far more plausible as a method of characterizing what such a scheme must be. Much can be said in favor of applying the difference principle in the adjudication of conflicting claims on the world's natural resources and in favor of applying something like the principle of liberty in the resolution of conflicting life-styles—that is, by working out compromises that require all of us to modify our plans as little as possible.

Even if we accept Rawls's account of societal justice, we are not committed to his view on international justice. To begin with, notice that unless we require them to ignore the question of the distribution of goods (say because these matters are to be decided at an earlier phase), then, as Beitz argues in Chapter 2, national representatives in the original position clearly would adopt a far more robust set of principles of international justice than that envisioned by Rawls. These representatives would want to redistribute both shares in natural resources as well as goods produced by relatively well-off nations, even if they assumed that nations are entirely self-contained. Self-containment, after all, does not entail self-sufficiency, and the representatives would realize that some nations might be unable to meet their basic needs.

More fundamentally, we must decide whether to select principles of international justice as Rawls suggests—namely, in an original position occupied by representatives of entire societies—or whether to select them in something more like the *original* original position, which is occupied by representatives of individual people. One consideration in favor of the latter is the fact that Rawls's approach gives us no way to deal with conflicts between the basic rights and liberties granted to citizens of one nation and those granted to citizens of other nations. Such conflicts are inevitable given that in Rawls's plan the representatives in the original position are to ignore the existence of other nations and hence will grant rights that are incompatible with the existence of a crowded world. For example, these representatives might advocate highly unrestricted fishing and property rights, which would be workable only if the world's population were small enough and there were far more territory available to each person. These conflicts are unresolvable on Rawls's tack because decisions made in the *original* original position (in which other nations are ignored) must be taken for granted by the representatives deciding on international justice.[12]

Another argument against Rawls's plan of settling the issues of intranational justice in isolation from and prior to those of international justice is that Rawls's theory arbitrarily assumes that a just global order will include autonomous nations as chief components. His theory also arbitrarily sets the scope of virtually all the requirements of distributive justice at the national level because those requirements are determined by representatives who ignore the possible needs of people in other nations. Even if all the requirements dealing with the distribution of the benefits and burdens of cooperation (as opposed to other constraints such as natural duties) were limited in scope to cooperating groups, which Rawls may believe, there would be no reason to focus on the national level because it is certainly possible (and arguably entirely permissible) for subcommunities within nations to refuse to join the cooperative enterprise of others in the nation. It is also possible for there to be cooperating groups that include several nations (for example, the European Economic Community) and groups that cut across national boundaries (such as Greenpeace and multinational corporations).

It is difficult to see how Rawls could defend the view that natural duties and principles for the basic structure of society should be selected in the *original* original position without contending that other moral principles should also be selected there, including ones that describe the basic structure of a just global order. If it is there that we decide on the significance of city, county, regional, and state boundaries and conclude, for example, that the difference principle extends to people regardless of those boundaries and that people within such boundaries do not have political sovereignty over themselves or the right to determine who will be allowed to settle in their communities, why should it not be there that we decide on the significance of national boundaries? Given that the communities within city and state boundaries would be granted so little autonomy by the representatives in the original position, it is unlikely that the representatives would want to bring about a global order of autonomous nations.

KANT ON JUSTICE

So far we have explored ways to support the claim that the requirements of international justice are rather minimal compared to the demands within nation-states. But of course there are strong arguments suggesting that no such disparity exists. Some arguments do so by concluding that the demands of justice on the international and national levels are both quite substantial, others by concluding that neither is. Let us consider two arguments of the first sort, one Kantian and one utilitarian, and then one of the second sort, namely a libertarian one.

It is useful to begin with Kant's view because Rawls considers his theory to be Kantian yet believes that there is a disparity in strength between the demands of justice on the national versus international levels. As is well known, Kant's moral conception is summed up in his categorical imperative. However, the categorical imperative is given more than one formulation and two of them are quite distinct in content although Kant seems to believe that the three are equivalent. The greatest discrepancy comes between the "universal law" and the "end in itself" formulations, which are so distinct as to inspire substantially distinct conclusions.

According to the universal law formulation, it is permissible to act as we intend only if our intention (the "maxim" behind our action) is universalizable in a certain sense. The exact nature of that sense is highly controversial; what follows is an interpretation that draws on writings by Rawls.[13]

In order to determine if the maxim behind our planned act is universalizable in the relevant sense, we must perform a thought experiment. We must work out the *world our maxim yields*, that is, the world as it would be if (a) everyone acted from our maxim as if by a psychological law and (b) the fact that everyone did so was public knowledge.[14] In Kant's view,[15] our maxim is universalizable if and only if neither of two "contradictions" occurs: First, there is no contradiction in "conception," meaning that in the world our maxim yields, circumstances would continue to arise in which individuals might find themselves acting from the maxim. Second, there is no contradiction in "will," meaning that we could meet the needs and goals we have strictly as rational beings if we were part of the world yielded by our maxim.

That Kant requires the possibility of our meeting needs of some sort in the world described in the preceding thought experiment is suggested by his discussion of the maxim of indifference. While considering someone who decides never to harm anyone but also never to "contribute anything to [anyone's] well-being," Kant notes that "although it is possible that a universal law of nature could subsist in harmony with this maxim, yet it is impossible to *will* that such a principle should hold everywhere as a law of nature. For [the will of a person who] decided in this way would be in conflict with itself, since many a situation might arise in which the [person] needed love and sympathy from others."[16]

The needs Kant speaks of—love and sympathy—seem peculiar to human beings. Is there a way to reconcile the importance Kant attributes to them with his claims that "duty has to be a practical, unconditioned necessity of action; it must therefore hold for all rational beings,"[17] and "everything that is empirical is, as a contribution to the principle of morality . . . wholly unsuitable"?[18] There is. We need only attribute to Kant the view that all rational beings by their very nature have the desire to (become and) remain happy and rational. Consistently with this desire, rational beings cannot choose to bring about a law of nature that precludes their (becoming and) remaining happy and rational. Human beings, Kant thinks, require love and sympathy in order to be happy and rational.

My interpretation of Kant is easy to substantiate. That he thought all rational creatures necessarily want to (become and) remain rational is suggested by his claim that "rational nature exists as an end in itself. Ths is the way in which [every rational being] necessarily conceives his own existence."[19] Moreover, Kant is explicit in saying that rational beings by their nature wish to be happy: "There is . . . *one* end that can be presupposed as actual in all rational beings . . . and thus there is one purpose which . . . they all *do* have by a natural necessity—the purpose, namely, of *happiness*."[20] Nonetheless, although rational creatures necessarily want to be happy, there is not much determinate content to their notion of happiness; they want to be happy, but there is an indefinite number of things in which their happiness could consist: "The concept of happiness is so indeterminate . . . that although every man wants to attain happiness, he can never say definitely . . . what it really is that he wants and wills."[21] Thus, the rational person's goal of happiness must not be understood as the desire to achieve happiness of a specific sort (such as the accomplishment of a particular specified life plan), but rather as the desire to achieve happiness of one form or another. Kant's ban on maxims that produce contradictions in "will" must be read in light of this discussion. A contradiction of the "will" occurs if and only if in the world yielded by our maxim we could not become and remain rational beings who achieve happiness of one form or another.

So interpreted, Kant's moral theory unfortunately generates inconsistencies and thus yields no clear implications concerning the character and relative strength of principles of justice on the national versus the international levels. (Moreover, it falls far short of motivating strong duties, which Kant defends, such as the duty of beneficence, which requires us to adopt the happiness of others as an end.) First, note that people in relatively poor nations would favor bringing about a global order in which everyone acts from the maxim that goods should be fairly equally distributed (call this the maxim of equity). After all, if the poor came to be part of the world yielded by this maxim, they would greatly improve their chances of becoming and remaining happy and rational. However, people in rich nations would not favor the maxim of equity. In fact, such citizens would endorse a maxim of inequity, according to which wide disparities are tolerated, because being part of the world yielded by this maxim allows *them* to become and remain happy, rational beings.

A second and related inconsistency arises. People in France (say) could refuse to provide aid to those in other nations because the French could become and remain happy and rational were they part of a global order in which everyone acted from the maxim that all and only French people are to receive aid. The French could justify principles of international justice requiring that all nations of the world help the French and only the French. Moreover, because granting nations autonomy in the determination of their own affairs would allow nations other than France to resist helping the French, then the French could adopt principles of international justice that grant autonomy only to France and that endow a strong and Francophilic international government with the power to overcome such resistance. On the other hand, people in Spain could use Kant's apparatus to justify principles of international justice requiring that all nations of the world help the Spanish and only the Spanish.

Kant's view can be relieved of these intolerable inconsistencies by adding to it a piece of apparatus borrowed from Rawls.[22] Suppose that neither the rich nor the poor know what their situation would be in the world yielded by the maxim of inequity. They do not know whether they will end up living in a poor country or in a wealthy one. Neither the wealthy nor the poor would endorse such a world because in it they might find themselves unable to become and remain happy and rational.

Hence, Kant's account can be repaired by altering Kant's requirement that no contradiction in "will" occur. We can understand it as the injunction that *even if we were situated behind a veil of ignorance* we would find becoming part of the world yielded by our maxim consistent with our goal of becoming and remaining happy, rational beings. That is, we must find entering that world consistent with our goal *even though we do not know where in that world we will be.* Better yet, Kant's injunction could be read as the requirement that *everyone* in the world yielded by our maxim can become and remain happy and rational.

Thus revised, Kant's account favors a rather equitable distribution of goods across the entire world. This account provides no reason whatever to select national boundaries or membership in cooperative schemes as the limits to concerns about the distribution of goods. Likewise, this account provides no reason to grant nations sovereignty. However, other aspects of Kant's position complicate matters. Recall that he provides a second formulation of the categorical imperative that is quite different from the first:

"Act in such a way that you always treat humanity, whether in your own person or in the person of any other, never simply as a means, but always at the same time as an end."[23] This second formulation is vague enough to support arguments for *and* against egalitarianism.

In his discussion of the second formulation, Kant made it clear that it is not enough to avoid treating people simply as a means. We must treat them as ends, which, he appears to have thought, also prevents us from treating anyone as a mere means. To treat people as mere means is to use them as a means toward an end they do not share;[24] it is "deliberately impairing their happiness."[25] To treat others as ends is to pursue ends they can share,[26] to adopt "humanity as an end in itself" by attempting, as far as possible, "to further the ends of others."[27]

If the second formulation is the requirement that we are to do our best to further the ends of others, it is like the first in demanding a substantially equitable distribution of the world's goods. If all of us are committed to adopting and pursuing the ends of others "as far as possible," we will certainly give everyone a roughly equal share in the means necessary to people's goals. However, the second formulation also demands that people never get used as mere means, and it is by no means clear that instituting equity is consistent with never treating people as mere means.

The point is this: Aside from extreme altruists, to require people to do their best to adopt and further the ends of others *is* to use them as a means toward ends they do not share and it *is* to impair their happiness! Requiring us to deal with others as ends ensures our not using *them* as mere means; however, Kant may not have noticed that imposing this requirement on us guarantees that *we* are used as a mere means. He may not have realized that requiring everyone to treat others as ends entails using everyone as a mere means. If he *did* realize this and meant the second formulation to permit the use of people as means in the course of treating others as ends, then he must have thought that using us as mere means for others is all right because others are treating *us* as ends (although getting used as well). Left unexplained is why Kant did not think it enough that no one gets used at all. Presumably the explanation is that the *first* formulation requires us to treat people as ends (although it does not require furthering their ends as far as *possible*) because the universalizability of our maxims entails their yielding a world in which everyone is happy and rational. Unfortunately, this explanation simply draws our attention to the fact that anyone who denies the permissibility of using others as mere means must reject Kant's first formulation.

My discussion of Kant's second formulation helps us sort through a famous controversy between John Rawls and Robert Nozick. Rawls argues that his brand of egalitarianism, as expressed by his difference principle, treats people as ends by accepting social advantages only when they are to the benefit of everyone in society; treating people as mere means is to force them to accept disadvantages for the sake of the greater good of others.[28] Nozick, on the other hand, provides a single criterion for treating people as ends and not simply as means, namely, never using them "for the achieving of other ends without their consent."[29] Therefore, forcibly taking from the wealthy and giving to the poor in order to eliminate an inequitable distribution of goods that arose through voluntary exchanges uses the wealthy as mere means.

In my view Rawls has not shown that his difference principle never treats people as mere means. Forcing those who wish to raise their situation above the baseline of equality to do so only if they can find a way that simultaneously improves the prospects of the least well-off is indeed to treat them as ends (on his criterion). However, forcing them to do this also imposes on them "lower prospects of life for the sake of the higher expectations of others," which conforms to Rawls's own criterion of use as mere means. Some people are forced to forego improving their situation through methods that are inconsistent with maximizing the well-being of others. It seems evident that any method of achieving an equal distribution of goods will have the same fault.

I conclude that there is strong reason to think that two of Kant's formulations of the categorical imperative sanction considerably distinct global (and social) arrangements. The first formulation (repaired along the lines suggested previously) requires equity while the second does this only if we eliminate its ban on using people as mere means. Moreover, I would suggest that this ban articulates a deep moral truth. The role of the requirements of legitimate interference is to prevent us from using each other as mere means; to interfere illegitimately with the plans of others is to act as if their interests could be sacrificed for the sake of ours. But to force those who scrupulously honor the requirements of legitimate interference to contribute the fruits of their labor toward the well-being of others is also to act as if the former's interests can be sacrificed for the sake of others. Our autonomy ought to extend to decisions about when and toward what (and whom) we shall contribute our time, effort, and, if it comes to it, our lives.

UTILITARIANISM AND JUSTICE

Classical utilitarianism resolves any issue on the basis of a single general principle: The best, most just arrangement, the one we are obligated to bring about, is the one that would produce the greatest total amount of happiness or satisfaction in the long run.[30] If this principle of utility is correct, then the world is very unjust indeed, and considerable redistribution should take place. Utilitarians such as Peter Singer claim that in a world in which some people are suffering terribly while others are well-off, the more fortunate are dutybound to sacrifice in order to improve the situation of the less fortunate up to the point at which any further sacrifices would make the misery of the former equal to that of the latter, this being the way to maximize the total happiness in the world.[31]

Such odious sacrifices are not mere charity. Utilitarians cannot make sense of a notion of doing good that is above and beyond the call of duty because doing as much good as possible *is* everyone's duty. The utilitarian would even insist that people in no position to help others are morally obligated to maximize their *own* happiness. The enormous implausibility of this contention should lead us to reject utilitarianism, for if we are not morally obligated to maximize our *own* happiness, how can we possibly be required to maximize that of others? (Similarly with Rawls's difference principle: The least well-off are not bound to maximize their own prospects, so justice cannot require the maximization of their well-being.)

Clearly, utilitarianism is much more demanding than is the universalization construction of Kant; that construction would certainly impose some limits on the amount of good we are required to do for others.[32] A fortiori, the utilitarian is prepared to violate Kant's injunction against using people as mere means.[33] Indeed, given that Rawls's theory violates Kant's injunction, it is ironic that Rawls believes the central defect of utilitarianism to be that it does not ensure that "the greater gains of some should not compensate for the lesser losses of others."[34] Nevertheless, by assigning priority to the principle of liberty over the difference principle, he ensures that no one's basic liberties are sacrificed for the sake of the greater economic welfare of others, which remains a distinct possibility under the utilitarian scheme.[35]

One of the main concerns about utilitarianism is that it assigns value to the liberties (such as the freedoms of thought, conscience, speech, association, movement) only insofar as they help create the maximal amount of happiness, which in certain situations may not be much value. J. S. Mill was worried enough about the undervaluation of liberty to devote one of his last essays, *On Liberty*, to defending the libertarian claim that an individual's freedom may be restricted only toward the end of preventing harm to others. Impressive as Mill's arguments are, however, he does virtually nothing to base this principle on the principle of utility. Even today, about the only utilitarian consideration against creating a highly paternalistic society run by a centralized technocratic government on the basis of "scientific" evidence about how best to make people happy is J. S. Mill's argument that people themselves know best what will make them happy.

The utilitarian view does not merely require that people sacrifice for those who are in great need. Even if everyone in the world had at least enough goods to live decent but modest lives, there could be great discrepancies in the amount of goods each person held. In response, utilitarians argue that given the phenomenon of declining marginal utility, any departure from an equal distribution of goods among individuals across the world is very likely to decrease the total amount of happiness and satisfaction, and so will need special defense. An example of such a defense is the neo-Malthusian argument that if a more equitable distribution of goods only enabled the world's starving to produce so many offspring that they outstrip all existing food sources, and hence initiate an even greater round of starvation and misery, then on utilitarian grounds we should avoid equity.[36] Thus, it is incumbent on utilitarian defenders of equity to either rebut the neo-Malthusian claim or link aid to the needy to some sort of birth control program and to address the issue of whether coercion or deception (such as providing food containing a concealed drug that causes sterilization) should be used if the needy are willing to take the aid offered but refuse to adopt any birth control policy.

Additional difficulties faced by utilitarianism concern the relative importance of the happiness of people vis-à-vis that of animals and of autonomy compared to happiness. According to utilitarians, whether a creature is due moral consideration depends entirely on its capacity to produce pleasure (or satisfy desires). Therefore, all creatures capable of producing the same amount of pleasure as human beings (whether individually or collectively) are equal to people in value. Resistance to this conclusion must be attributed by utilitarians to bigotry, to "speciesism" (to borrow a term made famous by Singer[37]). Such considerations made utilitarians (notably Jeremy Bentham) the earliest defenders of animal rights. But although it is indeed plausible to say that animals have certain rights (such as the right not to be tortured), the utilitarian view attributes too much importance to animals. It implies that (other things being equal) in a situation in which one or the other must die, a group of animals that is capable of producing more pleasure than a human being must be given priority. This implication is even less plausible than the contention that when one or the other human being must die the person who is capable of greater happiness must live.[38]

Nor would it be acceptable to use surgical or genetic engineering techniques to produce a group of human beings who would derive great pleasure from being the slaves of others. Producing such people is unacceptable even if the total amount of happiness and desire satisfaction would be increased. We value people's authority so much that we would not consider such a policy.[39]

Doubts about the acceptability of utilitarianism abound; I have referred to only some of them. But let us put these aside and sum up what implications the utilitarian view would have for global justice. Because it is so strongly egalitarian, utilitarianism would require a great deal of redistribution of the world's goods, including natural resources, technological expertise, and manufactured commodities. Utilitarianism also would favor short-term sacrifices by all for massive projects that no individual would dream of attempting, such as worldwide provisions for health care, communications, agriculture, and transportation. This view would not allow others to stand by while starvation and curable disease run rampant, but would require that those who are in a position to help do so and continue to do so until further sacrifices render the helpers as much in need as those they have helped. Obviously, many people would not be willing to make such sacrifices, but the utilitarian has no objection in principle to coercion and would favor a very strong centralized world government that would have the power to achieve such egalitarian aims. The world government would also be sizable, so as to oversee grand projects designed to increase the total happiness of people; to enforce the sorts of paternalistic laws that people often resist, such as bans on drugs and alcohol; and to promulgate other laws dreamed up by "experts" on human happiness, who may adopt various views on who ought to marry whom, who must and must not have children, and how children must and must not be reared.

The present order of sovereign nation-states would no doubt be revised dramatically. First, geographical boundaries are of no moral significance to the utilitarian; at best some boundaries (such as borders along oceans and mountains) are convenient places to divide up the world for administrative purposes, and at worst other boundaries only help foster feelings of nationalism, which interfere with people's ability to identify with the happiness of everyone in general and no one in particular. Second, national autonomy is no more important to the utilitarian than is individual autonomy. To grant each nation sovereignty over its own affairs is to bring about an inevitable situation in which some nations insist on pursuing their own nonutilitarian visions, which would prevent the world government from bringing about the order that its experts deem necessary to maximize the total happiness.

LIBERTARIANISM AND JUSTICE

Perhaps the strongest case against egalitarian conceptions of justice is made by libertarians such as Robert Nozick. Nozick claims that individual rights are inviolable; their nonviolation is a "side constraint" on action in that we may not violate them even if doing so would lead to a situation in which violations were less frequent.[40] Side constraints exist because people are (in Kant's phrase) ends, not mere means; therefore, it is not permissible to sacrifice or use people toward a goal without their consent,[41] even if that goal is the good of others. Forcing people to aid others (by say, taxing the relatively well-off in order to help the needy) turns them into mere means in spite of the fact that others benefit. Thus, in effect, Nozick uses Kant against Kant; Nozick appeals to the second formulation of the categorical imperative in order to reject the principle of mutual aid that is justifiable using the first formulation.

Even if requiring people to contribute the fruits of their labor to others is ruled out, it does not follow that some holdings may not be transferred; these may be shares in natural resources, which are not produced by anyone.[42] Actually, almost all holdings are likely to be neither purely the fruits of an individual's labor nor natural resources but rather a combination of the two— that is, the product of the application of labor to the provisions of nature. Thus, the case against redistribution is not complete as yet.

Nozick advanced a separate argument, however, against the view that states may redistribute goods (whether natural resources or the fruits of labor) in pursuit of equity (although he would also say that redistributing the fruits of people's labor in pursuit of equity is out of bounds because it treats people as mere means). He maintains that only a minimal state is legitimate inasmuch as more extensive states violate people's rights. A minimal state is one with a de facto monopoly on the use of force in a region and whose function is limited essentially to the protection of the rights of those living in that region. In particular, a state will violate people's rights and is therefore too extensive if it redistributes goods for the purpose of achieving equity or virtually any other pattern of distribution—except with everyone's consent.

A complete defense of this view would require that Nozick provide a clear account of rights, so that we can see that some must be violated by a greater than minimal state. Nozick declines to give such a theory. However, it would suffice for Nozick's purposes that people have the right to engage in all of the "capitalistic acts between consenting adults"[43] they choose, as Nozick believes—that is, that they have the right to keep any goods that have been legitimately and voluntarily transferred to them, such as an inheritance, and the right to give such goods away, such as in exchange for services rendered, out of love for another, or (monklike) out of abhorrence for worldly possessions.

To see how these rights must be violated by any state that sustains a pattern of distribution such as equality, let us imagine that you and I are in a state that has achieved its favored pattern of distribution and hence are entitled to our present set of goods. If I give some of my goods to you (or throw them away), say in exchange for a different quantity of goods or for some set of services from you, then I will have destroyed the pattern. The only way to preserve the pattern is to prevent such pattern-breaking exchanges from occurring, thus violating my right to give goods away and your right to keep what has been voluntarily transferred to you, or else to constantly intervene by taking from the holdings of other people (violating their rights) and transferring those goods elsewhere.

This argument appears to be stronger than it is, however, for we have ignored the sketch Nozick gives of legitimate acquisition of holdings. Here he borrows from John Locke's *Treatise.* Locke thought it better that originally God, being the creator of the world, owned everything and had political jurisdiction over everyone. He subsequently gave the world to humankind as community property.[44] But, according to Locke, God must have intended to allow for private property because people must have it in order to survive and God has made it apparent that we are to survive. Hence, people may acquire some of those items as private property. People may do so by mixing their labor with those items as long as the act of acquisition leaves "enough and as good for others"[45]—so that the situation of others is not worsened— and as long as they do not waste the items (of which God would disapprove). The system of private property, according to Locke, was and will remain in everyone's interest; otherwise he presumably would have said that the world's resources—land, minerals, wild animals—would one day revert back to common ownership. As others have noticed,[46] this is a primitive theory of fairness applied to property acquisition, one that is entirely consistent with of Rawls's difference principle.

From this beginning Nozick develops what amounts to a theory of fair property acquisition of his own. He borrows the view that we may acquire a hitherto unowned item so long as in doing so we do not worsen the situation of others (except by limiting their opportunities to appropriate things[47]), which condition he terms the Lockean proviso. Nozick also claims that the system of private property is in everyone's interest, and he presumably would say that if that system ever worsened people's situations, then property rights would be voided. Thus, according to his view, I may acquire one of several water holes in a desert and exclude others from using it without worsening anyone's position because other sources of water remain, but I lose my rights if all of the other water holes subsequently dry up.

Suppose that Columbus and his crew had been the very first to set foot in the New World. Perhaps they could have divided it all up for themselves and for their descendants without worsening the situation of anyone else except in the sense of limiting others' opportunities to appropriate. However, in Nozick's theory neither they nor their descendants could bar from the New World other people whose lives depended on having land, any more than I and my descendants could exclude others from the single desert water hole. For the same sort of reason that I would lose the right to own the desert water hole, presumably Columbus's descendants would lose their claim to the land passed on to them once the world's population became so great that the need for land was great. Land is a necessity of life, and no person or group of people may possess it all and exclude the rest. Similar reasoning applies to other essential resources. At best, then, Nozick's theory of acquisition justifies the temporary private ownership of the world's resources when people are so few and the resources so abundant that everyone can have as much as he or she needs. Nozick's theory cannot legitimate permanent transferable property rights. (If it did, the United States would owe a lot—not just land—to the descendants of the Indians who were in the New World first![48]) If his theory has any implications for today's situation in which nearly 5 billion people vie for as great a share as possible, it would appear to be that the world's resources are owned by no one.[49]

Moreover, once we see Nozick's theory as a theory of fair property acquisition, it can be criticized if it turns out to be unfair. Clearly, it would be unfair if it implied that the only people who may directly benefit from ownership of the world's resources are those lucky enough to have inherited a share.

It is apparent, then, that libertarians have a great deal of work left to do before they can present an adequate theory of legitimate interference, including an account of how to adjudicate our conflicting claims on the world's resources. The libertarians' stronger suit is presumably their theory of legitimate cooperation, which holds essentially that aside from honoring the rights granted to others by the requirements of legitimate interference, our obligations are limited to those agreements we have made that are above board in the sense of involving no deception or coercion. Therefore, we are free to withhold from, give to, or exchange with others our labor and goods. According to this view, it is unjust to require people to work toward the welfare of others—unjust, that is, to use taxation to forcibly transfer the fruits of people's labors, which, Nozick suggests, treats people as mere means. Therefore, although the libertarian theory of legitimate interference has (unintended) redistributive implications, the libertarian theory of legitimate cooperation does not.

Needless to say, libertarians would be no more tolerant of mandatory redistribution of the fruits of labor on the global level than on the national level. There, as on the national level, the minimal state would be the only justifiable regime, although this is compatible with a range of governmental forms. Thus, the global arrangement might be one in which subcommunities of people are largely self-governing but answerable to a central authority, which ensures that no communities can annex other communities or their members or property, and which adjudicates intercommunity disputes.

Nevertheless, it is important to notice that while libertarians take a jaundiced view of intercommunity redistribution, they are far more tolerant with respect to particular subcommunities within the nation; the latter "may have many restrictions unjustifiable on libertarian grounds."[50] Presumably, a similar claim could be made if the minimal state were implemented across the globe, so that it presides over many subcommunities. One of the paradoxes of democracy is that people may democratically make themselves the subjects of a totalitarian regime; Hobbes had such a process in mind when he suggested that people would agree unanimously to subject themselves to the sovereign. Global libertarianism would allow such totalitarian regimes to come about; a libertarian global state would allow people to form any group of communities they wished to on any terms they preferred so long as remaining a member of the community were not compulsory. Thus, so long as a group of people unanimously preferred an egalitarian community with mandatory redistribution through taxation, they could set one up and require everyone in the community to submit to the arrangement or leave and join some other community more to their liking (if one is available) or attempt to attract others to join them in starting one up. No one's rights would be violated. Moreover, the right to leave also ensures that the terms of association for a community will not be draconian because such a community would be abandoned. But while any sort of community may be initiated, existing ones may not change their terms of association without compensating dissenters.[51] In effect, then, Nozick is suggesting that the foreign policy of the libertarian and classical liberal ought to be one of toleration of most types of national government so long as they allow their citizens to emigrate and compensate citizens who dissent from radical changes in national policy.

Because people have a wide range of preferences, values, and visions of the good life, which are more easily realized in some sorts of associations than in others, and because a diversity of types of community enables the discovery of what sorts are best for which people, it is likely that within a global minimal state a wide range of communities would develop, each with its own terms of association. According to Nozick, such a situation would be as close to utopian as is possible in the actual world.

CONCLUSION

We are obligated to cooperate with others to the extent of avoiding illegitimate interference with their projects. This claim, variously stated, has been the main emphasis of libertarians and is certainly correct. But our obligations do not end there. Although it is entirely up to us whether to engage in further cooperative schemes for mutual advantage, we are obligated to restrict ourselves to legitimate ones. Moreover, libertarians have not provided an adequate account of legitimate interference; especially salient is their failure to provide an adequate account of how natural resources may legitimately be acquired. The upshot (ignoring acquisition through violence) is that through a policy resembling "first come, first served" these resources get acquired, and they get transferred down to future generations without regard to fairness. Those with control of natural resources can (as Marx famously says) exploit the labor of those with none because the latter must get access to these goods and must do so on any terms set by the former. On the global level, this means that resource-poor nations cannot complain, on grounds of justice, that they find themselves at the mercy of resource-rich ones. The former must accept whatever exploitation or charity comes their way or make do with domestic resources. Resource-poor nations have the right, however, to set any social goals that are achievable using available resources and may even require redistribution through taxation as long as dissenters are compensated and allowed to leave.

In spite of Rawls's demurrals, his theory, like Kant's (construed as universalizing) and like utilitarianism, requires an end to substantial global inequities of resources. Unfortunately, these theories also require massive redistribution in order to alleviate inequities in virtually all types of distributable goods, including the fruits of labor. Thus, these theories also favor societies and an international order that treat some of those who meet the requirements of noninterference as a mere means by forcing them to add their labor to social schemes designed to benefit other people.

The libertarian view is inadequate because it suggests that we have more liberty than we do. On the other hand, the Kantian, Rawlsian, and utilitarian views all restrict our liberty too much. I suggest that we would reach a far better conception of justice if we adopted a Kantian-Rawlsian conception of legitimate interference and a rather libertarian conception of legitimate cooperation. When we find our life plans clashing, in fairness we ought to resolve our disputes in favor of a scheme that allows us to pursue our individual plans to the greatest extent possible. In settling on the proper distribution of shares in the world's natural goods, fairness calls for equality unless inequality is to the advantage of the least well-off—such is the result of seeking a conception of legitimate interference using the apparatus of the original position. Sharing the world's natural resources alleviates the kind of exploitation described by Marx. But to require people to add their labor to projects designed to benefit others is to institute another type of exploitation, another form of treating people as mere means; better by far is the libertarian policy of allowing people to form associations and cooperative groups of any sort they choose and on any terms they prefer, so long as their agreements are above board and so long as the requirements of legitimate interference are met. My suggestion that helping others is not obligatory should not be construed as an uncritical abandonment of the needy, however. The point is that those who ignore the needy should be criticized as callous and narrowminded, not as immoral or evil. There is more to being a good person than meeting obligations.

NOTES

I wish to thank Charles R. Beitz and Winfred Phillips for helpful comments about and criticisms of this chapter.

1. This view was perhaps borrowed from Epicurus; see his *Principal Doctrines*, numbers 31–35.

2. In the First Supplement to *Perpetual Peace.*

3. "Justice as Fairness: Political Not Metaphysical," *Philosophy and Public Affairs* (1985):223–251 (Section VI is especially important, but see p. 225 as well). It is worth mentioning that in footnote 3 on p. 3 of Rawls's "The Idea of an Overlapping Consensus," *Oxford Journal of Legal Studies* 7 (1987):1–24, he accepts Kant's view that a world state would have to be "an oppressive autocracy." This claim is odd given the fact (accepted by Rawls [ibid., p. 10]) that pluralist societies need not be autocratic.

4. *A Theory of Justice* (Cambridge, Mass.: Harvard University Press, 1971), p. 4.

5. Ibid., p. 114.

6. Ibid., p. 115.

7. Ibid.

8. A full discussion of this point would require drawing Rawls's distinction between duty and obligation (see Sections 18 and 19 of *A Theory of Justice*). Mention should also be made of the fact that whereas Rawls thinks it permissible to force (through conscription) citizens to defend the liberties of people in other societies, he does not think it acceptable to use conscription to create or protect other features of a just society (ibid., p. 380).

Kant goes so far as to say that "everyone may use violent means to compel another to enter into a juridical state of society." See *The Metaphysical Elements of Justice,* trans. J. Ladd (Indianapolis, Ind.: Bobbs-Merrill, 1965), Section 44. See also Appendix I of *Perpetual Peace.* Hobbes and Locke would say that entry is by consent.

9. The difference principle is constrained by the just-savings principle; I ignore it here (see Section 44 of *A Theory of Justice*).

10. In Section 58 of *A Theory of Justice.*

11. This objection to using the original position apparatus is mitigated but not eliminated by the fact that the difference principle certainly would not be adopted in social circumstances less favorable than those Rawls assumes to hold (as a simplifying move). Perhaps the representatives would select the difference principle given that they are dealing with a society that never experiences substantial scarcity and whose citizens are fully motivated to participate their efforts to the social product, but I would argue that once these highly artificial restrictions are dropped so must the difference principle be. The matter is too complicated for an adequate discussion

here, but the main idea is this: Each representative must consider the possibility that the citizen he or she is looking after is in the worst social position and so would try to ensure that the least well-off have a fully adequate standard of living, but representatives must also take into account the possibility that they represent someone who is not least well-off, and hence would certainly limit the sacrifices they demand of the better-off somewhere short of the difference principle.

12. Ibid., pp. 110, 377.

13. See Section 40 of *A Theory of Justice.*

14. As Rawls notes (ibid., p. 133, note 8), the publicity requirement is made explicit by Kant in *Perpetual Peace*, Appendix II.

15. See *Groundwork of the Metaphysic of Morals*, H. J. Paton, trans. (New York: Harper Torchbooks, 1964), p. 91; Prussian Academy edition (hereafter PA), p. 424.

16. Ibid., p. 91; PA, p. 423.

17. Ibid., p. 92; PA, p. 425.

18. Ibid., p. 93; PA, p. 426.

19. Ibid., p. 96; PA, p. 429.

20. Ibid., p. 83; PA, p. 415.

21. Ibid., p. 85; PA, p. 418.

22. Rawls suggests that a veil of ignorance is implicit in Kant's ethics (*A Theory of Justice*, p. 140).

23. *Groundwork*, p. 96; PA, p. 429.

24. Ibid., p. 97; PA, pp. 429–430.

25. Ibid., p. 98; PA, p. 430.

26. Ibid., p. 97; PA, p. 430.

27. Ibid., p. 98; PA, p. 430.

28. Ibid., p. 180.

29. *Anarchy, State and Utopia* (Cambridge, Mass.: Basic Books, 1974), p. 31.

30. See, for example, J. Narveson, *Morality and Utility* (Baltimore, Md.: Johns Hopkins University Press, 1967).

31. Peter Singer, "Famine, Affluence, and Morality," *Philosophy and Public Affairs* 1, no. 3 (1972):229–244.

32. Given our goal of becoming and remaining rational and happy, we would bring about a world in which the greatly needy receive aid because we may find ourselves needy, but none of us would bring about a world in which the required sacrifices are too great because we may find ourselves having to do the sacrificing. Clearly, we would want to strike a balance.

33. Thus, the utilitarian J. J. Smart objected to Rawls's difference principle by raising the rhetorical question, "If it is rational for me to choose the pain of a visit to the dentist in order to prevent the pain of toothache, why is it not rational of me to choose a pain for Jones if that is the only way in which I can prevent a pain for Robinson?" *Utilitarianism: For and Against* (Cambridge, Mass.: Cambridge University Press, 1973), p. 37.

34. *A Theory of Justice*, p. 26.

35. Rawls recently adjusted his position concerning the value of liberty vis-à-vis economic welfare, however. Worries about the infelicity of speaking of greater and lesser "amounts" of liberty have in recent years led Rawls to change the formulation of his first principle so that it now guarantees a fully adequate package of equal basic liberties, where "adequate" is explained in terms of the resources necessary to develop and exercise moral personality. (See "The Basic Liberties and Their Priority," *Tanner Lectures on Human Values III* [Salt Lake City: University of Utah Press, 1982]).

In this new formulation only the basic liberties are given priority. Notice also that this new formulation avoids the following obvious difficulty confronting the old one: Given that a just society must give priority to maximizing the size of the package of equal liberties granted to its citizens, would it not follow that people have the right not to contribute to the well-being of others because this liberty certainly would be a possible part of a maximal package of liberties available to all (my liberty not to help anyone does not interfere with anyone else's)?

36. See Garrett Hardin, "Lifeboat Ethics: The Case Against Helping the Poor," *Psychology Today* (1974).

37. *Animal Liberation* (New York: New York Review of Books, 1975).

38. In *Anarchy, State and Utopia,* pp. 35–42, Nozick suggested Kantianism for people and utilitarianism for animals, but I am none too sure that animals should be any more content with utilitarianism than should people.

39. In "Annihilation," *The Philosophical Quarterly* 37 (1987):233–252, I press the point that we would not take a drug that would make us happy (pleasure-filled) slaves. The utilitarian, however, must say that if we can convert ourselves or others into a type of creature that experiences greater happiness than does a normal human being, we are obligated to do so (other things being equal).

40. But "the question of whether these side constraints are absolute is one I hope largely to avoid." *Anarchy, State and Utopia,* p. 31.

41. Ibid., pp. 30–31.

42. A similar point was made and discussed briefly by Hillel Steiner in "Justice and Entitlement," *Ethics* (1977):150–152, reprinted in Jeffrey Paul, ed., *Reading Nozick* (Totowa, N.J.: Rowman and Littlefield, 1981), pp. 380–382.

43. *Anarchy, State and Utopia,* p. 163.

44. Compare Locke's view with the following remark made by Jean-Jacques Rousseau in *Discourse on the Origin of Inequality,* Part Two: "The first man who, having enclosed a piece of ground, bethought himself of saying 'This is mine,' and found people simple enough to believe him, was the real founder of civil society. From how many crimes, wars and murders . . . might not any one have saved mankind, by . . . crying to his fellows, 'Beware of listening to this imposter. . . . The fruits of the earth belong to us all, and the earth itself to nobody.'"

45. *The Second Treatise of Government,* section 27.

46. See, for example, J. L. Mackie in *Ethics: Inventing Right and Wrong* (Harmondsworth, England: Penguin Books, 1977), Chapter 8.

47. *Anarchy, State and Utopia,* p. 178.

48. See David Lyons's critique in "The New Indian Claims and Original Rights to Land," *Social Theory and Practice* 4 (1977):249–272.

49. Alternatively, Nozick's theory might legitimate the private ownership of negligibly small amounts of the world's natural resources (such as a few grains of sand and a wild berry or two each) as consistent with the principle, suggested by Steiner, that "no individual's appropriation of unowned natural objects may ever be so great as to preclude any other present or future individual from making a similar appropriation" ("Justice and Entitlement," p. 382).

Another criticism is relevant here: Natural resources are very much like the manna from heaven that Nozick discusses on p. 198, for (1) no one has any special entitlement to raw resources, (2) we must all agree on some distribution of them, and (3) some resources even "fall" from the sky (nitrogen, etc.). Yet Nozick comes very close to saying that manna should be distributed in accordance with the difference principle.

50. *Anarchy, State and Utopia,* p. 320.

51. Ibid., p. 324.

PART ONE

World Resources and Distributive Justice

1

International Distributive Justice

CHARLES R. BEITZ

In Part Three of his book Political Theory and International Relations, *almost all of which is reproduced here, Charles Beitz argues that the duties of well-off nations are extensive. Although his argument relies heavily on work by John Rawls, Beitz rejects Rawls's conclusion that international justice does not demand substantial redistributions of goods from one nation to another. In doing so, Beitz joins several authors, including Brian Barry (in* The Liberal Theory of Justice *[Oxford: Clarendon Press, 1973]) and Thomas Scanlon (in "Rawls' Theory of Justice," University of Pennsylvania Law Review 121 [1973]).*

Beitz's position is that if nations were more or less self-contained, then the requirements of justice on the international level would be relatively weak. Nonetheless, even then requirements would exist in addition to those discussed by Rawls. Most importantly, a redistribution of natural resources would be necessary. Even more substantial demands can be defended once we see that Rawls's self-containment thesis is false. In defending the resource redistribution principle, Beitz pretends that the self-containment thesis is correct, but in fact he thinks that nations are not nearly as disconnected as Rawls seems to suppose. Once we admit that international interaction is almost as complex as intranational interaction, Beitz claims, we will also have to admit that the difference principle should hold across the globe.

It is no part of the morality of states that residents of relatively affluent societies have obligations founded on justice to promote economic development elsewhere. Indeed, the tradition of international political theory is virtually silent on the matter of international distributive justice. The most that might be said, consistently with the morality of states, is that the citizens of relatively affluent societies have obligations based on the duty of mutual aid to help those who, without help, would surely perish. The obligation to contribute to the welfare of persons elsewhere, on such a view, is an obligation of charity.

Obligations of justice might be thought to be more demanding than this, to require greater sacrifices on the part of the relatively well-off, and perhaps sacrifices of a different kind as well. Obligations of justice, unlike those of mutual aid, might also require efforts at large-scale institutional reform. The rhetoric of the General Assembly's "Declaration on the Establishment of a New International Economic Order" suggests that it is this sort of obligation that requires wealthy countries to increase substantially their contributions to less-developed countries, and radically to restructure the world economic system. Do such obligations exist? . . .

I shall argue that a strong case can be made on contractarian grounds that persons of diverse citizenship have distributive obligations to one another analogous to those of citizens of the same state. International distributive obligations are founded on justice and not merely on mutual aid. As a critique and reinterpretation of Rawls's theory of justice,[2] the argument explores in more detail the observation . . . that international relations is coming more and more to resemble domestic society in several respects relevant to the justification of principles of (domestic) social justice. The intuitive idea is that it is wrong to limit the application of contractarian principles of social justice to the nation-state; instead, these principles ought to apply globally.[3] The argument raises interesting problems for Rawls's theory, and, more important, it illuminates several central features of the question of global distributive justice. In view of increasingly visible global distributive inequalities, famine, and environmental deterioration, it can hardly be denied that this question poses one of the main political challenges of the foreseeable future. . . .

---

1. SOCIAL COOPERATION, BOUNDARIES, AND THE BASIS OF JUSTICE

Justice, Rawls says, is the first virtue of social institutions. Its "primary subject" is "the basic structure of society, or more exactly, the way in which the major social institutions distribute fundamental rights and duties and determine the division of advantages from social cooperation."[4]

The central problem for a theory of justice is to identify principles by which the basic structure of society can be appraised. The two principles proposed as a solution to this problem are:

1. Each person is to have an equal right to the most extensive total system of equal basic liberties compatible with a similar system of liberty for all.
2. Social and economic inequalities are to be arranged so that they are both: (a) to the greatest benefit of the least advantaged, consistent with the just savings principle [the "difference principle"], and (b) attached to offices and positions open to all under conditions of fair equality of opportunity.[5]

These principles are Rawls's preferred interpretation of the "general conception" of justice, which applies in a wider range of circumstances than those in which the two principles are appropriate.[6] . . .

Like Hume, Rawls regards society as a "cooperative venture for mutual advantage."[8] Society is typically marked by both an identity and a conflict of interests. Everyone (or almost everyone) in society shares an interest in having access to the various goods that social activity can provide. At the same time, people's claims to these scarce goods may conflict. Principles are needed to identify institutions that will fairly distribute the benefits and burdens of social life.

The model of society as a cooperative scheme is very important for Rawls's theory, but it must not be taken too literally. It is important because it explains the social role of justice and specifies the characteristics of human activity by virtue of which the requirements of justice apply. Thus, principles of justice determine a fair distribution of the benefits and burdens produced by "social cooperation." If there were no such "cooperation," there would be no occasion for justice, since there would be no joint product with respect to which conflicting claims might be pressed, nor would there be any common institutions (e.g., enforceable property rights) to which principles could apply. But Rawls's model must not be taken too literally, since all of the parties to a particular social scheme may not actually *cooperate* in social activity, and each party may not actually be advantaged in comparison with what his or her position would be in the absence of that scheme. For example, there is no doubt that the *polis* of ancient Greece constituted a scheme of social cooperation to which the requirements of justice should apply, yet its slaves were neither willing cooperators in social life, nor were they necessarily advantaged in comparison with what their situations would have been outside of their society. (For that matter, none of the parties may be advantaged. Perhaps there are societies in which everyone's position is depressed. Such a society would be strange, but there is no obvious reason why judgments about its justice, or lack of it, would be inappropriate.) To say that society is a "cooperative venture for mutual advantage" is to add certain elements of a social ideal to a description of the circumstances to which justice applies. These additional elements unnecessarily narrow the description of these circumstances. It would be better to say that the requirements of justice apply to institutions and practices (whether or not they are genuinely cooperative) in which social activity produces relative or absolute benefits or burdens that would not exist if the social activity did not take place. Henceforth, I shall take Rawls's characterization of society as a cooperative scheme as an elliptical description of social schemes meeting this condition. . . .

Rawls assumes that "the boundaries" of the cooperative schemes to which the two principles apply "are given by the notion of a self-contained national community." This assumption "is not relaxed until the derivation of the principles of justice for the law of nations."[11] In other words, the assumption that national communities are self-contained is relaxed when international justice is considered. What does this mean? If the societies of the world are now to be conceived as open, fully interdependent systems, the world as a whole would fit the description of a scheme of social cooperation, and the arguments for the two principles would apply, a fortiori, at the global level. The principles of justice for international politics would be the two principles for domestic society writ large, and this would be a very radical result, given the tendency to equality of the difference principle. On the other hand, if societies are thought to be *entirely* self-contained—that is, if they are to have no relations of any kind with persons, groups, or societies beyond their borders—then why consider international justice at all? Principles of justice are supposed to regulate conduct, but if, *ex hypothesi*, there is no possibility of international conduct, it is difficult to see why principles of justice for the law of nations should be of any interest whatsoever. Rawls's discussion of justice among nations suggests that neither of these alternatives describes his intention in the passage quoted. Some intermediate assumption is required. Apparently, nation-states are now to be conceived as "more or less"[12] self-sufficient, but not entirely self-contained. Probably he imagines a world of nation-states which interact only in marginal ways; perhaps they maintain diplomatic relations, participate in a postal union, maintain limited cultural exchanges, and so on. Certainly the self-sufficiency assumption requires that societies have no significant trade or other economic relations. . . .

For the purpose of justifying principles for nations, Rawls reinterprets the original position as a sort of international conference:

> One may extend the interpretation of the original position and think of the parties as representatives of different nations who must choose together the fundamental principles to adjudicate conflicting claims among states. Following out the conception of the initial situation, I assume that these representatives are deprived of various kinds of information. While they know that they

represent different nations, each living under the normal circumstances of human life, they know nothing about the particular circumstances of their own society. . . . Once again the contracting parties, in this case representatives of states, are allowed only enough knowledge to make a rational choice to protect their interests but not so much that the more fortunate among them can take advantage of their special situation. This original position is fair between nations; it nullifies the contingencies and biases of historical fate.[15]

While he does not actually present arguments for any particular principles for nations, he claims that "there would be no surprises, since the principles chosen would, I think, be familiar ones."[16] The examples given are indeed familiar; they include principles of self-determination, nonintervention, the *pacta sunt servanda* rule, a principle of justifiable self-defense, and principles defining *jus in bello.*[17] These are supposed to be consequences of a basic principle of equality among nations, to which the parties in the reinterpreted original position would agree in order to protect and uphold their interests in successfully operating their respective societies and in securing compliance with the principles for individuals that protect human life.[18] . . .

2. ENTITLEMENTS
TO NATURAL RESOURCES

Thus far, the ideal theory of international justice bears a striking resemblance to that proposed in the Definitive Articles of Kant's *Perpetual Peace.*[23] Accepting for the time being the assumption of national self-sufficiency, Rawls's choice of principles seems unexceptionable. But would this list of principles exhaust those to which the parties would agree? Probably not. At least one kind of consideration, involving natural resources, might give rise to moral conflict among states even in the absence of substantial social cooperation among them, and thus be a matter of concern in the international original position. The principles given so far do not take account of these considerations.

We can appreciate the moral importance of conflicting resource claims by distinguishing two elements that contribute to the material advancement of societies. One is human cooperative activity itself, which can be thought of as the human component of material advancement. The other is what Sidgwick called "the utilities derived from any portion of the earth's surface," the natural component.[24] While the first is the subject of the domestic principles of justice, the second is morally relevant even in the absence of a functioning scheme of international social cooperation. The parties to the international original position would know that natural resources are distributed unevenly over the earth's surface. Some areas are rich in resources, and societies established in such areas can be expected to exploit their natural riches and to prosper. Other societies do not fare so well, and despite the best efforts of their members, they may attain only a meager level of well-being because of resource scarcities.

The parties would view the distribution of resources much as Rawls says the parties to the domestic original-position deliberations view the distribution of natural talents. In that context, he says that natural endowments are "neither just nor unjust; nor is it unjust that men are born into society at any particular position. These are simply natural facts. What is just or unjust is the way that institutions deal with these facts."[25] A caste society, for example, is unjust because it distributes the benefits of social cooperation according to a rule that rests on morally arbitrary factors. Rawls's objection is that those who are less advantaged for reasons beyond their control cannot be asked to suffer the pains of inequality when their sacrifices cannot be shown to advance their position in comparison with an initial position of equality.

Reasoning analogously, the parties to the international original position would view the natural distribution of resources as morally arbitrary.[26] The fact that someone happens to be located advantageously with respect to natural resources does not provide a reason why he or she should be entitled to exclude others from the benefits that might be derived from them. Therefore, the parties would think that resources (or the benefits derived from them) should be subject to redistribution under a resource redistribution principle. This view is subject to the immediate objection that Rawls's treatment of natural talents is troublesome. It seems vulnerable in at least two ways. First, it is not clear what it means to say that the distribution of talents is "arbitrary from a moral point of view."[27] While the distribution of natural talents is arbitrary in the sense that one cannot deserve to be born with the capacity, say, to play like Rubinstein, it does not obviously follow that the possession of such a talent needs any justification. On the contrary, simply having a talent seems to furnish prima facie warrant for making use of it in ways that are, for the possessor, possible and desirable. A person need not justify the possession of talents, despite the fact that one cannot be said to deserve them, because they are already one's own; the prima facie right to use and control talents is fixed by natural fact.

The other point of vulnerability is that natural capacities are parts of the self, in the development of which a person might take a special kind of pride. A person's decision to develop one talent, not to develop another, as well as his or her choice as to how the talent is to be formed, and the uses to which it is to be put, are likely to be important elements of the effort to shape an identity. The complex of developed talents might even be said to constitute the self; their exercise is a principal form of self-expression. Because the development of talents is so closely linked with the shaping of personal identity, it might seem that one's claim to one's talents is protected by considerations of personal liberty. To interfere with the development and use of talents is to interfere with a self. Or so, at least, it might be argued.

Both of these are reasons to think that Rawls's discussion of natural talents is problematic. Perhaps it can be defended against objections like these, but that is not my concern here. I want to argue only that objections of this sort do not apply to the parallel claim that the distribution of natural resources is similarly arbitrary. Like talents, resource endowments are arbitrary in the sense that they are not deserved. But unlike talents, resources are not naturally attached to persons. Resources are found "out there," available to the first taker. Resources must be appropriated before they can be used, whereas, in the talents case, the "appropriation" is a *fait accompli* of nature over which persons have no direct control. Thus, while we might feel that the possession of talents confers a right to control and benefit from their use, we feel differently about resources. Appropriation may not always need a justification; if the resources taken are of limited value, or if, as Locke imagined, their appropriation leaves "enough and as good" for everyone else, appropriation may not present a problem. In a world of scarcity, however, the situation is different. The appropriation of valuable resources by some will leave others comparatively, and perhaps fatally, disadvantaged. Those deprived without justification of scarce resources needed to sustain and enhance their lives might well press claims to equitable shares.

Furthermore, resources do not stand in the same relation to personal identity as do talents. It would be inappropriate to take the sort of pride in the diamond deposits in one's back yard that one takes in the ability to play the *Appassionata*. This is because natural resources come into the development of personality (when they come in at all) in a more casual way than do talents. As I have said, talents, in some sense, are what the self is; they help constitute personality. The resources under one's feet, because they lack this natural connection with the self, seem more like contingent then necessary elements in the development of personality. Like talents, resources are used in this process; they are worked on, shaped, and benefited from. But they are not there, as parts of the self, to begin with. They must first be appropriated, and prior to their appropriation, no one has any special natural claim on them. Considerations of personal liberty do not protect a right to appropriate and use resources in the same way that they protect the right to develop and use talents as one sees fit. There is no parallel, initial presumption against interference with the use of resources, since no one is initially placed in a naturally privileged relationship with them.

I conclude that the natural distribution of resources is a purer case of something being "arbitrary from a moral point of view" than the distribution of talents. Not only can one not be said to deserve the resources under one's feet; the other grounds on which one might assert an initial claim to talents are absent in the case of resources, as well.

The fact that national societies are assumed to be self-sufficient does not make the distribution of natural resources any less arbitrary. Citizens of a nation that finds itself on top of a gold mine do not gain a right to the wealth that might be derived from it *simply* because their nation is self-sufficient. But someone might argue that self-sufficiency, nevertheless, removes any possible grounds on which citizens of other nations might press claims to equitable shares. A possible view is that no justification for resource appropriation is necessary in the global state of nature. If, so to speak, social cooperation is the root of all social obligations, as it is in some versions of contract theory, then the view is correct. All rights would be "special rights" applying only when certain conditions of cooperation obtain.[28]

I believe that this is wrong. It seems plausible in most discussions of distributive justice because their subject is the distribution of the benefits of social cooperation. Where there is no social cooperation, there are no benefits or burdens of cooperation, and hence no problem of conflicting distributive claims concerning the fruits of cooperation. (This is why a world of self-sufficient national societies is not subject to something like a global difference principle.) But there is nothing in this reasoning to suggest that we can *only* have moral ties to those with whom we share membership in a cooperative scheme. It is possible that other sorts of considerations might come into the justification of moral principles. Rawls himself recognizes this in the case of the natural duties, which are said to "apply to us without regard to our voluntary acts," and, apparently, without regard to our institutional memberships.[29]

In the case of natural resources, the parties to the international original position would know that resources are unevenly distributed with respect to population, that adequate access to resources is a prerequisite for successful operation of (domestic) cooperative schemes, and that resources are scarce. They would view the natural distribution of resources as arbitrary in the sense that no one has a natural prima facie claim to the resources that happen to be under one's feet. The appropriation of scarce resources by some requires a justification against the competing claims of others and the needs of future generations. Not knowing the resource endowments of their own societies, the parties would agree on a resource redistribution principle that would give each society a fair chance to develop just political institutions and an economy capable of satisfying its members' basic needs.

There is no intuitively obvious standard of equity for such matters; perhaps the standard would be population size, or perhaps it would be more complicated, rewarding societies for their members' efforts in extracting resources and taking account of the different resource needs of societies with different economies. The underlying principle is that each person has an equal prima facie claim to a share of the total available resources, but departures from this initial standard could be justified (analogously to the operation of the difference principle) if the resulting inequalities were to the greatest benefit of those least advantaged by the inequality.[30] In any event, the resource redistribution principle would function in international society as the difference principle functions in domestic society. It provides assurance to persons in resource-poor societies that their adverse fate will not prevent them from realizing economic conditions sufficient to support just social institutions and to protect human rights guaranteed by the principles for individuals. In the absence of this assurance, these nations might resort to war as a means of securing the resources necessary to establish domestic justice, and it is not obvious that wars fought for this purpose would be unjust.[31] . . .

3. INTERDEPENDENCE AND GLOBAL DISTRIBUTIVE JUSTICE

The case for an international resource redistribution principle is consistent with the assumption that states are self-sufficient cooperative schemes. Aside from humanitarian principles, like that of mutual aid, a global resource redistribution principle seems to be the strongest distributive principle applicable to a world of self-sufficient states.

Now, of course, the world is not made up of self-sufficient states. States participate in complex international economic, political, and cultural relationships that suggest the existence of a global scheme of social cooperation. As Kant notes, international economic cooperation creates a new basis for international morality.[34] If social cooperation is the foundation of distributive justice, then one might think that international economic interdependence lends support to a principle of global distributive justice similar to that which applies within domestic society. In this section I explore this idea.

International interdependence is reflected in the volume of transactions that flow across national boundaries—for example, communications, travel, trade, aid, and foreign investment. Although there has been some disagreement about the significance of the increase, the level of interdependence, measured by transaction flows and ratios of trade to gross national products, appears to have risen since 1945, reversing an interwar trend on the basis of which some have argued that rising interdependence is a myth. Furthermore, there is every reason to believe that the rising trend, if not the rate of increase, will continue in the years ahead.[35]

The main features of contemporary international interdependence relevant to questions of justice are the results of the growth of international investment and trade. Capital surpluses are not confined to reinvestment in the societies where they are produced, but instead are reinvested wherever conditions promise the highest yield without unacceptable risks. It is well known, for example, that large American corporations have systematically transferred significant portions of their capitalization to European, Latin American, and East Asian societies where labor costs are lower or markets are better. As a result of the long-term decline in tariffs and in nontariff barriers to trade, the rise of international advertising, and the development of rapid international communications, a world market has grown in which demand for finished goods is relatively insensitive to their place of manufacture, and international trade has increased substantially. The main organizational form to evolve in response to these trends is, of course, the multinational corporation, which makes possible greater refinements in the global allocation of capital investment, the coordination of production, and the development of markets.[36]

It is clear that interdependence in trade and investment produces substantial aggregate economic benefits in the form of a higher global rate of economic growth as well as greater productive efficiency. These results would be predicted by neoclassical economic theory and seem to be confirmed by empirical studies, even those that recognize the presence of various political constraints on trade and of extensive oligopolistic practices among multi-national corporations that might be thought to invalidate the predictions of economic theory.[37]

It is easier to demonstrate that a pattern of global interdependence exists, and that it yields substantial aggregate benefits, than to say with certainty how these benefits are distributed under existing institutions and practices or what burdens these institutions and practices impose on participants in the world economy. There is considerable controversy about these matters, and it is only possible here to offer some illustrative observations. There are several reasons for thinking that interdependence widens the income gap between rich and poor countries even though it produces absolute gains for almost all of them. Because states have differing factor endowments and varying access to technology, even "free" trade can lead to increasing international distributive inequalities (and, on some views, to absolute as well as relative declines in the well-being of the poorest classes) in the absence of continuing transfers to those least advantaged by international trade.[38] . . .

In some cases, participation in the world economy produces political inequality as well. Let us say that a party to some relationship is vulnerable to the extent that the relationship would be costly for that party to break. When breaking a relationship would impose higher costs on one party than on another, the relatively less vulnerable party can use the threat to break the relationship as a form of power over the more vulnerable party. In international trade, the most vulnerable parties are usually those with a heavy concentration of exports in a few products and a heavy concentration of export markets in a few countries. The most striking political inequalities arising from asymmetrical vulnerability involve industrial countries and non-oil-exporting developing countries (although it is worth noting that such vulnerability is neither distributed equally among developing countries nor limited to them).[42] . . .

Perhaps the most damaging burdens of interdependence have to do with its domestic consequences. These fall into two main classes. First, domestic governments are likely to experience difficulty in controlling their own economies, since domestic economic behavior is influenced by economic developments elsewhere. For example, the global monetary system allows disturbances (like price inflation) in some countries to be transmitted to others, complicating economic planning and possibly undercutting employment and incomes policies.[43] The other class of burdens involves the domestic distributive and structural effects of participation in the world economy. It is impossible to generalize in this area because the effect of trade and investment on domestic income distribution is a function of features peculiar to particular countries, such as relative factor endowments, domestic market imperfections, and government investment, tariff, and tax policies. However, with specific reference to the resource-poor developing countries, it is fair to say that participation in international trade and investment has often contributed to domestic income inequality in at least two separate ways:

first, under prevailing political conditions, the gains from trade and the retained profits of foreign-owned firms have tended to be concentrated in the upper income classes; second, the political influence of foreign investors has (either directly or indirectly) supported governments committed to inegalitarian domestic distributive policies.[44] . . .

International interdependence involves a complex and substantial pattern of social interaction, which produces benefits and burdens that would not exist if national economies were autarkic. In view of these considerations, Rawls's passing concern for the law of nations seems to miss the point of international justice altogether. In an interdependent world, confining principles of social justice to domestic societies has the effect of taxing poor nations so that others may benefit from living in "just" regimes. The two principles, so construed, might justify a wealthy society in denying aid to needy peoples elsewhere if the aid could be used domestically to promote a more nearly just regime. If the self-sufficiency assumption were empirically acceptable, such a result might be plausible, if controversial on other grounds.[50] But if participation in economic relations with the needy society has contributed to the wealth of the "nearly just" regime, its domestic "justice" seems to lose moral significance. In such situations, the principles of domestic "justice" will be genuine principles of justice only if they are consistent with principles of justice for the entire global scheme of social cooperation. Note that this conclusion does not require that national societies should have become entirely superfluous, or that the global economy should be completely integrated.[51] It is enough, for setting the limits of cooperative schemes, that some societies are able to increase their level of well-being via global trade and investment while others with whom they have economic relations do not fare so well.[52]

How should we formulate global principles? It has been suggested that Rawls's two principles, suitably reinterpreted, could themselves be applied globally.[53] The reasoning is as follows: if evidence of global economic and political interdependence shows the existence of a global scheme of social cooperation, we should not view national boundaries as having fundamental moral significance. Since boundaries are not coextensive with the scope of social cooperation, they do not mark the limits of social obligations. Thus the parties to the original position cannot be assumed to know that they are members of a particular national society, choosing principles of justice primarily for that society. The veil of ignorance must extend to all matters of national citizenship, and the principles chosen will therefore apply globally.[54] As Barry points out, a global interpretation of the original position is insensitive to the choice of principles.[55] Assuming that Rawls's arguments for the two principles are successful, there is no reason to think that the content of the principles would change as a result of enlarging the scope of the original position so that the principles would apply to the world as a whole. In particular, if the difference principle ("social and economic inequalities are to be arranged so that they are . . . to the greatest benefit of the least advantaged") would be chosen in the domestic original position, it would be chosen in the global original position as well. . . .

It is important to be clear who are the subjects of a global difference principle, especially because it has been questioned whether such a principle should apply to states rather than persons.[57] It seems obvious that an international difference principle applies to persons in the sense that it is the globally least advantaged representative person (or group of persons) whose position is to be maximized.[58] If one takes the position of the least-advantaged group as an index of distributive justice, there is no a priori reason to think that the membership of this group will be coextensive with that of any existing state. Thus, a global difference principle does not *necessarily* require transfers from rich countries as such to poor countries as such. While it is almost certainly the case that an international difference principle would require reductions in intercountry distributive inequalities, this would be because these inequalities are consequences of impermissible interpersonal inequalities. Furthermore, because the difference principle applies in the first instance to persons, it would also require intrastate inequalities to be minimized if necessary to maximize the position of the (globally) least-advantaged group.

It is not inconsistent with this view to understand states as the primary "subjects" of international distributive responsibilities.[59] For it may be that states, as the primary actors in international politics, are more appropriately situated than individual persons to carry out whatever policies are required to implement global principles. Perhaps intercountry redistribution should be viewed as a second-best solution in the absence of a better strategy for satisfying a global difference principle. In any event, it should be understood that the international obligations of states are in some sense derivative of the more basic responsibilities that persons acquire as a result of the (global) relations in which they stand.[60]

4. CONTRASTS BETWEEN INTERNATIONAL AND DOMESTIC SOCIETY

The conclusion that principles of distributive justice apply globally follows from the premise that international economic interdependence constitutes a scheme of social cooperation like those to which requirements of distributive justice have often been thought to apply. This is the most important normative consequence of my argument that international relations is more like domestic society than it is often thought to be. One might accept this premise but reject the conclusion on either of two grounds. First, one might hold that interdependence is a necessary but not a sufficient condition for the global application of principles of justice, and that other necessary conditions (like the existence of political institutions or of a capacity for a sense of justice) do not obtain in international relations. Second, one might argue that special features of social cooperation within national societies organized as states override the requirements of global principles, so that these cannot be understood as ultimate. In this and the following sections, I explore these objections.

There is no doubt that the main difference between international relations and domestic society is the absence in the former case of effective decision-making and decision-enforcing institutions. There is no world constitution analogous to those explicit or implicit codes that define the structure of authority within states. And there is no world police force capable of enforcing compliance with world community policies. Instead, there is an array of processes and institutions through which states and other political actors attempt to influence one another and which, directly or indirectly, affect the prospects of the persons who live within their scope. These processes and institutions range from war and coercive diplomacy to ad hoc bargaining and transnational organizations. Even in the last case, which most resembles the political institutions of domestic society, there is a significantly diminished capacity to make decisions and enforce them against offenders. Although one must grant that the international realm includes various capacities for sanctions and enforcement of community decisions, one cannot plausibly argue that these are similar in extent to those characteristic of most domestic societies. In particular, there is at present no reliable way of enforcing compliance with international redistributive policies. (The United Nations, for example, has been unable to persuade rich countries to contribute even three-quarters of one percent of their gross products to international development efforts.)

A related contrast between the international and domestic realms is the absence of what might be called an international sense of community. Within domestic society, the sense of community is an important motivational basis for compliance with laws and official decisions. Rawls recognizes this in arguing that compliance with the principles of justice rests on the fact that persons have a capacity for a sense of justice, and that this capacity would be developed by participation in the life of a well-ordered society (i.e., one whose basic structure conformed to the two principles).[61] In international relations, there is no similar sense of community; nor are most people moved to act by any commitment to ideals like global justice. One might think that the world is simply too large, and its cultures too diverse, to support a global sense of justice. Unifying symbols are scarce while sectional ones are all too available; and, in any event, it is a commonplace that the political force of a symbol decreases in proportion to the degree of abstraction of the symbol from the immediate needs and interests of individuals and small groups. Thus, it is unlikely that a sense of global community comparable to the sense of national community will develop.

How are these contrasts relevant to the argument for international distributive justice? Objections to global principles might be constructed following the precept that morality cannot demand the impossible. As Rawls points out, the parties to the original position would not choose principles they know they cannot live by.[62] Nor, surely, would they choose principles that cannot be implemented. If the lack of effective, global political institutions, or of a sense of world community, makes impossible the implementation of global principles, then the parties would not agree to them.

Such objections are not persuasive because they misunderstand the relation between ideal theory and the real world. Ideal theory prescribes standards that serve as goals of political change in the nonideal world, assuming that a just society can, in due course, be achieved. The ideal cannot be undermined simply by pointing out that it cannot be achieved at present. One needs to distinguish two classes of reasons for which it may be impossible to implement an ideal. One class includes impediments to change that are themselves capable of modification over time; the other includes impediments that are unalterable and unavoidable. Only in the second case can one appeal to the claim of impossibility in arguing against an ideal, since, in the former case, such an argument can be defeated by pointing out the mutability of those social facts that are supposed to render the ideal unattainable in the present.

Both of the objections sketched seem to rely on impediments to implementation of a global difference principle that are capable of modification over time. There is no evidence that it is somehow given in the nature of things that people can neither develop sufficient motivation for compliance nor evolve institutions capable of enforcing global principles against offenders. I am not claiming that either of these would be easy or that we can foresee the dynamics by which they may come about. But this is not what ideal theory requires. It requires only that the necessary changes be possible, and it is at least not demonstrably false that this is the case.[63]

A different interpretation of these objections is that neither authoritative global institutions, nor a sense of global justice, would be desirable even if they were attainable. Perhaps authoritative institutions on such a scale would be radically inefficient, or unavoidably oppressive, politics being what it is.[64] Or, perhaps the sense of justice is important not only as a motive for compliance with principles of justice, but also as a source of a people's common, and distinctive, identity. This might be thought to be an important good because it speaks to people's need to belong to a group that is smaller than the whole population of the world.[65] If this is true, then a sense of global justice might seem to carry allegiance to political ideals farther than is desirable.

In response to these objections it might be pointed out that the institutions and sentiments on which compliance with global principles is based need not bear too close a resemblance to their domestic analogues. In each case, some function must be fulfilled to make possible the implementation of global principles, but these functions need not be fulfilled through mechanisms like those familiar in domestic society. It is a mistake to identify too closely the scope of the principles and the scope of the institutions necessary to implement them, for a variety of configurations of institutions can be imagined (for example, a coordinated set of regional institutions) that would implement the principles. Similarly, the supposed undesirability of a sense of global justice rests on a conflation of the regulative role of the sense of justice and many other functions fulfilled by loyalties to subgroups of the species. While a common allegiance to justice is necessary to promote compliance with its norms and to regulate institutions that implement them, there is no obvious reason why this would be inconsistent with the persistence of those loyalties to smaller groups necessary to feelings of belonging and identity.[66]

The contrasts between international and domestic society, then, do not damage the argument for a global application of the difference principle. But the effect of distinguishing ideal from nonideal theory for the purpose of defeating such objections does not make the objections disappear; it merely recognizes that their relevance is not to the ideal of global distributive justice, but rather to the problem of realizing this ideal. In general, this problem is likely to be more difficult in international relations than in domestic society because the institutional framework of international relations is less capable of bringing about the shifts in the distribution of wealth and power required by the global difference principle. Below, I shall consider this problem in more detail. For the present, I would like briefly to illustrate one way in which the relative weakness of international institutions complicates nonideal theory. The illustration is of general interest because it involves the relation of fair coercive institutions to the sacrifices that can be required of people by moral principles.

An important feature of fair coercive institutions (that is, coercive institutions that are just or nearly just) is that they give assurance to those whom they call upon to make sacrifices that others in similar circumstances will be compelled to make similar sacrifices. So far as it is possible, such institutions seek to remove the unfairness inherent in the possibility that some of their members can avoid contributing their fair share by becoming free riders.[67] It is not only fairness that makes this a significant feature of coercive institutions; the perception that such institutions can assure a fair distribution of the burdens of social cooperation is likely to be an important source of the motivation for compliance. One reason that obligations of charity often seem weaker than obligations of justice is that charity is more often voluntary in the sense that its demands are not backed up by the coercive power of the state. One can beg off on the grounds that he or she would be unfairly disadvantaged by his or her contribution in comparison with others who do not contribute, or that his or her contribution, in the absence of cooperation by others, would be futile. But these alternatives are not available when there is assurance that each will be compelled to contribute his or her fair share.

Now in international relations this assurance is often absent. In this limited respect, the problem of bringing about international distributive justice is similar to that of escaping a Hobbesian state of nature. In both cases, the absence of fair coercive institutions—which makes more probable the absence of reliable expectations of reciprocal compliance—undermines the motivational basis for compliance with principles of justice. In both cases, the solution of the assurance problem is effective coordination of the actions of all of the actors involved. But there are important differences as well. First, the risks of voluntary compliance are different. Moral persons in Hobbes's state of nature risk death, while in international relations they risk relative deprivation. Hobbes's problem is survival, while the problem in the present case is international distributive justice. Second, . . . there are greater possibilities for coordination in international relations than in the state of nature. The assurance problem is more easily solved. Third, international relations involves a variety of institutions, which can be adjusted to improve the justice of the distribution they produce, while the state of nature lacks analogous institutions bearing on personal security. In sum, one can imagine a variety of intermediate solutions to the problem of implementing international distributive principles—intermediate in the sense of bringing the actual distribution closer to the ideal than it is at present—but it is hard to see what an intermediate solution would mean in the state of nature.

Thus the relevance of the contrasts between international relations and domestic society is to be found in the area of nonideal theory. These contrasts do not undermine the argument for a global application of principles of justice, but rather complicate the moral reasoning as well as the political action involved in the effort to realize the ideal. Unlike the partially analogous problem of escaping from a Hobbesian state of nature, however, the complications in the nonideal theory of international relations render justified political action more difficult, but not impossible in principle. . . .

Although conceding all that I have said so far, someone might object that there is still an important difference between domestic and international "social cooperation." While the terms of participation in domestic society apply to its members regardless of their consent and may therefore appropriately be assessed from the standpoint of justice, it might be thought that participation in the world economy is considerably more voluntary. After all, no state is required to participate in international trade or to accept foreign investment, and any state could withdraw at will (following the example, say, of Albania or Cambodia). By participating, states might be said to have accepted the terms of participation offered them, making further moral criticism of those terms otiose.

The objection seems plausible only because it locates the alleged voluntariness of international economic relations in the wrong place. Of course it is usually true that a party to some ongoing pattern of exchange can withdraw if the terms of exchange are too costly, but this is not the respect in which most international economic relationships are nonvoluntary from the point of view of their worse-off participants. Relationships might also be nonvoluntary if the relatively weaker partner lacks the resources to bargain effectively for different terms of exchange. In effect, the terms are set by the more powerful partner; they appear as a *fait accompli* to those who are unable to change them. Since withdrawal may be immensely costly (as, for example, it would be to a vulnerable poor country with only one export crop), there may be no practical alternative to accepting the terms of trade that are effectively dictated by those with greater power. This is not a situation to which one can be morally indifferent, because the reasons for the weak state's relative vulnerability are usually beyond its control, having to do, for example, with the uneven distribution of wealth-producing resources or the effects of past injustices.[68] It is a victim of natural and historical facts, from which others have no moral right to benefit. Thus, one needs to ask by what standards of fairness the international economic order can be assessed.

5. THE RIGHTS OF STATES

I turn now to another set of objections, according to which considerations of social cooperation at the national level justify distributive claims capable of overriding the requirements of a global difference principle. Typically, members of a wealthy nation might claim that they deserve a larger share than that provided by a global difference principle because of their superior technology, economic organization, and efficiency.[69]

Objections of this general sort might take several forms. First, it might be argued that even in an interdependent world, national society remains the primary locus of one's political identification. If one is moved to contribute to aggregate social welfare at any level, this level is most likely to be the national level. Therefore, differential rates of national contribution to the global welfare ought to be rewarded proportionally. This is a plausible form of the objection; the problem is that in this form it may not be an objection at all. The difference principle itself recognizes the probability that differential rates of reward may be needed as incentives for contribution; it requires only that the distributive inequalities that arise in such a system be to the greatest benefit of the world's least-advantaged group. To the extent that incentives of the kind demanded by this version of the objection actually do raise the economic expectations of the least advantaged without harming them in other ways, they would not be inconsistent with the difference principle.

Such objections only count against a globalized difference principle if they hold that a relatively wealthy nation could claim more than its share under the difference principle. That is, the objection must hold that some distributive inequalities are justified even though they are not to the greatest benefit of the world's least advantaged group. How could such claims be justified? One justification is on grounds of personal entitlement, appealing to the intuition that value created by someone's unaided labor or acquired through voluntary transfers is properly one's own, assuming that the initial distribution was just.[70] This second sort of argument yields an extreme form of the objection. It holds that a nation is entitled to its relative wealth because each of its citizens has complied with the relevant rules of justice in acquiring raw materials and transforming them into products of value. These rules might require, respectively, that an equitable resource redistribution principle has been implemented, and that no one's rights have been violated (for example, by imperial plunder) in the process of acquisition and production leading to a nation's current economic position. (Note that my arguments for a resource principle . . . are not touched by this sort of objection and would impose some global distributive obligations even if the personal-entitlement view were correct in ruling out broader global principles.)

This interpretation of the objection is analogous to the conception of distributive justice that Rawls calls the "system of natural liberty." His objection to such views is that they allow people to compete for available positions on the basis of their talents, making no attempt to compensate for deprivations that some suffer because of natural chance and social contingencies. These things, as I have said, are held to be morally arbitrary, and hence unacceptable as standards for distribution.[71] I shall not rehearse this argument further here. But two things should be noted. The argument seems even more plausible from the global point of view since the disparity of possible starting points in world society is so much greater. The balance between "arbitrary" and "personal" contributions to my present well-being seems decisively tipped toward the arbitrary ones by the realization that, no matter what my talents, education, life goals, etc., I would have been virtually precluded from attaining my present level of well-being if I had been born in a much less developed society. Also, if Rawls's counterargument counts against natural-liberty views in the domestic case, then it defeats the present objection to a globalized difference principle as well. Citizens of a society cannot base their claims to a larger distributive share than that warranted by the difference principle on morally arbitrary factors.

A third, and probably the most plausible, form of this objection is that a wealthy nation may retain more than its share under a global difference principle, provided that some compensation for the benefits of global social cooperation is paid to less fortunate nations, and that the amount retained by the producing nation is used to promote domestic justice—for example, by increasing the prospects of the nation's own least favored group. The underlying intuition is that citizens owe some sort of special obligation to the less fortunate members of their own society that is capable of overriding their general obligation to improve the prospects of less advantaged groups elsewhere. This intuition is distinct from that in the personal-entitlement case, for it does not refer to any putative individual right to the value created by one's labor or acquired through voluntary transfers. Instead, we are here concerned with supposedly conflicting rights and obligations that arise from membership in nested schemes of social cooperation, one embedded in the other.

An argument along these lines needs an account of how obligations to the sectional associations arise. It is tempting, though unhelpful, to bring in psychological considerations here: for example, one might point out that the sentiment of nationality is stronger than that of humanity and argue that the difference principle therefore applies in full force only inside national societies.[72] Now those who would pursue this line must recognize that any account of how institutional obligations arise that is sufficiently psychological to make plausible a general conflict of global and sectional obligations will probably be too psychological to apply to the large modern state.[73] If this is true, then proponents of this view face a dilemma: either they must endorse the strongly counterintuitive conclusion that obligations of justice may not even hold within large modern states and are appropriate primarily within smaller solidaristic communities or organic groups; or they must agree that obligations of justice may be justified by considerations other than those of strong common sentiment. The first alternative seems clearly unacceptable, but the second implies that domestic and international obligations cannot be distinguished with reference to the supposedly unique psychological features of membership in national societies.

Even if this last point is incorrect, there is a more fundamental problem with the suggestion that sentiments of nationality support especially strong intranational distributive obligations. The difficulty is that it is not obvious why we should attach objective moral weight to national sentiments even where they are widely felt. Why should sectional loyalties diminish global obligations based on participation in the world economy? (This question should be distinguished from that . . . concerning the realism of the assumption that persons are motivationally capable of acting on a global difference principle.)

To attempt to answer this question, it is necessary to look behind the sentiments that people experience to the forms of social interaction in which they take part. Accordingly, one might say that the greater degree or extent of social cooperation in national societies (compared with that in international society) justifies stronger intranational principles of justice. Imagine a world of two self-sufficient and internally just societies, A and B. Assume that this world satisfies the appropriate resource redistribution principle. Imagine also that the least-advantaged representative person in society A is considerably better off than his counterpart in society B. While the members of A may owe duties of mutual aid to the members of B, it is clear that they do not also have duties of justice, because the two societies, being individually self-sufficient, do not share membership in a cooperative scheme. Now suppose that the walls of self-sufficiency are breached very slightly; A trades its apples for B's pears. Does this mean that the difference principle suddenly applies to the world that comprises A and B, requiring A to share all of its wealth with B, even though almost all of its wealth is attributable to economic interaction within A? It seems not; one might say that an international difference principle can only command redistribution of the benefits derived from international social cooperation or economic interaction. It cannot touch the benefits of domestic cooperation.

It may be that some such objection will turn out to require modifications of a global difference principle. But there are reasons for doubting this. Roughly, it seems that there is a threshold of interdependence above which distributive requirements like a global difference principle are valid, but below which significantly weaker principles hold. To see why this formulation has intuitive appeal, consider another hypothetical case. Suppose that, *within* a society, there are closely knit local regions with higher levels of internal cooperation than the level of cooperation in society as a whole. Certainly there are many such regions within a society like the United States. The argument rehearsed above, applied to closely knit localities within national societies, would seem to give members of the localities special claims on portions of their wealth. This seems implausible, especially since such closely knit enclaves might well turn out to contain disproportionate numbers of the society's most advantaged classes. Why does this conclusion seem less plausible than that in the apples and pears case? It seems to me that the answer has to do with the fact that the apples and pears case looks like a case of voluntary, free market bargaining, which has only a marginal effect on the welfare of the members of each society, whereas we assume in the intranational case that there is a nonvoluntary society-wide system of economic institutions, which defines starting positions and assigns economic rights and duties. It is these institutions—what Rawls calls "the basic structure"[74]— that stand in need of justification, because, by defining the terms of cooperation, they have such deep and pervasive effects on the welfare of people to whom they apply regardless of consent.

The apples and pears case, of course, is hardly a faithful model of the contemporary world economy. Suppose that we add to the story to make it resemble the real world more closely. As my review of the current situation . . . makes clear, we would have to add just those features of the contemporary world economy that find their domestic analogues in the basic structure to which principles of justice apply. As the web of transactions grows more complex, the resulting structure of economic and political institutions acquires great influence over the welfare of the participants, regardless of the extent to which any particular one makes use of the institutions. These features make the real world situation seem more like the case of subnational, closely knit regions, than like the apples and pears case.

These considerations suggest that the amount of social and economic interaction in a cooperative scheme does not provide a straightforward index of the strength of the distributive principle appropriate to it. The existence of a nonvoluntary institutional structure, and its pervasive effects on the welfare of the cooperators, seem to provide a better indication of the strength of the appropriate distributive requirements. This sort of consideration would not necessarily support a globalized difference principle in the apples and pears case; but it does explain why, above a threshold measure of social cooperation, the full force of the difference principle may come into play despite regional variations in the amount of cooperation.[75]

Someone might think that a fourth version of the objection could be formulated by taking into account considerations about capital accumulation on behalf of future generations within national societies. The argument would be that people have a right to assurance that the capital they save for the sake of their descendants will actually be used for that purpose, rather than be distributed globally as the global difference principle might require. The idea here is that national societies can be conceived as cooperative schemes extending over time, in which earlier generations make sacrifices to raise the level of well-being of succeeding generations.[76] On reflection, however, it should be clear that this view is not distinct from versions of the objection previously considered. In fact, it is parasitic on them; if the previous versions are found wanting, considerations about domestic capital accumulation do not strengthen them.

The key question is why these considerations are thought to undermine the argument for global redistribution. There seem to be two possible replies. First, on the model of inheritance, one might visualize capital accumulation as the result of saving within a family, with wealth passed from one generation to the next in a series of private transfers. On this view, considerations about capital accumulation count against global redistribution for the same reason that they count against all redistribution: redistribution involves a violation of rights of inheritance. But rights of inheritance, in this sense, are simply species of the more general right of voluntary transfer on which natural-liberty and personal-entitlement views are based. The rejection of such views takes with it the justification of unrestricted rights of inheritance and therefore dissolves the foundation of the related objections to global redistribution.

The other reply to the question about why considerations about capital accumulation undermine the argument for global redistribution involves the model of social savings. Capital accumulated by one generation is passed on within a society but is distributed according to the society's allocative decision procedure. The explanation of why social savings should be used for the benefit of the members of the society in which they were generated rather than be redistributed globally must be that members of a national society have special claims to (portions of) their wealth, perhaps based on a supposed obligation to give special attention to the needs of the less fortunate members of their own society. But, again, such a view needs an account of how special obligations to sectional associations arise, and the attempt to supply such an account will encounter the same problems discussed with respect to the third interpretation of the objection. It follows that considerations about capital accumulation on behalf of future generations do not lend any independent strength to the objection that members of domestic societies have special rights to portions of their own product that undermine a global difference principle.

I have considered several versions of the objection that relatively well-off states have special claims on portions of their domestic products that would offset their global redistributive obligations. None of these versions of the objection appears to damage the argument for a global difference principle. However, it is worth pointing out that global redistributive obligations would not be entirely extinguished even if one or another of these versions of the objection could be made convincing. Suppose, for example, that the second version, based on individual entitlement, could be defended. It would not follow that there are no international redistributive obligations founded on justice because that version of the objection involves two premises that are probably contrary to fact: first, that the distribution of natural resources conforms to the requirements of the global resource principle, and second, that the effects of past injustices (stemming either from resource exploitation or violation of the relevant principles of justice in acquisition and transfer) have been rectified. A showing that either premise is false would lend support to an argument for some global redistribution to compensate for the uneven distribution of natural resources or to rectify past injustices. Or suppose that the third version of the objection, based on the greater intensity of social cooperation inside as compared to across national boundaries, could be defended. At a minimum it would still follow from my previous arguments that a global resource principle applies and that that portion of the global product actually attributable to global (as opposed to domestic) social cooperation should be redistributed according to a suitably restricted difference principle. In any event, if this general line of objection could somehow be made good, the question would not be whether there are global distributive obligations founded on justice, but rather to what extent considerations relevant to the special features of cooperation within national societies modify the strongly egalitarian tendencies of the global standard. And, in view of the large distributive inequalities that currently exist, it seems likely that the existing distribution would still be unjust.

6. APPLICATIONS TO THE NONIDEAL WORLD

Thus far, we have reached two main conclusions. First, assuming national self-sufficiency, Rawls's derivation of the principles of justice for the law of nations is incomplete. He neglects resource redistribution, a subject that would surely be on the minds of the parties to the international original position. But second, the self-sufficiency assumption, upon which Rawls's entire consideration of the law of nations rests, is not justified by the facts of contemporary international relations. The state-centered image of the world has lost its normative relevance because of the rise of global economic interdependence. Hence, principles of distributive justice must apply in the first instance to the world as a whole, and derivatively to nation-states. The appropriate global principle is Rawls's difference principle, perhaps modified by some provision for intranational redistribution in relatively wealthy states once a threshold level of international redistributive obligations has been met. In conclusion, I would like to consider the implications of this ideal theory for international politics and global change in the nonideal world.

We might begin by asking, in general, what relevance social ideals have for politics in the real world. Their most obvious function is to describe a goal toward which efforts at political change should aim. A very important natural duty is the natural duty of justice, which "requires us to support and to comply with just institutions that exist and . . . constrains us to further just arrangements not yet established, at least if this can be done without too much cost to ourselves."[77] By supplying a description of the nature and aims of a just world order, ideal theory "provides . . . the only basis for the systematic grasp of these more pressing problems."[78] Ideal theory, then, supplies a set of criteria for the formulation and criticism of strategies of political action in the nonideal world, at least when the consequences of political action can be predicted with sufficient confidence to establish their relationship to the social ideal. Clearly, this task is not easy, given the complexities of social change and the uncertainties of prediction in political affairs. There is the additional complication that social change is often wrongly conceived as a progressive approximation of actual institutions to ideal prescriptions in which people's welfare steadily improves. An adequate social theory must avoid both the pitfalls of a false incrementalism and what economists call the problem of second best.[79] But a coherent social ideal is a necessary condition of any attempts to conquer these difficulties.

Ideal justice, in other words, comes into nonideal politics by way of the natural duty to secure just institutions where none presently exist. The moral problem posed by distinguishing ideal from nonideal theory is that in the nonideal world, the natural duty of justice is likely to conflict with other natural duties, while the theory provides no mechanism for resolving such conflicts. For example, it is possible that a political decision that is likely to make institutions more just may also involve violations of other natural duties, like the duty of mutual aid or the duty not to harm the innocent. Perhaps reforming some unjust institution will require disappointment of expectations formed under the old order. The principles of natural duty in the nonideal world are relatively unsystematic, and we have no way of knowing which should win out in case of conflict. Rawls recognizes the inevitability of irresolvable conflicts in some situations, but, as Feinberg has suggested, he underestimates the role that an intuitive balancing of conflicting duties must play in nonideal circumstances.[80] It may be that the solution to problems of political change in radically unjust situations must rely on a consequentialist calculation of costs and benefits.[81] If this is true, then political change in conditions of great injustice marks one kind of limit of the contract doctrine, for in these cases the principles of justice collapse into consequentialism. Nevertheless, these considerations shed light on the normative problems we encounter in coping with global injustice, as I shall try to show briefly with respect to the question of development aid and international economic reform.

The duty to further just institutions where none exist endows certain political claims made in the nonideal world with a moral seriousness that does not derive merely from the duties that bind people regardless of the existence of cooperative ties. When the contract doctrine is interpreted globally, claims made by, or on behalf of, the less advantaged in today's nonideal world appeal to principles of global justice as well as to the duty of mutual aid. Those who are in a position to respond to these claims must take account of the reasons provided by the principles of justice in weighing their response. Furthermore, by interpreting the principles globally, we remove a major source of justifying reasons for not responding more fully to such claims. These reasons derive from statist concerns—for example, from a supposed right to reinvest domestic surpluses in national societies that are already relatively favored from a global point of view. Obviously, political considerations may make unavoidable levels of domestic reinvestment in excess of those that would be ideally just. But it should not be argued that citizens of wealthy nations have general rights to retain their domestic products, which override their obligations to advance the welfare of less-advantaged persons elsewhere.

These theoretical points have several practical consequences. Most clearly, the existence of global redistributive obligations strengthens the moral case for foreign aid. In the past, aid has often been regarded as a kind of international charity. Like charitable contributions, contributions to the economic development of poor countries have been understood to be morally discretionary and properly subject to various kinds of political restrictions. Moreover, the duty to give aid could be acknowledged without compromising the moral basis of existing legal property rights. Once the existence of global redistributive obligations founded on justice is recognized, however, the view of aid as charity must be given up. It is inappropriate to regard foreign assistance as discretionary in the way charitable contributions are, nor can the attachment of political conditions be easily defended (except in one sort of case, noted below). Furthermore, one cannot acknowledge a duty of justice to contribute to economic development elsewhere without acknowledging that existing legal property rights lack a firm moral foundation. Aid should not be regarded as a voluntary contribution of a portion of a state's own wealth, but rather as a transfer of wealth required to redress distributive injustice.[82] . . .

NOTES

. . .

2. John Rawls, *A Theory of Justice* (Cambridge: Harvard University Press, 1971).

3. Such criticisms have been suggested by several writers. For example, Brian Barry, *The Liberal Theory of Justice* (Oxford: Clarendon Press, 1973), pp. 128–33; Peter Danielson, "Theories, Intuitions, and the Problem of World-Wide Distributive Justice," *Philosophy of the Social Sciences* 3, No. 4 (1973), pp. 331–40; Thomas M. Scanlon, "Rawls' Theory of Justice," *University of Pennsylvania Law Review* 121, No. 5 (1973), pp. 1,066–67. For a discussion, see Robert Amdur, "Rawls' Theory of Justice: Domestic and International Perspectives," *World Politics* 29, No. 3 (1977), pp. 438–61.

4. Rawls, *A Theory of Justice*, p. 7.

5. Ibid., pp. 302–3.

6. The general conception reads: "All social primary goods—liberty and opportunity, income and wealth, and the bases of self-respect—are to be distributed equally unless an unequal distribution of any or all of these goods is to the advantage of the least favored" (ibid., p. 303). For the purposes of this discussion, I ignore the problem of when (and why) the two principles are to be preferred to the general conception, and the problems that might result if the general conception were applied globally.

. . .

8. Ibid., p. 4. Compare David Hume, *A Treatise of Human Nature* [1739–1740], ed. L. A. Selby-Bigge (Oxford: Clarendon Press, 1888), III, II, ii, pp. 484–89.

. . .

11. Ibid., p. 457.

12. Ibid., p. 4.

. . .

15. Ibid., p. 378.

16. Ibid.

17. These principles form the basis of traditional international law. See the discussion, on which Rawls relies, in J. L. Brierly, *The Law of Nations*, ed. H. Waldock (Oxford: Clarendon Press, 1963), esp. chs. 3–4.

18. Rawls, *A Theory of Justice*, pp. 378 and 115.

. . .

23. Immanuel Kant, *Perpetual Peace* [1795], in *Kant's Political Writings*, ed. H. Reiss, trans. H. B. Nisbet (Cambridge: Cambridge University Press, 1971), pp. 98–115.

24. Henry Sidgwick, *The Elements of Politics* [1891], 4th ed., (London: Macmillan & Co., 1919), p. 255; quoted in S. I. Benn and R. S. Peters, *The Principles of Political Thought* (New York: Free Press, 1965), p. 430. Sidgwick's entire discussion of putative national rights to land and resources is relevant here. See *Elements*, pp. 252–57.

25. Rawls, *A Theory of Justice*, p. 102.

26. Compare Kant, *Perpetual Peace*, p. 106, where it is claimed that persons "have a right to communal possession of the earth's surface."

27. Rawls, *A Theory of Justice*, p. 72.

28. William N. Nelson construes Rawlsian rights in this way in "Special Rights, General Rights, and Social Justice," *Philosophy and Public Affairs* 3, No. 4 (1974), pp. 410–30.

29. Rawls, *A Theory of Justice*, p. 114.

30. Compare ibid., p. 151.

31. On this account, U. N. General Assembly Resolution 1,803 (XVII), which purports to establish "permanent sovereignty over natural resources," would be prima facie unjust. However, there are important mitigating factors. This resolution, as the text and the debates make clear, was adopted to defend developing nations against resource exploitation by foreign-owned businesses, and to support a national right of expropriation (with compensation) of foreign-owned mining and processing facilities in some circumstances. While the "permanent sovereignty" doctrine may be extreme, sovereignty-for-the-time-being might not be, if it can be shown (as I think it can) that resource-consuming nations have taken more than their fair share without returning adequate compensation from their own surpluses. United Nations General Assembly, *Official Records: Seventeenth Session*, Supp. no. 17 (A/5,217) (New York, 1963), pp. 15–16.

. . .

34. Immanuel Kant, *The Metaphysical Elements of Justice* [1797], Part I of *The Metaphysics of Morals*, trans. J. Ladd (Indianapolis: Bobbs-Merrill, 1965), pp. 124–29. See also Kant, *Perpetual Peace*, pp. 106–8.

35. Peter J. Katzenstein, "International Interdependence: Some Long-term Trends and Recent Changes," *International Organization* 29, No. 4 (1975), pp. 1,021–34. See also R. Rosecrance, et al., "Whither Interdependence?" *International Organization* 31, No. 3 (1977), esp. pp. 432–41. For a skeptical view see Kenneth N. Waltz, "The Myth of National Interdependence," *The International Corporation*, ed. C. P. Kindelberger (Cambridge: MIT Press, 1960), pp. 205–26. Waltz's view is challenged in Richard Rosecrance, "Interdependence: Myth or Reality," *World Politics* 26, No. 1 (1973), pp. 1–27, which also provides a review of some other relevant literature.

36. The main texts on multinationals are Raymond Vernon, *Sovereignty at Bay* (New York: Basic Books, 1971) and C. Fred Bergsten, Thomas Horst, and Theodore H. Moran, *American Multinationals and American Interests* (Washington, D.C.: The Brookings Institution, 1978). There is a more critical discussion in Richard Barnet

and Ronald Müller, *Global Reach* (New York: Simon and Schuster, 1974), esp. chs. 1–2.

37. In this regard, a stronger empirical case can be made for the aggregate gains from foreign investment than for those from trade. On the gains from trade, see Richard N. Cooper, "Economic Assumptions of the Case for Liberal Trade," *Toward a New World Trade Policy*, ed. C. F. Bergsten (Lexington: Lexington Books, 1975), pp. 19–31. On the role of foreign investment in promoting global efficiency and growth, see Robert O. Keohane and Van Doorn Ooms, "The Multinational Firm and International Regulation," *International Organization* 29, No. 1 (1975), pp. 172–76.

38. Ronald Findlay, *Trade and Specialization* (Harmondsworth: Penguin, 1970), pp. 118–22. For the view that trade absolutely impoverishes the global poor, see Michael Barratt Brown, *The Economics of Imperialism* (Harmondsworth: Penguin, 1974), esp. ch. 5, pp. 96–126, and the references cited there.

. . .

42. Kal J. Holsti, "A New International Politics?" *International Organization* 32, No. 2 (1978), p. 516. For a more detailed discussion of the relative weakness of the poor countries, see Tony Smith, "Changing Configurations of Power in North-South Relations since 1945," *International Organization* 31, No. 1 (1977), esp. pp. 7–15.

43. For a discussion, see Richard N. Cooper, "Economic Interdependence and Foreign Policy in the Seventies," *World Politics* 24, No. 2 (1972), esp. pp. 164–67.

44. Keohane and Ooms, "The Multinational Firm," pp. 179–80.

. . .

50. For example, on consequentialist grounds. See Peter Singer, "Famine, Affluence, and Morality," *Philosophy and Public Affairs* 1, No. 3 (1972), pp. 229–43.

51. This conclusion would hold even if it were true that wealthy nations like the United States continue to be economically self-sufficient, as Kenneth Waltz has (mistakenly, I think) argued. To refute the claim I make in the text, it would be necessary to show that all, or almost all, nations are self-sufficient in the sense given above, and that such foreign relations as they engage in produce no significant external effects. This, plainly, is not the case. Waltz, "The Myth of National Interdependence," pp. 205–23.

52. In some cases the situation may be worse than this. It has been argued that some poor countries' relations with the rich have actually worsened economic conditions among the poor countries' worst-off groups. This raises the question of whether interdependence must actually benefit everyone involved to give rise to questions of justice. I think the answer is clearly negative; countries A and B are involved in social cooperation even if A (a rich country) could get along without B (a poor country), but instead exploits it, while B gets nothing out of its "cooperation" but exacerbated class divisions and Coca-Cola factories. This illustrates my remark (section 1, part three) that Rawls's characterization of a society as "a cooperative venture for mutual advantage" (*A Theory of Justice*, p. 4) may be misleading, since everyone need not be advantaged by the cooperative scheme in order for requirements of justice to apply.

53. Barry, *The Liberal Theory of Justice*, pp. 128–32; and Scanlon, "Rawls' Theory of Justice," pp. 1,066–67.

54. David Richards also argues that the principles apply globally. But he fails to notice the relationship between distributive justice and the morally relevant features of social cooperation on which its requirements rest. This relationship is needed to explain why the original position parties should be kept ignorant of their nationalities, and thus why Rawlsian principles of social justice should apply globally. See David

A. J. Richards, *A Theory of Reasons for Action* (Oxford: Clarendon Press, 1971), pp. 137–41.

55. Barry, *The Liberal Theory of Justice*, p. 129.

. . .

57. For example, by Robert W. Tucker, *The Inequality of Nations* (New York: Basic Books, 1977), pp. 62–64.

58. This would be obscured if one supposed (as has Christopher Brewin) that the parties to the international original position "would be masterless or sovereign states." But the supposition is incorrect (and perhaps incoherent); the parties are *persons,* and the international original position is distinguished from the domestic one by stipulating the parties' ignorance of their citizenship. Brewin, "Justice in International Relations," *The Reason of States,* ed. M. Donelan (London: George Allen and Unwin, 1978), p. 147.

59. As Tucker suggests. *The Inequality of Nations,* pp. 62–64.

60. The relation of individual and group responsibilities is a difficult issue, involving a variety of complications. I cannot pursue it here. See Joel Feinberg, "Collective Responsibility," *Journal of Philosophy* 65, No. 21 (1968), 674–88; and Virginia Held, "Can A Random Collection of Individuals Be Morally Responsible?" *Journal of Philosophy* 67, No. 14 (1970), 471–81.

61. Rawls, *A Theory of Justice,* pp. 496–504.

62. Ibid., p. 145.

63. "[T]he idea that something which has hitherto been unsuccessful will never be successful does not justify anyone in abandoning even a pragmatic or technical aim. . . . This applies even to moral aims, which, so long as it is not demonstrably impossible to fulfil them, amount to duties." Kant, "On the Common Saying: 'This May be True in Theory, but it does not Apply in Practice'" [1793], *Kant's Political Writings,* p. 89.

64. Such a view is suggested by Kenneth N. Waltz, *Man, The State, and War* (New York: Columbia University Press, 1959), p. 228; and Inis L. Claude, *Power and International Relations* (New York: Random House, 1962), pp. 206–28.

65. See, e.g., Sigmund Freud, *Civilization and its Discontents* [1930], trans. J. Strachey (New York: Norton, 1961), p. 61; and Emile Durkheim, *Moral Education* [1925], trans. E. K. Wilson and H. Schnurer (New York: Free Press, 1961), pp. 74–77. Durkheim does not draw the extreme conclusion that the need for state-centered loyalties entirely undermines international morality. In fact, he claims that domestic society "can enjoy moral primacy only on the condition that it is not conceived as an unscrupulous self-centered being." *Moral Education,* p. 79.

66. As Herbert Kelman points out in "Education for the Concept of a Global Society," *Social Education* 32 (1968), p. 661. Compare Rawls's discussion of this issue as it arises in domestic society: "[T]he institutional scheme in question may be so large that particular bonds never get widely built up. In any case, the citizen body as a whole is not generally bound together by fellow feeling between individuals, but by the acceptance of public principles of justice." (*A Theory of Justice,* p. 477.) There is nothing in the global interpretation that defeats this reasoning; if it is plausible at the national level, it is plausible at the global level as well.

67. For a general discussion, see James M. Buchanan, *The Demand and Supply of Public Goods* (Chicago: Rand McNally, 1968), pp. 77–99, and the references cited there.

68. Should a state be held responsible for its vulnerability or poverty to the extent that these are caused by the absence of effective population-control policies? I think not, but cannot argue it here. For a penetrating discussion, see Henry Shue, "Food,

Population and Wealth: Toward Global Principles of Justice," paper presented at the annual meeting of the American Philosophical Association, Chicago, Sept. 2–5, 1976.

69. More crudely: "[N]ational wealth is something that is earned by the capacities of the country's people and the policies of its Government; it is not something that is just shifted around." Robert Moss, "Let's Look Out for No. 1!", *The New York Times Magazine* (May 1, 1977), p. 100.

70. This is Robert Nozick's view in *Anarchy, State and Utopia* (New York: Basic Books, 1974), ch. 7.

71. Rawls, *A Theory of Justice,* pp. 66–72.

72. For a suggestive account of a similar problem, see Michael Walzer, "The Obligation to Disobey," *Obligations: Essays on Disobedience, War, and Citizenship* (Cambridge: Harvard University Press, 1970), pp. 3–23.

73. Compare Rawls, *A Theory of Justice,* p. 477.

74. Ibid., pp. 7–11.

75. I do not claim to have resolved entirely the problem that underlies this objection, although I believe that my remarks point in the right direction. It should be noticed, however, that what is at issue here is really a general problem for any theory that addresses itself to institutional structures rather than to particular transactions. One can always ask why institutional requirements should apply in full force to persons who make minimal use of the institutions they find themselves living under.

76. Such an argument is made by W. H. Hutt, "Immigration under 'Economic Freedom,' " p. 36, quoted in Danielson, "Theories, Intuitions, and [the Problem of] World-Wide Distributive Justice," p. 335.

77. Rawls, *A Theory of Justice,* p. 155.

78. Ibid., p. 9.

79. On the problem of second best, see Brian Barry, *Political Argument* (London: Routledge and Kegan Paul, 1965), pp. 261–62.

80. Rawls, *A Theory of Justice,* p. 303; Joel Feinberg, "Duty and Obligation in the Nonideal World," *Journal of Philosophy* 70 (1973), pp. 263–75.

81. As Rawls implies. *A Theory of Justice,* pp. 352–53.

82. See Thomas Nagel, "Poverty and Food: Why Charity Is Not Enough," *Food Policy: The Responsibility of the United States in the Life and Death Choices,* ed. Peter G. Brown and Henry Shue (New York: Free Press, 1977), pp. 54–61. . . .

2

The Uneasy Case
for Global Redistribution

ERIC MACK

*Eric Mack rejects Charles Beitz's arguments for a resource
redistribution principle and a global difference principle. On Mack's
interpretation of Rawls and Beitz, a defense of a claim of justice can
successfully be made from the point of view of the original position only
when that claim applies to a set of cooperating agents. Yet Beitz argues
that the resource redistribution principle applies among societies even in
the absence of economic cooperation; thus, Beitz's use of the original
position concept in defense of resource redistribution among completely
self-sufficient nations is illegitimate.*

*Mack's rejection of the global difference principle begins with Beitz's
assumption that among self-sufficient nations there are no demands of
redistributive justice (with the possible exception of the distribution of
resources) and thus that each nation is entitled to the share of goods it
has regardless of inequity across nations. Doesn't this assumption imply
that each country has the right to refuse leaving this state of
independence and the right to cooperate only with nations of its choice
at levels of cooperation of its choice? If so, then surely nations can
bargain about who shall be their partners and about what shall be the
terms of their interactions, terms likely to be inconsistent with a global
difference principle.*

In Part Three of *Political Theory and International Relations,* Charles
Beitz offers a two-tiered justification for the international redistribution of
wealth.[1] The first tier of justification is concerned with natural resources
and seeks to establish a "resource redistribution principle" that would require
transfers of natural resources (or a proportion of the benefits derived from
natural resources) from those societies, nations, or nation-states that find
themselves with more than their "fair" share of natural resources to those
societies, nations, or nation-states that find themselves with less than their
"fair" share. The second part of the justification is concerned with income
in general and seeks to establish a "global difference principle" that would
require global income to be redistributed so as to maximize the long-term
income of the economically least advantaged.

A crucial feature of the first tier justification for the resource redistribution
principle is that, within it, Beitz explicitly eschews any appeal to cooperative
interaction among the parties subject to the principle. Conflicting resource
claims among societies would exist even in a world of self-sufficient states;
and even in such a world, these conflicts should be resolved by the resource
redistribution principle. Beitz does point out that the national self-sufficiency
assumed by John Rawls is not a matter of states being "entirely self-contained."
Rather, self-sufficient states are somewhat cooperative—for example, they
establish postal unions. Therefore, states are "more or less" self-sufficient.
But Beitz is not at all interested in basing the resource redistribution principle
on the small degree of cooperation implied by a "more or less" self-sufficiency.
This would base the resource principle on social cooperation while Beitz is
at pains to emphasize that this principle of justice does not rest on such
cooperation.[2] In contrast, within the second tier of justification, Beitz's
argument for the global difference principle explicitly appeals to cooperative
interaction among the parties subject to the principle. Given that this is a
principle of *distributive* justice, it must be founded on social cooperation
among the parties subject to it because, Beitz holds, social cooperation is
the foundation of distributive justice.

Beitz's justifications for international redistribution represent Rawlsian
attempts to overthrow Rawls's own surprising conclusion in *A Theory of
Justice* that justice does not call for the redistribution of income among
nations.[3] Essentially, Rawls arrives at this conclusion by assuming that national
boundaries set off discrete, self-sufficient schemes of social cooperation and
by holding to the principle that only those agents who are mutually engaged
in a scheme of social cooperation will be subject to principles of distributive
justice that mandate how income wealth should be divided among them.
Beitz's first tier justification involves the denial of this social cooperation
requirement with respect to the resource distribution principle. Beitz's second
tier justification proceeds by rejecting the self-sufficiency assumption. The
rejection of the self-sufficiency assumption is supposed to put the case of
international redistribution on a par with the case for intranational redistribution.

I find each tier of justification unpersuasive. I will argue that any (even
initially) plausible contractarian argument for a given principle must posit

social cooperation among the parties subject to that principle.[4] Thus, Beitz's denial of this social cooperation requirement in connection with the resource redistribution principle deprives him of recourse to any *contractarian* argument for that principle and leaves him with only an unsatisfactory noncontractarian argument. Against the second tier justification, I shall argue that much more than the existence of some international cooperation is needed to put the case for a global difference principle on a par with the case, whatever its strength, for an intranational difference principle. I shall argue that, especially in the international case, the acknowledgment that there would be no foundation for the difference principle in a world of self-sufficient agents provides a barrier to the rational acceptance of that principle.[5]

THE RESOURCE REDISTRIBUTION PRINCIPLE

Beitz's case for the resource redistribution principle appeals to two distinct Rawlsian arguments that Beitz tends to conflate.[6] According to the argument from moral arbitrariness, because the existing distribution of natural resources among societies is merely a matter of "advantageous location," this distribution is morally arbitrary, and, therefore, either this distribution itself or the equally arbitrary allocation of wealth produced by this distribution ought to be nullified. The contractarian argument invites us to conceive each society[7] as a rational agent concerned with advancing its own interests in the possession and use of natural resources. According to this view, each such society bargains, behind a veil of mutual ignorance about the actual distribution of those resources, about what its respective shares of those resources will be and agrees to some egalitarian rule for distributing those resources (or the proceeds of those resources). The projection of this hypothetical agreement is supposed to indicate the actual justice of such an egalitarian rule.

In Rawls, the moral arbitrariness argument appears within his sketch of a "preferred interpretation" of his second principle,[8] and, as Rawls makes clear, his invocation of the undesirability of the morally arbitrary is not to be confused with the contractarian original position argument. As Rawls puts it, "None of the . . . remarks [in favor of the "democratic conception" as the "preferred interpretation"] are an argument for this conception. . . . All arguments, strictly speaking, are to be made in terms of what it would be rational to choose in the original position."[9] Such rational negotiators do not care whether a distribution is morally arbitrary or not. Such notions have no force in their essentially premoral condition.

Beitz's argument from moral arbitrariness is the only one appropriate to his resource redistribution principle because any plausible contractarianism contends that only the actual or prospective cooperation among agents sets the stage for the elaboration of principles of justice binding among those agents. This actual or prospective engagement requires some mutually acceptable rules for conducting this interaction or for evaluating its benefits and burdens. Interaction or the prospect of interaction, under conditions of scarcity but with the prospect of mutual advantage, makes it rational for mutually disinterested agents to agree upon, adopt, and thereby create principles of justice.[10] It then is essential to the contractarian idea that a particular set of moral rules hold among and only among agents who, because of their actual or prospective cooperation, have a rational need to reach and abide by some terms of accommodation. This is to say that any plausible contractarianism incorporates the "social cooperation requirement."[11] Thus, if Beitz wants to maintain that a resource redistribution principle holds among societies whether or not there is economic cooperation among them— that is, even if the social cooperation requirement is not satisfied with respect to that principle—he may not support that principle by appeal to a contractarian argument.

This leaves Beitz with the ever vague moral arbitrariness argument. The following seems to be the core statement of that argument for resource redistribution between societies:

> The parties to the international original position would view the natural distribution of natural resources as morally arbitrary. The fact that someone happens to be located advantageously with respect to natural resources does not provide a reason why he or she should be entitled to exclude others from the benefits that might be derived from them. *Therefore*, the parties would think that the resources (or the benefits derived from them) should be subject to redistribution under a resource redistribution principle [emphasis added].

The moral arbitrariness of "the natural distribution" of resources is inferred by Beitz from the denial that advantageous location vindicates entitlements to natural resources, and "redistribution under a resource redistribution principle" is inferred by Beitz from the moral arbitrariness of "the natural distribution."

Let us begin with the second inference, then return to the first. Clearly, it does not follow from the proposition that no one is entitled to particular bundles of resources that resources "should"—indeed, as a matter of justice, must—be redistributed. It is positively odd to hold that because no one has any entitlement to any particular natural resources, everyone (or every society) is entitled to a certain share of the totality of resources. If the natural distribution of resources is "morally arbitrary," their (supposed) easy availability to or possession by specific agents is, in a phrase that Rawls applies to the distribution of natural talents, "neither just nor unjust. . . . These are simply natural facts."[12] Such facts alone cannot ground a principle of distributive justice. Rawls, of course, immediately goes on to say that "what is just or unjust is the way that institutions deal with these facts."[13] Beitz cites Rawls's apparent volte-face regarding the moral significance of the facts about natural talents to support his parallel assertions about the justice or injustice of ways of dealing with the (supposed) natural facts about natural resources. What is to be made of this sort of move?

In his discussion, Rawls goes on to say, "Aristocratic and caste societies are unjust because they make these contingencies ["the distribution of natural talents and the contingencies of social circumstance"] the ascriptive basis for belonging to more or less enclosed or privileged classes. The basic structure of these societies incorporates the arbitrariness found in nature. But there is no necessity for men to resign themselves to these contingencies."[14] Putting aside the special injustices of the social enclosures and privileges of "aristocratic and caste societies," what rationale is suggested here for moving from the "natural facts," which add up to a distribution of natural talents, to the justice or injustice of ways of dealing with these facts? Certain ways of dealing with these morally arbitrary facts are said to incorporate the arbitrariness found in nature. But what is unjust about either the process or the product of such an incorporation? It might, of. course, be a mistake to assert that the process or product of incorporating morally arbitrary facts into a basic social structure is just. But the nonjustice of the incorporation does not imply its injustice. Although it is true that people need not "resign" themselves to any particular response to the natural facts, the question remains whether justice requires that people not so "resign" themselves. This question remains unanswered because nothing in the arbitrariness argument justifies describing the incorporating response as unjust or describing certain nullifying or compensating responses are just.

It may be that Rawls recognizes the need for an independent argument for the injustice of the system that incorporates the "neither just nor unjust" natural facts and for the justice of some alternative response. For almost immediately he turns back to a contractarian argument when he declares that "in justice as fairness men agree to share one another's fate. In designing institutions they undertake to avail themselves of the accidents of nature and social circumstances only when doing so is for the common benefit."[15]

Within this argument the moral arbitrariness of those "accidents" plays no role. People agree to share one another's fate for the same sort of reasons that people take out insurance policies. Rawls has legitimate access to this independent contractarian argument because the subjects of its conclusion are agents interacting under the circumstances of justice. But Beitz, by renouncing appeal to economic cooperation as part of the basis for his resource redistribution principle, denies himself legitimate access to an analogous contractarian appeal. He is left, therefore, with the bare and implausible inference that because the distribution of natural resources is a nonjust natural fact, its incorporation into a social structure is unjust and nullification of or compensation for this natural fact is just.

Let us turn back briefly to the first inference—that is, the distribution of holdings that redistribution purports to rectify is morally arbitrary. This inference falsely presupposes that the only or most plausible alternative to the moral arbitrariness of "the natural distribution" is the doctrine that advantageous location grounds entitlement. This inference also falsely presupposes entitlements to "the natural distribution" must be proved nonarbitrary. These presuppositions misleadingly characterize the entitlement alternative to the arbitrariness of "the natural distribution."

An entitlement theorist maintains that individuals can acquire rights over particular, otherwise unowned, portions of nature by entering into certain relationships with and by performing certain sorts of actions on those respective segments. Such a theory differs fundamentally from the view that entitlement rests on the fact that someone happens to be located advantageously with respect to natural resources. This latter view represents a nonhistorical patterned principle while an entitlement view is historical and nonpatterned. Moreover, because in entitlement theory particular rights depend upon the specific ways individuals have claimed, used, transformed, and created objects, the entitlements supported by such a theory are not well described as entitlements to "the natural distribution."

A precise formulation of a given theorist's favored principle of initial acquisition depends, among other things, on the background moral theory from which that theorist operates. An advocate of Lockean rights over one's person and labor proceeds differently than an advocate of Humean principles of justice that are ultimately justified by their long-term, indirect contribution to social utility. A streamlined Lockean entitlement view (without complicating requirements about initial acquirers' leaving "enough and as good" for others) provides a sample of an alternative to the doctrine of advantageous location. Such a Lockean maintains that initially nature is thoroughly unowned. No one, either individually or collectively, has title to any parts of it whether he or she is advantageously or disadvantageously located. Rights over purposively transformed segments of previously unowned nature arise through the process of purposive transformation. The seizure of such a transformed object from transforming agents wrongfully interferes with their rightful control over their lives and activities. Agents "acquire" a right to the transformed object by virtue of the wrongfulness of such interfering seizures.[16]

According to this view, no one ever is entitled to natural resources as such—to raw segments of nature. There are no entitlements to "the natural distribution." The initial, transforming rightholder and his or her "resource" (the material that has been made into a resource) are linked through the rightholder's economic insight, effort, risk-taking, and skill—through the agent's making his or her "location" advantageous. Therefore, entitlement to resources is far less arbitrary in this view than in a theory such as Beitz's, that accords each person (or society) an entitlement to a "fair" share by virtue of presence in a world in which some individuals (or societies) have made resources "available"—which is to say, have created valuable resources out of raw segments of nature.

Beitz is rightly skeptical of Rawls's view that the natural distribution of talents is morally arbitrary and therefore not rightfully held. Beitz seems to hold that even if the possession of a talent is arbitrary, having the talent seems to endow the possessor with prima facie warrant to make use of the talent in desirable ways. Likewise, the possession of "natural capacities" is not arbitrary because "a person might take a special kind of pride" in their development. But, if simply having a talent provides a prima facie entitlement to it, why does not simply having a segment of nature provide a comparable entitlement to it? Moreover, Beitz himself insists that natural resources are not naturally attached to persons. Resources, which are available to the first taker, must be appropriated, according to Beitz, before they can be used. In the case of talents, by contrast, the "appropriation" is a fait accompli over which persons have no direct control. Beitz concludes that possession of talents confers a right to control and benefit from their use, but this is not the case with resources.

But surely a very different conclusion is called for than the one Beitz provides. Beitz himself asserts that appropriation of talents is a mere fait accompli while the appropriation of resources is under an agent's "direct control." To this, according to the present argument, we can add that so-called natural resources are not taken but rather are created out of natural material by activities that characteristically display effort, insight, and skill in which, and in the products of which, a person might take pride. Thus, if any conclusion is called for, it is that the case for individual entitlements to "appropriated" resources is stronger than is the acknowledged prima facie case for individual entitlements to talents.

Thus, the argument from moral arbitrariness, which is the only Rawlsian argument available to Beitz for supporting the resource redistribution principle, provides no plausible basis for that principle. We have reason to question the claim that the natural distribution of resources is arbitrary, in particular more arbitrary than the natural distribution of talents. We have no reason to believe that the arbitrariness of the distribution of natural resources would provide any positive support for a resource redistribution principle.

THE GLOBAL DIFFERENCE PRINCIPLE

Although Beitz asserts that his international difference principle applies in the first instance to persons and not to states, his discussion of the principle proceeds in terms of nations and states and their economic cooperation and not in terms of persons (or even "representative persons"[17]) and their transnational interactions. I believe that proceeding in terms of nations or states is unfortunate because it assumes nations or states are helpful units of economic analysis and accepts statist presumptions that certain segments of the economic world belong to certain nations, states, or governments whose job is to manage them. But, in this section, I adopt Beitz's language in order to argue that he fails to make plausible the claim that nations are bound by a global difference principle. The adoption of the language of nations, states, and their "shares" may make it seem that in rejecting Beitz's principle, I am asserting that nations, states, or societies are entitled to certain other shares of the world's income. But I could mean that only if I thought nations, states, or societies were entitled to anything.

In order to argue for a global difference principle, Beitz finds it necessary to deny John Rawls's self-sufficiency assumption. Beitz clearly affirms that were this a world of self-sufficient states, there would be no basis for the global difference principle. He maintains that social cooperation is the foundation of distributive justice. This commitment brings to the fore questions about how social cooperation lays the "foundation" for distributive justice and about what is properly subject to the divisions dictated by principles founded upon social cooperation. I shall argue that focusing on these questions reveals general (and well-known) difficulties with the thesis that cooperation within a group of agents lays the foundation for their being subject, among themselves, to a difference principle. Further, I shall argue that there is least hope of overcoming these difficulties in connection with the more specific thesis that international cooperation provides a foundation for a global difference principle.

In his discussion of the connection between economic cooperation and the applicability of principles of distributive justice, Rawls does not distinguish between the division of the cooperation "surplus" among the cooperating parties and the division of the total income generated by such parties.[18] Nevertheless, his claim that a perch for principles of distributive justice is established only with the advent of cooperation (like Beitz's claim that there would be no basis for principles of distributive justice in a world of self-sufficient agents) would lead us to expect that those principles would take agents' precooperative "shares" as given and would address only the distribution of the cooperative surplus. This would leave room only for a surplus difference principle, which theoretically is quite different from the standard difference principle.

Yet Rawls uses his difference principle to specify the just distribution of the total income of the cooperating parties. Although we might conclude that this amalgamation of precooperative shares and cooperative surplus is unjustified, we can still cite a number of reasons in support of this amalgamation for the specific case of *individuals and their respective societies.* First, in intensely and complexly cooperative situations, it may be exceedingly difficult to identify agents' precooperative shares.[19] Thus, it may be infeasible in practice for the difference principle to take the precooperative shares as given—that is, as portions of the income of economic agents that are not subject to the distributive principle. Second, especially in intensely and complexly cooperative situations, the cooperative surplus will exceed enormously the sum of the precooperative shares of the individuals involved in that cooperative scheme.[20] Thus, even in principle, very little of what falls under the sway of an amalgamating difference principle ought not do so. Third, each individual's precooperative share would be very small. Thus, there is little danger that a distribution of total income will leave people worse off than they were in their precooperative state.

But, in general, parallel reasons do not exist for individual nations and international cooperation. First, it does seem possible to identify a nation's gains from international cooperation and therefore to estimate what a nation's precooperative income would have been. Second, the international cooperative surplus probably does not enormously exceed (indeed, it may be dwarfed by) the sum of the precooperative shares of individual nations because those precooperative national shares are enormously enhanced by intranational cooperation. Third, again because of the enhancement of some nations' precooperative income through their respective intranational cooperation, there is a considerable danger that what some nations would receive under a global distribution principle that exercised authority over total global income would be less than their respective precooperative incomes.[21] Thus, especially in the international case, the amalgamation of precooperative shares and the cooperative surplus is unjustified. At the very most, international cooperation opens the door to a global surplus difference principle, and such a principle would be, both in theory and in practice, strikingly different from the less constrained global difference principle.

However, the recognition that one's favorite distributive principles do not extend to precooperative shares, which is only to recognize the implications of the claim that such principles have no application among self-sufficient agents, opens the door to a competing entitlement principle about how the benefits of exchange and joint production ought to be divided. The competing principle holds that the cooperative benefits should be divided in accordance with the particular agreements that are negotiated by the parties involved in specific cooperative endeavors. I want to indicate how precluding the application of distributive principles to precooperative incomes opens the door to this antidistributive entitlement principle. To do so here, I must pay the price of having accepted Beitz's units of analysis—nations or states— and of having argued that on the international level it is especially appropriate to recognize that even one's favorite distributive principle does not extend to national precooperative incomes. I must proceed, then, to talk about what nations have, bargain for, and have entitlements over. The claim against Beitz can be put conditionally: If nations were the sort of agents suggested by Beitz's language, then their precooperative incomes would not be subject to any global difference principle, and this opens the door to the entitlement view that even nations' cooperative surplus would not be subject to this principle.

The idea that self-sufficiency excludes any redistributive principle implies that no autarkic nation would have any obligation to enter into any scheme of international economic cooperative, no matter how great the mutual benefits of that scheme. It is a short and plausible step from this implication to the proposition that each currently cooperative nation is morally at liberty to abstain from future interaction as long as any redistributive obligations generated by past cooperation are fulfilled. Thus, at any time, any nation is entitled to bargain with any other nation or group of nations about the terms of their possible economic interaction. If the nations are entitled to bargain with each other and to withhold their cooperation until a bargain is struck, each nation is also entitled to the fulfillment of the terms of whatever bargains are struck. This includes entitlements to the specific division of the benefits of exchange or to the specific division of the proceeds from the joint product that are established by the voluntary agreements of such nations. If two nations cooperate, their cooperative product has the status of a precooperative "share" vis-à-vis any third nation. Thus, no third nation has even a prima facie claim to share in their cooperative surplus. In short, cooperative activity, exchanges of goods, or jointly productive activities must proceed through mutual agreement, and when they do, each party's "fair" share is the share that has been agreed upon among them.

While continuing to speak the misleading language of cooperation between nations, we should not think that whether cooperation exists among a number of nations is a matter of the existence or nonexistence of a single, comprehensive scheme accompanied by an equally comprehensive agreement about the divisions of the benefits from that scheme. Rather, any overall cooperative scheme will simply be the union of many intersecting cooperative arrangements, each of which particular nations enter and each of which provides the nations involved with certain of its entitlements. There is no comprehensive division of the benefits of international cooperation that is to be made in accord with some comprehensive actual or hypothetical agreement. Thus, still speaking the misleading language of nations, international justice would consist in whatever distribution of income would arise among nations that, starting with the natural materials that those nations discovered, gathered, and/or transformed, proceeded to engage in and abide by voluntary market interactions with one another. In short, international economic justice would be the justice of a laissez-faire market society writ large.[22]

I have argued here that, especially in the international case, the doctrine that self-sufficiency undercuts the difference principle leads quite naturally to an entitlement conception of the just division of benefits of international cooperation. This argument builds on a dilemma facing any contractarian argument—the need for rules for the division of the benefits of cooperation and only the need for such rules makes it rational for cooperating agents to adopt and abide by such rules. But this implies that, absent further and countervailing reasons, whatever rules might be adopted may not reach into the precooperative holdings of those agents. This seems to leave agents free to dispose of their precooperative holdings (what were, to that point, precooperative holdings) as they respectively see fit. Thus, agents are free to cooperate in accordance with the terms negotiated within their particular endeavors and are not bound to divide the gains from that cooperation in accordance with any comprehensive "contract" about the division of total income or even the total cooperative surplus. I would be foolhardy to insist that there is no conceivable escape from this dilemma. I have suggested one way out in discussing what might justify Rawls's amalgamation of precooperative income and the cooperative surplus. But that way out, if it is a way out, is much more plausible for the domestic than for the international case. Thus, it provides no way out for Beitz.

Were Beitz to avoid this dilemma by simply abandoning contractarian arguments, he would be left only with arguments from moral arbitrariness. Yet Beitz's own skepticism about treating natural talents as morally arbitrary and as collective assets should carry over to a skepticism about treating the products of natural talents as common assets. For this is precisely what the difference principle does.[23] Hence, Beitz should be especially dubious about getting to a global difference principle by means of any moral arbitrariness argument. Uneasy is Beitz's case for global redistribution.

NOTES

This chapter was completed during the tenure of a summer research grant from the Murphy Institute for Political Economy of Tulane University.

1. Charles Beitz, *Political Theory and International Relations* (Princeton, N.J.: Princeton University Press, 1979).
2. Beitz explicitly denies that social cooperation is the root of all social obligations because he wants to maintain that we would be bound by the resource redistribution principle even were there no international social cooperation. Beitz does claim that social cooperation is the foundation of distributive justice. It is because distributive justice rests on cooperation and the resource principle does not that Beitz cannot classify, and does not classify, the resource principle as a principle of distributive justice.
3. John Rawls, *A Theory of Justice* (Cambridge, Mass.: Harvard University Press, 1971), especially pp. 378–379.
4. Beitz comes close to recognizing this, but retreats in his final phrase to a trivial claim when he argues that where social cooperation is absent, there are no benefits or burdens of cooperation, and thus that there are conflicting distributive claims concerning the fruits of cooperation. Also see note 11.
5. There are many aspects of Beitz's "worldview" that, although not central to any one of his philosophical arguments, provide them with a congenial collective setting. I provide a sample of these in order to indicate my dissent from them: Beitz's comfort with talk about a *society's* chances, a *nation's* wealth, a *state's* economy; his tendency to see international trade as (appropriately) trade among states, all of whom should be free of difficulty in controlling their own economies; his readiness to assign distributive shares (at least derivatively) to states—that is, to politicians, as though the endowment of this already well-positioned class has any positive relation to the well-being of its subjects; his impartial rationalism, which sees people's stronger ties to nearby individuals and small groups than to the global community as irrational impediments to the implementation of a global difference principle.
6. For movement back and forth between the contractarian and the moral arbitrariness arguments see the third and fourth paragraphs of Beitz's section on "Entitlements to Natural Resources."
7. It is unclear to me whether Beitz takes individuals or societies to be the primary subjects of the resource redistribution principle. I follow those passages in Beitz that discuss resource redistribution in the language of individuals.
8. Rawls, *A Theory of Justice*, p. 66 and pp. 65–75 generally.
9. Ibid., p. 75.
10. Cf., ibid., pp. 126–130.
11. This is the nub of my philosophical dispute with Beitz. He notes the existence of versions of contract theory according to which social cooperation is the root of all social obligations. He rejects these versions, although he says nothing in defense of his conclusion that there can be obligations that are not based on social cooperation *and* that are to be affirmed on the basis of some *contract* argument. I emphasize that I am not endorsing one of the versions of contract theory that Beitz rejects. I am merely claiming that such versions are the plausibly motivated versions of contract theory.
12. Rawls, *A Theory of Justice*, p. 102.
13. Ibid.
14. Ibid.

15. Ibid.

16. An advocate of such an entitlement view, while opposing redistribution for its own sake, may well condemn many existing holdings—for example, nationalized natural resources or privately held resources obtained through political means—as violating entitlement principles and may well call for rectifying transfers.

17. Beitz's search for the *globally* least-well-off "representative man" should be more difficult than the search for a given society's least-well-off "representative man." Is he the hunter-gatherer, the unemployed and unskilled urbanite, or the collective farm worker?

18. Cf. Robert Nozick, *Anarchy, State and Utopia* (New York: Basic Books, 1974), pp. 183–189.

19. As Nozick points out, this proposition clashes with the prominent idea in Rawls that rational social judgments can be made about who should be offered what incentives.

20. Agents' precooperative income is not their income when they are engaged in a cooperative scheme minus the income "due to" that cooperation. For had they not been engaged in that cooperative scheme, they would have pursued other noncooperative activities. If the United States were to cease all international trade, its income would drop less than the amount that is currently "due to" that trade.

21. Won't a nation that is offered less in exchange for international cooperation than its precooperative income lack any incentive for international cooperation? Only if that nation is allowed to keep its autarkic income should it opt for the autarkic path. But an amalgamating global difference principle will not allow this.

22. As a classical liberal I favor laissez faire writ small—that is, as a domestic and an international economic order based on individuals' entitlements over themselves, their talents, their precooperative products, and those products or shares that accrue to individuals in accordance with all the cooperative schemes they choose to enter into both intranationally and transnationally. What such an economic order would look like and how it would *not* incorporate the many injustices introduced by (attempted) state control of both national economies and transnational economic activity is a project for another time and another author.

23. Rawls, *A Theory of Justice*, p. 101.

3

Hunger, Needs, and Rights

ONORA O'NEILL

Are those of us who live in affluent countries obligated to help the hungry of the world? Certainly some group would be obligated if the needy had a right to receive help, but it is difficult to establish the existence of any such right. The main ethical theories do not help much toward establishing either a right to receive needed aid or an obligation to give it. Onora O'Neill thinks that the question of whether the desperate have a right to have their needs met is best addressed indirectly, by asking what people's obligations are. A general theory of obligations will give us an answer to the more specific question of our obligations toward the needy. Such a theory must begin with the Kantian assumption that everyone has the same obligations, so that everyone is to act only on obligation-specifying principles that can be acted on by all. But a commitment to act on shared principles must include a commitment to develop the capacities to act and to assist those whose capacities are insufficient or faltering. Hence, O'Neill concludes, we do have an obligation to help the needy. We must help them to become and remain moral agents.

In the 1980s, there are hundreds of millions of human beings who go hungry. At most times, there are millions whose hunger is so severe that they starve, become ill, and may die. Where there is famine, many starve. The publicity given to these events often suggests that hunger and famine

are natural disasters, produced by floods, droughts, blights, and other forces
of nature. However, in the mid-1980s it is increasingly clear that bad weather
and pests alone need not and do not produce massive human disasters.
Weather and pests do so only when social and economic structures are too
fragile to cope with normal fluctuations. Where social and economic structures
are robust enough to provide for harsh climates and other recurrent difficulties
we do not accept high death rates as natural. Nobody would accept the
deaths of many southern Californians because they live in a natural desert
or of Minnesotans because of severe winters. The problems of hunger and
famine in other parts of the world are also not irremediable natural realities.

Given that these disasters are remediable, we can raise many practical
questions about them. The questions most often asked are "how" questions.
How can hunger be reduced? Is it a matter of advances in agriculture?
Of higher investment in poor economies? Of reducing population growth?
Of reforming systems of land tenure? Of preventing migration to the cities?
Of massive transfer of resources from rich to poor countries? These questions
are complicated; probably different answers are needed for different situations
and different parts of the world.

Before we reach the "how" questions, however, we must answer certain
"why" questions. Why should we take steps to deal with world hunger? Is
world hunger perhaps a problem for those who are hungry, but of no concern
to those of us who have enough to eat? What claims have the hungry on
us? Is it wrong to do nothing? Why? If we come to the conclusion that
there is nothing wrong with leaving the hungry to starve, then there is little
reason to ask "how" questions. This chapter will look at some of the ways
in which we might approach the "why" questions. If we find that there are
good reasons to help the hungry, we will not have "the answers," but we
at least will have reason for putting energy and resources into answering
the "how" questions.

NEEDS AND HAPPINESS

Imagine that your doorbell rings one evening and you find on the doorstep
an emaciated family. They obviously are hungry and desperate. Few of us
would hesitate. We are clear enough about the urgency of need when it is
in front of our eyes. Of course, we might not have enough food, or we
might hope to hand the problem over to welfare officials quickly; but for
most of us the thought of turning a starving person from our homes is
repugnant. Those of us who have grown up with the traditions and parables
of Jewish or Christian life see refusal to help those in great need as a
paradigm of wrongdoing. We remember the parable of the Good Samaritan,
who helped the man that fell among thieves. We remember that neither the
priest nor the Levite helped, and we know the implied answer to Christ's
question, "Which of these was neighbor to him that fell among thieves?"
In Christian and Jewish thought, and in other religious traditions also,
meeting others' *needs*, including the needs of strangers, is and has always
been a central matter of ethical concern.

Yet when we turn to present-day ethical theories, we find that need is often no longer a central category. This transformation of popular and philosophical ethical thinking has taken various forms, of which utilitarian reasoning and human rights theories are probably the most significant today, at least in the English-speaking world.

Utilitarian thinking concentrates on seeking those optimal lines of action that will secure the greatest total happiness. Of course, meeting needs is often one way of producing happiness, but it is not the only way, and for utilitarians, meeting needs has no automatic priority over other ways of making people happy. If maximal happiness were produced by action that leaves some people in need—or even exacerbates their needs—then, according to utilitarian thinking, it would be wrong to meet those needs.

This harsh conclusion is often blurred. Sometimes meeting needs will maximize happiness; sometimes it is quite unclear which line of action would maximize happiness. Utilitarian writers disagree about which policies are optimal. Some hold that a massive transfer of resources from rich to poor will maximize happiness. These theorists suggest (invoking standard marginalist considerations) that a given sum of money or other resources yields more happiness for those who start with less. But other utilitarian thinkers have reasoned that transfer payments will produce economic dependence and (they suggest) fuel population growth, which ultimately outstrips all possible aid and so will lead to dire misery in the long run.[1] According to this view, maximal happiness would be produced by leaving those in greatest need to suffer the consequences. Even if utilitarians could settle their disputes, they would still be committed to the production of happiness rather than the alleviation of need. All utilitarian thinking sets as much store by increasing the happiness of somebody who is in no way needy as by equivalent increases of happiness produced by meeting needs.

Utilitarianism is a mode of ethical thinking that takes a subjective view of what is good. What matters is happiness, the experiences that we subjectively have. Thinking about human needs is a matter of thinking about what is objectively required for fulfilled human life. Sometimes people want and would be made happy by things that stand in the way of their needs being met. They may want cigarettes more than good health or their traditional way of life more than a modern one that reduces poverty or increases food supplies.

Here we begin to see some of the deeper reasons why the category of need has faded from modern ethical thought. We hesitate to declare that we can know what is objectively good. We have lost the certainties of classical and of religious ethics about what human beings need in order to lead good and flourishing lives. If we cannot be sure what the good is, how can we claim that human beings need certain things and that meeting their needs should take priority over the pursuit of happiness? The category of need became marginal in modern ethical thinking with the rejection of the Aristotelian and Christian picture of a determinate human nature, whose flourishing or fulfillment would be thwarted if certain conditions—those that humans need—were not met. In its place much modern political and ethical thought placed the pursuit of happiness. Indeed, much modern liberal thinking claims to be "agnostic about the good for man."²

NEEDS AND RIGHTS

Utilitarian thinking is not the only modern approach to ethical issues in which the category of need has become marginal. Theories of human rights, which have become immensely influential in the 1970s and 1980s, also place little weight on meeting human needs. Of course, if we could show that everybody has a right to have his or her needs met, including a right to food, or more comprehensively, as the U.N. Universal Declaration of Human Rights puts it, "a right to a standard of living adequate for the well being of himself and his family, including food," all would be plain sailing. But we cannot show that everybody has some right merely by pointing to a document—however grand—that states that everybody has that right. When we talk about human rights, we are talking about those fundamental rights (if there are any) that justify or prohibit the establishment of certain sorts of statutory or positive rights. We cannot establish fundamental rights by pointing to existing legal documents. By contrast, if we can show that there are certain fundamental rights, we will have standards by which to judge and revise charters, constitutions, and policies.

What does it take to show that people have some right? One necessary requirement is surely to show that others have obligations to respect or fulfill that right. If nobody has such obligations, there just is no right at all. There cannot be a right not to be assaulted unless others have an obligation not to assault. There cannot be a right to vote unless others have an obligation not to interfere with voting. You have no right to the bank paying out the money you have deposited unless the bank has an obligation to do so. This is commonplace and uncontroversial. So we could begin the task of showing that everybody has a right to food by showing that there is a counterpart obligation to provide that food to which everybody has a right. Here we find a major obstacle.

We have a right if we are entitled to claim certain sorts of action or forebearance from whomever holds the counterpart obligation. There is a right to food only if there is some agent or institution that has the obligation to provide food to those who are hungry. Who has such an obligation? We can imagine a wide variety of answers. For example, the obligation to feed the hungry belongs to their own families or communities; to the government of the country in which they live; to the United Nations or to other corporate, voluntary, or political international organizations; or to the citizens of more prosperous parts of the world. Usually when people are really hungry it is pointless to suggest that their families or local communities have an obligation to provide food. Real hunger occurs precisely when local resources are exhausted. However, who else has the obligation? Unless we can answer this question, asserting that there is a right to food or a right to have one's basic needs met is mere, and callous, rhetoric.

Two conflicting answers are currently given to this question by writers on human rights. One answer, which I label the libertarian answer, is that nobody has an obligation to feed the hungry, and consequently the hungry have no right to food, unless they have entered into special relationships by which others incurred special obligations to feed them. The other answer I call the welfare answer, which contends that because there is a right to food (and to other necessities of life), every person and every political entity, including each nation-state, have obligations to make good on this right by assigning and then enforcing obligations to provide food for the hungry. These two visions of human rights have radically different implications for problems of world hunger. I shall sketch these before turning to the arguments that we might use for or against either vision.

TWO VISIONS OF THE RIGHTS OF THE HUNGRY

The libertarian vision of human rights sees all fundamental rights as *liberty rights* or freedoms from others' interference. Rights are simply entitlements not to be interfered with. Because needs cannot be met merely by a policy of noninterference, there can be no right to have one's needs met. The hungry have no right to food. The only way anybody can acquire a right to some positive action or service from another is when the two have entered some special relationship. For example, if somebody hungry has bought food, he or she is entitled to have it delivered and the vendor has an obligation to deliver; if somebody is a member of a family that has food supplies, he or she has the customary entitlements of relatives to share in the available food. Those who are really hungry usually lack special rights to food.

Within a libertarian vision of rights there is no required response to others' need, however dire. At the same time, libertarians often will remind those who criticize them as harsh or callous that they leave room for, and indeed admire, voluntary charitable action undertaken by individuals and that charity may save the hungry.

This appeal to charity is unconvincing for two reasons. The first reason is that as things are in the world today, hunger is far too large a problem, and far too closely connected with major issues of political and economic power and policy, to be remedied by individual voluntary action. Charity may help in the short run where there has been major political or economic failure, but charity cannot substitute for the sustained working of effective institutions and policies that prevent hunger. Even when nothing better can be offered in the short term, charity cannot substitute for good development policies.

The illusion that charity is the appropriate response to world hunger is sustained by comparisons made in the media (also in the publicity of major charities) between one-time emergencies, such as earthquakes, floods, or wars, and long-term, systemic problems, such as world hunger. The comparison is apt in one way: Like natural disasters and wars, world hunger causes hideous suffering and shortens lives. But in other ways the comparison is inept. Most hungry people have not suffered any sudden disruption or disaster that can be remedied by emergency relief. Alas, the hungry are mostly living their normal lives, with their normal resources and their ordinary social and economic relations, which are too fragile to sustain what are often quite minor ups and downs of climate, harvest, or market forces. We all know that slight declines in supplies can trigger large price rises, create incentives to hoard, and leave the weakest unable to compete in the market. When the market we are talking about is the market for the means of life, these abstract economic forces end lives. Short-term relief of the sorts charities aim to organize can prevent immediate deaths, but cannot produce the social or economic transformations that sustain lives.

The second problem with relying on charity as a response to hunger or other major human needs is that charity is not taken seriously within the libertarian vision. Traditional religious views of charity saw it as a matter of obligation. Obligations of charity were not "perfect" obligations, to which rights correspond; yet they were considered real, if "imperfect" obligations. In the Western religious tradition, there was no suggestion that "imperfect" obligations were optional. These obligations were called imperfect only to indicate that they were incomplete. Given that we cannot provide all help that is needed by all others on all occasions, our obligations to help meet needs must be incomplete in the sense that we cannot do everything and cannot (in the abstract) specify whom we should help when and how much. Because we cannot identify who among the possible recipients of help is entitled to help from which others, we cannot speak of rights to be helped. By contrast, obligations not to interfere can be complete—it is possible to refrain from battering, killing, or defrauding *all* others at *all* times, so here we can talk of corresponding rights. In traditional views, help to the needy and justice are both obligatory, but justice can be accorded to all, while help can be given only to some. Hence, the allocation of justice assigns rights to the recipients, but the allocation of help does not.

It is an interesting intellectual, or perhaps ideological, curiosity of the present day that many people profess commitment to two incompatible ethical positions. Many advocate a libertarian vision of rights, which takes seriously only those obligations not to interfere that correspond to liberty rights. Yet the same people also claim to be committed to religious traditions that take a wider view of obligations and think it obligatory to help meet the needs of others, including the needs of strangers. Laissez faire is embraced together with the parable of the Good Samaritan. Those who are aware of the conflicts between these visions of human obligations sometimes try to resolve the conflicts by insisting that the libertarian vision is correct for public affairs and the religious vision for the private domain. There is a long chapter of Western intellectual history behind this attempted reconciliation of incompatibles. Although a discussion of this attempted reconciliation is beyond the scope of this chapter, I can point out some of the central questions such a discussion would have to raise. How should we distinguish between public and private spheres? If we relegate a religious vision to a private sphere and deny its application to matters public and political, are we taking the vision seriously? In particular, is an interpretation of the parable of the Good Samaritan that limits its applicability to private and local matters consonant with the actual message of the parable? Or does such a privatized interpretation tacitly subordinate the Christian vision to the libertarian one?

The second widely discussed contemporary vision of human rights also sees liberty rights as central human rights. Unlike the libertarian view, however, this second vision asserts that there are also rights to certain sorts of goods and services, and in particular to the fulfillment of basic needs. For example, some maintain that there are rights to food, rights to basic health care, and rights to education. These rights are commonly referred to as welfare rights. The label is an ill-chosen one because the term *welfare* has been put to various uses, including (especially in the United States) that of indicating goods and services to which people are *not* entitled. For those who take the term to mean something like handout or undeserved benefit, the thought that there could be welfare rights must appear puzzling indeed. This, however, is no more than one of those unhappy historical accidents that happen to quite respectable words. In any case, the claim that there are rights to have basic needs met cannot be rejected by calling such rights welfare rights and then pointing out that the very idea of a welfare right is paradoxical if one assumes a certain interpretation of "welfare."

Welfare rights cannot be dismissed out of hand. But establishing that there are such rights is another matter. Appeal to grand international or constitutional documents is no more decisive here than it is for the libertarian vision of all rights as liberty rights. If we are to settle the debates about fundamental rights, we have to go beyond the charters and proclamations.

It hardly needs saying that it will matter a great deal to those who are hungry how this issue is decided. Behind the ebb and flow of current politics and economic struggles lie legal and institutional structures and policies whose form reflects (no doubt imperfectly) certain conceptions of human obligations. If we could show that our only obligations are to respect liberty rights, we could vindicate a laissez-faire policy toward the needs of the hungry. All that the poor and hungry would be owed are the same freedoms from interference that those with plenty are owed. If, on the other hand, we could establish that there are welfare as well as liberty rights, obligations would not be met and justice could not be achieved by institutions or policies that take a laissez-faire approach to others' needs. Justice to those in need might demand arduous and specific action on the part of those who have the obligations to meet those needs. It is no idle theoretical concern that leads us to consider the fundamental arguments offered by various theories of human rights. I shall look in turn at the prospects for establishing a libertarian rights and a broader conception of human rights that includes welfare rights.

LIBERTARIAN CONSTRUCTIONS OF RIGHTS

Libertarian thinking takes the notion of liberty as fundamental and interprets this liberty in a quite restricted way as a matter of freedom from interference. Human rights are defined as the set of arrangements needed to guarantee equal and maximal liberty for all. Modern interpretations of this thought are sophisticated and clear. Unlike the eighteenth century documents, such as Tom Paine's *The Rights of Man* or the Declarations of Rights of the American and French revolutions, present-day interpretations do not base rights on a mixture of appeals to self-evidence, human nature, or divine authority. Contemporary theories of human rights try to justify a specific list of rights by constructing the set of rights that would constitute the best realization of equal liberty for all. Of course, some people doubt whether liberty, however interpreted, should be given this fundamental status. I propose to leave that issue aside and consider whether, if we accepted that liberty was fundamental, the libertarian construction would work. If the construction works, we then will need to check whether the platform on which it rests—the priority given to (a certain interpretation of) liberty— is sound. If the construction does not even work, we can spare ourselves that labor.

The construction of a libertarian account of human rights requires that we find the *largest* set of liberties that is *consistently extendable to everybody*.[3] It is easy to see how this standard can be used to rule out certain rights as spurious. Liberty rights are consistently extendable only when the counterpart obligations not to interfere are compatible with the exercise of the right. We can see that there can be no rights to privileges, or rights to success, or rights to win in competitive activities, for all these rights would require that others grant us privileges or successes that would prevent them having a like right. Such bogus rights in principle could not be held by all.

However, we cannot provide a libertarian construction of rights just by ruling out those spurious rights that cannot be extended to all. We also would have to show which one of many mutually consistent, universally extendable sets of rights should be preferred. This stage of the libertarian construction faces serious difficulties. There is no unique set of rights that includes all others. Because liberty rights can themselves be in conflict, we cannot construct a consistent set that includes all possible liberty rights. For example, there cannot be both an unconditional right of access to public places *and* an unconditional right of assembly in public places for political purposes. If both rights were unconditional, they would conflict with one another. Hence, one or the other of these possible rights must be excluded from any consistent set of rights. There are many ways in which rights of assembly and of access can be accommodated to one another. The same holds true for other sets of liberty rights. To determine which rights human beings actually have, we need to work out which set of mutually consistent, universally holdable rights is *largest*. Yet there is no ready way to do this, for there is no metric that tells us which rights or sets of rights are larger or more extensive than other rights or sets of rights.

Given this lack of metric, it is puzzling that rights theorists make such widespread use of the idea of the most extensive liberty. What creates the impression that we can tell which set of liberty rights is the largest? I believe that the impression is due in very large part to the constant use of a set of *spatial* or *territorial* and often *proprietary* metaphors in discussions of rights. Rights constantly are spoken of as "spheres" or "territories," which right-holders are entitled to defend by excluding others. Those who violate rights are said to "invade" others' rights or to "cross borders."

These metaphors have a long history. They arose in seventeenth and eighteenth century Europe, whose central political concerns were the power and conflicts of nation-states and their territorial integrity, and whose economic development often centered on the enclosure of land whose use had once been either common or unassigned. In such a world, as well as in the New Worlds, where conquest and colonization, "clearing" native peoples and establishing plantations, and homesteading, ranching, and vanishing frontiers obtained, it was all too easy to think of all rights on the model of property rights and of property rights on the model of owning a piece of land—what came to be called "a property." This history encouraged the illusion that rights themselves, rather than some things that people (may) have (exclusive) rights to use, have spatial dimensions. Illusion it is, however. Even rights in landed property do not literally have size or shape. They are rights to use certain resources in certain ways to the exclusion of others. A right is not any larger when it is exercised over a larger area or object. Somebody who buys both a loaf of bread and a roll does not have a larger right to the loaf.

If rights do not literally have a spatial structure, we cannot determine which set of possible liberty rights is the greatest. Distinct rights can be made mutually consistent in varied, mutually exclusive ways; hence, we can find no all encompassing set of rights. Nor is there even a core set of basic liberty rights that is included in all consistent sets of liberty rights. Consider any two putative members of such a core set of rights. They, too, could be mutually adjusted in varied ways, thereby forming alternative core sets and precluding any unique core set. Therefore, we cannot establish what human rights there are by looking for a largest consistent set of liberty rights.

This argument meets those who advocate a libertarian interpretation of rights on their chosen ground. The point is not that libertarians fail to pay enough attention to human needs and welfare, for libertarian advocates would retort that justice requires no attention to needs or welfare. Rather, libertarian accounts of justice fail in their chosen objective of providing an account of maximal liberty. Nevertheless, the critical argument advanced here does not provide us with an adequate account of human rights. The inadequacy of libertarian constructions does not show that other accounts of human rights succeed; it shows only that the libertarian construction of rights does not work.

WELFARE RIGHTS CONSTRUCTIONS

An alternative approach to constructing a theory of rights is used by those who think that there are welfare as well as liberty rights. One promising line of argument is the following: Rights of all sorts are of use and value only to those who can act. Even paradigmatic liberty rights, such as rights to vote or to speak freely, are useless to those who cannot act. Those who are starving, physically weak, or abysmally ignorant cannot use such liberty rights. Hence, if there are *any* rights, there must be *basic rights* to have needs met. Basic rights are rights to those goods, services, or liberties that are needed if human beings are to become and remain agents. Human agency fails to develop if children are starved or grossly deprived of socialization; hence, it would be a basic right that these needs be met. Human agency is destroyed by severe damage to health, by hunger and oppression; hence, it would be a basic right that needs for survival, including basic health, food, and minimal physical security, be met. Some basic rights must be welfare rights.

This is an impressive line of reasoning that has been developed and refined by several recent writers[4] and is conceived as a critique of the libertarian view of rights. This critique confronts anybody who already holds that there are rights with reasons to think that these must include welfare as well as liberty rights. It insists that human beings are not ideal, disembodied agents, but material beings whose agency depends on their material needs being met. However, those not already committed to thinking that there are human rights are given no reasons to conclude that there are. The argument, as sketched, might lead in either of two directions. We might conclude (1) that because there are rights there are also basic welfare rights or (2) that neither basic welfare nor other rights have been established.

What reason can those who hold the first view give for thinking that there are any rights? If these theorists are to be convincing, they must at least show who bears the obligations that are the counterpart to such rights. Advocates of a libertarian conception of justice have no difficulty in showing to whom the counterpart obligations are allocated. Because libertarians hold that all rights are liberty rights, the only recognized obligations are negative obligations not to interfere, which fall universally on all individuals and all institutions. The obligations that correspond to liberty rights can and must be universal obligations; liberty is curtailed if anybody or any institution is permitted to infringe it. But advocates of welfare rights cannot plausibly use this line of argument. The obligations that must exist if there are any welfare rights are obligations to provide goods and services to particular persons at particular places. It would be absurd to claim that everyone has an obligation to provide a morsel of food or a fraction of an income to each deprived person. Goods and services have to be rendered by particular persons or institutions to some others.

Advocates of welfare rights face the problem that allocation *cannot* here be universal and thus remains undetermined. Some have argued that this raises no problem once we address the institutionalization of rights.[5] All rights, even liberty rights, can be enforced only by allocating specific powers and obligations to particular agents and institutions. In this respect, there is nothing special about welfare rights. However, we cannot move on to questions of enforcement until we know what human rights there are. For we would not know what should be enforced.

There is a real asymmetry between welfare and liberty rights that cannot be overcome by postponing the question of who has obligations to meet whose basic needs and treating it as a matter that arises only in contexts of enforcing and institutionalizing rights. Yet we cannot simply assume that existing institutions (states? international agencies? transnational corporations? charities?) should meet welfare rights. First, current institutional structures may be sources of world hunger rather than of its remedy; hence, allocating obligations to meet needs on the basis of the status quo may backfire. Second, appeals to existing laws and institutions in the course of an argument to discover what rights there are only beg questions; such appeals commit what is often called the naturalistic fallacy.

THE PERSPECTIVE OF OBLIGATIONS

The project of constructing a determinate account of human rights looks unpromising. Even a libertarian theory of rights is indeterminate, and theories that include welfare rights face further difficulties in allocating the obligations that correspond to welfare rights. Yet if obligations are unallocated, we have no more than the rhetoric of charters and manifestos. In addition, theories that make rights fundamental are mute on the subject of imperfect obligations.

These two problems are closely linked. Imperfect obligations were supposed to be obligations to help and support others. If all ethical relations are grounded in rights and all rights are liberty rights, then imperfect obligations vanish. This is a point to which proponents of welfare rights are sensitive. These proponents take seriously the libertarian criticism that no rights correspond to imperfect obligations, which are therefore no matter of justice, and undertake to show that help and support to others in need is, after all, a matter of perfect obligation and therefore is as central to justice as the recognition of liberty rights. If the argument had succeeded, we would at least have less need for a theory of imperfect obligations; those in need would find in welfare rights better arguments for demanding others' help than they could have mustered within the terms of any theory of imperfect obligation.

However, if the argument for welfare rights also fails to allocate the corresponding obligations, our best strategy may be to stay within a conceptual framework that takes imperfect obligations seriously. This cannot be done within the framework of any theory that makes rights the fundamental ethical category because no rights correspond to imperfect obligations. However, by reversing our perspective we can reach a standpoint that affords a view of imperfect obligations. The alternative perspective can be explored by constructing a theory of obligations rather than of rights.

78   *Onora O'Neill*

If we were able to construct a theory of obligations, the problem of the allocation of obligations would be solved in the process of construction, although it would still be the case that imperfect obligations lacked counterpart rights. This, however, might not be a practical disaster. Those who have obligations can seek to fulfill them whether or not particular others have rights to the performance of those obligations. Imperfect obligations can even be enforced, although their performance cannot be claimed by particular right-holders. (Of course, we may conclude that imperfect obligations ought not to be enforced, but that is a further question.) While rights without counterpart obligations are mere rhetoric, obligations without counterpart rights provide agents with solid reasons to act.

A change of perspective from rights to obligations makes agents and agency central. Theories of rights indeed see agents as indispensable (without agents, no rights could be recognized or respected), yet oddly focus on those who are to *receive* rather than on those who are to *act*. There are political and rhetorical reasons why this focus is sometimes useful. When the aim is to exert pressure from below to secure the performance of obligations that are not acknowledged, the best or only strategy may be to galvanize the powerless to claim others' action. Galvanizing may work best when the powerless see themselves as holders of rights. Yet no amount of galvanizing would have effect if the (relatively) powerful could not act, for pressure and encouragement could not then bring them to do so.

If we take a long view, we can see that the perspective of agents and their obligations, rather than that of right-holders and their entitlements, is not only conceptually more basic but has been historically more important. The notion of obligation has been part of all ethical and political thought, secular and religious, since antiquity. The notion of rights is a seventeenth century innovation, and the notion that rights are ethically basic is an eighteenth century one. Yet neither innovation gained new ground. Even an incomplete theory of obligations—the part that deals only with perfect obligations—provides all that is needed to ground rights; a more complete theory of obligations captures matters that must be ignored by those who make rights fundamental. Nothing then is lost by adopting the broader perspective of obligations, and something may be gained.

THE UNIVERSALIZING CONSTRUCTION

How could we construct a theory of human obligations? A first move might be the exact counterpart of the one used to construct theories of rights. We could begin by insisting that all should have the same fundamental obligations (whose specific requirements might vary with circumstance). This amounts only to denying that some are by nature privileged or by nature subordinate. If we are neither natural slaves nor natural masters, it is reasonable that we should have the same obligations. This thought can be expressed in a different way by aiming to construct *principles of obligation* that could hold for all human beings. Universal human obligations cannot be based on principles that presume privilege for some; an articulation of universal obligations must reject principles of action that cannot be shared by all.

By itself this may seem a slender basis for any theory of human obligations. Nevertheless, the insistence that human obligations require us to reject principles that cannot be acted on by all is not new. It is the very standard Immanuel Kant used in the late eighteenth century when he constructed the first account of human obligations that appealed neither to tradition nor to religion. Following Kant's lead we may label this method for constructing the outline of an account of human obligations a universalizing construction. Of course, venerable antecedents are no guarantee of sound argument; we had better move slowly in considering the possibility of constructing a theory of universal obligations. We can begin by rehearsing what it is to have an obligation.

When we have an obligation, we are required to do or omit some type of action. Sometimes we are required to do or omit this type of action for *all* others. Sometimes we are required to do or omit it for *specified* others. Sometimes we are required to do or omit the action for *unspecified* others, but not for *all* others. Obligations of the first two sorts—universal and special-perfect obligations—may be thought of as having corresponding rights. Obligations of the third sort cannot plausibly be thought of as having corresponding rights; they are (whether universal or special) imperfect obligations. All of this is just a review of terrain we have explored, which is now mapped from the perspective of the agent rather than from the perspective of those entitled to receive action of a certain type from others.

What sorts of principles of action are ruled out by reliance on a universalizing construction? Can principles that are acted on by each be acted on by all? Will any exceptions that refer to unique achievements or particular objects be trivial? To be sure, not everyone can eat the same loaf or live in the same house. However, we do not expect principles of action to be peculiar to individual cases. Principles of action are presumably fairly indeterminate; they are formulated to apply to a range of cases, not to a unique or privileged situation. A universalizing construction of obligations demands not that any (or every) principle of action that uses some arbitrary description of a given act be universally adoptable, but that the fundamental principles that govern the choice of particular actions be so.[6]

Not every fundamental principle of action is universally adoptable. There are certain principles that can be acted on by any one person, but cannot be acted on by all. Consider the principle of deceiving (whose varied modes include fraud, false promising, and cheating). Deceit only works against a background of trust; trust would be destroyed by universal deceit; hence, successful deceit requires that not everybody deceive. A principle of deceit cannot be universalized; the universalizing construction shows that it is a human obligation to avoid action that is based on principles of deceit.

An analogous argument shows that the rejection of principles of coercion is also a matter of obligations. Coercion, too, has many modes, which include the use of force, threat and, more specifically, slavery, torture, and forced labor. Each mode of coercion denies or destroys the agency of its victims. This reveals that a principle of coercion cannot be universally acted on. Principles can be universally acted on only when others' agency is respected, and the core of respect for agency is not to destroy or override it.

These two arguments are closely connected to those by which libertarian thinkers establish human rights. Libertarian arguments also establish obligations that are universally held and are owed to all other agents. Noncoercion and nondeceit are generally a matter of not interfering with others' agency, either by circumventing it (deceit) or by overriding or destroying it (coercion). These are perfect obligations, matters of justice that are owed by all to all. In this domain, constructivist accounts of obligations are the mirror image of constructivist accounts of rights. Each construction is a demonstration that those who do not have ethical relations that reflect privilege and subordination have mutual rights and obligations that exclude destroying, coercing, or deceiving one another.

These principles of obligation cast a severe light on the European penetration and annexation of other continents in the early modern period. Colonizers standardly did serious injustice to the native peoples whose lives they disrupted and ended and whose land they took. Deceit and coercion, even slavery, were the order of the day. From Connecticut to the Congo, genocide was frequent. Those of us who are descendants of the explorers and colonists can look back in shame.

We can also wonder how much rectification is owed for undoubted injustices. If those who did the wrongs and their victims were still alive, we would surely think that restitution and compensation were necessary and appropriate; they would be urgent matters of rectificatory justice, analogous to questions about punishment of Nazi war criminals and compensation for their victims. However, we are now by and large so distant from the crimes of colonialism that we cannot tell who ought to make what restitution to whom. So many victims have perished, often without descendants; so many crimes are unrecorded. We doubt whether the sins of the fathers should be visited on the children and often cannot identify the children. Perhaps some or much of the hunger of today can be traced in part to ancient wrongs; but too much is obscure for us to work out just what restitution and punishment are appropriate.

If ancient wrongs cannot now be righted, can we assume that we have met our obligations to those who are hungry provided we now refrain from deceit and coercion? Does the universalizing construction of obligations conform to the libertarian construction of perfect rights and demand no more than policies of national noncoercion and commercial laissez faire? Would such policies be enough to secure justice for the poverty-stricken parts of the world?

Laissez faire—noninterference—is hardly possible in an interdependent world. For laissez faire is not just a matter of refusing help to others, but of not interfering in their action in *any* way. The powerful nations and institutions that determine conditions of manufacture, credit, and trade for the poor world do not practice laissez faire; these actors fix the conditions of life and survival for others.

The distance between the refusal of help that passes for laissez faire and genuine noninterference shows that the universalizing construction of obligations and the libertarian construction of rights are only superficially similar. The libertarian construction looks at what should be received and provides arguments for (supposedly) specific freedoms from interference. Here the emphasis is entirely on noninterference, and the reliance on spatial metaphors appears to allow a simple interpretation of noninterference as a matter of keeping out, of staying away, of doing nothing.

A constructivist account of obligations, by contrast, focuses on actions; it demands that action be based on universally adoptable principles, such as nondeceit and noncoercion. These standards cannot be satisfied merely by policies of selective laissez faire, such as neglect of others' needs. Genuine laissez faire would require complete severance of relations with others. The reality of what is dishonestly now called laissez faire is that powerful nations, institutions, and individuals coerce and deceive weaker ones. It is tempting and fairly easy for the powerful—be they transnational corporations or village moneylenders—to coerce or deceive the weak. Those who live on the margins of survival are so vulnerable that a commitment to refrain from coercing or deceiving them demands much more than noninterference and routine bureaucratic and commercial good practice. What looks outwardly like open bargaining and negotiation between parties with unequal power can mask deception or coercion. The first great advantage of approaching issues of justice by way of an account of obligations is that we see more readily that general principles of justice make different demands in different contexts and that just action and policies often demand more than noninterference.

OBLIGATIONS AND NEEDS

A second great advantage of approaching questions of poverty and hunger by way of a theory of obligations is that we are not restricted to considering those perfect obligations that correspond to human rights. The universalizing construction can also be used to construct principles of imperfect obligation; specifically, the construction can consider human needs.

Human agents are not the abstract rational agents so beloved of social and political science. They are (as advocates of welfare rights emphasize) embodied rational beings whose rationality and agency only develop and survive in adequate material and social conditions. Adequate social conditions themselves collapse without adequate material conditions. Wherever there is endemic hunger, and the poor health and raised death rates that hunger brings, we know that the material conditions necessary for human agency to grow and survive are fragile and failing. If we are to act only on principles that can be acted on by all, we must then do more than refrain from deceit and coercion. Even scrupulous and sensitive adherence to these principles of justice and their appropriate application cannot guarantee that we act on shared standards where some find their very capacities to act threatened. Because human beings are vulnerable and needy, a commitment to act on principles that can be shared by all has to include a commitment to develop capacities to act and to assist those whose capacities to act are insufficient or faltering. It is a matter of obligation to refrain from making a principle that neglects human potential or denies the help needed for agency to survive.

Neither developing human potential nor offering needed help can be a matter of justice. Nor could either be a matter of perfect obligation for the standard reason that neither is the sort of policy that we can enact completely. We cannot develop all the potential of all human beings; indeed, we cannot even develop all of our own potential (some developments will rule out others) or some potential for everybody. Similarly, we cannot provide all others all the help that they may need in all circumstances if they are to remain agents. Both development of potential and help to those who need it must be selective; neither can be more than a matter of imperfect obligation. Nevertheless, imperfect obligations are obligations; they are not optional forms of self-expression or heroic action that exceeds all obligation.

When we look at the vast scale of human hunger and misery, we may feel that principles of imperfect obligation are just not enough. Surely, we may feel, those who try to establish welfare rights are on the right track. For they try to show that the poor have rights to have their needs met. If welfare rights could be established, they would provide more complete reasons for action to end hunger than principles of imperfect obligation provide. However, if welfare rights cannot be determined, we have good reason to look at the framework of obligations within which rights have a place, but not the whole place. Principles of imperfect obligation are not a trivial matter. They offer not a complete account of what is owed, but an addition to an account of perfect obligations. Helping others and developing human potential are not *substitutes for* but *supplements to* just action. If we are to meet our obligations, we must act to help develop human potential as well as to meet human needs.

We may find courage for these tasks if we realize that our obligation is to do something, not to do everything. For doing something lies within our powers, while doing everything does not. Those of us who are less vulnerable, who hold offices in institutions that have some power, and who are citizens of nations that are not powerless or highly vulnerable may find that quite a lot lies within our powers. We may also find it liberating to think in terms of an account of human obligations that is congruent with the older currents of Western religion and tradition and does not demand that we divide our ethical life into separate public and private spheres and govern them by conflicting principles.

NOTES

1. For various utilitarian views on world hunger, see Peter Singer, "Famine, Affluence, and Morality," *Philosophy and Public Affairs* 1 (1972): 229–243; Tony

Jackson, *Against the Grain* (Oxfam: Oxford, 1982); Garrett Hardin, "Lifeboat Ethics: The Case Against Helping the Poor," *Psychology Today* (1974). I have discussed these disagreements among utilitarians and other difficulties with ethical reasoning about world hunger in *Faces of Hunger: An Essay on Poverty, Development and Justice* (London: George Allen and Unwin, 1986).

2. See Ronald Dworkin, "Liberalism," in Stuart Hampshire, ed., *Public and Private Morality* (Cambridge: Cambridge University Press, 1978), pp. 113–143. The theme is most deeply explored in Alasdair MacIntyre, *After Virtue: A Study in Moral Theory* (London: Duckworth, 1981).

3. The origins of the construction are to be found in the writings of Jean-Jacques Rousseau and Immanuel Kant; it is inserted into rather different, liberal (but nonlibertarian) contexts by J. S. Mill and recently by John Rawls and used in a wide variety of ways by contemporary libertarian writers.

4. See, for example, Henry Shue, *Basic Rights: Subsistence, Affluence and U.S. Foreign Policy* (Princeton, N.J.: Princeton University Press, 1980); Alan Gewirth, "Starvation and Human Rights," in *Human Rights: Essays on Justification and Application* (Chicago: University of Chicago Press, 1982). Gewirth offers reasons why those who take themselves to be agents must hold that they, and so others, have some rights.

5. See Shue, ibid.

6. For further clarification of some problems with universalizing constructions, see O'Neill, *Faces of Hunger*.

4

World Hunger, Benevolence, and Justice

WILLIAM AIKEN

William Aiken raises doubts about Onora O'Neill's Kantian argument that we are obligated to help the needy. Nonetheless, he agrees with her claim that we are obligated to help them. He thinks that O'Neill is too quick to dismiss the view that people have welfare rights. The answer to O'Neill's question about the bearer of the obligation to meet the requirements imposed by these rights is simple, according to Aiken: Everyone has this obligation, including people who live far from those in need. Because we do, we must create international institutions capable of meeting the requirements of the needy.

The world hunger problem is very complicated, and it is not at all clear what steps should be taken to alleviate it. Nevertheless, a detailed, country-by-country analysis of the causes of hunger is needed. Such a study would examine agricultural and trade history, demographic data and trends, economic arrangements and infrastructures, sociopolitical policies and practices, and roles in and relationships to international economics. On the basis of such an in-depth analysis, careful country-specific plans could be devised to reduce starvation and malnourishment. Then strategies for effective implementation could be created that stress the importance of mustering the necessary political will and economic resources. It is at this point that we could talk about the concrete steps we could take to eliminate world hunger.

It seems to me that these tough "how to" questions are of utmost importance. They should be of primary concern to international policymakers, planners, and economists. But as Onora O'Neill points out in "Hunger, Needs, and Rights," these "how to" questions presuppose that we *ought* to try doing something about world hunger. In her chapter, she asks the prior question, Why should we take steps to deal with world hunger? and she offers an analysis of moral theories rather than an exercise in applying moral principles to the practice of international affairs. She argues that to account for our initial intuition that it is wrong not to help people in need, we must abandon the current moral theories that make rights fundamental and exhaustive of moral responsibility, and we must embrace a moral theory that makes agents and their obligations fundamental. She argues that such a shift will better account for our perfect obligations of justice and our imperfect obligations of benevolence. I will critique her discussion of benevolence and then examine her analysis of justice.

A MATTER OF BENEVOLENCE

O'Neill discusses three theories of benevolence: utilitarianism, libertarian-charity, and her own imperfect obligation approach. Although utilitarianism is grounded in benevolence, it fails to prioritize the alleviation of human needs. Because it adopts a subjective view of the good for humans, it cannot specify some needs as objectively required for human beings to flourish, and thus it does not necessarily prescribe helping hungry people meet their food needs. Although I would argue that rule utilitarianism does prioritize action to alleviate human need (because of marginal utility considerations[1]), I concur with O'Neill's assessment that there is much controversy among utilitarians about what is morally required. This is especially the case when the interests of future generations are included in the calculations. Even though she might have given considerably more attention to the utilitarian argument, I believe that her general critique is well made; it is not clear that utilitarianism places priority on alleviating the food needs of the desperately poor.

According to O'Neill, the libertarian's view of charity is defective because it is optional rather than obligatory (it is supererogatory or "good to do but not wrong not to do"). Because this view is inappropriately privatized (separated from public action), it is ineffective in altering the social and economic relations that contribute to the creation of world hunger and thus is inadequate to meet the needs of the hungry. I agree with her criticism of this view of charity.

O'Neill sees both the utilitarian and the libertarian views of benevolence not only as inadequate to meet effectively the needs of the hungry, but also as erroneous accounts of our obligations of benevolence. In their place, she offers a Kantian theory of imperfect obligation that is neither supererogatory nor, she argues, necessarily privatized. Although she grants that adopting her view of benevolence may not lead to the complete elimination of hunger in the world, she does offer it as a better, more effective, alternative view of our duties of benevolence.

Because O'Neill holds that neither developing human potential nor offering needed help can be a matter of justice when no coercion or deceit is involved, her case for helping the poor ultimately rests on her theory of benevolence. If her theory of benevolence does not stand up well under criticism, then we will be thrown back on one of the rejected theories of benevolence; we will have to turn to some theory of justice to provide moral reasons for why we should help the needy; or we will have to abandon the intuition that it is "wrong to do nothing" about world hunger. I will show that her theory of benevolence is susceptible to substantial criticisms and thus cannot provide adequate reasons for acting to assist the needy.

Let us suppose that she can establish that we have an imperfect obligation to help develop human potential or to meet human needs. Is this obligation of benevolence more effective than the libertarian's notion of charity? Her most forceful criticism of the charity view is that it is ineffectual because it leads to a split between public and private action. In this split, the public domain operates solely by the rules of noninterference, and the meeting of strangers' needs is relegated solely to the sphere of private action. This is ineffectual because the world hunger problem is far too large and too closely connected with major issues of political and economic power to be remedied by individual voluntary action. She assumes that by grounding the duty of benevolence in an imperfect obligation that is not optional (but is selective), we will be able to develop social policies in the "public" domain that will discharge this obligation and that we will be able to generate the social and economic transformations necessary to sustain lives.

But will a government ever enact an international policy that would involve substantial expenditures of taxpayers' money in order to benefit citizens of other nations without thereby gaining some kind of political advantage? Realist assumptions about international politics (that is, that governments determine their international policies exclusively on the grounds of strategic, economic, political, or ideological grounds) would seem to make this unlikely. But perhaps we could say that governments *ought* to act on grounds of benevolence, even though currently they frequently do not. Perhaps some humanitarian famine or disaster relief could be provided solely for benevolent reasons. But this is not the same as effecting substantial social or economic transformations. Radical structural changes are very likely to be perceived by the governments of rich nations as counter to their national interest. Given that the imperfect obligation to be benevolent allows us to be selective in the discharge of this duty, the governments of rich nations would not instigate radical structural changes on grounds of benevolence when those changes would be adverse to the interests of these nations. Rather, they would choose to discharge this duty only when not damaging to their interests. How will the general obligation of benevolence, even if adopted in the public world of policy formation, change the political, social, and economic structures that contribute to world hunger? Will benevolence be any more effective than private voluntary action in this respect?

Given that the production of social and economic transformations in another country where many are starving cannot be done without some compliance by the government of that country, the problem of national sovereignty also arises. If a rich nation attempted to enact, for example, a policy for land reform in a poor country against the expressed will of the government of that country, would this not be an instance of unjustified interference? In light of the lack of an international political community that transcends the sovereignty of each nation-state, such action becomes problematic. It is akin to violating the obligations of justice in dealing with individuals because it would involve coercion. Can benevolence ever justify coercion? On Kantian grounds, it is hard to see how the obligation of benevolence could override the perfect obligations of justice. Of course, one could argue that a government that failed to agree to structural changes that would help to end its citizens' starvation would be unjust and therefore not entitled to autonomy rights. But this will not do in all cases. There are many cultures that do not share our intolerance for life-threatening poverty; rather, they see it as part of the metaphysical order of the world. For instance, a belief in reincarnation and a rigid socioeconomic caste system provide a very different attitude toward human suffering and need. If economic and social structures that generate hunger are rooted in traditional religious beliefs and the only way to alter the economic structures is to challenge the religious beliefs, then it becomes problematic for outsiders to attempt implementing change without being charged with cultural imperialism. Once again, this causes problems with the notion of "autonomy" and the perfect obligations of justice. Will an imperfect obligation of benevolence ever justify such paternalistic changes?

But suppose that coercion is not necessary, that pressure and inducement could persuade another government to agree to the implementation of radical changes. For example, developmental assistance loans could be tied to a radical land reform policy. Provided that rectificatory justice for ancient wrongs is inappropriate, the current landowners whose land will be expropriated and redistributed in the land reform program have legitimate property rights in that land. To seize this land for redistribution would be unjust (it violates a perfect obligation of noncoercion). If these landowners choose not to sell their land to the government, will the imperfect obligation of benevolence justify forcing them to relinquish their holdings? Here again we have a clash between a policy based on an imperfect obligation and the general perfect obligations of justice. Because the imperfect obligation is selective and the perfect is not, would not this require us to choose to discharge our duty of benevolence elsewhere where we can avoid such conflicts with duties of justice? How then are radical changes in social, political, and economic structures going to be effected by this imperfect obligation of benevolence? I just do not see how this obligation is going to justify helping, in any significant way, the world's poor to meet their basic food needs.

We have been assuming that O'Neill can establish the imperfect obligation of benevolence. But it is not clear that she has succeeded in this. She argues that because human agents depend on adequate material and social conditions for the development of their agency, we must not neglect human potential or deny help needed for agency itself to survive. She justifies this by appeal to the "universalizing construction," which demands that action be based on universally adoptable principles. She also contends that because human beings are vulnerable and needy, a commitment to act on shared principles has to include a commitment to develop capacities to act and to assist those whose capacities are insufficient or faltering. Therefore, according to her view, we have an obligation to help develop human potential as well as to meet human needs.

But why? How does the universalizing construction yield this result? To show that a principle of action cannot be adopted by all seems to show that it is either self-contradictory (like deceit) or denies and destroys the agency of its victim (like coercion). How is it self-contradictory or destructive of agency to not help others who are in material need? All who are agents can act on a principle of action that excludes benevolence. To cause another to die of want would be to destroy his or her agency, but if you did not cause the need, how does your failure to alleviate need deny or destroy that person's agency? How does it treat that person as a means? A nonbenevolence principle can be universalized. It is not clear how the fact of our agency being contingent upon material conditions can introduce the obligations to assist others by no other appeal than to the universalizing construction. Furthermore, this focus upon agency bypasses the very difficult problem of young children who, it can be argued, are not yet moral agents but whose welfare is nonetheless contingent upon material conditions. Given that a substantial portion of the world's starving are very young children, this is a problem. The argument would have to be extended to include the obligation to assist those who are not yet, but could become, moral agents. Although this extension could be made, it is not clear that the universalizing construction alone can justify this obligation to assist these needy individuals either.

Immanuel Kant's account of the imperfect obligation to aid the needy (his fourth example in *The Foundations of the Metaphysics of Morals*) does not fare much better.[2] He grants that principles of action that refuse to render assistance to others in time of need can be a universal law of nature (they pass the consistency test) and that the human race could exist under them (they pass the agency-destroying test). But, he says, it is impossible to will such a principle, "for a will which resolved this would conflict with itself, since instances can often arise in which he would need the love and sympathy of others, and in which he would have robbed himself, by such a law of nature springing from his own will, of all hope of the aid he desires."[3]

It appears that he is saying that if you willed a world without the duty of assistance, you may live to regret it. This seems to be a hypothetical imperative that is dependent upon our desire (inclination) for our own self-preservation. This then would be a rule of prudence and not of morality. He may not be saying this, but at least it is not apparent in Kant's version (which O'Neill relies upon) how the categorical imperative generates the duty of benevolence. His version does add the aspect of consistent willing of the principle of action, whereas O'Neill only requires that the principle of action be one that can be universally adopted. This may not be a significant difference, but it seems to render O'Neill's version weaker than Kant's.[4]

Kant's second discussion of the example of benevolence is closer to O'Neill's point. He says,

> Humanity might indeed exist if no one contributed to the happiness of others, provided he did not intentionally detract from it; but this harmony with humanity as an end in itself is only negative rather than positive if everyone does not also endeavor, so far as he can, to further the ends of others. For the ends of any person, who is an end in himself, must as far as possible also be my end, if that conception of an end in itself is to have its full effect on me.[5]

Kant is prescribing positive obligations here. He thinks these obligations follow from the practical imperative ("Act so that you treat humanity, whether in your own person or in that of another, always as an end and never as a means only"[6]). But I do not see how his imperative requires me to make others' ends as far as possible my own. It is understandable that many have picked up on Kant's explanation of perfect obligations and relegated his imperfect obligations to the category of the supererogatory.[7]

What might make his view of identifying with the interests of others work would be an explanation that appealed to the sentiment of sympathy, a sentiment that provokes us to identify with the ends, needs, and hopes of others. Of course this would take us back before Kant, to David Hume or more appropriately to Jean-Jacques Rousseau, and we would no longer be attempting to ground the obligation to help others in need on the universalizing construction performed by reason. Rather, the feeling that it would be wrong not to help another in need would be explained by appeal to the "natural" (or at least cultivated) sentiment of sympathy and to the prescription that we ought to act on our sentiments.

I think this next step in the direction of sympathy is the natural consequence of the way that O'Neill set up the problem. By starting with the intuition that most of us would hesitate to turn a starving family from our doorsteps, she searches through the popular moral theories to see if they can show that turning away needy people is a paradigm of wrongdoing. None of the theories she examines can show this. Likewise, the theory she proposes also fails to establish a paradigm of wrongdoing because O'Neill has not derived the obligation of benevolence from her universalizing construction.

Perhaps a straightforward, sentiment-based ethical theory would help to explain why we feel it would be wrong to turn a starving family from our doors. Let us return to the original scenario proposed by O'Neill: Your doorbell rings one evening and you find an emaciated family on the doorstep.

They are hungry and desperate. Few of us would hesitate to help because the thought of turning a starving person from our homes is repugnant.

Why? Because we pity them, we feel for them, we want to help them, and we would feel guilty if we refused such help. We feel sympathy for them; we may even try to put ourselves in their place and to empathize with them, realizing that "there, but for the grace of God, go I."

Where does this feeling come from? O'Neill points out that those raised in the Jewish or Christian traditions will recognize the feeling as a central part of those traditions, and she cites the parable of the Good Samaritan in support of that contention. Perhaps we derive these feelings from our religious traditions. Or perhaps Rousseau was correct in suggesting that sympathy is a natural moral sentiment, that man "has an innate abhorrence to see beings suffer that resemble him."[8] Although it would be difficult to empirically verify such a claim, let us grant that the sentiment of compassion is a common human feeling. But then so are other feelings. J. S. Mill warns us that there is nothing particularly moral in all of our natural sentiments (for instance, the "natural feeling of retaliation or vengeance").[9] The question is, Should we act on these feelings or not? That we have them is one thing; whether we ought to act on them is quite another. When it comes to revenge, we willingly allow the split between feeling and action, but to raise this distinction in the case of compassion seems about as mean-hearted as answering "No" to the question Am I my brother's keeper? But the link between feelings and prescriptions for action is not automatic. The feelings just are; the prescriptions must be justified. This is best brought out in the world hunger situation by utilitarian objectors to food aid (such as Joseph Fletcher[10]) who argue that in the long run acting on such feelings of compassion will prove detrimental to the recipients of that aid. This is so because it will create dependency; or disrupt local agriculture and produce a net negative effect on the plight of the poor; or exacerbate population growth problems, which eventually will result in more starvation; or prolong the power of corrupt governments by pacifying the desperately poor. Even a moral theory like utilitarianism that makes benevolence its fundamental moral principle does not take the sentiment of sympathy as an automatic justification for acting upon that feeling. Compassion alone is not a reliable guide for acting. Sometimes it would be wrong to act on this feeling.

We could even push the point further and ask if there is any link at all between the moral sentiments and what we ought to do. O'Neill cites the parable of the Good Samaritan, which we all identify as a paradigmatic act of compassion, as an illustration of meeting the needs of others. The parable was told by Jesus in response to the question, And who is my neighbor? But this question was asked to get clear on the moral prescription "Love your neighbor as yourself."[11] Our feelings of compassion do not prescribe action; the divine commandment grounds the moral obligation to help others. In the parable, Luke establishes the obligation of benevolence in a divine-command moral theory. We have retained the sentiment generated by this way of looking at the needs of others without retaining the divine-command moral theory from which it arose. Sentiments can and often do reinforce moral principles and can provide a motivational impetus to act on moral principles.[12] But it is not clear that sentiments alone have any necessary connection to moral responsibility. Therefore, a sentiment-based ethics with any semblance of justification for why we ought to act cannot merely appeal to our feelings of compassion for others.

There is a new sentiment-based moral theory currently under development that is attempting to circumvent the appeal to moral principles in order to justify action. It has been called the ethics of caring and is based on the work of Carol Gilligan. This theory stresses the role of caring interpersonal relationships in informing our moral judgments. The theory replaces the abstract universal moral principles of rule-oriented moral theories with the concrete experience of responding to others and therefore "begins with a self who is enmeshed in a network of relations to others, and whose moral deliberation aims to maintain these relations."[13] This theory avoids the problem of seeking justifying principles for acting upon our feelings by denying that abstract principles are particularly relevant to the concrete moral relationships between people. Feeling compassion for someone in need and responding appropriately to alleviate that need are common moral experiences between people; these experiences are what caring relationships are all about, and they do not need to be "justified."

Although this new ethical perspective is most naturally applicable to our relationships with family and friends, it can have some application to our treatment of strangers. The agencies that encourage those in rich nations to "adopt" a child from a poor nation by sending monthly support checks know well the importance of establishing personal relationships to convert compassion into action; the "adopted" child writes letters and sends photographs to the adoptive parents. Establishing concrete human relationships promotes caring responses that can sustain and nourish those relationships.

This ethics of caring might explain in part why turning away a starving family from our homes would feel unacceptable. The family's very presence at my door implies that I am somewhat personally involved with these individuals. My caring response may be provoked even though they are at the very margin of my personal network of relationships. Of course, I may be suspicious that this is just a ruse to gain access to my home in order to burglarize it, and my intention to protect my sleeping children from potential harm may cause me to turn the family from my door. But it is not hard to see how the caring response that has been nurtured in special relationships can be generalized to include concern for those who are virtual strangers.

This theory may help to explain personal caring action in face-to-face contact between people, but it does little to support the claim that we ought to aid distant, unknown strangers with whom we have no contact. The appropriate attitudes or sentiments and the resultant actions that flow from these attitudes attach to concrete individuals. There are numerous barriers between individuals in different lands: geographic distance, lack of personal contact, inability to act directly, inability to share or even understand fundamental beliefs, values, or life-styles due to cultural, religious, class, or ideological differences. These barriers make the possibility of establishing any concrete network of interpersonal relationships with a significant number of distant people quite remote. But to the extent that such a network is required to explain the response of caring as a means of circumventing the need for moral principles, this approach will fail to provide a basis for acting to solve the problem of world hunger.

This theory does not prescribe that we create personal relationships in order to care for others; rather, it stresses that to the extent that we do have close relationships with others, we will care for them. Thus, we could avoid the caring response with its moral responsibility by avoiding any relationships with distant strangers in need. Furthermore, such a personal approach to the world hunger problem is not likely to provide the justification for the radical socioeconomic changes that O'Neill and others envision as necessary to abolish chronic poverty and its resultant starvation. Dealing with complex institutions and structures and acting to modify them for the sake of unknown and virtually unknowable strangers in other lands require a moral passion much more abstract than the passion for caring relationships. Hence, there does not seem to be a viable moral theory based solely on sentiments that can show that it would be wrong to do nothing about world hunger.

To sum up my discussion so far: O'Neill's theory of imperfect obligation does not convincingly establish the obligation to assist distant, needy strangers (especially to the point of altering socioeconomic arrangements). Her initial intuition that it is wrong not to help needy strangers seems best explained by a moral sentiment theory, but there are no unproblematic versions of this theory.

A MATTER OF JUSTICE

If, as I have tried to show, treating the world hunger problem as a matter of benevolence is inadequate, can it be a matter of justice? The strongest case here, as O'Neill points out, would be to show that people have welfare rights to basic goods and services. If all people had such rights, then it would be wrong to prevent people from attaining the goods and services necessary for their lives and well-being. It may even be necessary to provide people with these things. From this perspective, current socioeconomic structures and arrangements (including some property institutions) that inappropriately prevent people from acquiring the goods necessary to meet their needs would be unjust. Similarly, international trade arrangements that are disadvantageous to the poor and local governments that fail to prioritize the meeting of human needs would be unjust. Even patterns of distribution of wealth that tolerate an affluent privileged class whose wealth does not serve to better the material conditions of the impoverished would be unjust. The world hunger problem would indeed be a matter of justice if welfare rights could be shown to exist.

But O'Neill does not think that there are any convincing defenses of a theory of welfare rights. She has two general criticisms. First, most contemporary versions are formulated so as to make welfare rights contingent upon the assertion that we have moral rights. The reasoning is this: If there are any rights, there must be basic rights to have needs met because material needs must be met if human beings are to become and remain agents. Of course, this presupposes that we already believe that humans do have rights. Thus, she challenges advocates of welfare rights to ground them in something. Her skeptical challenge to defenders of rights as "moral facts" to provide a grounding within some normative discourse is well made. Her challenge is probably unanswerable without some type of appeal to an "objective" moral order or moral law.

Her second criticism of welfare rights is that in making such a claim of entitlement one must be able to specify who has the correlative obligation. She argues that welfare rights advocates cannot do this. She denies that welfare rights can be universal (that is, that all others have a correlative obligation to honor these rights). She says that it would be absurd to claim that everyone is obliged to provide some food or income to each deprived person.

I question the claim that welfare rights cannot be rendered meaningfully as universal rights—ones that all in a position to do so are obligated to honor. I have argued elsewhere that a universal entitlement right is claimable against all persons, although conditions of unawareness, nonaccess to effective means of remedy, and competing equivalent need could relieve one from acting on the obligation.[14] Even though an entitlement right would be met most effectively by family or immediate community, remote persons are obligated nonetheless if there are no other means of meeting these needs. I do not see the logical absurdity of endorsing universal welfare rights or universal moral obligations correlative to these rights, although I grant that it is currently popular among (liberal) rights theorists to reject this view as an inappropriate use of rights language.

This leads to another point. O'Neill is particularly concerned with documents, such as the U.N. Declaration of Rights, that simply proclaim that people have a right to food but that make no effort to specify who has the correlative obligation to meet this right. She says that unless we can specify this obligation, asserting that there is a right to food or a right to have one's basic needs met is callous rhetoric. This is certainly true; simply declaring a list of rights will not feed hungry people. But I do not think that in such manifestos or charters the use of rights language is hollow rhetoric if these proclamations are taken seriously. These lists of rights present a statement of a broader vision of what a just world order would ensure to all people. The declarations state a moral view of the world that serves as a goal. It is up to us to create the institutions and structures necessary to ensure that these claims can be met. The economic and political mechanisms we adopt should be means to achieve this end and should be judged according to their ability to promote it. Such a vision of a just world order can serve as a means to critique current institutions and practices that do not honor these rights. Thus, I do not think that appeal to universal welfare rights is hollow rhetoric. But I agree with O'Neill that grounding such claims of rights and justifiying such moral visions of a just world order are difficult tasks.

After rejecting welfare rights, O'Neill develops her own theory of justice, which is based on perfect obligations. Like the libertarian rights theory of justice, it equates justice with the avoidance of wrongful acts against others, and like the libertarian theory, her theory requires restitution for clearly specified past wrongs. But her theory differs from the libertarian theory in its assessment of current wrongs by rich people against poor people. The libertarian theory, she argues, only demands policies of national noncoercion and commercial laissez faire. But the latter is inadequate because laissez faire is hardly possible in an interdependent world. The powerful nations and institutions that determine economic conditions for the poor world do not practice laissez faire. Indeed, she says, the reality is that powerful nations, institutions, and individuals coerce and deceive weaker ones. The libertarian theory seems to justify current actions that her theory designates as wrongs to be avoided.

It is not clear what her theory prescribes. If we are only to avoid deceit and coercion, then it would seem that genuine laissez faire, which is a complete severance of relations with others, would satisfy the demands of justice. Thus, an absolute refusal to interact economically with an impoverished nation would be to treat it justly. There are some voices in the world hunger debate who call for this type of solution of total noninterference. They claim that world hunger is caused solely by the interference of the rich, who are pursuing their own interests; thus, total noninterference would eliminate the cause and thereby solve the problem of world hunger.[15] I doubt that this solution would lead to a satisfactory resolution of the economic problems of many desperately poor nations. However, if we read O'Neill as prescribing genuine laissez faire, we do not have to ask whether this will completely solve the problem. Her theory of justice only requires that the rich act justly, not that the poor receive any benefit.

There is, however, another way to read O'Neill's theory. Although she seems to imply that justice requires us to roughly equalize the power and knowledge between parties, thus giving the poor a claim of entitlement to a redistribution of wealth that would give them equal economic power, I do not believe this is her view. Rather, I think she is merely cautioning us against subtle forms of structural and institutional deceit and coercion that the powerful can exercise over the vulnerable. I suspect that she has in mind "offers" and inducements that the poor cannot afford not to accept—instances where unfair advantage is taken of another's desperate situation, where another's weakness is exploited.

Because O'Neill restricts her concept of injustice to coercion and deceit, she must try to render all instances of exploitation in these terms. But are they all clearly cases of coercion or deceit? The condition of the neediest and most vulnerable may have been worsened in the long run by economic arrangements that they had little choice but to accept, but if they were not intentionally deceived, was their acceptance of these arrangements necessarily the result of coercion? To say yes would be to adopt a very controversial use of the term *coercion*—one that would be hotly disputed by advocates of free market capitalism. Given that so much of O'Neill's criticism of taking unfair advantage hinges on her notion of coercion, it should have been given further articulation and defense. It is certainly not obvious that all policies, institutions, and arrangements that result in negative long-term effects upon the powerless are due to coercion and deceit. Some (perhaps a very large number) will pass her test of justice, even though they can certainly be seen as exploitation of the vulnerability of the powerless. Thus, these will not be unjust.

Because O'Neill's theory of justice focuses exclusively on wrongs, it cannot even consider gross material inequality per se as relevant to justice. The welfare of the neediest per se also is not a relevant consideration of justice. Her theory cannot assess the fairness of patterns of material distribution but, like the libertarian theory, must concentrate on discovering injustice in the accumulation of wealth. In this, O'Neill's theory differs from John Rawls's theory of justice and socialistic theories of justice that do consider patterns of material distribution and the welfare of the neediest as relevant to justice. O'Neill did not examine these alternative, more egalitarian theories of justice. Of course, she could not be expected to consider every theory in one chapter, but it is important to point out this omission for two reasons. First, simply because she has shown that in the context of a libertarian rights, welfare rights, or Kantian theory of justice neither developing human potential nor offering needed help can be a matter of justice, it does not follow that these concerns are not matters of justice. Nor does it follow that we have no other option than to turn to benevolence to explain why we should take steps to alleviate world hunger. To reach the conclusion that these concerns are not matters of justice, she would have to show that Rawlsian, socialistic, and Marxist theories of justice either fail to establish them as such or are false theories.

Second, failure to consider these theories tends to render the discussion somewhat parochial. Given the political fact that much of the international debate about the world hunger problem (and the international economic order that is linked to it) centers precisely on this clash between liberal and egalitarian (and needs-based) theories of justice, the failure to even address the egalitarian theories could be seen as a refusal to engage in dialogue. Or even worse, O'Neill's discussion could be seen as a mere apologia for Western affluence. Given O'Neill's other work on the world hunger problem, such charges would be entirely unfair. Yet the present analysis does not provide a broad enough context from which to resolve the crucial but difficult "why" questions about the alleviation of world hunger. World hunger is an international issue; adequate discussion of it must take seriously the perspectives on justice of all the disputants in the international forum.

NOTES

1. Peter Singer's analysis, "Famine, Affluence, and Morality," *Philosophy and Public Affairs* 1, no. 5 (Spring 1972):229–243, is very persuasive on this point.

2. Immanuel Kant, *Foundations of the Metaphysics of Morals* (New York: Bobbs-Merrill, 1959), p. 41.

3. Ibid., p. 41.

4. John Rawls's inclusion of the motive of self-interest in his "veil of ignorance" universalizing construction may better explain Immanuel Kant's understanding of being able to "will" the maxim than does Onora O'Neill's notion of "adoption" of the principle.

5. Kant, *Foundations*, pp. 48–49.

6. Ibid., p. 47.

7. For an interesting recent discussion of this, see Marcia Barron, "Kantian Ethics and Supererogation," *The Journal of Philosophy* 84, no. 5 (May 1987):237–262.

8. Jean-Jacques Rousseau, *The Social Contract and Discourse on the Origin of Inequality* (New York: Washington Square Press, 1967), p. 201.

9. John Stuart Mill, *Utilitarianism* (Indianapolis, Ind.: Hackett Publishing, 1979), p. 50.

10. Joseph Fletcher, "Give If It Helps But Not If It Hurts," in *World Hunger and Moral Obligation*, William Aiken and Hugh LaFollette (eds.) (Englewood Cliffs, N.J.: Prentice-Hall, 1977), pp. 104–114.

11. The Good Samaritan parable is found in the Gospel according to Luke, 10: 25–37.

12. Jane English makes this point effectively in "Abortion and the Concept of a Person," reprinted in *Feminism and Philosophy*, Mary Vetterling-Braggin et al. (eds.) (Totowa, N.J.: Littlefield Adams, 1978), p. 425.

13. From the introduction of *Women and Moral Theory*, Eva Feder Kittay and Diana T. Meyers, (eds.) (Totowa, N.J.: Rowman and Littlefield, 1987), p. 10.

14. See my "The Right to be Saved from Starvation," in Aiken and LaFollette, *World Hunger*, pp. 85–102.

15. This seems to be the position of both Frances Moore Lappé in *Food First* (Boston: Houghton Mifflin, 1977); and Susan George in *How the Other Half Dies* (Totowa, N.J.: Rowman and Allanheld, 1977).

C. THE RESPONSIBILITIES
OF INTERNATIONAL CORPORATIONS

5

The Moral Obligations of Multinational Corporations

NORMAN BOWIE

Corporations that do business in more than one country are faced with the question, Whose moral rules ought they to obey—those of their home country or those of the host countries in which they are conducting business? According to Norman Bowie, multinationals would be obligated to follow the rules of host countries if a theory called cultural relativism were true, but this theory is incorrect. By cultural relativism Bowie means the view that a practice is morally permissible in a country if that country's culture permits it, wrong just in case the culture forbids it, and obligatory if the culture requires it. One problem with cultural relativism is that it is difficult to justify it over ethnocentrism. Rather than honoring the relativist principle "When in Rome, do as the Romans instead of doing as you would at home," ethnocentrists, like Richard Rorty, suggest that we subscribe to the principle "When in Rome or anywhere else, do as you would at home."

There is a more substantial problem with relativism. The fact is, according to Bowie, that moral universalism is correct, the view that there are moral rules that hold universally, regardless of country or culture. As to how we can determine what the universal morality is, Bowie suggests that an important part of it can be established by examining the conditions (called by Bowie the "morality of the market")

97

under which the business market can exist. Multinationals must honor
such moral requirements no matter what land they find themselves in.

Now that business ethics is a fashionable topic, it is only natural that the behavior of multinational corporations should come under scrutiny. Indeed, in the past few decades multinationals have allegedly violated a number of fundamental moral obligations. Some of these violations have received great attention in the press.

Lockheed violated an obligation against bribery. Nestle violated an obligation not to harm consumers when it aggressively and deceptively marketed infant formula to uneducated poor women in Third World countries. Union Carbide violated either an obligation to provide a safe environment or to properly supervise its Indian employees.

Other violations have received less attention. After the Environmental Protection Agency prohibited the use of the pesticide DBCP, the American Vanguard Corporation continued to manufacture and export the product in Third World countries. U.S. cigarette companies are now aggressively marketing their products abroad. Such actions have been criticized because they seem to treat the safety of foreigners as less important than the safety of U.S. citizens. Other charges involve the violation of the autonomy of sovereign governments. Companies such as Firestone and United Fruit have been accused of making countries dependent on one crop, while Union Miniere and ITT were accused of attempting to overthrow governments.[1]

The charges of immoral conduct constitute a startling array of cases where multinationals are alleged to have failed to live up to their moral obligations. However, the charges are of several distinct types. Some have also been brought against purely domestic U.S. firms—for example, issues involving a safe working environment or safe products. Other charges are unique to multinationals—the charge that a multinational values the safety of a foreigner less than the safety of a home country resident. Still others are charges that companies try to justify behavior in other countries that is clearly wrong in the United States, for example, the bribing of government officials.

In this chapter, I will focus on the question of whether U.S. multinationals should follow the moral rules of the United States or the moral rules of the host countries (the countries where the U.S. multinationals do business). A popular way of raising this issue is to ask whether U.S. multinationals should follow the advice "When in Rome, do as the Romans do." In discussing that issue I will argue that U.S. multinationals would be morally required to follow that advice if the theory of ethical relativism were true. On the other hand, if ethical universalism is true, there will be times when the advice would be morally inappropriate. In a later section, I will argue that ethical relativism is morally suspect. Finally, I will argue that the ethics of the market provide some universal moral norms for the conduct of multinationals. Before turning to these questions, however, I will show briefly that many of the traditional topics discussed under the rubric of the obligations of multinationals fall under standard issues of business ethics.

OBLIGATIONS OF MULTINATIONALS THAT APPLY TO ANY BUSINESS

As Milton Friedman and his followers constantly remind us, the purpose of a corporation is to make money for the stockholders—some say to maximize profits for the stockholders. According to this view, multinationals have the same fundamental purpose as national corporations. However, in recent years, Friedman's theory has been severely criticized. On what moral grounds can the interests of the stockholders be given priority over all the other stakeholders?[2] For a variety of reasons, business ethicists are nearly unanimous in saying that no such moral grounds can be given. Hence, business executives have moral obligations to all their stakeholders. Assuming that Friedman's critics are correct, what follows concerning the obligations of multinationals?

Can the multinationals pursue profit at the expense of the other corporate stakeholders? No; the multinational firm, just like the national firm, is obligated to consider all its stakeholders. In that respect there is nothing distinctive about the moral obligations of a multinational firm. However, fulfilling its obligations is much more complicated than for a national firm. A multinational usually has many more stakeholders. It has all the classes of stakeholders a U.S. company has but multiplied by the number of countries in which the company operates.[3]

It also may be more difficult for the multinational to take the morally correct action. For example, one of the appealing features of a multinational is that it can move resources from one country to another in order to maximize profits. Resources are moved in order to take advantage of more favorable labor rates, tax laws, or currency rates. Of course, the pursuit of such tactics makes it more difficult to honor the obligation to consider the interests of all stakeholders. Nonetheless, the increased difficulty does not change the nature of the obligation; multinationals, like nationals, are required to consider the interests of all corporate stakeholders.

Should a multinational close a U.S. plant and open a plant in Mexico in order to take advantage of cheap labor? That question is no different in principle from this one: Should a national firm close a plant in Michigan and open a plant in South Carolina in order to take advantage of the more favorable labor climate in South Carolina? The same moral considerations that yield a decision in the latter case yield a similar decision in the former. (Only if the interests of Mexican workers were less morally significant than were the interests of U.S. workers could any differentiation be made.)

These examples can be generalized to apply to any attempt by a multinational to take advantage of discrepancies between the home country and the host country in order to pursue a profit. Any attempt to do so without considering the interests of all the stakeholders is immoral. National firms and multinational firms share the same basic obligations. If I am right here, there is nothing distinctive about the many problems faced by multinationals, and much of the discussion of the obligations of multinationals can be carried on within the framework of traditional business ethics.

DISTINCTIVE OBLIGATIONS

Certain obligations of multinationals do become distinctive where the morality of the host country (any country where the multinational has subsidiaries) differs from or contradicts the morality of the home country (the country where the multinational was legally created). The multinational faces a modern version of the "When in Rome, should you do as the Romans do?" question. That question is the focus of this chapter.

On occasion, the "when in Rome" question has an easy answer. In many situations the answer to the question is yes. When in Rome a multinational is obligated to do as the Romans do. Because the circumstances Romans face are different from the circumstances Texans face, it is often appropriate to follow Roman moral judgments because it is entirely possible that Romans and Texans use the same moral principles, but apply those principles differently.

This analysis also works the other way. Just because a certain kind of behavior is right in the United States does not mean that it is right somewhere else. Selling infant formula in the United States is morally permissible in most circumstances, but, I would argue, it is not morally permissible in most circumstances to sell infant formula in Third World countries. U.S. water is safe to drink.

Many moral dilemmas disappear when the factual circumstances that differentiate two cultures are taken into account. It is important to note, however, that this judgment is made because we believe that the divergent practices conform to some general moral principle. The makers of infant formula can sell their product in an advanced country but not in a Third World country because the guiding principle is that we cannot impose avoidable harm on an innocent third party. Selling infant formula in underdeveloped countries would often violate that common fundamental principle; selling the formula in developed countries usually would not.

This situation should be contrasted with cases where the home and the host country have different *moral* principles. Consider different moral principles for the testing of new drugs. Both countries face the following dilemma. If there are fairly lax standards, the drug may have very bad side effects, and if it is introduced too quickly, then many persons who take the drug are likely to be harmed—perhaps fatally. On the other hand, if a country has very strict standards and a long testing period, the number of harmful side effect cases will be less, but a number of people who could have benefited from benign drugs will have perished because they did not survive the long testing period. Where is the trade-off between saving victims of a disease and protecting persons from possible harmful side effects? To bring this problem home, consider a proposed cure for cancer or for AIDS. Two different countries could set different safety standards such that plausible moral arguments could be made for each. In such cases, it is morally permissible to sell a drug abroad that could not yet be sold in the United States.

If all cases were like this one, it would always be morally permissible to do as the Romans do. But alas, all cases are not like this one. Suppose a country totally ignores the problem of side effects and has no safety standards at all. That country "solves" the trade-off problem by ignoring the interests of those who might develop side effects. Wouldn't that country be wrong, and wouldn't a multinational be obligated not to market a drug in that country even if the country permitted it?

If the example seems farfetched, consider countries that are so desperately poor or corrupt that they will permit companies to manufacture and market products that are known to be dangerous. This is precisely the charge that was made against American Vanguard when it exported the pesticide DBCP. Aren't multinationals obligated to stay out even if they are permitted?

That question leads directly to the question of whether multinationals always should do in Rome as the Romans do. To sort through that issue, Figure 5.1 may be useful. Thus far, I have focused on I and IIA. The remainder of the chapter considers the range of ethical problems found in IIB.

In IIB4, the multinational has an obligation to follow the moral principles of the host country because on the issue at hand those of the host country are justified while those of the home country are not. Although Americans may believe that there are few such obligations because their moral principles are far more likely to be justified, it is not hard to think of a contrary case. Suppose it is a moral obligation in a host country that no corporation fire someone without due cause. In other words, in the host country employment at will is morally forbidden. Although I shall not argue for it here, I think the employment-at-will doctrine cannot stand up to moral scrutiny. Hence, in this case, multinationals are obligated to follow the moral principle of the host country. Except for economic reasons (falling demand for one's product), a multinational is morally obligated not to fire an employee without just cause.

As for IIB3, if the moral principles with respect to a given issue are not justified, then the multinational is under no moral obligation to follow them (except in the weak sense where the multinational is under a legal obligation and hence under a moral obligation to obey the law). Actually, IIB3 can be further subdivided into cases where the moral principles are not justified and where the moral principles cannot be justified. Theocratic states with moral principles based on revelation but not in contradiction with rationally justified moral principles are examples of the former. When the "moral" principles based on revelation are in contradiction with rationally justified moral principles, we have an example of the latter. In this latter case, a multinational is obligated not to follow the moral principles of the host country. In these cases, when in Rome, multinationals are not to do as the Romans do.

102   *Norman Bowie*

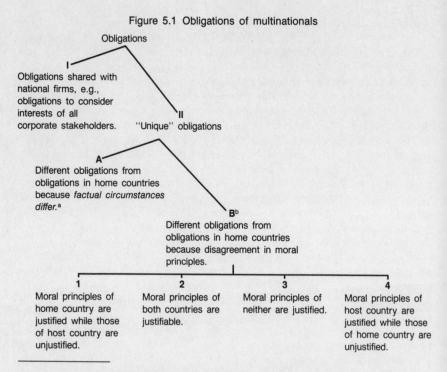

Figure 5.1 Obligations of multinationals

[a]In my view, different obligations still conform to universal principles.
[b]It is assumed that the different moral principles referred to here and below refer to
the same moral issue. It is also stipulated that "unjustified" in IIB1 and IIB4 means
that the unjustified principles are in conflict with the canons of justification in ethics.

In Case IIB2, multinationals may do in Rome as the Romans do. In this
case, the moral principles of the host country are justified.

Finally, in case IIB1, the multinational is obligated not to follow the
moral principles of the host country. In these cases, the principles of the
host country are contrary to the canons of ethics.

In summary, then, U.S. multinationals are obligated to do as the Romans
do in IIB4, are permitted to do as the Romans do in IIB2 and in IIB3
where the moral principles of the Romans are consistent with what morality
would justify. U.S. multinationals are obligated *not* to do as the Romans
do in IIB1 and IIB3 where the moral principles of the Romans are inconsistent
with what morality would justify.

Notice, however, that the entire analysis assumes there is some means of
justifying ethical principles independent of the fact that a society believes
they are justified. Otherwise, for example, I could not say that the moral
principles of a home country are not justified while those of the host country
are. But who is to say whether the moral principles of a country are justified
or when they run counter to universal morality. Besides, perhaps there is
no universal morality. What then?

RELATIVISM

Cultural relativism is the doctrine that what is right or wrong, good or bad, depends on one's culture. If the Irish consider abortion to be morally wrong, abortion *is* morally wrong in Ireland. If the Swedes do not consider abortion to be morally wrong, then abortion *is not* morally wrong in Sweden. There is no universal principle to which the Swedes and the Irish can appeal that determines whether abortion really is wrong or not.

If a person is a cultural relativist, then the implications for our discussion may seem quite clear. A corporation has an obligation to follow the moral principles of the host country. When one is in Rome, one is obligated to do as the Romans do. On our chart, IIB1, IIB3, and IIB4 have no referents. There are no members of those classes just as there are no members of the class of unicorns.

The officers and managers of many multinationals often speak and act as if cultural relativism were true. Who are we, they argue, to impose our moral standards on the rest of the world? For example, the U.S. Foreign Corrupt Practices Act, which prohibits the payment of unrecorded bribes to foreign governments or officials, has come under intense attack. After all, if the payment of bribes is morally acceptable in country X, why should we impose our moral views about bribery on that country. Besides if U.S. multinationals do not bribe, German and Japanese multinationals will—or so the argument goes. Former president Jimmy Carter's attempt to include a country's record on violating or not violating fundamental human rights when making foreign policy decisions came under the same kind of criticism. Who is the United States to impose its moral values on others?

This relativistic way of thinking has always been prominent in the thinking of many social scientists. After all, discoveries by anthropologists, sociologists, and psychologists have documented the diversity of moral beliefs and punctured some of the pseudo-justifications that had been given for the superiority of white Western male ways of thinking. Philosophers, by and large, welcomed the corrections to prejudicial moral thinking, but, nonetheless, found the doctrine of cultural relativism seriously flawed.

Recently, however, the situation in philosophy has taken a surprising turn. A number of prominent philosophers have either seemed to embrace cultural relativism or have been forced by the "critics" to admit that their own philosophical positions may be consistent with it. Three examples should make the point.

In 1971, John Rawls published his monumental work *A Theory of Justice*. In that work, Rawls intended to develop a procedure (the original position) that would provide principles for a just society. Although these principles might be implemented in different ways by different societies, Rawls seemed to think that *any* just society would conform to these principles. In part, Rawls held this view because he believed the original position provided a universal justification for the principles of justice the original position produced. Early critics charged that the assumptions behind the original

position were individualistic, liberal, Western, and democratic. The original
position was biased in favor of individualistic Western democracies; it did
not provide a universal method of justification. In a 1985 article in *Philosophy
and Public Affairs*, Rawls admitted that his critics were right.

> In particular justice as fairness is framed to apply to what I call the basic
> structure of a modern constitutional democracy. . . . Whether justice as fairness
> can be extended to a general political conception for different kinds of societies
> existing under different historical and social conditions or whether it can be
> extended to a general moral conception . . . are altogether separate questions. I
> avoid prejudging these larger questions one way or the other.[4]

Another highly influential book in ethics, Alasdair MacIntyre's *After Virtue*,
argued that the recent emphasis by ethicists on utilitarianism and deontology
was seriously skewed. MacIntyre argued that a full moral theory must give
a central place to the virtues. His own account was rich in description of
the place of virtue in various societies (an emphasis on the cultural setting
that appeared in Michael Walzer's *Spheres of Justice*). However, MacIntyre's
critics pointed out that what was considered a virtue in one society was
frequently not considered a virtue in another—indeed one culture's virtue
might be another culture's vice. MacIntyre now concedes that his earlier
attempts to avoid these relativistic implications have largely failed.[5]

In theory, a cultural relativist could have two responses to CEOs of
multinationals who wanted to know whether their personnel should behave,
when in Rome, as the Romans do. Given that the morality of one culture
cannot be shown to be superior to the morality of another, the personnel
should follow the moral principles of the host country. Such an attitude of
tolerance is the traditional response of most relativists.

But another response is possible. Even though the morality of one culture
cannot objectively be shown to be superior to the morality of another, rather
than embrace tolerance, one could simply assert the superiority of one's own
culture. This is the approach taken by Richard Rorty, who has written
extensively on the pretensions to objectivity in philosophy. In his 1984
article "Solidarity or Objectivity," he points out that the objectivist tries to
create a dilemma for any subjectivist position. The dilemma is that

> either we attach a special privilege to our own community, or we pretend an
> impossible tolerance for every other group. I have been arguing that we
> pragmatists should grasp the ethnocentric horn of this dilemma. We should say
> that we must, in practice, privilege our own group, even though there can be
> no noncircular justification for doing so. . . . We Western liberal intellectuals
> should accept the fact that we have to start from where we are, and that this
> means that there are lots of views which we simply cannot take seriously.[6]

But how would Rorty's quotation strike the CEO of a U.S. multinational?
In this case, the personnel of a multinational should *not* follow the moral
principles of the host country unless they are consistent with U.S. principles.

But what would this mean in terms of business practice? Given that in U.S. culture, the capitalist Friedmanite principle—maximize profits!—is the cultural norm, a U.S. multinational with a plant in South Africa would not refuse to follow the rules of apartheid or pull out. It would locate in South Africa and conform to local custom so long as it could make a profit.

Although I argued earlier that the classical view of profit maximization is seriously flawed, I did not do so from Rorty's ethnocentric position. I assumed an objective universal moral standpoint, as have those who have criticized the classical view. If Rorty's theory is correct, there is no transcultural objective perspective; because the classical view is a central principle in U.S. business and legal culture, I assume Rorty would have to accept it.

Hence, whether we are cultural relativists or ethnocentrists, some disconcerting implications seem to follow.

1. A corporation has no obligation to follow the Sullivan principles[7] in South Africa.
2. A corporation that wants to do business with the Arabs has no moral obligation to refuse participation in a boycott against Israel as a condition for doing business with the Arabs.
3. A corporation has no obligation to refrain from doing business with a state that is in systematic violation of human rights.

If these implications do follow, there seems to be something wrong with the position that entails them. Even Ronald Reagan has forbidden U.S. firms from doing business with Libya. Some set of criteria is needed for indicating when multinationals are permitted to follow the moral principles of the host country and when multinationals are forbidden to follow host-country principles. What is also needed are some principles that tell U.S. multinationals when they have an obligation to refrain from doing business either *with* a foreign (host) government or *in* a host country. However, unless cultural relativism is false, these principles will never be forthcoming.

THE ADEQUACY OF
CULTURAL RELATIVISM

Although our primary concern is the obligations of multinationals, some considerations of the adequacy of cultural relativism must be made before we can speak meaningfully about the obligations of multinationals. As a starting point, I adopt a strategy used by Derek Parfit to undermine the doctrine of prudentialism.[8] Consider a continuum with three positions:

Individual Relativism	Cultural Relativism	Universalism

Individual relativism is the view that what is right or wrong, good or bad, depends on the feelings or attitudes of the individual. If an individual believes abortion is wrong, then abortion is wrong for that individual. If another individual believes abortion is not wrong, then abortion is not wrong for that individual. There is no valid cultural norm that will tell us which individual is objectively right.

The strategy is to show that any argument the cultural relativist uses against universalism can also be used by the individual relativist against cultural relativism. Similarly, any argument the cultural relativist uses against the individual relativist can be used by the universalist against the cultural relativist. As Parfit would say, the cultural relativist is constantly fighting a war on two fronts.

In this discussion, one example of this strategy will have to suffice. First, against an individual relativist, a cultural relativist would often argue that if individual relativism were the prevailing view, a stable society would be impossible. Arguments from Thomas Hobbes or decision theory would prove the point. If individual relativism were the prevailing norm, life would be "nasty, brutish, and short."

But in the present world, any arguments that appeal to social stability will have to be applied universally. In the atomic age and in an age where terrorism is an acceptable form of political activity, the stability problems that afflict individual relativism equally afflict cultural relativism. If the necessity for social stability is a good argument for a cultural relativist to use against an individual relativist, it is an equally good argument for a universalist to use against a cultural relativist.

This brief argument has not refuted relativism. It has only shown that if the stability argument works for the cultural relativist against the individual relativist, the argument also works for the universalist against the cultural relativist. Moreover, to accept the argument this far is only to show that some universal moral norms are required for stable relationships. The argument itself does not provide those universal moral norms. Multinational CEOs are likely to accept the argument thus far, however, because multinationals need a stable international environment if they are to make a profit in the long run. As any adviser for any multinational will verify, one of the chief factors affecting an investment decision in a foreign country is the political stability both of that individual country and of the region surrounding it. An unstable country or region is highly inimical to the conduct of international business.

THE MORAL MINIMUM FOR SOCIETY

Thus far we have established that multinational business requires stability and that commonly accepted moral rules are necessary for stability. But what specifically are these moral rules? To answer that question I will appeal to conceptual arguments that will assist in providing answers.

One argument that is especially effective against the charge of moral imperialism develops the point that some universal standards of conduct already have been accepted by all parties. Despite appearances to the contrary, a great deal of morality has already been internationalized either explicitly through treaty, through membership in the U.N., or implicitly through language and conduct.

Whereas the explicit acceptance of a universal morality has often been commented upon, the implicit acceptance of universal standards has not. Nonetheless, this type of moral argument has a long tradition that goes back at least to David Hume. Hume points out that our very use of language indicates that we accept the notion of an impartial outside observer. Hence, we recognize the distinction between behaving in our interest and behaving in ways that would be justified by an impartial observer. Often the two ways of behaving overlap, but not always. Hume's observations are not limited to the speakers of English.

Note the following: The word *democracy* or *democratic* has become an honorific term. Nearly all national states claim they are democracies—people's democracies, worker democracies, but democracies nonetheless. The August 4, 1986, *Newsweek* carried a story about repression and the denial of civil rights in Chile. The president of Chile responded to his critics by calling his dictatorship "a democratic government with authority." I have yet to come across a state that brags it is not a democracy and has no intention of being one. (Some nations do indicate they do not want to be a democracy like the United States.) Hence, there is no moral imperialism involved in saying that host countries should be democracies. The controversy involves the question, What must a government be like to be properly characterized as a democracy?

A notion of shared values can be of assistance here as well. There is a whole range of behavior, such as torture, murder of the innocent, and racism, that nearly all agree is wrong. A nation-state accused of torture does not respond by saying that a condemnation of torture is just a matter of subjective morality. The state's leaders do not respond by saying, "We think torture is right, but you do not." Rather, the standard response is to deny that any torture took place. If the evidence of torture is too strong, a finger will be pointed either at the victim or at the morally outraged country. "They do it, too." In this case the guilt is spread to all. Even the Nazis denied that genocide took place. What is important is that *no* state replies there is nothing wrong with genocide or torture. Hence, the head of a multinational need have no fear of cultural imperialism when she or he takes a stand in favor of democracy and against torture and genocide.

This conceptual argument is buttressed by another. Suppose an anthropologist discovers a large populated South Pacific island. How many tribes are on the island? Part of the answer to that question will be determined by observing if such acts as killing and murder are permitted and if they are permitted, against whom are they permitted? If they are not permitted, that counts as evidence that there is only one tribe. If people on the northern half of the island permit stealing directed against southerners but do not permit northerners to steal from one another, that provides evidence that there are at least two tribes. What often distinguishes one society from another is the fact that society A does not permit murder, lying, and stealing against members of A—society A could not permit that and still be a society—but society A does permit that kind of behavior against society B. What this strategy shows is that one of the criteria for having a society is that there be a shared morality among the individuals that make up the society.

What follows from this is that there are certain basic rules that must be followed in each society—for example, do not lie; do not commit murder. There is a moral minimum in the sense that if these specific moral rules are not generally followed, then there will not be a society at all. These moral rules are universal, but they are not practiced universally. That is, members of society A agree that they should not lie to each other, but they think it is okay to lie to the members of other societies. Such moral rules are not relative; they simply are not practiced universally.

However, multinational corporations are obligated to follow these moral rules. Because the multinational is practicing business in the society and because these moral norms are necessary for the existence of the society, the multinational has an obligation to support those norms. Otherwise, multinationals would be in the position of benefiting from doing business with the society while at the same time engaging in activity that undermines the society. Such conduct would be unjust.

THE MORALITY OF THE MARKETPLACE

Given that the norms constituting a moral minimum are likely to be few in number, it can be argued that the argument thus far has achieved something—that is, multinationals are obligated to follow the moral norms required for the existence of a society. But the argument has not achieved very much—that is, most issues surrounding multinationals do not involve alleged violations of these norms. Perhaps a stronger argument can be found by making explicit the morality of the marketplace. That there is an implicit morality of the market is a point that is often ignored by most economists and many businesspersons.

Although economists and businesspersons assume that people are basically self-interested, they must also assume that persons involved in business transactions will honor their contracts. In most economic exchanges, the transfer of product for money is not simultaneous. You deliver and I pay or vice versa. As the economist Kenneth Boulding put it: "without an integrative framework, exchange itself cannot develop, because exchange, even in its most primitive forms, involves trust and credibility."[9]

Philosophers would recognize an implicit Kantianism in Boulding's remarks. Kant tried to show that a contemplated action would be immoral if a world in which the contemplated act was universally practiced was self-defeating. For example, lying and cheating would fail Kant's tests. Kant's point is implicitly recognized by the business community when corporate officials despair of the immoral practices of corporations and denounce executives engaging in shady practices as undermining the business enterprise itself.

Consider what John Rawls says about contracts:

> Such ventures are often hard to initiate and to maintain. This is especially evident in the case of covenants, that is, in those instances where one person is to perform before the other. For this person may believe that the second party will not do his part, and therefore the scheme never gets going. . . . Now in these situations there may be no way of assuring the party who is to perform first except by giving him a promise, that is, by putting oneself under an obligation to carry through later. Only in this way can the scheme be made secure so that both can gain from the benefits of their cooperation.[10]

Rawls's remarks apply to all contracts. Hence, if the moral norms of a host country permitted practices that undermined contracts, a multinational ought not to follow them. Business practice based on such norms could not pass Kant's test.

In fact, one can push Kant's analysis and contend that business practice generally requires the adoption of a minimum standard of justice. In the United States, a person who participates in business practice and engages in the practice of giving bribes or kickbacks is behaving unjustly. Why? Because the person is receiving the benefits of the rules against such activities without supporting the rules personally. This is an example of what John Rawls calls freeloading. A freeloader is one who accepts the benefits without paying any of the costs.

> In everyday life an individual, if he is so inclined, can sometimes win even greater benefits for himself by taking advantage of the cooperative efforts of others. Sufficiently many persons may be doing their share so that when special circumstances allow him not to contribute (perhaps his omission will not be found out), he gets the best of both worlds. . . . We cannot preserve a sense of justice and all that this implies while at the same time holding ourselves ready to act unjustly should doing so promise some personal advantage.[11]

This argument does not show that if bribery really is an accepted moral practice in country X, that moral practice is wrong. What it does show is that practices in country X that permit freeloading are wrong and if bribery can be construed as freeloading, then it is wrong. In most countries I think it can be shown that bribery is freeloading, but I shall not make that argument here.

The implications of this analysis for multinationals are broad and important. If activities that are permitted in other countries violate the morality of the marketplace—for example, undermine contracts or involve freeloading on the rules of the market—they nonetheless are morally prohibited to multinationals that operate there. Such multinationals are obligated to follow the moral norms of the market. Contrary behavior is inconsistent and ultimately self-defeating.

Our analysis here has rather startling implications. If the moral norms of a host country are in violation of the moral norms of the marketplace, then the multinational is obligated to follow the norms of the marketplace. Systematic violation of marketplace norms would be self-defeating. Moreover, whenever a multinational establishes businesses in a number of different countries, the multinational provides something approaching a universal morality—the morality of the marketplace itself. If Romans are to do business with the Japanese, then whether in Rome or Tokyo, there is a morality to which members of the business community in both Rome and Tokyo must subscribe—even if the Japanese and Romans differ on other issues of morality.

THE DEFENSE OF
MARKETPLACE MORALITY

Up to this point I have argued that multinationals are obligated to follow the moral minimum and the morality of the marketplace. But what justifies the morality of the marketplace? Unless the marketplace morality can be justified, I am stuck in Rorty's ethnocentrism. I can start only where I am, and there are simply a lot of views I cannot take seriously. If a CEO of a U.S. multinational should adopt such an ethnocentric position, she or he would be accused of cultural imperialism. The claim of objectivity remains the central issue for determining the obligations of multinationals.

One possible argument is that capitalism supports democratic institutions. For example, Milton Friedman argues in *Capitalism and Freedom* that capitalism institutionally promotes political freedom.

> Economic arrangements play a dual role in the promotion of a free society. On the one hand freedom in economic arrangements . . . is an end in itself. In the second place economic freedom is also an indispensable means toward the achievement of political freedom. . . .
> No one who buys bread knows whether the wheat from which it is made was grown by a Communist or a Republican, by a constitutionalist or a Fascist, or for that matter by a Negro or a white. This illustrates how an impersonal market separates economic activities from political views and protects men from being discriminated against in their economic activities for reasons that are irrelevant to their productivity—whether these reasons are associated with their views or their color.[12]

Friedman also points out that freedom of speech is more meaningful so long as alternative opportunities for employment exist. However, these alternatives are impossible if the government owns and operates the means of production. In a private diversified economic community someone has a better chance to publish views that are contrary to the views of a given editor, the government, or even a majority of the public. Usually one can find some audience that is interested. Moreover, even publishers who disagree might still publish. Fear of competition often overcomes the distaste for certain ideas.

Indeed, one of the arguments for morally permitting multinationals to operate in nondemocratic countries is an extension of Friedman's point. Capitalism is allegedly a catalyst for democratic reform. If capitalism promotes democracy, then a moral argument can be made to justify capitalist investment in repressive regimes because investment will serve the moral end of making the government less repressive. This is precisely the argument that many have used to justify U.S. investment in South Africa. Indeed, the South African situation can serve as an interesting case study. The point of the Sullivan principles is to provide moral guidelines so that a company may be morally justified in having plants in South Africa without becoming part of the system of exploitation. The Sullivan principles also prevent profit-seeking corporations from morally justifying immoral behavior. No company can passively do as the South Africans do and then claim that its presence will bring about a more democratic, less racist regime. After all, if it is plausible to argue that capitalism can help create a democracy, it seems equally plausible to argue that a totalitarian regime may corrupt capitalism. The Sullivan principles help keep multinationals with South African facilities morally honest.

Moreover, the morality of the Sullivan principles depends on an empirical claim that profit-seeking corporations behaving in accordance with marketplace morality and acknowledging universally recognized human rights will in fact help transform totalitarian or repressive regimes into more democratic, more humane regimes. If that transformation does not take place within a reasonable amount of time, the moral justification for having facilities in that country disappears. Leon Sullivan recognized that point when he set May 31, 1987, as the deadline for reform of the South African government. When that reform was not forthcoming, he insisted that U.S. companies suspend operations in South Africa.

At this point, some special remarks must be made about the U.S. relationship with the Soviet Union. If we take the position that there is little evidence that doing business with the Soviets will end their oppressive regime, then we must conclude that the United States should not do business with the USSR. However, the ability the two nations possess to destroy one another perversely binds them in a special relationship. Even if increased business transactions between the two countries do not transform the Soviet system of government, moral justification for doing business with the Soviets remains. If such business transactions lessen the chance of war between the United States and the USSR, then such business activity is justified on that ground alone. Hence, there need be no inconsistency in saying that a multinational has an obligation not to do business in South Africa but does not have a similar obligation with respect to the Soviet Union. What is needed is a similar code or set of codes for doing business in other repressive countries. There should be a Sullivan code for doing business in the Soviet Union or in any other nondemocratic country. The existence of such a code would go far toward promoting the required consistency.

What about the issue of human rights? Can multinationals ignore that question? No, they cannot. Part of what it means to be a democracy is that respect be shown for fundamental human rights. The only justification for a multinational's doing business with a regime that violates human rights is the claim that in so doing, the country's human rights record will improve. Again, business activity under that justification will have to be judged on results.

Even if the "contribution to democracy argument" is not convincing, there is another argument on behalf of the morality of the marketplace. On the assumption that a multinational business agreement is a voluntary exchange, the morality of the marketplace is voluntarily accepted. Economic prosperity seems to be highly desired by all countries. Given that multinational business is a device for achieving prosperity, participating countries voluntarily accept the morality of the market.

CONCLUSION

I have argued that on occasion multinationals have obligations that would require them *not* to do in Rome as the Romans do—for example, in those cases where Roman practice is in violation of marketplace morality. I have also provided arguments on behalf of marketplace morality, although those arguments require that businesses have obligations to pull out of oppressive countries if there is little hope of reform.

But the appeal to the morality of the marketplace has an added benefit. What often is forgotten by business is that the market is not a morally neutral, well-oiled machine; rather, it is embedded in morality and depends upon the acceptance of morality for its success. Ultimately, the obligations of multinationals, whether in Rome, Tokyo, or Washington, are the obligations required by the market. If corporations live up to those obligations, and if capitalism really could advance the cause of democracy and human rights throughout the world, then the morally responsible multinational could be a force for social justice. However, I regret to say that I am discussing a goal and a hope rather than a current reality.

NOTES

I wish to thank Steven Luper-Foy for his helpful comments on an earlier version of this chapter.

1. See "There's No Love Lost Between Multinational Companies and the Third World," *Business and Society Review* (Autumn 1974).

2. For the purpose of this discussion, a stakeholder is a member of a group without whose support the organization would cease to exist. The traditional list of stakeholders includes stockholders, employees, customers, suppliers, lenders, and the local community where plants or facilities are located.

3. Of course, one large U.S. company with 10 plants in 10 different states has more classes of stakeholders than 1 U.S. company with 1 U.S. plant and 1 foreign subsidiary.

4. John Rawls, "Justice as Fairness: Political not Metaphysical," *Philosophy and Public Affairs* 14, no. 3 (Summer 1985):224–225. Also see John Rawls, *A Theory of Justice* (Cambridge, Mass.: Harvard University Press, 1971).

5. The most explicit charge of relativism is made by Robert Wachbroit, "A Genealogy of Virtues," *Yale Law Journal* 92, no. 3 (January 1983):476–564. For Alasdair MacIntyre's discussion, see "Postscript to the Second Edition" in *After Virtue*, 2nd ed. (Notre Dame: University of Notre Dame, 1984) and his Eastern Division American Philosophical Association Presidential Address, "Relativism, Power and Philosophy" in *Proceedings and Addresses of the American Philosophical Association* 59, no. 1 (September 1985):5–22. Also see Michael Walzer, *Spheres of Justice* (New York: Basic Books, 1983).

6. Richard Rorty, "Solidarity or Objectivity," in *Post-Analytic Philosophy*, John Rajchman and Cornel West, eds. (New York: Columbia University Press, 1985), pp. 12–13.

7. The Sullivan code affirms the following principles: (1) that there be nonsegregation of the races in all eating, comfort, and work facilities; (2) that equal and fair employment practices be instituted for all employees; (3) that all employees doing equal or comparable work for the same period of time receive equal pay; (4) that training programs be developed and implemented that will prepare substantial numbers of blacks and other nonwhites for supervisory, administrative, technical, and clerical jobs; (5) that the number of blacks and other nonwhites in management and supervisory positions be increased; and (6) that the quality of employees' lives outside the work environment be improved—this includes housing, transportation, schooling, recreation, and health facilities.

8. See Derek Parfit, *Reasons and Persons* (New York: Oxford University Press, 1986), pp. 126–127.

9. Kenneth E. Boulding, "The Basis of Value Judgments in Economics," in *Human Values and Economic Policy*, Sidney Hook, ed. (New York: New York University Press, 1967), p. 68.

10. John Rawls, *A Theory of Justice* (Cambridge: Mass.: Harvard University Press, 1971), p. 569.

11. Ibid., p. 497.

12. Milton Friedman, *Capitalism and Freedom* (Chicago: University of Chicago Press, 1962), pp. 8, 21.

6

Exorcising the Demon of Cultural Relativism

PETER FRENCH

Norman Bowie maintained that there is a set of moral rules that hold universally and that because the "morality of the marketplace" is at least a large component of these universal rules, we can then identify universal rules by identifying the morality presupposed by the successful operation of the marketplace. Peter French points out that the notion of a universal rule is ambiguous and that on the one hand it might mean a rule acknowledged by everyone regardless of culture or on the other a rule that is morally binding on everyone regardless of culture. Universal rules exist only in the latter sense of the term; thus, while a universally binding morality exists, there is no consensus as to what it is. To some extent this may be mitigated if it turns out that radical moral disagreement among cultures is impossible, as French argues using apparatus developed by Donald Davidson. But the impossibility of radical disagreement still leaves open a great deal of room for disagreement affecting the behavior of corporations. The remainder of French's chapter is largely devoted to undermining Bowie's defense of marketplace morality. Thus, for example, French denies that capitalism supports democratic institutions by adducing the cases of South Africa and Chile, which he says are capitalistic but far from democratic.

The moral problems of multinational corporations are said to focus on the question, By what set of principles and rules ought a corporation play when doing business in a foreign country? This issue most dramatically arises when the foreign (or host) country is one whose inhabitants hold what appear to be radically different moral beliefs than we do. A standard example is bribery, where the corporation's defense of its payments to foreign government officials or the agents of foreign customers in order to garner contracts is that such a practice is acceptable or even expected in the host country. Norman Bowie refers to this as the "When in Rome, do as the Romans do" principle (call it the R-principle).

The R-principle is not, of course, a moral principle. It may be used to tell a visitor whether to wear short skirts in the town square or to almost completely cover her body and walk with her head down in the presence of men. She may discern what is permitted, or common, or stylish, or expected, or forbidden. Suppose she is an American who regards the customary dress and rules of behavior of women in her host country as demeaning. Although the R-principle may counsel that she adopt local dress, it provides no moral reason for her to do so. In fact, that is the deficiency of the R-principle as it is usually stated. The R-principle is truncated. It is, it seems, a hypothetical imperative with a missing antecedent. The U.S. visitor may decide that if she wants to be liked by her hosts, or if she wants to gain their confidence, or if she wants to honor them and their customs, or if she wants to mock them, that she ought to do as they do. In other words, she may have some prudential or whimsical reasons for invoking the R-principle that we may encourage in some cases. But suppose her suppressed antecedent is that she wants to behave morally, that she wants to do the morally proper and justifiable thing. The principle then becomes "If you want to do what is morally justifiable, when in Rome, do as the Romans." When viewed in this light, the R-principle seems to be far less than what is wanted. In fact, it seems to assault our moral intuitions.

Assume that the host country is one in which women are treated as pieces of property. Women submit to being bought, sold, scrapped. Our U.S. visitor, let us say, was stranded by a misfortunate booking by a travel agent in this country. Most assuredly, we would think it the farthest thing from morality were she to submit to such practices in order to be moral. How can location so drastically change her moral obligations, even her moral status?

Our intuition is that location generally is morally irrelevant. Of course, we must allow for differences in the environment that can affect what is morally proper from place to place. Infant formula can be marketed where drinking water is not contaminated, but in those regions where water is more likely than not to be polluted, infant formula morally ought not to be sold. In such a case, it is interesting that the R-principle usually is not really invoked. Something like a no-harm-to-innocents principle is used cross-culturally.

What may well be happening when we endow the R-principle with genuine moral weight is that we are confusing morality with law. In law, location is crucial. If I am in Saudi Arabia, then I am subject to Saudi law. The fact that I am an alien in that country does not exempt me from obedience, although it may excuse some of my ignorance. On this point, as is well known, a clash between the two great traditions of legal theory could be imagined. The natural law theorist might argue that one has an obligation to obey only the morally legitimate laws of the host country, while the legal positivist insists that the alien is subject to all of the properly enacted laws of the land, except those expressly excluding the noncitizen. I do not think it productive to detail how such an encounter could proceed. Instead, all we need to note is that the positivist's argument is aligned with the R-principle, and although that may make good legal theory, it makes, as the great positivist of the century, H.L.A. Hart knew, bad morality.

THE BOWIE DOCTRINE

But why should it be the case that the R-principle is a valuable guide in legal matters and a washout in moral ones? Suppose that there is no disagreement between two cultures with respect to what sorts of actions constitute bribery. But in culture A, in general, bribery is morally wrong, while in B, bribery is morally permissible. A corporation, whose home is in A, doing business in both cultures, may consider the advantages of bribing in culture B. Bowie thinks that some method needs to be devised in order to guide a multinational corporation in such circumstances. He offers a diagram to illustrate the possibilities and then argues that if the moral principle of B is justified but that of A is not, or if both are justified, then the multinational ought (has a moral obligation) to act in accordance with B's moral principle.

All of this sounds fine, but as Bowie wonders, how is one to determine whether a culture's moral principle is justified? Fairness would seem to require a method of evaluating moral principles that is independent of any culture. But if we could gain access to such an independent moral point of view, we would have no need to raise questions about the moral status of B's principles in the first place. Bowie thinks we do have something like an independent set of moral principles. He assigns that role to what he calls "the morality of the marketplace." He then recommends that multinationals heed the "morality of the marketplace" wherever on the globe they operate. In the process of doing so, he expects that they will improve the morality of host countries by advancing the cause of democracy and human rights.

UNIVERSAL MORALITY

Bowie also claims that the morality of the marketplace approaches a universal morality. But we need to distinguish between a universally shared morality and a universally binding morality. I want to argue that whether there is a universally shared morality is a factual matter. Clearly there is not, or the moral problems of multinationals would never arise. However, it may be the case, as I think it is, that there is a universally binding morality, and thus the fact that it is not shared by all cultures is irrelevant to the authority of its principles. I further want to argue that cultures that do not evidence the principles of that universally binding morality do not have alternative moralities. They have no morality at all. Put otherwise, radically different universally binding moral principles do not exist, if by "radically different" we mean that the principles in question are about the same situation while demanding incompatible behavior.

Bowie worries that his position degenerates into ethnocentrism unless he can independently justify the morality of the marketplace. This leads him to argue for the moral virtues of capitalism. Not only is his doing so unnecessary; he is just wrong about capitalism.

Bowie would have us believe that capitalism supports democratic institutions and that such institutions promote the primary principles of morality. It may well be true that democracy encourages the concepts and principles that we believe to be fundamental in morality, such as respect for persons, or keeping promises and contracts, but it is just historically inaccurate to say that capitalism "is a catalyst for democratic reform." South Africa, Chile, and a number of other contemporary states are capitalistic, but hardly democratic. Also, capitalism emerged in Western European states that were, by and large, monarchies or oligarchies. In fact, if equality and basic rights are the cornerstones of the universally binding morality, then Bowie might better look at the rise of Protestantism as its wellspring.

Grasping the ethnocentric horn of the dilemma is not suspiciously anti-liberal, as Bowie fears. We start from our own morality, and, as I hope to show, we need not apologize for ending there. Furthermore, we can exorcise the demon of cultural relativism without having to distinguish between essential and accidental aspects of a morality and certainly without any recourse to the R-principle, even in a limited number of cases.

DAVIDSONIAN CHARITY
AND MORAL BELIEFS

Attacks on radical relativism have been made with respect to alternative logics, the Sapir-Whorf hypothesis (the theory that people who speak substantially different languages see the world differently), and so on. Some of the most persuasive have taken as their point of departure Donald Davidson's well-known argument that not many of the beliefs of a culture can be false. "The reason for this is that a belief is identified by its location in a pattern of beliefs; it is this pattern that determines the subject matter of the belief, what the belief is about."[1]

Davidson's point is that if more than a few of a person's beliefs about some subject can be false, then almost all of that person's beliefs about that subject can be false. Davidson notes, however, that "false beliefs tend to undermine the identification of the subject matter."[2] Simply, if we were to admit to the possibility that someone (or some culture) could hold beliefs about a subject that were mostly false, we would have to conclude that we had misidentified the subject of those beliefs.

Suppose the subject matter in question has to do with the way people ought to behave.[3] Further, let us stipulate that we hold a number of beliefs about how people morally ought to behave and that members of another culture hold beliefs that are incompatible with ours. What must we conclude? Because we cannot hold that most of our moral beliefs are false and the same must be said of their beliefs, then we must either have misunderstood their beliefs or misunderstood at what features of the circumstances their moral beliefs were directed. In the latter case, we may expect to discover our error and then revise our original judgment that radical disagreement exists between us. In the former case, we must conclude that their beliefs just are not moral ones. David Cooper has seen the outcome of this argument: "We can only identify another's beliefs as moral beliefs about X if there is a massive degree of agreement between his and our beliefs. Hence, there is no chance of radical moral diversity."[4]

WHEN A CULTURE HAS A MORALITY

Such a strategy against the relativist will fail, however, if, rather than distinguishing moral beliefs and judgments from others in terms of content, we identify moral judgments as those having certain formal features such as that popular Kantian favorite: universalizability. It will certainly be conceivable that the people of culture B might make universalizable judgments on a subject (and there is no serious doubt about our translation), yet their judgments are radically different from, that is, incompatible with, our judgments on the subject.

Although the formalistic position has had many advocates, it has been the target of devastating criticism in recent years. Philippa Foot has argued that formal features do not mark off moral judgments from others.[5] For Foot, judgments are moral if they express principles that connect to issues of human welfare, happiness, and so on. But Foot's approach, although it offers an escape from formalistic criteria, as David Cooper notes,[6] does not escape the suspicion that it is but an exercise in stipulation. "Attractive as the stipulation that moral principles *must* display a concern for welfare, happiness, etc., might be, to the extent that it remains a stipulation, the formalist can remain unimpressed."[7]

The Davidsonian-styled approach that both Cooper and I[8] have advocated will arrive at the same destination as did Foot, but without the appearance of arbitrary stipulation. The full argument depends upon a complicated theory of meaning and interpretation that need not burden us here, but in lieu of which some rudiments should be assembled.

Imagine that the people of culture B have not developed any geometrical concepts that are even roughly equivalent to the familiar forms of Euclidian geometry. Instead of square, triangle, circle, they use the notion of "blob." "Blob" has different meanings in different contexts. They talk about forming a blob, the angles of a blob, and whether a blob of one sort would be preferable to that of another. (I have no idea how this is done.) Importantly, however, we can interpret what they say when they talk of blobs in imprecise, although correct, geometric expressions. Under such conditions we would be right in claiming that they have a geometry, of a sort.

What cannot be imagined is that the people of culture B have substituted aesthetic or some other kind of beliefs for our beliefs about geometry. Lacking geometric concepts and beliefs, they simply have no geometry. Aesthetics is not an alternative geometry.

Analogously, a concept or belief is a moral one if it fits in a system of moral beliefs that, to a large degree, resembles our system of moral beliefs. If b (a person of culture B) reports that he believes that businesspersons ought to bribe public officials to secure sales contracts, we first need to ascertain whether b and we use the term *bribery* in reference to the same sort of activity. Suppose we do. The next, and natural, move is to determine what force "ought" has when b uses it to express his belief. That he is prepared to universalize his judgment is not relevant to our problem, for, as suggested previously, such formal criteria have proved unreliable as marks of the moral.

Before continuing, certain things need to be clarified. First, I am not claiming that it is a criterion of a culture's having a morality that its members believe that businesspersons ought not to engage in bribery. (I have discussed elsewhere different types of truncated moralities and will not reiterate that here.[9]) No specific moral belief is essential to a culture's having a morality, that is, genuine moral beliefs. That b's beliefs about the permissibility of bribery are radically different from our own does not prove either that b has no morality or that b's moral principles are incompatible with ours. All it may show is that when b insists that bribery is permissible, he is not expressing one of the moral beliefs of culture B.

Second, behavioral criteria are not sufficient to distinguish moral from nonmoral beliefs. There are at least three reasons why. Suppose that b tells us he approves of bribery. He thinks it should not be illegal, and he does not object or refuse to do business with anyone whom he suspects of attempting bribery. Does his approval of bribery arise from moral considerations? Perhaps he has (as do most other members of culture B) religious views that encourage acts of bribery. From behavioral clues alone we are not likely to be able to determine that his attitudes are moral ones. But even if we could identify, solely on behavioral grounds, when he was exhibiting his moral attitudes, we will not be likely, on the same grounds, to tell what moral beliefs b actually holds. Does b really believe that bribery in business is not morally wrong, or is it not that he thinks bribery is morally permissible?

To answer such a question, we need to know more than that b exhibits certain attitudes. We have to ascertain the object of those attitudes. That is unlikely to be a simple observational project. To borrow an example from both John Searle[10] and David Cooper,[11] can we suppose that the people in culture B disapprove of keeping promises or contracts? That seems hard to imagine for we first should have to suppose that they engage in, or at least have the concepts of, promising and contracting. It is hard to see how the people of culture B could have the concept of contract or promise and not believe that the parties are obligated with respect to either. Yet it is not simply a matter of definition that promise-keeping must be morally approved. Nevertheless, if the evidence seems to support the conclusion that members of B disapprove of what we identify in their activities as contracting and promising, we should first question whether we have properly identified what they disapprove. It may be some other feature of the practices that regularly are associated with those activities. Perhaps members of culture B disapprove of hand shaking or the typical linguistic form in which the promise is couched. Perhaps we have utterly failed to understand their social life.

DISAGREEMENT WITHOUT RELATIVISM

The force of the Davidsonian approach is that radical moral disagreement is not possible between cultures. However, with respect to specific issues, there could be a considerable amount of divergence of opinion. After all, a range of viewpoints exists in our culture about abortion, euthanasia, and myriad other issues, and on these matters our morality has not pronounced final sentence.

Contrast these with a concept about which there is no reasonable dispute, for example, murder. A primary reason for the existence of this concept is to mark off as unjustifiable certain kinds of homicides. Perpetrators of homicides that are correctly described as murders perform deeds that are indisputably morally wrong. "Murder is wrong" is, I have argued,[12] necessarily true, uninformative, and certainly not a matter of debate. "Euthanasia is wrong" is quite another story. That clearly is debatable. One form of argument in support of it identifies euthanasia with murder; another draws an analogy between euthanasia and murder. The moral status of euthanasia is not morally resolved, but we should not conclude that because Steven and I disagree about whether euthanasia is wrong that we must have different moralities. We may share a morality while engaging in such a debate. In fact, our common nest of moral beliefs provides the background that makes our disagreement sensible.

Suppose, however, Steven argues that *murder* is not wrong. Can he be expressing a moral belief, even one from an alternative moral system? The Davidsonian argument is intended to explain why the answer should be negative. (One might imagine trying to teach a child that murder is wrong and getting into some sort of argument with the child about whether it really is wrong. The disagreement would not signal that the child has a radically different morality, only that she has not yet learned her lessons in morality.) Within the scope of morality certainly there is considerable space for disagreement. Bribery, like euthanasia, may be debatable without deserting the moral sphere.

A representative of a multinational corporation might question an official in a host country about a bribe attempt by saying something like, "Bribery is wrong," and hear in response, "No, it is not; it is just a normal cost of doing business, a cementing of goodwill and friendship between seller and buyer." This is, to be sure, a genuine disagreement, but it does not signal that the disputants hold different moralities. Such a disagreement may not be resolved, although it is in principle resolvable. A judgment such as "Bribery is morally wrong" does not stand alone. It is not a matter of moral bedrock. It must be buttressed. On moral grounds, this judgment may be supported by appealing to moral concepts and principles or by arguing that the consequences (in business or human affairs generally) of the practice of bribery are morally relevant.

If the person from culture B says that bribery is gift-giving, that may be intended to move the practice to at least a morally neutral ground. If he says that it has the consequences of benefiting the less well-off because it is the only means in B to strike a deal from which jobs for the poor will be created (suppose the multinational wants to build a factory in culture B), he is offering what we may accept as morally relevant reasons for the bribe. This sort of defense of bribery by b reveals that he does not have a radically different morality than we do. If, however, b just spouts a version of the R-principle, "We just do this here, so do likewise," no moral ground has been plotted. Adopting such a strategy to defend bribery is simply deserting morality.

MARKETS AND MORALITY

Bowie claims that if the morality of a host country violates the moral norms of the marketplace, then the multinational is obligated to follow those norms. His reasons for offering what I think is an unintelligible recommendation are rather obscure. First, he tells us that systematic violation of marketplace norms would be self-defeating. Does Bowie mean to imply that all immoral actions are self-defeating? Surely, it would be a morally happy situation if morally wrong practices also were self-defeating. Doing them would defeat the purpose of doing them. But, sadly, we all know that is far from the way matters are. It is also important to note that within the marketplace, systematic violators often prosper, and it takes severe nonmarket forces, such as governmental regulation and adverse publicity, to get violators to alter their immoral behavior.

Second, Bowie advises that following marketplace morality as against that of a host country is preferable because to do so provides something approaching a universal morality. The multinational abiding by the "morality" of the marketplace becomes a kind of missionary for true morality. Bowie rightly notes that to make this a palatable claim, he needs to justify the morality of the marketplace, and to do so he offers his dubious "contribution to democracy argument." Democracy, we may agree, does embody the recognition of basic human rights; hence, Bowie's argument assumes that the concept of fundamental human rights is a characteristic of genuine morality or, in other words, a stipulation about the content of moral principles with respect to which neither the formalist nor the Davidsonian need be impressed. Furthermore, if we were going to end with rights protection, why not begin there? But that would be, of course, to stipulate the primary content of morality and thus make the whole multinational problem a nonstarter.

I do not see why a culture that has no interest in protecting individual human rights (for example, a Confucian culture) may not still be properly said to have a morality. If the culture does, its beliefs will not contradict all of our moral beliefs. Thus, a foundation of agreement will exist between us that can provide the basis for our conversion of those in that culture on the issue of rights protection. The marketplace could provide a kind of teaching situation in such a culture in which expansion of its moral beliefs might be accomplished. Conversely, the members of the other culture, while successfully operating in the marketplace, may convince us that the protection of individual human rights is not that morally important. Continued trade and business associations with China could lead to such a reevaluation of what those in the United States believe to be morally basic.

The bottom line, of which corporations are so fond of speaking, with regard to the R-principle is that it has no moral status, although it does have legal status. If a corporation wants to act morally, and we should encourage it to do so, then it need only ape the customs of the host country insofar as they affect matters of law, etiquette, goodwill, and so forth. When, however, local law or customs stand in opposition to Western moral principles, then a corporation may not excuse its adherence to local custom by use of the R-principle. The South African situation, as Bowie notes, is an excellent case in point. Corporate actions that support apartheid are morally unjustifiable even if legally enforced, and they are as immoral when done by the South Africans as when they are done by multinational corporations who are just doing in Johannesburg as the Johannesburgers do. It is tempting to argue that the multinational is more morally culpable than the native in such circumstances because the multinational's reasons for contributing to the exploitation of South African blacks is that it is a cost of making a profit in that country.

A final comment: Bowie's attempt to justify requiring corporate moral behavior in countries in which there are widespread and long-established rights violations—that it likely will make the host regime less repressive—is just bad moralizing. Suppose that as time passes there are no significant changes in the level of oppression. What then? What relevance should that fact have on the issue of whether a multinational ought then or ever to act in the morally proper way in that country? Surely we would not say, "Okay, you tried and it did no good, so when in Rome, do as the Romans." The level of repression in the host country is a totally independent matter from the morality of multinational corporate behavior. Repression becomes a relevant moral factor only if the corporation's regular business practice aggrandizes and supports those responsible for the repression. That is the crucial point of the Reverend Leon Sullivan's principles and the reason he has declared them a failure in South Africa and now recommends total divestment. To be sure, one of the dreams of many moralists is that the moral behavior of some will beget the moral behavior of most, and if the "some" includes large, powerful entities such as multinational corporations, the dream seems more realizable. But it is still just a dream and does not constitute much of an argument for being moral, especially in the face of the facts.

NOTES

1. Donald Davidson, "Thought and Talk," *Mind and Language*, ed. by S. Guttenplan (Oxford: Oxford University Press, 1975), pp. 20–21.
2. Ibid.
3. This supposition is contentious. Some will no doubt argue that moral beliefs (or the sentences that express them) do not admit to truth and falsity. This, however, is not the place to discuss such claims.
4. David E. Cooper, "Moral Relativism," *Midwest Studies in Philosophy* 3 (1978):101.
5. Philippa Foot, *Virtues and Vices* (Oxford: Basil Blackwell, 1978), especially Chapters 7–9, 11.
6. Cooper, "Moral Relativism."
7. Ibid., p. 104.
8. Peter A. French, *The Scope of Morality* (Minneapolis: University of Minnesota Press, 1979), Chapter 2.
9. Ibid.
10. John Searle, "How to Derive 'Ought' from 'Is,' " *The Philosophical Review* 73 (1964), reprinted in Wilfrid Sellars and John Hospers, eds., *Readings in Ethical Theory*, 2nd ed. (Englewood Cliffs, N.J.: Prentice-Hall, 1970), pp. 63–73.
11. Cooper, "Moral Relativism," p. 103.
12. French, "The Scope of Morality," Chapter 5.

7

Environmental Ethics
and International Justice

BERNARD E. ROLLIN

*People are conscious, sentient beings. They can feel pain, anxiety,
loneliness, and pleasure. They have interests, and their fate matters to
them; they can be harmed when others act against these interests. In
large part, these features lead us to attribute intrinsic value to human
beings, and features such as these make us think that people have moral
rights. But other animals possess these features, too, Bernard Rollin says.
Hence, he contends, animals have intrinsic value and moral rights. Rivers,
mountains, forests, species and ecosystems, by contrast, are not sentient
beings, are incapable of emotion, and cannot be harmed except in the
merely metaphorical sense that as equilibria their balance may be
disturbed. Hence, Rollin maintains, they do not have intrinsic value or
moral rights. Nonetheless, they do have instrumental value that in some
cases is enormous; thus, the argument against the destruction of the
nonsentient can be extremely strong.*

*In large measure, leading industrial nations have achieved a high
standard of living by exploiting the environment, and underdeveloped
countries seem to have no choice but to follow the same course if they
are to improve their standard of living. Environmental disasters, such as
the destruction of the rain forests, can be avoided only if an international
cooperative effort is made. The introduction of destructive, genetically*

engineered life forms into the environment is another example of a
potential disaster that can be avoided only with international cooperation.

The past two decades have witnessed a major revolutionary thrust in social
moral awareness, one virtually unknown in mainstream Western ethical
thinking, although not unrecognized in other cultural traditions; for example,
the Navajo, whose descriptive language for nature and animals is suffused
with ethical nuances; the Australian Aboriginal people; and the ancient
Persians. This thrust is the recognition that nonhuman entities enjoy some
moral status as objects of moral concern and deliberation. Although the
investigation of the moral status of nonhuman entities has sometimes been
subsumed under the global rubric of environmental ethics, such a blanket
term does not do adequate justice to the substantial conceptual differences
of its components.

THE MORAL STATUS OF
NONHUMAN THINGS

As a bare minimum, environmental ethics comprises two fundamentally
divergent concerns—namely, concern with individual nonhuman animals as
direct objects of moral concern and concern with species, ecosystems,
environments, wilderness areas, forests, the biosphere, and other nonsentient
natural or even abstract objects as direct objects of moral concern. Usually,
although with a number of major exceptions,[1] those who give primacy to
animals have tended to deny the moral significance of environments and
species as direct objects of moral concern, whereas those who give moral
primacy to enviro-ecological concerns tend to deny or at least downplay the
moral signficance of individual animals.[2] Significant though these differences
are, they should not cloud the dramatic nature of this common attempt to
break out of a moral tradition that finds loci of value only in human beings
and, derivatively, in human institutions.

Because of the revolutionary nature of these attempts, they also remain
somewhat undeveloped and embryonic. Writings in this area by and large
have tended to focus more on making the case for the attribution of moral
status to these entities than in working out detailed answers to particular
issues.[3] Thus, in order to assess these thrusts in relation to international
justice, one must first attempt to articulate a consensus concerning the basic
issue of attributing moral status to nonhumans, an attribution that, prima
facie, flies in the face of previous moral tradition. In attempting such an
articulation, one cannot hope to capture all approaches to these issues, but
rather to glean what appears most defensible when assessed against the
tribunal of common moral practice, moral theory attempting to explain that
practice, and common moral discourse.

The most plausible strategy in attempting to revise traditional moral theory and practice is to show that the seeds of the new moral notions or extensions of old moral notions are, in fact, already implicit in the old moral machinery developed to deal with other issues. Only when such avenues are exhausted will it make sense to recommend major rebuilding of the machinery, rather than putting it to new uses. The classic examples of such extensions are obviously found in the extension of the moral/legal machinery of Western democracies to cover traditionally disenfranchised groups such as women and minorities. The relatively smooth flow of such applications owes much of its smoothness to the plausibility of a simple argument of the form:

Our extant moral principles ought to cover all humans.
Women are humans.
∴ Our extant moral principles ought to cover women.

On the other hand, conceptually radical departures from tradition do not lend themselves to such simple rational reconstruction. Thus, for example, the principles of *favoring* members of traditionally disenfranchised groups at the expense of innocent members of nondisenfranchised groups for the sake of rectifying historically based injustice is viewed as much more morally problematic and ambivalent than simply according rights to these groups. Thus, it would be difficult to construct a simple syllogism in defense of this practice that would garner universal acquiescence with the ease of the one indicated previously.

Thus, one needs to distinguish between moral revolutionary thrusts that are ostensibly paradoxical to common sense and practice because they have been ignored in a wholesale fashion, yet are in fact logical extensions of common morality, and those revolutionary thrusts that are genuinely paradoxical to previous moral thinking and practice because they are not implicit therein. Being genuinely paradoxical does not invalidate a new moral thrust— it does, however, place upon its proponents a substantially greater burden of proof. Those philosophers, like myself, who have argued for a recognition of the moral status of individual animals and the rights and legal status that derive therefrom, have attempted to place ourselves in the first category. We recognize that a society that kills and eats billions of animals, kills millions more in research, and disposes of millions more for relatively frivolous reasons and that relies economically on animal exploitation as a mainstay of social wealth, considers talk of elevating the moral status of animals as impossible and paradoxical. But this does not mean that such an elevation does not follow unrecognized from moral principles we all hold. Indeed, the abolition of slavery or the liberation of women appeared similarly paradoxical and economically impossible, yet gradually both were perceived as morally necessary, in part because both were implicit, albeit unrecognized, in previously acknowledged assumptions.[4]

My own argument for elevating the status of animals has been a relatively straightforward deduction of unnoticed implications of traditional morality.

I have tried to show that no morally relevant grounds for excluding animals from the full application of our moral machinery will stand up to rational scrutiny. Traditional claims that rely on notions such as animals have no souls, are inferior to humans in power or intelligence or evolutionary status, are not moral agents, are not rational, are not possessed of free will, are not capable of language, are not bound by social contract to humans, and so forth, do not serve as justifiable reasons for excluding animals and their interests from the moral arena.

By the same token, morally relevant similarities exist between us and them in the case of the "higher" animals. Animals can suffer, as Jeremy Bentham said; they have interests; what we do to them matters to them; they can feel pain, fear, anxiety, loneliness, pleasure, boredom, and so on. Indeed, the simplicity and power of the argument calling attention to such morally relevant similarities has led Cartesians from Descartes to modern physiologists with a vested interest against attributing moral status to animals to declare that animals are machines with no morally relevant modes of awareness, a point often addressed today against moral claims such as mine. In fact, such claims have become a mainstay of what I have elsewhere called the "common sense of science." Thus, one who argues for an augmented moral status for animals finds it necessary to establish philosophically and scientifically what common sense takes for granted—namely, that animals *are* conscious.[5] Most people whose common sense is intact are not Cartesians and can see that moral talk cannot be withheld from animals and our treatment of them.

In my own work, appealing again to common moral practice, I have stressed our society's quasi-moral, quasi-legal notion of rights as a reflection of our commitment to the moral primacy of the individual, rather than the state. Rights protect what are hypothesized as the fundamental interests of human beings from cavalier encroachment by the common good—such interests as speech, assembly, belief, property, privacy, freedom from torture, and so forth. But those animals who are conscious also have fundamental interests arising out of *their* biologically given natures (or *teloi*), the infringement upon which matters greatly to them, and the fulfillment of which is central to their lives. Hence, I deduce the notion of animal rights from our common moral theory and practice and attempt to show that conceptually, at least, it is a deduction from the moral framework of the status quo rather than a major revision therein. Moral concern for individual animals follows from the hitherto ignored presence of morally relevant characteristics, primarily sentience, in animals. As a result, I am comfortable in attributing what Immanuel Kant called "intrinsic value," not merely use value, to animals if we attribute it to people.[6]

The task is far more formidable for those who attempt to make nonsentient natural objects, such as rivers and mountains, or, worse, quasi-abstract entities, such as species and ecosystems, into direct objects of moral concern. Interestingly enough, in direct opposition to the case of animals, such moves appear prima facie plausible to common morality, which has long expressed concern for the value and preservation of some natural objects, while condoning wholesale exploitation of others. In the same way, common practice often showed extreme concern for certain favored kinds of animals, while systematically exploiting others. Thus, many people in the United States strongly oppose scientific research on dogs and cats, but are totally unconcerned about such use of rodents or swine. What is superficially plausible, however, quite unlike the case of animals, turns out to be deeply paradoxical given the machinery of traditional morality.

Many leading environmental ethicists have attempted to do for nonsentient natural objects and abstract objects the same sort of thing I have tried to do for animals—namely, attempted to elevate their status to direct objects of intrinsic value, ends in themselves, which are morally valuable not only because of their relations and utility to sentient beings, but in and of themselves.[7] To my knowledge, none of these theorists has attempted to claim, as I do for animals, that the locus of such value lies in the fact that what we do to these entities matters to them. No one has argued that we can harm rivers, species, or ecosystems in ways that matter to them.

Wherein, then, do these theorists locate the intrinsic value of these entities? This is not at all clear in the writings, but seems to come down to one of the following doubtful moves:

1. Going from the fact that environmental factors are absolutely essential to the well-being or survival of beings that are loci of intrinsic value to the conclusion that environmental factors therefore enjoy a similar or even higher moral status. Such a move is clearly fallacious. Just because I cannot survive without insulin, and I am an object of intrinsic value, it does not follow that insulin is, too. In fact, the insulin is a paradigmatic example of instrumental value.

2. Going from the fact that the environment "creates" all sentient creatures to the fact that its welfare is more important than theirs. This is really a variation on (1) and succumbs to the same sort of criticism, namely, that this reasoning represents a genetic fallacy. The cause of something valuable need not itself be valuable and certainly not necessarily more valuable than its effect—its value must be established independently of its result. The Holocaust may have caused the state of Israel; that does not make the Holocaust more valuable than the state of Israel.

3. Confusing aesthetic or instrumental value for sentient creatures, notably humans, with intrinsic value and underestimating aesthetic value as a category. We shall return to this shortly, for I suspect it is the root confusion in those attempting to give nonsentient nature intrinsic value.

4. Substituting rhetoric for logic at crucial points in the discussions and using a poetic rhetoric (descriptions of natural objects in terms such as "grandeur," "majesty," "novelty," "variety") as an unexplained basis for according them "intrinsic value."

5. Going from the metaphor that infringement on natural objects "matters" to them in the sense that disturbance evokes an adjustment by their self-regulating properties, to the erroneous conclusion that such self-regulation,

being analogous to conscious coping in animals, entitles them to direct moral status.

In short, traditional morality and its theory do not offer a viable way to raise the moral status of nonsentient natural objects and abstract objects so that they are direct objects of moral concern on a par with or even higher than sentient creatures. Ordinary morality and moral concern take as their focus the effects of actions on beings who can be helped and harmed, in ways that matter to them, either directly or by implication. If it is immoral to wreck someone's property, it is because it is someone's; if it is immoral to promote the extinction of species, it is because such extinction causes aesthetic or practical harm to humans or to animals or because a species is, in the final analysis, a group of harmable individuals.

There is nothing, of course, to stop environmental ethicists from making a recommendation for a substantial revision of common and traditional morality. But such recommendations are likely to be dismissed or whittled away by a moral version of Occam's razor: Why grant animals rights and acknowledge in animals intrinsic value? Because they are conscious and what we do to them matters to them? Why grant rocks, or trees, or species, or ecosystems rights? Because these objects have great aesthetic value, or are essential to us, or are basic for survival? But these are paradigmatic examples of *instrumental* value. A conceptual confusion for a noble purpose is still a conceptual confusion.

There is nothing to be gained by attempting to elevate the moral status of nonsentient natural objects to that of sentient ones. One can develop a rich environmental ethic by locating the value of nonsentient natural objects in their relation to sentient ones. One can argue for the preservation of habitats because their destruction harms animals; one can argue for preserving ecosystems on the grounds of unforeseen pernicious consequences resulting from their destruction, a claim for which much empirical evidence exists. One can argue for the preservation of animal species as the sum of a group of individuals who would be harmed by its extinction. One can argue for preserving mountains, snail darters, streams, and cockroaches on aesthetic grounds. Too many philosophers forget the moral power of aesthetic claims and tend to see aesthetic reasons as a weak basis for preserving natural objects. Yet the moral imperative not to destroy unique aesthetic objects and even nonunique ones is an onerous one that is well ingrained into common practice—witness the worldwide establishment of national parks, preserves, forests, and wildlife areas.

Rather than attempting to transcend all views of natural objects as instrumental by grafting onto nature a mystical intrinsic value that can be buttressed only by poetic rhetoric, it would be far better to nurture public appreciation of subtle instrumental value, especially aesthetic value. People can learn to appreciate the unique beauty of a desert, or of a fragile ecosystem, or even of a noxious creature like a tick, when they understand the complexity and history therein and can read the story each life form contains. I am reminded of a colleague in parasitology who is loath to destroy worms he has studied upon completing his research because he has aesthetically learned to value their complexity of structure, function, and evolutionary history and role.

It is important to note that the attribution of value to nonsentient natural objects as a relational property arising out of their significance (recognized or not) for sentient beings does not denigrate the value of natural objects. Indeed, this attribution does not even imply that the interests or desires of individual sentient beings always trump concern for nonsentient ones. Our legal system has, for example, valuable and irreplaceable property laws that forbid owners of aesthetic objects, say a collection of Vincent Van Gogh paintings, to destroy them at will, say by adding them to one's funeral pyre. To be sure, this restriction on people's right to dispose of their own property arises out of a recognition of the value of these objects to other humans, but this is surely quite sensible. How else would one justify such a restriction? Nor, as we said earlier, need one limit the value of natural objects to their relationship to humans. Philosophically, one could, for example, sensibly (and commonsensically) argue for preservation of acreage from the golf-course developer because failure to do so would mean the destruction of thousands of sentient creatures' habitats—a major infringement of their interests—while building the golf course would fulfill the rarefied and inessential interests of a few.

Thus, in my view, one would accord moral concern to natural objects in a variety of ways, depending on the sort of object being considered. Moral status for individual animals would arise from their sentience. Moral status of species and their protection from humans would arise from the fact that a species is a collection of morally relevant individuals; moral status also would arise from the fact that humans have an aesthetic concern in not letting a unique and irreplaceable aesthetic object (or group of objects) disappear forever from our *Umwelt* (environment). Concern for wilderness areas, mountains, deserts, and so on would arise from their survival value for sentient animals as well as from their aesthetic value for humans. (Some writers have suggested that this aesthetic value is so great as to be essential to human mental/physical health, a point perfectly compatible with my position.[8])

Nothing in what I have said as yet tells us how to weigh conflicting interests, whether between humans and other sentient creatures or between human desires and environmental protection. How does one weigh the aesthetic concern of those who oppose blasting away part of a cliff against the pragmatic concern of those who wish to build on a cliffside? But the problem of weighing is equally thorny in traditional ethics—witness lifeboat questions or questions concerning the allocation of scarce medical resources. Nor does the intrinsic value approach help in adjudicating such issues. How does one weigh the alleged intrinsic value of a cliffside against the interests of the (intrinsic-value-bearing) homebuilders?

Furthermore, the intrinsic value view can lead to results that are repugnant to common sense and ordinary moral consciousness. Thus, for example, it follows from what has been suggested by one intrinsic value theorist that if a migratory herd of plentiful elk were passing through an area containing an endangered species of moss, it would be not only permissible but obligatory to kill the elk in order to protect the moss because in one case we would lose a species, in another "merely" individuals.[9] In my view, such a case has a less paradoxical resolution. Destruction of the moss does not matter to the moss, whereas elk presumably care about living or being injured. Therefore, one would give prima facie priority to the elk. This might presumably be trumped if, for example, the moss were a substratum from which was extracted an ingredient necessary to stop a raging, lethal epidemic in humans or animals. But such cases—and indeed most cases of conflicting interests—must be decided on the actual occasion. These cases are decided by a careful examination of the facts of the situation. Thus, our suggestion of a basis for environmental ethics does not qualitatively change the situation from that of current ethical deliberation, whereas granting intrinsic value to natural objects would leave us with a "whole new ball game"—and one where we do not know the rules.

In sum, then, the question of environmental ethics in relation to international justice must be analyzed into two discrete components. First are those questions that pertain to direct objects of moral concern—nonhuman animals whose sentience we have good reason to suspect—and that require the application of traditional moral notions to a hitherto ignored domain of moral objects. Second are those questions pertaining to natural objects or abstract natural objects. Although it is nonsensical to attribute intrinsic or direct moral value to these objects, they nonetheless must become (and are indeed becoming) central to our social moral deliberations. This centrality derives from our increasing recognition of the far-reaching and sometimes subtle instrumental value these objects have for humans and animals. Knowing that contamination of remote desert areas by pollutants can destroy unique panoplies of fragile beauty, or that dumping wastes into the ocean can destroy a potential source of antibiotics, or that building a pipeline can have undreamed-of harmful effects goes a long way toward making us think twice about these activities—a far longer way than endowing them with quasi-mystical rhetorical status subject to (and begging for) positivistic torpedoing.

THE ENVIRONMENT
AND INTERNATIONAL JUSTICE

How do both of these newly born areas of moral concern relate to issues of international justice? In the case of issues pertaining to moral awareness of the questions involved in the preservation and despoliation of nonsentient natural objects, processes, and abstract objects, the connection becomes increasingly clear as our knowledge increases. The interconnectedness of all things occupying the biosphere, the tenuousness and violability of certain natural objects and events whose permanence and invulnerability were long taken for granted have become dramatically clearer as environmental science has developed and the results of cavalier treatment of nature have become known.

Even those lacking any moral perspective on the instrumental values in nature now ought to have some prudential ones. Thus, even if one does not care about poisoning the air that other people and animals breathe, prudential reason would dictate that one realize that one is also poisoning oneself. Thus, the question of control of the actions of those who would or could harm another or everyone for the sake of selfish interests begins to loom large as our knowledge of environmental impact of individual actions begins to grow. These effects therefore enter into the dialectic of social justice. What constraints can legitimately be placed upon my freedoms in order to protect the environment? What social or individual benefits balance what costs to the environment or to natural objects? How much ought aesthetic values weigh against economic ones? Whole bureaucracies like the Environmental Protection Agency in the United States exist to ponder and regulate such questions in almost all civilized countries, and recent legal thinking has sought ways to codify the importance of natural objects in the law—for example, by granting them legal standing.[10] (Such a granting can and should be based on a realization of their instrumental value, not on intrinsic value; we already have such a precedent in legal standing for ships, cities, and corporations.)

Nevertheless, increased environmental knowledge has driven home a major but often ignored point: Environmental effects do not respect national boundaries. I recall traveling more than twenty years ago to the northernmost regions of eastern Canada that can be reached by road—areas inhabited almost exclusively by Native Americans to whom the benefits accruing from technological progress were manifestly limited. I was appalled to discover that in this land of few roads and fewer amenities, atmospheric pollutants such as sulfur dioxide and hydrogen sulfide reigned supreme—an unwelcome gift from factories hundreds of miles away across the U.S. border. I had no doubt that the respiratory systems of those native people were paying a heavy, and totally unjustified, price for another country's prosperity in which they did not share.

Similar examples abound. When propellant gases released by people in affluent societies (possibly) succeed in tearing a hole in the ozone layer, which hole then has cataclysmic effects on global weather, penetration of noxious rays, and so on, we again see that environmental damage does not respect national boundaries.

In a slightly different vein, one can consider underdeveloped countries struggling to raise the living standards of their populace. To do so, they must exploit and perhaps despoil resources and environments that, from the point of view of a detached observer, ought to be left alone or whose exploitation will or may in some measure ultimately threaten the whole biosphere. The detached observer may well be (and probably is) where he is in virtue of similar despoliation routinely engaged in by his country generations before environmental consciousness had dawned. Is the underdeveloped country to bear a burden of poverty just because its awakening is happening a hundred years late? Or is the new environmental knowledge to count for naught in the face of the need for development?

An excellent example of this point was recently given by an environmental scientist, Michael Mares, in an article in *Science*. Echoing the point we just made, Mares asserts that "broad-scale ecological problems have little to do with national boundaries. In our complex world, where multiple links of commerce, communications, and politics join all countries to a remarkable degree, the suggestion that ecological problems of large magnitude can or should be solved only at a local level is unrealistic. We are all involved in biospheric problems."[11]

Using the case of South America, for which massive extinction of species has been predicted and where wholesale destruction of rain forests has occurred, Mares points out that one cannot look at this situation strictly as South America's problem, but as one caused by global as well as local pressures with global and local consequences. With South American countries in economic difficulties, can one really expect governments there to take a long-run ecological perspective rather than acceding to short-term gain? If other countries in an immediate position to adopt a long-run perspective wish to do so, they must help South America with the requisite expertise as well as with significant financial assistance.

> South America's economies are in poor shape. Poverty is extensive, inflation rates in some countries are among the highest in the world, and the foreign debt is a crushing burden. Bare subsistence is often the only way of life. Impoverished farmers or unemployed workers engage in the illegal wildlife trade because they have nowhere else to turn. Their earnings, unlike the middle-level businessmen, are minimal, and they are frequently paid in goods, such as sugar or tobacco. Widespread poverty leads to desperation, and desperation causes people to eke out the barest of livings by using plant and animal resources, legally or illegally, with no thought to their renewability. The foreign debt, with its unending spiral fed by high interest rates, and the strict economic standards imposed by the International Monetary Fund on debtor nations lead to societal unrest and political instability, hopelessness, and increased poverty. When the United States demands repayment of loans, while telling the countries to increase their efforts at conservation, the reluctance or inability of South American countries to do more is understandable, as is the undercurrent of anti-American feeling that has increased over the last decade. Poor people and bankrupt countries have very little interest in conserving resources for themselves or for the richest nation on Earth. The poor economic panorama on the continent affects all areas of life. For example, educational opportunities decline as university budgets are cut back. Fewer students are trained in fields related to conservation needs. In addition, the continent is experiencing the most rapid human population growth in the world. This fact impacts negatively on all aspects of conservation biology.[12]

Mares points out that international cooperation is necessary in at least seven problem areas to solve the environmental problems of South America:

1. Lack of data
2. Lack of people trained in areas related to conservation
3. Lack of money
4. Lack of coordinated plans for the long term
5. Weak economics
6. The precedence of short-term planning strategies
7. An air of panic (suggesting that crisis is imminent and nothing can be done)[13]

Unlike many doomsayers, Mares argues that international cooperation can forestall the crisis: "We are all a part of this problem and must work together to find its solution. There is still time to act."[14]

The ultimate example is, of course, the ecological catastrophe of the nuclear winter that is projected to follow nuclear war. Those who would suffer from the effects of such a winter far outnumber the belligerents. Thus, nuclear war becomes a pressing matter not only to those nations with a penchant for annihilating one another, but even to those simple innocents thousands of miles and cultural light years away from the principals who have no notion of the ideological and economic disputes leading to the conflagration and no allegiance to either side.

Yet another striking example of the need for international cooperation and justice in environmental matters comes from the burgeoning area of biotechnology and genetic engineering. For some time, the United States has led in genetic engineering and also in attempts to create rules and guidelines for its regulation. Interest groups have brought suit against projects that might have untoward and unpredictable environmental consequences—for example, the ice nucleation experiments in California that use genetically engineered bacteria to protect crops from frost.[15] Demands for stringent federal regulation of such work have persisted, primarily on the grounds that such activities could wreak havoc with the environment in undreamed-of ways. What is all too often forgotten is that genetic engineering is a problem for international regulation, not merely for national rules. By and large, the technology for doing pioneering work in genetic engineering is relatively inexpensive, compared, for example, to the need for enormous amounts of capital to build particle accelerators. Thus, stringent regulation or even abolition of genetic engineering in a country such as the United States would not alone solve the problem; regulation would merely move genetic engineering into countries less concerned with potential national and global catastrophe. The net effect is that probably riskier, less supervised work would be done under less stringent conditions. Thus, by its very nature, genetic engineering must be controlled internationally if national control is to be effective.

The point about genetic engineering can be made even more strongly when one contemplates its use for military purposes. If there is a real possibility of environmental disaster arising adventitiously out of benign applications of biotechnology, this is a fortiori the case regarding those uses whose avowed purpose is destructive and whose sphere of effect is unpredictable. So much is manifest in the ratification of the Biological Weapons Convention of 1975, widely cited as the world's first disarmament treaty, "since it is the only one that outlaws the production and use of an entire class of weapons of mass destruction."[16] In October 1986, steps were taken to strengthen the verificational procedures of the treaty, but these essentially boil down to merely voluntary compliance, with no system of sanctions or enforcement.

The final example of environmental problems depending for their solution on some system of international justice concerns the extinction of species. Such problems fall into two distinct categories given the argument we have developed, although this distinction has traditionally been ignored. In my view, we must distinguish between threats of extinction involving sentient and nonsentient species. In the case of sentient species, the fact that a species is threatened is trumped by the fact that its members are sentient. First and foremost, the issue involves harming individual, direct objects of moral concern, just as genocide amounts to mass murder, not the elimination of an abstract entity.

Thus, from the point of view of primary loci of moral concern, killing *any* ten Siberian tigers is no different than killing the *last* ten. Our greater horror at the latter stems from invoking the relational value dimension to humans—no human will ever again be able to witness the beauty of these creatures; our world is poorer in the same way that it would be if one destroyed the last ten Van Goghs, not just any ten; the loss of the last ten tigers may lead to other losses of which we are not aware. But we should not lose sight of the fact that the greater harm is to the animals, not to us. For this reason, I will discuss the destruction of sentient species separately, along with cases where individual animals are destroyed and hurt without endangering the species.

This still leaves us with the case of species extinction involving nonsentient species—plants or animals in whom we have no reason to suspect the presence of consciousness. Such extinction is not necessarily an evil. Few (albeit some) bemoaned the eradication of the smallpox virus, and David Baltimore recently remarked that, in his view, all viruses could be eradicated with no loss (save perhaps to intrinsic value theorists).[17] On the other hand, most cases of extinction presumably would be cases of (relational) evil because nonsentient species that do not harm us or other sentient creatures directly or indirectly are at worst neutral, and their loss is both an aesthetic loss for their uniqueness and beauty (the humblest organisms often contain great beauty—in symmetry, adaptation, complexity, or whatever, as my friend the parasitologist discovered), or a loss of a potential tool whose value is not yet detected (as a source of medicine, dye, and so on), or as crucial to the ecosystem in some unrecognized way.

The destruction of myriad species is a major problem. The greatest threat lies in the tropics, where species diversity is both the richest and under the greatest threat. It has been estimated that only one in ten to one in twenty species in the tropics are known to science.[18] A hectare of land in the Peruvian Amazon rain forest contains 41,000 species of insect alone, according to a recent count.[19] A *single tree* contained 43 species of ant. In ten separate hectare plots in Borneo, 700 species of tree were identified, matching the count for all of North America![20] According to a report in *Science*, "The continued erosion of tropical rain forests—through small-scale slash and burn agriculture at one extreme to massive timber operations at the other— is . . . closing in on perhaps half the world's natural inventory of species. Most biologists agree that the world's rain forests will be all but obliterated at some point in the next century."[21] Furthermore, small parks and preserves could not harbor numbers and varieties of species proportional to their size. Thus, standard conservation compromises do not represent a viable solution to the problem.

Other habitats holding a large diversity of species also are threatened. These include coral reefs, coastal wetlands, such as those in California, and large African lakes. The last have been especially threatened by the attempt to cultivate within them varieties of fish not indigenous to the area. A mere documentation of species unknown to science and possibly threatened would require the life work of twenty-five thousand taxonomists; currently there are a mere fifteen hundred such individuals at work.[22] Standard techniques of conserving representative members of such species in zoos and herbaria or preserving germ plasm in essence represent the proverbial drop in the bucket, although they are of course better than nothing.

Scientists who have devoted a great deal of study to these issues again echo the point cited earlier from Mares: These concerns are not local, but international. Michael Robinson puts the point dramatically: "We are facing 'the enlightenment fallacy.' The fallacy is that if you educate the people of the Third World, the problem will disappear. It won't. The problems are not due to ignorance and stupidity. The problems . . . derive from the poverty of the poor and the greed of the rich."[23] *Science*, in concluding its analysis, asserted that "the problems are those of economics and politics. Inescapably, therefore, the solutions are to be found in those same areas."[24]

Some recognition of this politico-economic dimension of environmental problems has been slowly forthcoming politically. There are, for example, indications that policies of the World Bank, which lends development money to countries, are being restructured to take more cognizance of environmental concerns. The bank has been criticized for funding the Polonoroeste project in Brazil, which would have destroyed large forest areas in Brazil in order to allow mass migration of farmers from impoverished areas, and for funding cattle ranching projects in Africa that promote desertification.[25]

Thus, even a cursory examination of some major environmental issues affecting the nonsentient environment indicates that those problems are insoluble outside of the context of international justice. The question then becomes: What, if any, philosophical basis exists for a system of international justice in this area? History has shown, after all, that attempts to create viable machinery of international justice in any area, ranging from an end to genocide to the prevention of war, have run the gamut from laughable to ineffectual. Self-interest has always trumped justice; the situation among nations, it is often remarked, is essentially the Hobbesian "war of each against all." This historical point again blunts even the pragmatic justification for attributing intrinsic value to the nonsentient environment. After all, widespread recognition in the Western tradition of the intrinsic value of humans has not at all assisted in the development of effective mechanisms to ensure that such value is respected.

Ironically, if we begin with the Hobbesian insight, it actually may be easier to provide a rational (and pragmatically effective) basis for a system of international justice regarding environmental concerns rather than human rights. After all, there is no pragmatic reason for a nation to sacrifice its sovereignty in the international arena regarding matters of human rights. If a given country benefits significantly from oppressing all or some of its citizenry, what positive incentive is there for that nation to respond to other nations' protests, and what incentive is there for other nations to protest? In the latter case, of course, there may be moral or ideological reasons for a nation to protest another's human rights policies, but such concerns usually give way to more pragmatic pressures—for example, if the oppressive country stands in a mutually beneficial trade or defensive relationship with the concerned nation.

In the case of global environmental concerns—destruction of the ozone, pollution of air and water, nuclear winter, dangers arising out of genetic engineering, loss of species—*everyone* loses (or might lose) if these concerns are not addressed. A leitmotif of our discussion has been precisely the global nature of such concerns. We have, in the case of all of the examples cited previously, something closer to what game theorists call a game of cooperation rather than a game of competition. That is, if one nation loses its fight with an environmental problem, or simply does not address it, any other nation could, and in many cases would, be likely to suffer as well. Thus, if the United States, through excessive use of fluorocarbons, weakens the ozone barrier, the results will not be restricted to the United States, but will have global impact.

By the same token, even if a given nation X stands to gain by ignoring environmental despoliation, others may lose and, without a system of regulation, may in turn bear the brunt of Y's or Z's cavalier disregard of other aspects of the environment. Furthermore, there is good reason to believe that the short-run gains accruing to a nation by a disregard of environmental concerns may well be significantly outweighed in the long run by unforeseen or ignored consequences. Thus, the wholesale conversion of African grasslands into grazing lands for domestic animals not ecologically adapted to such an environment may yield short-term profits, but in the long run lead to desertification, which leaves the land of no use at all. By the same token, cavalier disregard of species loss in the deforestation of the tropics may certainly provide short-term windfall profits, but at the expense of far richer resources. *Time* magazine recounted a number of examples of these riches.

These threatened ecosystems have already proved a valuable source of medicines, foods and new seed stock for crops. Nine years ago, for example, a strain of perennial, disease-resistant wild maize named *Zea diploperennis* was found in a Mexican mountain forest, growing in three small plots. Crossing domestic corn varieties with this maize produces hardy hybrids that should ultimately be worth billions of dollars to farmers. A great many of the prescription drugs sold in the U.S. are based on unique chemical compounds found in tropical plants. For example, vincristine, originally isolated from the Madagascan periwinkle, is used to treat some human cancers. Scientists are convinced that still undiscovered forest plants could be the source of countless new natural drugs.[26]

The fundamental argument, however, is still the Hobbesian one of rational self-interest. Any country, if utterly unbridled in its pursuit of short-term economic gains, or in its cavalier disregard for the impact of its activities on other nations, can permanently harm the interests of other nations. An irresponsibly genetically engineered microorganism does not respect national boundaries or military power, nor does oceanic or atmospheric pollution. The consequences of lack of control of environmental damage can range from loss of potential benefits—such as loss of new medication derived from plants, or loss of the delight and wonder in seeing a fragile tundra aglow in wildflowers—to positive and serious harm—the dramatic rise in cancers or other diseases produced by environmental despoliation of air, water, or the food chain, or even to a new ice age or tidal waves resulting from destruction of the ozone. Given modern technology, virtually any nation can damage any or all nations in any number of these ways; hence, a situation ripe for Hobbesian contractualism is reached.

In Hobbesian terms, of course, individuals engaged in a war of each against all are rendered equal by their ultimate vulnerability to harm and death by action on the part of others or combinations of others. Thus, we rationally relinquish our natural tendency toward rapaciousness in recognition of others' similar tendency, and our vulnerability thereto. Unrestricted greed is sacrificed for security and protection from the unrestricted greed of others, and a sovereign who, as it were, builds fences protecting each from all is constituted by each individual surrendering a portion of his or her unbridled autonomy. As we have seen, a precisely analogous situation exists regarding environmental vulnerability, and thus rationality would dictate that each nation surrender some of its autonomy to an international authority in order to protect itself, or the whole world including itself, from major disaster. This is of course especially clear, as we have seen earlier, in matters pertaining to biological warfare, where any nation can effectively annihilate any or all others.

In summary, then, the relevance of a viable mechanism of international justice to environmental ethical concerns is manifest. Indeed, many if not most environmental issues, and certainly the most vexing and important ones, entail major global consequences and thus cannot be restricted to local issues of sovereignty. An environmental ethics is inseparable from a system of international justice, not only in terms of policing global dangers and verifying and monitoring compliance with international agreements, but also in terms of implementing the distributive justice necessary to prevent poor countries from looking only at short-term gains. The rain forests are not only a problem for the countries in which they are found; if other developed nations are to benefit from the continued existence of the rain forests, we must be prepared to pay for that benefit. No country should be expected to bear the full brunt of environmental concerns. Classical economics does not work for ecological and environmental concerns; each unit pursuing its own interest will not enrich the biosphere, but deplete and devastate it. As E. O. Wilson put it in a recent conference on biodiversity, "The time has come to link ecology to economic and human development. . . . What is happening to the rain forests of Madagascar and Brazil will affect us all."[27] In other words, if a tree is felled in a primeval forest and there is no one else around, one should care about it anyway.

ANIMALS AND INTERNATIONAL JUSTICE

But what of the other class of environmental moral issues—namely, those affecting nonhuman sentient beings? Does the solution of these issues require a system of international justice as well? Clearly, in many cases, the answer is an obvious yes. In the first place, animal populations do not always respect or adhere to geopolitical boundaries, the classic case being, of course, the numerous species of whales. Thus, any given country's commitment to protect the whales is meaningless in the face of other nations' commitment to "harvest" them, to use a common if odious locution. Thus, in such a case, some international guarantees are required to protect the animals. Such treaties, of course, currently exist, but, like the convention regulating biological weaponry, are readily and frequently abrogated in the face of national interest.

The whaling treaties, for example, are regularly ignored by various nations in the face of self-interest, and other nations look the other way because they are tied to the offending nation by ties of commerce and defense, which unequivocally trump the interests of the animals.[28] Only if some neutral, disinterested mechanism existed for enforcing such treaties could one assure that the interests of the animals were protected in the face of self-interest or even tradition—witness the recent case of the Faroe Islands whale slaughters, which are undertaken for fun, not meat or income.[29] Unfortunately, the surrender of the autonomy that makes such mechanisms possible does not, unlike the environmental areas of our previous discussion, follow plausibly from rational self-interest. The Japanese, for example, lose nothing by violating a treaty and killing whales; there is no parallel meaningful threat from other nations. The problem here is that concern for the animals does not rest upon rational self-interest, but on extended moral concern, similar to concern for human rights and their abridgment in other nations. Thus, we cannot even appeal to self-interest as a basis for moral concern; indeed, in such cases, moral concern may exact a cost in self-interest.

Nonetheless, the situation is not hopeless. The case of the Canadian harp seal hunt dramatically illustrates that nations can be motivated by a moral concern that is actually inimical to self-interest. The European Economic Community recently banned the importation of seal products derived from the barbaric Newfoundland hunt. This was done despite the fact that at least some European nations derived economic benefit from the seal hunt and despite the fact that the European public was a major traditional consumer of seal products. This case dramatically illustrates that human consciousness is being increasingly sensitized to the suffering and interests of animals.

Cynics might argue that the seal case derives from the sentiment attached to the furry cuteness of baby seals and the jarring image of their slaughter by clubbing—big eyes and blood on the white snow. Although there is some truth in this claim, it is by no means all. Until recently, moral concern as embodied in the "humane ethic" was highly selective and favored the cute, cuddly, and familiar. Thus, for example, the Animal Welfare Act of 1966 and 1970, the only legal constraint on animal research in the United States, exempted from its very limited purview (it concerned itself only with food, caging, transport, and so on and disavowed concern with the actual content and conduct of research) rats, mice, and farm animals, in fact, 90 percent of the animals used in research. For purposes of the act, a dead dog was defined as an animal, a live mouse was not. Recently, however, things have changed. With the rise of an articulated moral concern for sentient beings by philosophers such as Peter Singer, Tom Regan, Steven Sapontzis,[30] and myself, that concern has captured the social imagination nationally and internationally. New guidelines and laws extend concern even to the more prosaic and unlovely animals, and a new amendment to the Animal Welfare Act in the United States, which I helped to draft, now mandates control of pain, suffering, and distress, which is a direct insult to the ideology of science that treated these as unknowable. Similar thrusts have occurred in other countries; in Germany, a new law bans animal research for military and cosmetic purposes, as does a new Dutch law. By the same token, many countries, such as Britain, Switzerland, and Denmark, have put constraints on confinement agriculture—"factory farming"—even though a price is paid in "efficiency" and cost to the consumer.

We sometimes forget that there is an international dimension even to animal research and factory farming. Unilateral and major constraints on such practices by one country for the sake of moral concern for animals, with other countries not making similar moves, can lead, for example, to an erosion of the legislating country's agricultural economy if the constraints make its products prohibitively more expensive and drastically reduce a market for them. But a universal constraint applicable to all countries would merely put all competitors back at the same starting gate. Public education also can convince consumers to "put their money where their morality is."

In the case of animals in science, a parallel problem arises. Multinational corporations, and even individual researchers, when unable to do a particular kind of experiment in one country will simply go to another. Given that experimenters then are shifting the suffering from one animal to another who is not different morally, this is not a just solution. Here we cannot even use the rationalization we do with humans—"Their culture makes things tolerable to them that are not tolerable to us"—because, as a Dutch colleague of mine said, "All dogs bark in the same language." Thus, scientific research must also be regulated by internationally accepted rules, else the burden of injustice is merely shifted from one innocent animal to another who happens to be living in a different place. For this reason, the European Economic Community member nations are drafting rules designed to govern all member nations, which is a step in the right direction because it would probably be impractical for companies smarting under such rules to move out of Europe altogether to less enlightened countries.

There are many areas of animal abuse where the network of interests and thus the need for rules are obviously international. There are other cases— for example, a horrendous blood sport practiced in a small country—where there are fewer international connections and implications. Nonetheless, the key to stopping all such evils is, in the final analysis, the same. It lies in a widespread philosophical extension of widespread moral notions. Thus, the philosophical basis for a system of international justice that can stop, for example, the slaughter of rhinoceroses for frivolous consumer goods such as ornamental knives and aphrodisiacs (which reduced the black rhino population from 65,000 in 1970 to 4,500 today),[31] or the killing of the snow leopard for fur, lies in the expanded moral vision of many people in diverse nations. Such expanded awareness is contagious and creates a new gestalt on animals that finds expression in legislation, boycotts, embargos, and the like. Such concern is likely to manifest first on a national level, with demands for regulation of research and mandated protection of research animals (including recent demands for housing that respects their telos); legal constraints on agricultural practices that yield efficiency at the expense of animals' suffering; restriction of frivolous and painful testing on animals, such as the LD 50 and Draize tests used in developing cosmetics and the like; tighter controls imposed over zoos, circuses, and rodeos; and so on.

But as I said, animal exploitation does not stop at national boundaries, nor does moral concern for animals. Thus, such abuses as traffic in rare birds where vast shipments of them arrive dead and dying; unregulated transport of all varieties of animals; the murder of porpoises in pursuit of tuna; the slaughter of migrating whales in the Faroe Islands as a sport and "cultural tradition," will—whether happening in any or all countries—be subjected to international pressures for regulation. These inevitably will result in tighter monitoring and restriction of such activities, which in turn will require international cooperation of the sort that is starting to develop in order to control the drug traffic.

It is perhaps not totally utopian to suggest that expanded concern for animals, a concern crossing geopolitical barriers, may lead to expanded concern for other human beings in countries not one's own, in a lovely dialectical reversal of the traditional wisdom preached by St. Thomas Aquinas and Immanuel Kant, suggesting that concern for animals is merely disguised concern for human beings.

NOTES

1. See the chapters in Tom Regan, *All That Dwell Therein* (Berkeley: University of California Press, 1982).
2. See Aldo Leopold, *A Sand County Almanac* (Oxford: Oxford University Press, 1949); J. Baird Callicott, "Animal Liberation: A Triangular Affair," *Environmental Ethics* 2 (1980):311–338; Holmes Rolston III, *Philosophy Gone Wild* (Buffalo, N.Y.: Prometheus Books, 1986).
3. There are exceptions to this generalization—for example, my own work in abolishing multiple use of animals as a standard teaching practice in medical and veterinary schools and my efforts in writing and promoting new legislation on proper care of laboratory animals.
4. See the discussions of this point in Peter Singer, *Animal Liberation* (New York: New York Review of Books, 1975); and B. Rollin, *Animal Rights and Human Morality* (Buffalo, N.Y.: Prometheus Books, 1981).
5. See my "Animal Pain," in M. Fox and L. Mickley (eds.), *Advances in Animal Welfare Science 1985* (The Hague; Martinus Nijhoff, 1985); and my "Animal Consciousness and Scientific Change," *New Ideas in Psychology* 4, no. 2 (1986):141–152, as well as the replies to the latter by P. K. Feyerabend, H. Rachlin, and T. Leahey in the same issue, p. 153. See also my *Animal Consciousness, Animal Pain, and Scientific Change* (tentative title) (Oxford: Oxford University Press, forthcoming).
6. See my *Animal Rights*, Part I.
7. See the works mentioned in footnotes 1 and 2.
8. This point is made with great rhetorical force in Edward Abbey, *Desert Solitaire* (New York: Ballantine Books, 1971).
9. See Holmes Rolston, "Duties to Endangered Species," *Philosophy Gone Wild*.
10. See the seminal discussion in Christopher Stone, *Should Trees Have Standing? Toward Legal Rights for Natural Objects* (Los Altos, Calif.: William Kaufmann, 1974).
11. Michael Mares, "Conservation in South America: Problems, Consequences, and Solutions." *Science* 233 (1986):734.
12. Ibid., p. 738.
13. Ibid., p. 736.
14. Ibid., p. 739.
15. For a discussion of various ethical issues surrounding genetic engineering, see my "The Frankenstein Thing," in J. W. Evans and A. Hollaender (eds.), *Genetic Engineering of Agricultural Animals* (New York: Plenum, 1986).
16. *Science* 234 (1986):143.
17. *Time*, November 3, 1986, p. 74.
18. *Science* 234 (1986):149.
19. Ibid.
20. Ibid.
21. Ibid.
22. Ibid., p. 150
23. Ibid.
24. Ibid.
25. *Science* 234 (1986):813.
26. *Time*, October 13, 1986, p. 80.

27. Ibid.

28. Maxine McCloskey, "Wildlife on a Geopolitical Planet" (Presentation by U.S. delegate to the International Whaling Commission, at the Animal Protection Institute annual meeting, Sacramento, California, October 18, 1986). See also N. Carter and A. Thornton, *Pirate Whaling 1985, and a History of the Subversion of International Whaling Regulations* (Glasgow: SAVE International, 1985).

29. See A. Thornton and J. Gibson, *Pilot Whaling in the Faroe Islands* (London: CACE, 1986).

30. Steven Sapontzis, *Morals, Reason, and Animals* (Philadelphia: Temple University Press, 1987).

31. *Science* 234 (1986):147.

8

The Deep Ecology
Movement

ARNE NAESS

There is substantial agreement between Arne Naess and Bernard Rollin. Both think that animals have intrinsic value and hence have rights. Unlike Rollin, however, Naess claims that insentient objects may have intrinsic value. He maintains that ordinary people speak of such things having value for their own sakes, and he claims that philosophers have not shown that this manner of speaking is problematic. In addition, Naess provides a useful description of some of the progress that has occurred toward environmental justice.

The chapter by Bernard E. Rollin offers, in my opinion, a careful description of some of the prevalent views within what I have called the deep ecology movement. This is an international movement started about the time of the appearance of Rachel Carson's *Silent Spring* in 1962. This movement concentrates not on the health and well-being of humans *exclusively*, but on the diversity and richness of life on this planet. The supporters of the movement are deeply concerned about the decline of the conditions of life on the planet. This degradation and impoverishment of life may turn out to be worse than anything that has happened in the last thousand million years. Paradoxically, the present devastation has been caused by living beings with the capacity to experience every form of life and its long history.

Reversing the dominant trend does not call only for minor repairs and local fights against pollution. Changes of policies are needed that affect basic economic, technological, and ideological structures.[1] Moreover, a general appeal to sentiments against mistreating animals should be combined with a national and international demand that the entire ecosphere be treated *justly.*

Rollin has shown that many nonhuman things are objects of moral concern. The moral status of sentient creatures, he argues, is due to their intrinsic value. The status of insentient things is quite different in his view—while they have no intrinsic value, they are not valueless because they are useful to sentient beings. However, by resisting the view that insentient beings may possess intrinsic value he neglects an important consideration against mistreating them: Things such as plants and the ecosphere have intrinsic value— or so I shall argue.

THE INTRINSIC VALUE OF NONSENTIENT BEINGS

Rollin stresses the intrinsic value—not merely the use value for humans— of sentient animals. They are ends in themselves, not merely means. He considers it crucial that what we do to them matters to *them,* even if they serve no purpose to anyone else. But Rollin limits his application of intrinsic value to sentient beings.[2] However, among people who are not heavily influenced by certain philosophical or juridical terminology, it is common to be concerned about animals regardless of sentience and to value flowers, landscapes, or ecosystems for their own sakes. People often say that such things "belong there" or "are part of the whole," and these remarks are extended even to poisonous plants. Moreover, the intrinsic value many people attribute to nonsentients does not preclude that these "natural objects" also have instrumental value. In my view, this ordinary way of speaking is most persuasive. I agree that the flourishing of human and nonhuman life on earth, sentient or not, has intrinsic value. But beings such as ecosystems are also of value in themselves, independent of their narrow usefulness for human purposes.[3]

Some people speak about the usefulness of conserving free nature because people have a need to conserve such natural items for their own sake. According to this view, because what fulfills broad human needs is useful, such nature is useful, and conservation is justifiable from a broad utilitarian point of view. I have used the adjective *narrow* to avoid the interpretation that what has value in itself is necessarily independent of broad utilitarian value.

What Rollin calls aesthetic value may be a sort of value closely related to the intrinsic value discussed within the deep ecology movement. Humans and only humans form judgments concerning aesthetic value, but people tend to treat value as an "objective" property of the object itself, not as a property that disappears when humans do not appreciate it. As a philosopher, I think these people are right.

Elsewhere Rollin criticizes those who maintain that natural objects have intrinsic value on the grounds that such people see value as a mystic property. But even people without special mystical talents speak about intrinsic value of a sort that does not need to be buttressed by poetic rhetoric. I have the impression that Rollin refers to concepts of intrinsic value that are developed by professional metaphysicians. I do not need them. What Rollin says about parasitologists suggests that they appreciate the value of worms independent of any narrow use for humans. This is all I need for my concept of intrinsic value. The parasitologist has *respect* for life! "Let the worms live!" What Rollin calls the aesthetic value of the worms is scarcely experienced as aesthetic by the parasitologist. To him the worms *are* of value whatever their usefulness or lack of usefulness.

I do not think philosopical analysis has shown that we really do *not* affix any intrinsic value to a "noxious creature like a tick" but view it solely in its instrumental function. The so-called objective view (according to which natural objects have intrinsic value) is not easy to explain and justify philosophically, but the same also holds of the subjective view and of every basic view I know.

Nonetheless, I do not see any clear incompatibility between what Professor Rollin says and the deep ecology "platform formulation." This is a proposed set of eight points that are intended to formulate basic views characteristic of the deep ecology movement. The essentials of the eight points are as follows.[4] The first two affirm the intrinsic value of the richness and diversity of life on this planet and suggest that no species endowed with the capacity to understand has the right to treat such a planet as merely the resource for itself. The third and fourth points insist that only human vital needs could justify reducing the richness and diversity of life on earth. Such needs do not require a human population of many thousand million. If human behavior is not drastically changed, human population should decrease in order to increase the quality of life of other creatures. Current interference with others is excessive (point 5). Necessary changes of the human/planet relationship involve fundamental technological, economic, social, and political structures (point 6). The rich countries must shift priorities from a material standard of living to the quality of life (point 7). The activist aspect of the platform of the deep ecology movement is affirmed in the last point. Those who agree with the seven points have an obligation to do something for the implementation of the necessary changes—however modest in range and impact (point 8).

WORK IN PROGRESS

Let me briefly survey the progress in environmental justice. Work is in progress to move from international environmental cooperation to the creation of a system of international environmental conventions. The convention of Bern of September 19, 1979, furnishes an example. It covers the conservation of European plants and animals and of their habitats. It envisages far-reaching protection with heavy practical economic consequences. A growing section of the general public interprets this protection, whatever the usefulness of the plants and animals, as a protection of intrinsic values. Living beings have a right to be where they are. We as living beings also have this right, but there are limits to our legitimate interference.

Limits, yes, but exactly where are they? Abstract general criteria are not difficult to offer, but what is more difficult is the establishment of guidelines for behavior in definite localities. Consider this conflict: A winding road through a landscape is considered too narrow, too slow. A cost-benefit analysis concludes with the recommendation of a broad, straight highway. Disturbance of the life and geomorphology of the landscape will be considerable. Opinion against the construction of the highway is increasing, but opponents appear too late. The major destructive interference is carried out. Considering that such kinds of yearly interference in free nature covers more than the 80,000 square kilometers of yearly desert expansion, there is reason to take up the ethical aspect for reconsideration in every locality. The importance of local initiative ("Think globally; act locally!") stems partly from the self-defense that motivates initiative. A human being has an ego and a social self, but self-realization implies realization of an ecological Self comprising more than elements of human society. From ethics of altruism we are led to an enlightened ethics of Self-interest.[5]

Conventions comparable in thoroughness to that of Bern are desperately needed to cover the Third World. But there is no moral or other basis for requiring developing countries to adopt the environmental conventions of rich nations. Nations in Europe, since the time of the Roman Empire, have degraded and impoverished their own environments. Colonial powers have done the same with other regions. A few white settlers played havoc with the ecology of a continent, Australia, through their uncontrolled burnings. Consequently, justness, not pity, requires the rich nations to cooperate with the developing countries and to help finance the implementation of ecological conventions.

The cost is considerable. Consider the fairly small parks of Thailand. Illegal logging and decimation of wildlife go on. Wardens, badly paid but fond of nature, protect wildlife, but are sometimes shot by poachers hired by corrupt politicians. The poor are not against keeping wildlife protected, but it requires labor and money.

Thailand is only one country where laws are enacted but enforcement is feeble or absent. Rich nations can do a great deal to help the ecologically educated of these countries in their courageous fight. The new basic slogan "sustainable development" implies long-term, ecologically responsible development. The ethical imperative to assist the poor entails helping the poor ecologically, not just economically.

The mechanisms of international law and conventions like that of Bern are extremely important, according to the *World Conservation Strategy,* a summary of contemporary ecological problems, together with suggested solutions, worked out by the International Union for the Conservation of

Nature and Natural Resources, in cooperation with UNEP, FAO, and UNESCO.[6] Unhappily, even the short priority checklist of these actions is hardly known. I think it justifiable to list the first four in toto.

1. Review the coverage and effectiveness of international law relevant to living resources and develop new law to remedy any deficiencies.
2. Implement international conservation conventions.
3. Provide multilateral and bilateral assistance for reforestation, the restoration of degraded environments, and the protection of the support systems of fisheries and of genetic resources.
4. Provide multilateral and bilateral assistance for the design and implementation of ecologically appropriate policies and the establishment and maintenance of effective conservation procedures, laws, and organizations.

The rest of the list covers more specific actions, such as "the implementation of the Convention on the Prevention of Marine Pollution by Dumping of Wastes and Other Matter, of the Convention on the Regulation of Long-range Transboundary Air Pollution, and of analogous regional conventions." The term *implementation* is crucial. There are myriad conventions already in existence, but governments do not take them seriously. Little is done at the level of mass communication to inform the public about the reasons for the conventions. Still less has been done, until just recently, to appeal to the ethics of people, *including their sense of justice.* If the rich nations do not mend their ways, there is little hope.

NOTES

1. A. Naess, "The Deep Ecology Movement: Some Philosophical Aspects," *Philosophical Inquiry* 8 (1986):14.
2. For a recent comprehensive expression of this view, see E. Partridge, "Values in Nature: Is Anybody There?" *Philosophical Inquiry* 8 (1986):96.
3. Point 1 of an 8-point version in my *Ecology, Community, Lifestyle* (Cambridge University Press, forthcoming).
4. For details and comments, see, for example, Naess, "The Deep Ecology Movement," p. 13.
5. A. Naess, "Self-Realization: An Ecological Approach to Being in the World" (Keith Memorial Lecture, Murdoch University Press, 1986).
6. The excellent summary is obtainable from the International Union for Conservation of Nature and Natural Resources (IUCN), 1196 Gland, Switzerland, or from any local IUCN branch.

PART TWO

The Legitimate Use of Violence

9

The Theory of Aggression

MICHAEL WALZER

*By thinking of the community of nations as analogous to communities
of individuals, and the rights of the former as analogous to those of the
latter, Michael Walzer constructs a theory of aggression. He thinks that it
is a theory we have held for centuries and that it is acceptable once
altered in certain ways. Termed by Walzer the* legalist paradigm, *this
doctrine consists of the following tenets:*

1. *There exists an international society of independent states.*
2. *This international society has a law that establishes the rights of its
   members—above all, the rights of territorial integrity and political
   sovereignty.*
3. *Any use or threat of force by one state against the political
   sovereignty or territorial integrity of another constitutes aggression
   and is a criminal act.*
4. *Aggression justifies two kinds of violent response: a war of self-
   defense by the victim and a war of law enforcement by the victim
   and any other member of international society.*
5. *Nothing but aggression can justify war.*
6. *Once the aggressor state has been militarily repulsed, it can also be
   punished.*

*One alteration of the paradigm suggested by Walzer is a revision of
tenets 3 and 4 to make it clear that preventive war is sometimes
permissible. Another is clarification of the right of political sovereignty
mentioned in 2. In Walzer's view, there is a strong presumption that no*

foreign power may intervene in the internal affairs of another, but there are three exceptions: to aid secessions, to counter existing intervention, and to halt grievous violations of human rights. In a section not reproduced here, Walzer suggests an alteration of the last tenet of the legalist paradigm to make it clear that capturing and punishing political leaders is illegitimate. In rare instances, on the other hand, states can be justified in demanding the unconditional surrender of the initiators of war and even in reconstructing the defeated nations.

Law and Order
in International Society

AGGRESSION

Aggression is the name we give to the crime of war. We know the crime because of our knowledge of the peace it interrupts—not the mere absence of fighting, but peace-with-rights, a condition of liberty and security that can exist only in the absence of aggression itself. The wrong the aggressor commits is to force men and women to risk their lives for the sake of their rights. It is to confront them with the choice: your rights or (some of) your lives! Groups of citizens respond in different ways to that choice, sometimes surrendering, sometimes fighting, depending on the moral and material condition of their state and army. But they are always justified in fighting; and in most cases, given that harsh choice, fighting is the morally preferred response. The justification and the preference are very important: they account for the most remarkable features of the concept of aggression and for the special place it has in the theory of war.

Aggression is remarkable because it is the only crime that states can commit against other states; everything else is, as it were, a misdemeanor. There is a strange poverty in the language of international law. The equivalents of domestic assault, armed robbery, extortion, assault with intent to kill, murder in all its degrees, have but one name. Every violation of the territorial integrity or political sovereignty of an independent state is called aggression. It is as if we were to brand as murder all attacks on a man's person, all attempts to coerce him, all invasions of his home. This refusal of differentiation makes it difficult to mark off the relative seriousness of aggressive acts—to distinguish, for example, the seizure of a piece of land or the imposition of a satellite regime from conquest itself, the destruction of a state's independence (a crime for which Abba Eban, Israel's foreign minister in 1967, suggested the name "policide"). But there is a reason for the refusal.

Reprinted from Michael Walzer, *Just and Unjust Wars: A Moral Argument with Historical Illustrations* (copyright © 1977 by Basic Books, Inc.), pp. 51–63 and 86–108, by permission of Basic Books, Inc., Publishers.

All aggressive acts have one thing in common: they justify forceful resistance, and force cannot be used between nations, as it often can between persons, without putting life itself at risk. Whatever limits we place on the means and range of warfare, fighting a limited war is not like hitting somebody. Aggression opens the gates of hell. Shakespeare's *Henry V* makes the point exactly:[1]

> For never two such kingdoms did contend
> Without much fall of blood, whose guiltless drops
> Are every one a woe, a sore complaint
> 'Gainst him whose wrongs gives edge unto the swords
> That makes such waste in brief mortality.

At the same time, aggression unresisted is aggression still, though there is no "fall of blood" at all. In domestic society, a robber who gets what he wants without killing anyone is obviously less guilty, that is, guilty of a lesser crime, than if he commits murder. Assuming that the robber is prepared to kill, we allow the behavior of his victim to determine his guilt. We don't do this in the case of aggression. Consider, for example, the German seizures of Czechoslovakia and Poland in 1939. The Czechs did not resist; they lost their independence through extortion rather than war; no Czech citizens died fighting the German invaders. The Poles chose to fight, and many were killed in the war that followed. But if the conquest of Czechoslovakia was a lesser crime, we have no name for it. At Nuremberg, the Nazi leadership was charged with aggression in both cases and found guilty in both.[2] Once again, there is a reason for this identity of treatment. We judge the Germans guilty of aggression in Czechoslovakia, I think, because of our profound conviction that they ought to have been resisted—though not necessarily by their abandoned victim, standing alone.

The state that does resist, whose soldiers risk their lives and die, does so because its leaders and people think that they should or that they have to fight back. Aggression is morally as well as physically coercive, and that is one of the most important things about it. "A conqueror," writes Clausewitz, "is always a lover of peace (as Bonaparte always asserted of himself); he would like to make his entry into our state unopposed; in order to prevent this, we must choose war."[3] If ordinary men and women did not ordinarily accept that imperative, aggression would not seem to us so serious a crime. If they accepted it in certain sorts of cases, but not in others, the single concept would begin to break down, and we would eventually have a list of crimes more or less like the domestic list. The challenge of the streets, "Your money or your life!" is easy to answer: I surrender my money and so I save myself from being murdered and the thief from being a murderer. But we apparently don't want the challenge of aggression answered in the same way; even when it is, we don't diminish the guilt of the aggressor. He has violated rights to which we attach enormous importance. Indeed, we are inclined to think that the failure to defend those rights is never due to a sense of their unimportance, nor even to a belief (as in the street-challenge case) that they are, after all, worth less than life itself, but only to a stark conviction that the defense is hopeless. Aggression is a singular and undifferentiated crime because, in all its forms, it challenges rights that are worth dying for.

THE RIGHTS OF
POLITICAL COMMUNITIES

The rights in question are summed up in the lawbooks as territorial integrity and political sovereignty. The two belong to states, but they derive ultimately from the rights of individuals, and from them they take their force. "The duties and rights of states are nothing more than the duties and rights of the men who compose them."⁴ That is the view of a conventional British lawyer, for whom states are neither organic wholes nor mystical unions. And it is the correct view. When states are attacked, it is their members who are challenged, not only in their lives, but also in the sum of things they value most, including the political association they have made. We recognize and explain this challenge by referring to their rights. If they were not morally entitled to choose their form of government and shape the politics that shape their lives, external coercion would not be a crime; nor could it so easily be said that they had been forced to resist in self-defense. Individual rights (to life and liberty) underlie the most important judgments that we make about war. How these rights are themselves founded I cannot try to explain here. It is enough to say that they are somehow entailed by our sense of what it means to be a human being. If they are not natural, then we have invented them, but natural or invented, they are a palpable feature of our moral world. States' rights are simply their collective form. The process of collectivization is a complex one. No doubt, some of the immediate force of individuality is lost in its course; it is best understood, nevertheless, as it has commonly been understood since the seventeenth century, in terms of social contract theory. Hence it is a moral process, which justifies some claims to territory and sovereignty and invalidates others.

The rights of states rest on the consent of their members. But this is consent of a special sort. State rights are not constituted through a series of transfers from individual men and women to the sovereign or through a series of exchanges among individuals. What actually happens is harder to describe. Over a long period of time, shared experiences and cooperative activity of many different kinds shape a common life. "Contract" is a metaphor for a process of association and mutuality, the ongoing character of which the state claims to protect against external encroachment. The protection extends not only to the lives and liberties of individuals but also to their shared life and liberty, the independent community they have made, for which individuals are sometimes sacrificed. The moral standing of any particular state depends upon the reality of the common life it protects and the extent to which the sacrifices required by that protection are willingly accepted and thought worthwhile. If no common life exists, or if the state doesn't defend the common life that does exist, its own defense may have no moral justification. But most states do stand guard over the community of their citizens, at least to some degree: that is why we assume the justice of their defensive wars. And given a genuine "contract," it makes sense to say that territorial integrity and political sovereignty can be defended in exactly the same way as individual life and liberty.*

It might also be said that a people can defend its country in the same way as men and women can defend their homes, for the country is collectively as the homes are privately owned. The right to territory might be derived, that is, from the individual right to property. But the ownership of vast reaches of land is highly problematic, I think, unless it can be tied in some plausible way to the requirements of national survival and political independence. And these two seem by themselves to generate territorial rights that have little to do with ownership in the strict sense. The case is probably the same with the smaller properties of domestic society. A man has certain rights in his home, for example, even if he does not own it, because neither his life nor his liberty is secure unless there exists some physical space within which he is safe from intrusion. Similarly again, the right of a nation or people not to be invaded derives from the common life its members have made on this piece of land—it had to be made somewhere—and not from the legal title they hold or don't hold. But these matters will become clearer if we look at an example of disputed territory.

The Case of Alsace-Lorraine

In 1870, both France and the new Germany claimed these two provinces. Both claims were, as such things go, well founded. The Germans based themselves on ancient precedents (the lands had been part of the Holy Roman Empire before their conquest by Louis XIV) and on cultural and linguistic kinship; the French on two centuries of possession and effective government.[5] How does one establish ownership in such a case? There is, I think, a prior question having to do with political allegiance, not with legal titles at all. What do the inhabitants want? The land follows the people. The decision as to whose sovereignty was legitimate (and therefore as to whose military presence constituted aggression) belonged by right to the men and women who lived on the land in dispute. Not simply to those who owned the land: the decision belonged to the landless, to town dwellers

---

*The question of when territory and sovereignty can rightly be defended is closely connected to the question of when individual citizens have an obligation to join the defense. Both hang on issues in social contract theory. I have discussed the second question at length in my book *Obligations: Essays on Disobedience, War, and Citizenship* (Cambridge, Mass., 1970). See especially "The Obligation to Die for the State" and "Political Alienation and Military Service." But neither in that book nor in this one do I deal in any detail with the problem of national minorities—groups of people who do not fully join (or do not join at all) in the contract that constitutes the nation. The radical mistreatment of such people may justify military intervention (see ["Interventions," below]). Short of that, however, the presence of national minorities within the borders of a nation-state does not affect the argument about aggression and self-defense.

and factory workers as well, by virtue of the common life they had made. The great majority of these people were apparently loyal to France, and that should have settled the matter. Even if we imagine all the inhabitants of Alsace-Lorraine to be tenants of the Prussian king, the king's seizure of his own land would still have been a violation of their territorial integrity and, through the mediation of their loyalty, of France's too. For tenantry determines only where rents should go; the people themselves must decide where their taxes and conscripts should go.

But the issue was not settled in this way. After the Franco-Prussian war, the two provinces (actually, all of Alsace and a portion of Lorraine) were annexed by Germany, the French conceding German rights in the peace treaty of 1871. During the next several decades, the question was frequently asked, whether a French attack aimed at regaining the lost lands would be justified. One of the issues here is that of the moral standing of a peace treaty signed, as most peace treaties are signed, under duress, but I shall not focus on that. The more important issue relates to the endurance of rights over time. Here the appropriate argument was put forward by the English philosopher Henry Sidgwick in 1891. Sidgwick's sympathies were with the French, and he was inclined to regard the peace as a "temporary suspension of hostilities, terminable at any time by the wronged state." But he added a crucial qualification:[6]

> We must . . . recognize that by this temporary submission of the vanquished . . . a new political order is initiated, which, though originally without a moral basis, may in time acquire such a basis, from a change in the sentiments of the inhabitants of the territory transferred; since it is always possible that through the effects of time and habit and mild government—and perhaps through the voluntary exile of those who feel the old patriotism most keenly—the majority of the transferred population may cease to desire reunion. . . . When this change has taken place, the moral effect of the unjust transfer must be regarded as obliterated; so that any attempt to recover the transferred territory becomes itself an aggression.

Legal titles may endure forever, periodically revived and reasserted as in the dynastic politics of the Middle Ages. But moral rights are subject to the vicissitudes of the common life.

Territorial integrity, then, does not derive from property; it is simply something different. The two are joined, perhaps, in socialist states where the land is nationalized and the people are said to own it. Then if their country is attacked, it is not merely their homeland that is in danger but their collective property—though I suspect that the first danger is more deeply felt than the second. Nationalization is a secondary process; it assumes the prior existence of a nation. And territorial integrity is a function of national existence, not of nationalization (any more than of private ownership). It is the coming together of a people that establishes the integrity of a territory. Only then can a boundary be drawn the crossing of which is plausibly called aggression. It hardly matters if the territory belongs to someone else, unless that ownership is expressed in residence and common use.

This argument suggests a way of thinking about the great difficulties posed by forcible settlement and colonization. When barbarian tribes crossed the borders of the Roman Empire, driven by conquerors from the east or north, they asked for land to settle on and threatened war if they didn't get it. Was this aggression? Given the character of the Roman Empire, the question may sound foolish, but it has arisen many times since, and often in imperial settings. When land is in fact empty and available, the answer must be that it is not aggression. But what if the land is not actually empty but, as Thomas Hobbes says in *Leviathan*, "not sufficiently inhabited"? Hobbes goes on to argue that in such a case, the would-be settlers must "not exterminate those they find there but constrain them to inhabit closer together."[7] That constraint is not aggression, so long as the lives of the original settlers are not threatened. For the settlers are doing what they must do to preserve their own lives, and "he that shall oppose himself against [that], for things superfluous, is guilty of the war that thereupon is to follow."[8] It is not the settlers who are guilty of aggression, according to Hobbes, but those natives who won't move over and make room. There are clearly serious problems here. But I would suggest that Hobbes is right to set aside any consideration of territorial integrity-as-ownership and to focus instead on life. It must be added, however, that what is at stake are not only the lives of individuals but also the common life that they have made. It is for the sake of this common life that we assign a certain presumptive value to the boundaries that mark off a people's territory and to the state that defends it.

Now, the boundaries that exist at any moment in time are likely to be arbitrary, poorly drawn, the products of ancient wars. The mapmakers are likely to have been ignorant, drunken, or corrupt. Nevertheless, these lines establish a habitable world. Within that world, men and women (let us assume) are safe from attack; once the lines are crossed, safety is gone. I don't want to suggest that every boundary dispute is a reason for war. Sometimes adjustments should be accepted and territories shaped so far as possible to the actual needs of nations. Good borders make good neighbors. But once an invasion has been threatened or has actually begun, it may be necessary to defend a bad border simply because there is no other. We shall see this reason at work in the minds of the leaders of Finland in 1939: they might have accepted Russian demands had they felt certain that there would be an end to them. But there is no certainty this side of the border, any more than there is safety this side of the threshold, once a criminal has entered the house. It is only common sense, then, to attach great importance to boundaries. Rights in the world have value only if they also have dimension.

THE LEGALIST PARADIGM

If states actually do possess rights more or less as individuals do, then it is possible to imagine a society among them more or less like the society of individuals. The comparison of international to civil order is crucial to the theory of aggression. I have already been making it regularly. Every reference to aggression as the international equivalent of armed robbery or murder, and every comparison of home and country or of personal liberty and political independence, relies upon what is called the *domestic analogy.*[9] Our primary perceptions and judgments of aggression are the products of analogical reasoning. When the analogy is made explicit, as it often is among the lawyers, the world of states takes on the shape of a political society the character of which is entirely accessible through such notions as crime and punishment, self-defense, law enforcement, and so on.

These notions, I should stress, are not incompatible with the fact that international society as it exists today is a radically imperfect structure. As we experience it, that society might be likened to a defective building, founded on rights; its superstructure raised, like that of the state itself, through political conflict, cooperative activity, and commercial exchange; the whole thing shaky and unstable because it lacks the rivets of authority. It is like domestic society in that men and women live at peace within it (sometimes), determining the conditions of their own existence, negotiating and bargaining with their neighbors. It is unlike domestic society in that every conflict threatens the structure as a whole with collapse. Aggression challenges it directly and is much more dangerous than domestic crime, because there are no policemen. But that only means that the "citizens" of international society must rely on themselves and on one another. Police powers are distributed among all the members. And these members have not done enough in the exercise of their powers if they merely contain the aggression or bring it to a speedy end—as if the police should stop a murderer after he has killed only one or two people and send him on his way. The rights of the member states must be vindicated, for it is only by virtue of those rights that there is a society at all. If they cannot be upheld (at least sometimes), international society collapses into a state of war or is transformed into a universal tyranny.

From this picture, two presumptions follow. The first, which I have already pointed out, is the presumption in favor of military resistance once aggression has begun. Resistance is important so that rights can be maintained and future aggressors deterred. The theory of aggression restates the old doctrine of the just war: it explains when fighting is a crime and when it is permissible, perhaps even morally desirable.* The victim of aggression fights in self-defense, but he isn't only defending himself, for aggression is a crime against society as a whole. He fights in its name and not only in his own. Other states can rightfully join the victim's resistance; their war has the same

---

*I shall say nothing here of the argument for nonviolent resistance to aggression, according to which fighting is neither desirable nor necessary. This argument has not figured much in the development of the conventional view. Indeed, it poses a radical challenge to the conventions: if aggression can be resisted, and at least sometimes successfully resisted, without war, it may be a less serious crime than has commonly been supposed.

character as his own, which is to say, they are entitled not only to repel the attack but also to punish it. All resistance is also law enforcement. Hence the second presumption: when fighting breaks out, there must always be some state against which the law can and should be enforced. Someone must be responsible, for someone decided to break the peace of the society of states. No war, as medieval theologians explained, can be just on both sides.[10]

There are, however, wars that are just on neither side, because the idea of justice doesn't pertain to them or because the antagonists are both aggressors, fighting for territory or power where they have no right. The first case I have already alluded to in discussing the voluntary combat of aristocratic warriors. It is sufficiently rare in human history that nothing more need be said about it here. The second case is illustrated by those wars that Marxists call "imperialist," which are not fought between conquerors and victims but between conquerors and conquerors, each side seeking dominion over the other or the two of them competing to dominate some third party. Thus Lenin's description of the struggles between "have" and "have-not" nations in early twentieth century Europe: "Picture to yourselves a slave-owner who owned 100 slaves warring against a slave-owner who owned 200 slaves for a more 'just' distribution of slaves. Clearly, the application of the term 'defensive' war in such a case . . . would be sheer deception."[11] But it is important to stress that we can penetrate the deception only insofar as we can ourselves distinguish justice and injustice: the theory of imperialist war presupposes the theory of aggression. If one insists that all wars on all sides are acts of conquest or attempted conquest, or that all states at all times would conquer if they could, then the argument for justice is defeated before it begins and the moral judgments we actually make are derided as fantasies. Consider the following passage from Edmund Wilson's book on the American Civil War:[12]

> I think that it is a serious deficiency on the part of historians . . . that they so rarely interest themselves in biological and zoological phenomena. In a recent . . . film showing life at the bottom of the sea, a primitive organism called a sea slug is seen gobbling up small organisms through a large orifice at one end of its body; confronted with another sea slug of an only slightly lesser size, it ingurgitates that, too. Now the wars fought by human beings are stimulated as a rule . . . by the same instincts as the voracity of the sea slug.

There are no doubt wars to which that image might be fit, though it is not a terribly useful image with which to approach the Civil War. Nor does it account for our ordinary experience of international society. Not all states are sea-slug states, gobbling up their neighbors. There are always groups of men and women who would live if they could in peaceful enjoyment of their rights and who have chosen political leaders who represent that desire. The deepest purpose of the state is not ingestion but defense, and the least that can be said is that many actual states serve that purpose. When their territory is attacked or their sovereignty challenged, it makes sense to look for an aggressor and not merely for a natural predator. Hence we need a theory of aggression rather than a zoological account.

The theory of aggression first takes shape under the aegis of the domestic analogy. I am going to call that primary form of the theory the *legalist paradigm*, since it consistently reflects the conventions of law and order. It does not necessarily reflect the arguments of the lawyers, though legal as well as moral debate has its starting point here.[13] Later on, I will suggest that our judgments about the justice and injustice of particular wars are not entirely determined by the paradigm. The complex realities of international society drive us toward a revisionist perspective, and the revisions will be significant ones. But the paradigm must first be viewed in its unrevised form; it is our baseline, our model, the fundamental structure for the moral comprehension of war. We begin with the familiar world of individuals and rights, of crimes and punishments. The theory of aggression can then be summed up in six propositions.

1. *There exists an international society of independent states.* States are the members of this society, not private men and women. In the absence of a universal state, men and women are protected and their interests represented only by their own governments. Though states are founded for the sake of life and liberty, they cannot be challenged in the name of life and liberty by any other states. Hence the principle of non-intervention, which I will analyze later on. The rights of private persons can be recognized in international society, as in the U.N. Charter of Human Rights, but they cannot be enforced without calling into question the dominant values of that society: the survival and independence of the separate political communities.

2. *This international society has a law that establishes the rights of its members—above all, the rights of territorial integrity and political sovereignty.* Once again, these two rest ultimately on the right of men and women to build a common life and to risk their individual lives only when they freely choose to do so. But the relevant law refers only to states, and its details are fixed by the intercourse of states, through complex processes of conflict and consent. Since these processes are continuous, international society has no natural shape; nor are rights within it ever finally or exactly determined. At any given moment, however, one can distinguish the territory of one people from that of another and say something about the scope and limits of sovereignty.

3. *Any use of force or imminent threat of force by one state against the political sovereignty or territorial integrity of another constitutes aggression and is a criminal act.* As with domestic crime, the argument here focuses narrowly on actual or imminent boundary crossings: invasions and physical assaults. Otherwise, it is feared, the notion of resistance to aggression would have no determinate meaning. A state cannot be said to be forced to fight unless the necessity is both obvious and urgent.

4. *Aggression justifies two kinds of violent response: a war of self-defense by the victim and a war of law enforcement by the victim and any other*

member of international society. Anyone can come to the aid of a victim, use necessary force against an aggressor, and even make whatever is the international equivalent of a "citizen's arrest." As in domestic society, the obligations of bystanders are not easy to make out, but it is the tendency of the theory to undermine the right of neutrality and to require widespread participation in the business of law enforcement. In the Korean War, this participation was authorized by the United Nations, but even in such cases the actual decision to join the fighting remains a unilateral one, best understood by analogy to the decision of a private citizen who rushes to help a man or woman attacked on the street.

5. *Nothing but aggression can justify war.* The central purpose of the theory is to limit the occasions for war. "There is a single and only just cause for commencing a war," wrote Vitoria, "namely, a wrong received."[14] There must actually have been a wrong, and it must actually have been received (or its receipt must be, as it were, only minutes away). Nothing else warrants the use of force in international society—above all, not any difference of religion or politics. Domestic heresy and injustice are never actionable in the world of states: hence, again, the principle of nonintervention.

6. *Once the aggressor state has been militarily repulsed, it can also be punished.* The conception of just war as an act of punishment is very old, though neither the procedures nor the forms of punishment have ever been firmly established in customary or positive international law. Nor are its purposes entirely clear: to exact retribution, to deter other states, to restrain or reform this one? All three figure largely in the literature, though it is probably fair to say that deterrence and restraint are most commonly accepted. When people talk of fighting a war against war, this is usually what they have in mind. The domestic maxim is, punish crime to prevent violence; its international analogue is, punish aggression to prevent war. Whether the state as a whole or only particular persons are the proper objects of punishment is a harder question, for reasons I will consider later on. But the implication of the paradigm is clear: if states are members of international society, the subjects of rights, they must also be (somehow) the objects of punishment. . . .

NOTES

1. *Henry V,* 1:2, ll. 24–28.

2. The judges distinguished "aggressive acts" from "aggressive wars," but then used the first of these as the generic term: see *Nazi Conspiracy and Aggression: Opinion and Judgment* (Washington, D.C., 1947), p. 16.

3. Quoted in Michael Howard, "War as an Instrument of Policy," in Herbert Butterfield and Martin Wight, eds., *Diplomatic Investigations* (Cambridge, Mass., 1966), p. 199. Cf. *On War,* trans. Howard and Paret, p. 370.

4. John Westlake, *Collected Papers,* ed. L. Oppenheim (Cambridge, England, 1914), p. 78.

5. See Ruth Putnam, *Alsace and Lorraine from Caesar to Kaiser: 58 B.C.–1871 A.D.* (New York, 1915).

6. Henry Sidgwick, *The Elements of Politics* (London, 1891), pp. 268, 287.

7. *Leviathan*, ch. 30.

8. *Leviathan*, ch. 15.

9. For a critique of this analogy, see the two essays by Hedley Bull, "Society and Anarchy in International Relations," and "The Grotian Conception of International Society," in *Diplomatic Investigations*, chs. 2 and 3.

10. See Vitoria, *On the Law of War*, p. 177.

11. Lenin, *Socialism and War* (London, 1940), pp. 10–11.

12. Edmund Wilson, *Patriotic Gore* (New York, 1966), p. xi.

13. It is worth noting that the United Nations' recently adopted definition of aggression closely follows the paradigm: see the *Report of the Special Committee on the Question of Defining Aggression* (1974), General Assembly Official Records, 29th session, supplement no. 19 (A/9619), pp. 10–13. The definition is reprinted and analyzed in Yehuda Melzer, *Concepts of Just War* (Leyden, 1975), pp. 26ff.

14. *On the Law of War*, p. 170. . . .

Interventions

The principle that states should never intervene in the domestic affairs of other states follows readily from the legalist paradigm and, less readily and more ambiguously, from those conceptions of life and liberty that underlie the paradigm and make it plausible. But these same conceptions seem also to require that we sometimes disregard the principle; and what might be called the rules of disregard, rather than the principle itself, have been the focus of moral interest and argument. No state can admit to fighting an aggressive war and then defend its actions. But intervention is differently understood. The word is not defined as a criminal activity, and though the practice of intervening often threatens the territorial integrity and political independence of invaded states, it can sometimes be justified. It is more important to stress at the outset, however, that it always has to be justified. The burden of proof falls on any political leader who tries to shape the domestic arrangements or alter the conditions of life in a foreign country. And when the attempt is made with armed force, the burden is especially heavy—not only because of the coercions and ravages that military intervention inevitably brings, but also because it is thought that the citizens of a sovereign state have a right, insofar as they are to be coerced and ravaged at all, to suffer only at one another's hands.

SELF-DETERMINATION AND SELF-HELP

The Argument of John Stuart Mill

These citizens are the members, it is presumed, of a single political community, entitled collectively to determine their own affairs. The precise nature of this right is nicely worked out by John Stuart Mill in a short article published in the same year as the treatise *On Liberty* (1859) and especially useful to us because the individual/community analogy was very much in Mill's mind as he wrote.[1] We are to treat states as self-determining communities, he argues, whether or not their internal political arrangements are free, whether or not the citizens choose their government and openly debate the policies carried out in their name. For self-determination and political freedom are not equivalent terms. The first is the more inclusive idea; it describes not only a particular institutional arrangement but also the process by which a community arrives at that arrangement—or does not. A state is self-determining even if its citizens struggle and fail to establish free institutions, but it has been deprived of self-determination if such institutions are established by an intrusive neighbor. The members of a political community must seek their own freedom, just as the individual must cultivate his own virtue. They cannot be set free, as he cannot be made virtuous, by any external force. Indeed, political freedom depends upon the existence of individual virtue, and this the armies of another state are most unlikely to produce—unless, perhaps, they inspire an active resistance and set in motion a self-determining politics. Self-determination is the school in which virtue is learned (or not) and liberty is won (or not). Mill recognizes that a people who have had the "misfortune" to be ruled by a tyrannical government are peculiarly disadvantaged: they have never had a chance to develop "the virtues needful for maintaining freedom." But he insists nevertheless on the stern doctrine of self-help. "It is during an arduous struggle to become free by their own efforts that these virtues have the best chance of springing up."

Though Mill's argument can be cast in utilitarian terms, the harshness of his conclusions suggests that this is not its most appropriate form. The Millian view of self-determination seems to make utilitarian calculation unnecessary, or at least subsidiary to an understanding of communal liberty. He doesn't believe that intervention fails more often that not to serve the purposes of liberty; he believes that, given what liberty is, it *necessarily* fails. The (internal) freedom of a political community can be won only by the members of that community. The argument is similar to that implied in the well-known Marxist maxim, "The liberation of the working class can come only through the workers themselves."[2] As that maxim, one would think, rules out any substitution of vanguard elitism for working class democracy, so Mill's argument rules out any substitution of foreign intervention for internal struggle.

Self-determination, then, is the right of a people "to become free by their own efforts" if they can, and nonintervention is the principle guaranteeing that their success will not be impeded or their failure prevented by the intrusions of an alien power. It has to be stressed that there is no right to be protected against the consequences of domestic failure, even against a bloody repression. Mill generally writes as if he believes that citizens get the government they deserve, or, at least, the government for which they are "fit." And "the only test . . . of a people's having become fit for popular institutions is that they, or a sufficient portion of them, to prevail in the contest, are willing to brave labor and danger for their liberation." No one can, and no one should, do it for them. Mill takes a very cool view of political conflict, and if many rebellious citizens, proud and full of hope in their own efforts, have endorsed that view, many others have not. There is no shortage of revolutionaries who have sought, pleaded for, even demanded outside help. A recent American commentator, eager to be helpful, has argued that Mill's position involves "a kind of Darwinian definition [*The Origin of the Species* was also published in 1859] of self-determination as survival of the fittest within the national boundaries, even if fittest means most adept in the use of force."[3] That last phrase is unfair, for it was precisely Mill's point that force could not prevail, unless it were reinforced from the outside, over a people ready "to brave labor and danger." For the rest, the charge is probably true, but it is difficult to see what conclusions follow from it. It is possible to intervene domestically in the "Darwinian" struggle because the intervention is continuous and sustained over time. But foreign intervention, if it is a brief affair, cannot shift the domestic balance of power in any decisive way toward the forces of freedom, while if it is prolonged or intermittently resumed, it will itself pose the greatest possible threat to the success of those forces.

The case may be different when what is at issue is not intervention at all but conquest. Military defeat and governmental collapse may so shock a social system as to open the way for a radical renovation of its political arrangements. This seems to be what happened in Germany and Japan after World War II, and these examples are so important that I will have to consider later on how it is that rights of conquest and renovation might arise. But they clearly don't arise in every case of domestic tyranny. It is not true, then, that intervention is justified whenever revolution is; for revolutionary activity is an exercise in self-determination, while foreign interference denies to a people those political capacities that only such exercise can bring.

These are the truths expressed by the legal doctrine of sovereignty, which defines the liberty of states as their independence from foreign control and coercion. In fact, of course, not every independent state is free, but the recognition of sovereignty is the only way we have of establishing an arena within which freedom can be fought for and (sometimes) won. It is this arena and the activities that go on within it that we want to protect, and we protect them, much as we protect individual integrity, by marking out boundaries that cannot be crossed, rights that cannot be violated. As with individuals, so with sovereign states: there are things that we cannot do to them, even for their own ostensible good.

And yet the ban on boundary crossings is not absolute—in part because of the arbitrary and accidental character of state boundaries, in part because of the ambiguous relation of the political community or communities within those boundaries to the government that defends them. Despite Mill's very general account of self-determination, it isn't always clear when a community is in fact self-determining, when it qualifies, so to speak, for nonintervention.

No doubt there are similar problems with individual persons, but these are, I think, less severe and, in any case, they are handled within the structures of domestic law.* In international society, the law provides no authoritative verdicts. Hence, the ban on boundary crossings is subject to unilateral suspension, specifically with reference to three sorts of cases where it does not seem to serve the purposes for which it was established:

- when a particular set of boundaries clearly contains two or more political communities, one of which is already engaged in a large-scale military struggle for independence; that is, when what is at issue is secession or "national liberation;"
- when the boundaries have already been crossed by the armies of a foreign power, even if the crossing has been called for by one of the parties in a civil war, that is, when what is at issue is counter-intervention; and
- when the violation of human rights within a set of boundaries is so terrible that it makes talk of community or self-determination or "arduous struggle" seem cynical and irrelevant, that is, in cases of enslavement or massacre.

The arguments that are made on behalf of intervention in each of these cases constitute the second, third, and fourth revisions of the legalist paradigm. They open the way for just wars that are not fought in self-defense or against aggression in the strict sense. But they need to be worked out with great care. Given the readiness of states to invade one another, revisionism is a risky business.

Mill discusses only the first two of these cases, secession and counter-intervention, though the last was not unknown even in 1859. It is worth pointing out that he does not regard them as exceptions to the nonintervention principle, but rather as negative demonstrations of its reasons. Where these reasons don't apply, the principle loses its force. It would be more exact, from Mill's standpoint, to formulate the relevant principle in this way: *always act so as to recognize and uphold communal autonomy.* Nonintervention is most often entailed by that recognition, but not always, and then we must prove our commitment to autonomy in some other way, perhaps even by

*The domestic analogy suggests that the most obvious way of not qualifying for nonintervention is to be incompetent (childish, imbecilic, and so on). Mill believed that there were incompetent peoples, barbarians, in whose interest it was to be conquered and held in subjection by foreigners. "Barbarians have no rights as a *nation* [i.e. as a political community]." Hence utilitarian principles apply to them, and imperial bureaucrats legitimately work for their moral improvement. It is interesting to note a similar view among the Marxists, who also justified conquest and imperial rule at certain stages of historical development. (See Shlomo Avineri, ed., *Karl Marx on Colonialism and Modernization,* New York, 1969.) Whatever plausibility such arguments had in the nineteenth century, they have none today. International society can no longer be divided into civilized and barbarian halves; any line drawn on developmental principles leaves barbarians on both sides. I shall therefore assume that the self-help test applies equally to all peoples.

sending troops across an international frontier. But the morally exact principle is also very dangerous, and Mill's account of the argument is not at this point an account of what is actually said in everday moral discourse. We need to establish a kind of *a priori* respect for state boundaries; they are, as I have argued before, the only boundaries communities ever have. And that is why intervention is always justified as if it were an exception to a general rule, made necessary by the urgency or extremity of a particular case. The second, third, and fourth revisions have something of the form of stereotyped excuses. Interventions are so often undertaken for "reasons of state" that have nothing to do with self-determination that we have become skeptical of every claim to defend the autonomy of alien communities. Hence the special burden of proof with which I began, more onerous than any we impose on individuals or governments pleading self-defense: intervening states must demonstrate that their own case is radically different from what we take to be the general run of cases, where the liberty or prospective liberty of citizens is best served if foreigners offer them only moral support. And that is how I shall characterize Mill's argument (though he characterizes it differently) that Great Britain ought to have intervened in defense of the Hungarian Revolution of 1848 and 1849.

SECESSION

The Hungarian Revolution

For many years before 1848, Hungary had been a part of the Hapsburg Empire. Formally an independent kingdom, with a Diet of its own, it was effectively ruled by the German authorities in Vienna. The sudden collapse of those authorities during the March Days—symbolized by the fall of Metternich—opened the way for liberal nationalists in Budapest. They formed a government and demanded home rule within the Empire; they were not yet secessionists. Their demand was initially accepted, but controversy developed over the issues that have always plagued federalist schemes: the control of tax revenue, the command of the army. As soon as "order" was restored in Vienna, efforts began to reassert the centralist character of the regime, and these soon took the familiar form of military repression. An imperial army invaded Hungary, and the nationalists fought back. The Hungarians were now rebels or insurgents; they quickly established what international lawyers call their belligerent rights by defeating the Austrians and taking control of much of old Hungary. In the course of the war, the new government shifted leftwards; in April 1849, a republic was proclaimed under the presidency of Lajos Kossuth.[4]

The revolution might be described, in contemporary terms, as a war of national liberation, except that the boundaries of old Hungary included a very large Slavic population, and the Hungarian revolutionaries seem to have been as hostile to Croat and Slovene nationalism as the Austrians were to their own claims for communal autonomy. But this is a difficulty that I am going to set aside, for it did not appear as such at the time; it did not enter into the moral reflections of liberal observers like Mill. The Hungarian Revolution was greeted with enthusiasm by such men, especially in France, Britain, and the United States, and its emissaries were eagerly received. Governmental response was different, in part because nonintervention was the general rule to which all three governments subscribed, in part because the first two were also committed to the European balance of power and therefore to the integrity of Austria. In London, Palmerston was formal and cold: "The British government has no knowledge of Hungary except as one of the component parts of the Austrian Empire."[5] The Hungarians sought only diplomatic recognition, not military intervention, but any British dealings with the new government would have been regarded by the Austrian regime as an interference in its internal affairs. Recognition, moreover, had commercial consequences that might have engaged the British more closely on the side of Hungary, for the revolutionaries hoped to purchase military supplies on the London market. Despite this, the establishment of formal ties, once the Hungarians had demonstrated that "a sufficient portion of them" were committed to independence and willing to fight for it, would not have been difficult to justify in Millian terms. There can be no doubt of the existence (though there was a reason to doubt the extent) of the Hungarian political community; it was one of the oldest nations in Europe, and its recognition as a sovereign state would not have violated the moral rights of the Austrian people. Military supply to insurgent armies is indeed a complex issue, and I will come back to it with reference to another case, but none of the complexities are apparent here. Soon enough, however, the Hungarians needed far more than guns and ammunition.

In the summer of 1849, the Austrian emperor asked for the help of Tsar Nicholas I, and Hungary was invaded by a Russian army. Writing ten years later, Mill argued that the British should have responded to this intervention with an intervention of their own.[6]

> It might not have been right for England (even apart from the question of prudence) to have taken part with Hungary in its noble struggle against Austria; although the Austrian government in Hungary was in some sense a foreign yoke. But when, the Hungarians having shown themselves likely to prevail in this struggle, the Russian despot interposed, and joining his force to that of Austria, delivered back the Hungarians, bound hand and foot, to their exasperated oppressors, it would have been an honorable and virtuous act on the part of England to have declared that this should not be, and that if Russia gave assistance to the wrong side, England would aid the right.

The qualification "in some sense a foreign yoke" with regard to Austrian rule in Hungary is curious, for whatever its meaning, it must also qualify the nobility and rightness of the Hungarian struggle for independence. Since Mill does not intend the latter qualification, we need not take the former seriously. The clear tendency of his argument is to justify assistance to a secessionist movement at the same time as it justifies counter-intervention—

indeed, to assimilate the one to the other. In both cases, the rule against interference is suspended because a foreign power, morally if not legally alien, is already interfering in the "domestic" affairs, that is, in the self-determinations of a political community.

Mill is right, however, to suggest that the issue is easier when the initial interference involves the crossing of a recognized frontier. The problem with a secessionist movement is that one cannot be sure that it in fact represents a distinct community until it has rallied its own people and made some headway in the "arduous struggle" for freedom. The mere appeal to the principle of self-determination isn't enough; evidence must be provided that a community actually exists whose members are committed to independence and ready and able to determine the conditions of their own existence.[7]* Hence the need for political or military struggle sustained over time. Mill's argument doesn't cover inarticulate and unrepresented peoples, or fledgling movements, or risings quickly suppressed. But imagine a small nation successfully mobilized to resist a colonial power but slowly being ground down in the unequal struggle: Mill would not insist, I think, that neighboring states stand by and watch its inevitable defeat. His argument justifies military action against imperial or colonial repression as well as against foreign intervention. Only domestic tyrants are safe, for it is not our purpose in international society (nor, Mill argues, is it possible) to establish liberal or democratic communities, but only independent ones. When it is required for the sake of independence, military action is "honorable and virtuous," though not always "prudent." I should add that the argument also applies to satellite regimes and great powers: designed for the first Russian intervention in Hungary (1849), it precisely fits the second (1956).

But the relation between virtue and prudence in such cases is not easy to make out. Mill's meaning is clear enough: to threaten war with Russia might have been dangerous to Britain and hence inconsistent "with the regard which every nation is bound to pay to its own safety." Now, whether or not it actually was dangerous was surely for the British to decide, and we would judge them harshly only if the risks they declined to run were very slight indeed. Even if counter-intervention is "honorable and virtuous," it is not morally required, precisely because of the dangers it involves. But one can make much more of prudence than this. Palmerston was concerned with the safety of Europe, not only of England, when he decided to stand

---

*There is a further issue here, having to do with the natural resources that are sometimes at stake in secessionist struggles. I have argued that "the land follows the people." But the will and capacity of the people for self-determination may not establish a right to secede if the secession would remove not only land but also vitally needed fuel and mineral resources from some larger political community. The Katangan controversy of the early 1960s suggests the possible difficulties of such cases—and invites us to worry also about the motives of intervening states. But what was missing in Katanga was a genuine national movement capable, on its own, of "arduous struggle." (See Conor C. O'Brien, *To Katanga and Back*, New York, 1962.) Given the existence of such a movement, I would be inclined to support secession. It would then be necessary, however, to raise more general questions about distributive justice in international society.

by the Austrian empire. It is perfectly possible to concede the justice of the Millian position, and yet opt for nonintervention on what are currently called "world order" principles.[8] So justice and prudence are (with a certain worldly relish) set in opposition to one another in a way that Mill never imagined they could be. He thought, naively perhaps, that the world would be more orderly if none of its political communities were oppressed by foreign rule. He even hoped that Britain would one day be powerful enough, and have the necessary "spirit and courage," to insist "that not a gun [should] be fired in Europe by the soldiers of one Power against the revolted subjects of another," and to put itself "at the head of an alliance of free peoples." Today, I suppose, the United States has succeeded to those old-fashioned liberal pretensions, though in 1956 its leaders, like Palmerston in 1849, thought it imprudent to enforce them.

It might also be said that the United States had (and has) no right to enforce them, given the self-serving ways in which its government defines freedom and intervention in other parts of the world. Mill's England was hardly in a better position. Had Palmerston contemplated a military move on behalf of the Hungarians, Count Schwarzenberg, Metternich's successor, was prepared to remind him of "unhappy Ireland." "Wherever revolt breaks out within the vast limits of the British Empire," Schwarzenberg wrote to the Austrian ambassador in London, "the English government always knows how to maintain the authority of the law . . . even at the price of torrents of blood. It is not for us," he went on, "to blame her."[9] He sought only reciprocity, and that kind of reciprocity among great powers is undoubtedly the very essence of prudence.

To set prudence and justice so radically at odds, however, is to misconstrue the argument for justice. A state contemplating intervention or counter-intervention will for prudential reasons weigh the dangers to itself, but it must also, *and for moral reasons,* weigh the dangers its action will impose on the people it is designed to benefit and on all other people who may be affected. An intervention is not just if it subjects third parties to terrible risks: the subjection cancels the justice. If Palmerston was right in believing that the defeat of Austria would shatter the peace of Europe, a British intervention ensuring that defeat would not have been "honorable and virtuous" (however noble the Hungarian struggle). And clearly, an American threat of atomic war in 1956 would have been morally as well as politically irresponsible. Thus far prudence can be, and has to be, accommodated within the argument for justice. But it should be said that this deference to third party rights is not at the same time a deference to the local political interests of the great powers. Nor does it involve the acceptance of a Schwarzenbergian reciprocity. Britain's recognition of Austria's imperial claims does not entitle it to a similar recognition. The prudential acceptance of a Russian sphere of influence in Eastern Europe does not entitle the United States to a free hand in its own sphere. Against national liberation and counter-intervention, there are no prescriptive rights.

CIVIL WAR

If we describe the Hungarian Revolution as Mill did, assuming that Palmerston was wrong [and] ignoring the claims of Croats and Slovenes, it is virtually a paradigm case for intervention. It is also, so described, an historically exceptional, indeed, it is now an hypothetical case. For these circumstances don't often arise in history: a national liberation movement unambiguously embodying the claims of a single, unified political community; capable at least initially of sustaining itself on the battlefield; challenged by an unambiguously foreign power; whose intervention can however be deterred or defeated without risking a general war. More often history presents a tangle of parties and factions, each claiming to speak for an entire community, fighting with one another, drawing outside powers into the struggle in secret, or at least unacknowledged, ways. Civil war poses hard problems, not because the Millian standard is unclear—it would require a strict stand-offishness—but because it can be and routinely is violated by degrees. Then it becomes very difficult to fix the point at which a direct and open use of force can plausibly be called a counter-intervention. And it is difficult also to calculate the effects of such a use of force on the already distressed inhabitants of the divided state and on the whole range of possible third parties.

In such cases, the lawyers commonly apply a qualified version of the self-help test.[10] They permit assistance to the established government—it is after all, the official representative of communal autonomy in international society—so long as it faces nothing more than internal dissension, rebellion, and insurgency. But as soon as the insurgents establish control over some substantial portion of the territory and population of the state, they acquire belligerent rights and an equality of status with the government. Then the lawyers enjoin a strict neutrality. Now, neutrality is conventionally regarded as an optative condition, a matter of choice, not of duty. So it is with regard to wars between states, but in civil wars there seem to be very good (Millian) reasons for making it obligatory. For once a community is effectively divided, foreign powers can hardly serve the cause of self-determination by acting militarily within its borders. The argument has been succinctly put by Montague Bernard, whose Oxford lecture "On the Principle of Non-intervention" ranks in importance with Mill's essay: "Of two things, one: the interference in the case supposed either turns the balance, or it does not. In the latter event, it misses its aim; in the former, it gives the superiority to the side which would not have been uppermost without it and establishes a sovereign, or a form of government, which the nation, if left to itself, would not have chosen."[11]

As soon as one outside power violates the norms of neutrality and nonintervention, however, the way is open for other powers to do so. Indeed, it may seem shameful not to repeat the violation—as in the case of the Spanish Civil War, where the noninterventionist policies of Britain, France, and the United States did not open the way for a local decision, but simply allowed the Germans and Italians to "turn the balance."[12] Some military response is probably required at such moments if the values of independence and community are to be sustained. But though that response upholds values shared throughout international society, it cannot accurately be described as law enforcement. Its character is not readily explicable within the terms of the legalist paradigm. For counter-intervention in civil wars does not aim at punishing or even, necessarily, at restraining the intervening states. It aims instead at holding the circle, preserving the balance, restoring some degree of integrity to the local struggle. It is as if a policeman, instead of breaking up a fight between two people, should stop anyone else from interfering or, if he cannot do that, should give proportional assistance to the disadvantaged party. He would have to have some notions about the value of the fight, and given the ordinary conditions of domestic society, those would be strange notions for him to have. But in the world of states they are entirely appropriate; they set the standards by which we judge between actual and pretended counter-interventions.

The American War in Vietnam ·

I doubt that it is possible to tell the story of Vietnam in a way that will command general agreement. The official American version—that the struggle began with a North Vietnamese invasion of the South, to which the United States responded in accordance with its treaty obligations—follows the legalist paradigm closely, but is on its surface unbelievable. Fortunately, it seems to be accepted by virtually no one and need not detain us here. I want to pursue a more sophisticated version of the American defense, which concedes the existence of a civil war and describes the U.S. role, first, as assistance to a legitimate government, and secondly, as counter-intervention, a response to covert military moves by the North Vietnamese regime.[13] The crucial terms here are "legitimate" and "response." The first suggests that the government on behalf of which our counter-intervention was undertaken had a local status, a political presence independent of ourselves, and hence that it could conceivably win the civil war if no external force was brought to bear. The second suggests that our own military operations followed upon and balanced those of another power, in accordance with the argument I have put forward. Both these suggestions are false, but they point to the peculiarly confined character of counter-intervention and indicate what one has to say (at least) when one joins in the civil wars of other states.

The Geneva Agreement of 1954, ending the first Vietnamese war, established a temporary frontier between the North and the South, and two temporary governments on either side of the line, pending elections scheduled for 1956.[14] When the South Vietnamese government refused to permit these elections, it clearly lost whatever legitimacy was conferred by the agreements. But I shall not dwell on this loss, nor on the fact that some sixty states nevertheless recognized the sovereignty of the new regime in the South and opened embassies in Saigon. I doubt that foreign states, whether they act independently or collectively, sign treaties or send ambassadors, can establish or disestablish the legitimacy of a government. What is crucial is the standing of that government with its own people. Had the new regime been able to rally support at home, Vietnam today would have joined the dual states of Germany and Korea, and Geneva 1954 would be remembered only as the setting for another cold war partition. But what is the test of popular support in a country where democracy is unknown and elections are routinely managed? The test, for governments as for insurgents, is self-help. That doesn't mean that foreign states cannot provide assistance. One assumes the legitimacy of new regimes; there is, so to speak, a period of grace, a time to build support. But that time was ill-used in South Vietnam, and the continuing dependence of the new regime on the U.S. is damning evidence against it. Its urgent call for military intervention in the early 1960's is more damning evidence still. One must ask of President Diem a question first posed by Montague Bernard: "How can he impersonate [represent] his people who is begging the assistance of a foreign power in order to reduce them to obedience?"[15] Indeed, it was never a successful impersonation.

The argument might be put more narrowly: a government that receives economic and technical aid, military supply, strategic and tactical advice, and is still unable to reduce its subjects to obedience, is clearly an illegitimate government. Whether legitimacy is defined sociologically or morally, such a government fails to meet the most minimal standards. One wonders how it survives at all. It must be the case that it survives because of the outside help it receives and for no other, no local reasons. The Saigon regime was so much an American creature that the U.S. government's claim to be committed to it and obligated to ensure its survival is hard to understand. It is as if our right hand were committed to our left. There is no independent moral or political agent on the other side of the bond and hence no genuine bond at all. Obligations to one's creatures (except insofar as they pertain to the personal safety of individuals) are as insignificant politically as obligations to oneself are insignificant morally. When the U.S. did intervene militarily in Vietnam, then, it acted not to fulfill commitments to another state, but to pursue policies of its own contrivance.

Against all this, it is argued that the popular base of the South Vietnamese government was undermined by a systematic campaign of subversion, terrorism, and guerrilla war, largely directed and supplied from the North. That there was such a campaign, and that the North was involved in it, is clearly true, though the extent and timing of the involvement are very much in dispute. If one were writing a legal brief, these matters would be critically important, for the American claim is that the North Vietnamese were illegally supporting a local insurgency, with both men and material, at a time when the U.S. was still providing only economic assistance and military supply to a legitimate government. But that claim, whatever its legal force, somehow misses the moral reality of the Vietnamese case. It would be better to say that the U.S. was literally propping up a government—and shortly a series of governments—without a local political base, while the North Vietnamese were assisting an insurgent movement with deep roots in the countryside. We were far more vital to the government than they were to the insurgents.

Indeed, it was the weakness of the government, its inability to help itself even against its internal enemies, that forced the steady escalation of American involvement. And that fact must raise the most serious questions about the American defense: for counter-intervention is morally possible only on behalf of a government (or a movement, party, or whatever) that has already passed the self-help test.

I can say very little here about the reasons for insurgent strength in the countryside. Why were the communists able, and the government unable, to "impersonate" Vietnamese nationalism? The character and scope of the American presence probably had a great deal to do with this. Nationalism is not easily represented by a regime as dependent as Saigon was on foreign support. It is also important that North Vietnamese moves did not similarly brand those they benefited as foreign agents. In nations divided as Vietnam was, infiltration across the dividing line is not necessarily regarded as outside interference by the men and women on the other side. The Korean War might look very different than it does if the Northerners had not marched in strength across the 38th parallel, but had made covert contact, instead, with a Southern rebellion. In contrast to Vietnam, however, there was no rebellion—and there was considerable support for the government—in South Korea.[16] These cold war dividing lines have the usual significance of an international border only insofar as they mark off, or come in time to mark off, two political communities within each of which individual citizens feel some local loyalty. Had South Vietnam taken shape in this way, American military activity, in the face of large-scale Northern connivance at terrorism and guerrilla war, might have qualified as counter-intervention. At least, the name would have been an arguable one. As it is, it is not.

It remains an issue whether the American counter-intervention, had it been such, could rightly have assumed the size and scope of the war we eventually fought. Some notion of symmetry is relevant here, though it cannot be fixed absolutely in arithmetic terms. When a state sets out to maintain or restore the integrity of a local struggle, its military activity should be roughly equivalent to that of the other intervening states. Counter-intervention is a balancing act. I have made this point before, but it is worth emphasizing, for it reflects a deep truth about the meaning of responsiveness: *the goal of counter-intervention is not to win the war.* That this is not an esoteric or obscure truth is suggested by President Kennedy's well-known description of the Vietnam War. "In the final analysis," Kennedy said, "it is their war. They are the ones who have to win it or lose it. We can help them, we can give them equipment, we can send our men out there as advisors, but they have to win it—the people of Vietnam against the Communists."[17] Though this view was reiterated by later American leaders, it is not, unhappily, a definitive exposition of American policy. In fact, the United States failed in the most dramatic way to respect the character and dimensions of the Vietnamese civil war, and we failed because we could not win the war as long as it retained that character and was fought within those dimensions. Searching for a level of conflict at which our technological superiority could be brought to bear, we steadily escalated the struggle, until finally it was an American war, fought for American purposes, in someone else's country.

HUMANITARIAN INTERVENTION

A legitimate government is one that can fight its own internal wars. And external assistance in those wars is rightly called counter-intervention only when it balances, and does no more than balance, the prior intervention of another power, making it possible once again for the local forces to win or lose on their own. The outcome of civil wars should reflect not the relative strength of the intervening states, but the local alignment of forces. There is another sort of case, however, where we don't look for outcomes of that sort, where we don't want the local balance to prevail. If the dominant forces within a state are engaged in massive violations of human rights, the appeal to self-determination in the Millian sense of self-help is not very attractive. That appeal has to do with the freedom of the community taken as a whole; it has no force when what is at stake is the bare survival or the minimal liberty of (some substantial number of) its members. Against the enslavement or massacre of political opponents, national minorities, and religious sects, there may well be no help unless help comes from outside. And when a government turns savagely upon its own people, we must doubt the very existence of a political community to which the idea of self-determination might apply.

Examples are not hard to find; it is their plenitude that is embarrassing. The list of oppressive governments, the list of massacred peoples, is frighteningly long. Though an event like the Nazi holocaust is without precedent in human history, murder on a smaller scale is so common as to be almost ordinary. On the other hand—or perhaps for this very reason—clear examples of what is called "humanitarian intervention" are very rare.[18] Indeed, I have not found any, but only mixed cases where the humanitarian motive is one among several. States don't send their soldiers into other states, it seems, only in order to save lives. The lives of foreigners don't weigh that heavily in the scales of domestic decision-making. So we shall have to consider the moral significance of mixed motives.* It is not necessarily an argument against humanitarian intervention that it is, at best, partially humanitarian, but it is a reason to be skeptical and to look closely at the other parts.

---

*The case is different, obviously, when the lives at stake are those of fellow nationals. Interventions designed to rescue citizens threatened with death in a foreign country have conventionally been called humanitarian, and there is no reason to deny them that name when life and death are really at issue. The Israeli raid on Entebbe airport in Uganda (July 4, 1976) seems likely to become a classic case. Here there is, or ought to be, no question of mixed motives: the only purpose is to rescue *these* people towards whom the intervening power has a special commitment.

Cuba, 1898, and Bangladesh, 1971

Both these cases might be taken up under the headings of national liberation and counter-intervention. But they each have a further significance because of the atrocities committed by the Spanish and the Pakistani governments. The brutal work of the Spaniards is easier to talk about, for it fell short of systematic massacre. Fighting against a Cuban insurgent army that lived off the land and apparently had large-scale peasant support, the Spaniards first worked out the policy of forced resettlement. They called it, without euphemism, *la reconcentración*. General Weyler's proclamation required that[19]

> all inhabitants of rural areas or areas outside the lines of fortified towns will be concentrated within the towns occupied by troops at the end of eight days. All individuals who disobey or who are found outside the prescribed areas will be considered as rebels and judged as such.

I will ask later on whether "concentration" in itself is a criminal policy. The immediate crime of the Spaniards was to enforce the policy with so little regard for the health of the people involved that thousands of them suffered and died. Their lives and deaths were widely publicized in the United States, not only in the yellow press, and undoubtedly figured in the minds of many Americans as the major justification for the war against Spain. Thus the Congressional resolution of April 20, 1898: "Whereas the abhorrent conditions which have existed for more than three years in the island of Cuba, so near our own borders, have shocked the moral sense of the people of the United States."[20] But there were other reasons for going to war.

The chief of these were economic and strategic in character, having to do, first, with American investment in Cuban sugar, a matter of interest to a section of the financial community; and second, with the sea approaches to the Panamanian Isthmus where the canal would one day be, a matter of interest to the intellectuals and politicians who championed the cause of American expansion. Cuba was a minor element in the plans of men like Mahan and Adams, Roosevelt and Lodge, who were more concerned with the Pacific Ocean than the Caribbean Sea. But the canal that would connect the two gave it a certain strategic value, and the war to win it was worthwhile insofar as it accustomed Americans to imperialist adventures (and led also to the conquest of the Philippines). By and large, the historical debate over the causes of the war has focused on the different forms of economic and political imperialism, the search for markets and investment opportunities, the pursuit of "national power for its own sake."[21] It's worth remembering, however, that the war was also supported by anti-imperialist politicians— or rather, that Cuban freedom was supported and then, in consequence of Spanish brutality, the humanitarian intervention of American military forces [was supported]. The war we actually fought, however, and the intervention urged by populists and radical Democrats were two rather different things.

The Cuban insurgents made three requests of the United States: that we recognize their provisional government as the legitimate government of Cuba, that we provide their army with military supplies, and that American warships blockade the Cuban coast and cut off the supplies of the Spanish army. Given such help, it was said, the insurgent forces would grow, the Spaniards could not long hold out, and the Cubans would be left to reconstruct their country (with American help) and manage their own affairs.[22] This was also the program of American radicals. But President McKinley and his advisors did not believe the Cubans capable of managing their own affairs, or they feared a radical reconstruction. In any case, the U.S. intervened without recognizing the insurgents, invaded the island, and quickly defeated and replaced the Spanish forces. The victory undoubtedly had humane effects. Though the American military effort was remarkably inefficient, the war was short and added little to the miseries of the civilian population. Relief operations, also remarkably inefficient at first, began as soon as the battles were won. In his standard account of the war, Admiral Chadwick boasts of its relative bloodlessness: "War of itself," he writes, "cannot be the great evil; the evil is in the horrors, many of which are not necessarily concomitant. . . . The war now beginning between the United States and Spain was one in which these greater horrors were largely to be absent."[23] The horrors were indeed absent; far more so, at least, than in the long years of the Cuban Insurrection. But the invasion of Cuba, the three years of military occupation, the eventual granting of a drastically limited independence (under the provisions of the Platt Amendment) go a long way toward explaining the skepticism with which America's professions of humane concern have conventionally been regarded. The entire course of action, from 1898 to 1902, might be taken as an example of benevolent imperialism, given the "piratical times," but it is not an example of humanitarian intervention.[24]

The judgments we make in cases such as this don't hang on the fact that considerations other than humanity figured in the government's plans, or even on the fact that humanity was not the chief consideration. I don't know if it ever is, and measurement is especially difficult in a liberal democracy where the mixed motives of the government reflect the pluralism of the society. Nor is it a question of benevolent outcomes. As a result of the American victory, the *reconcentrados* were able to return to their homes. But they would have been able to do that had the U.S. entered the war on the side of the Spaniards and, together with them, decisively defeated the Cuban insurgents. "Concentration" was a war policy and would have ended with the war, whatever the war's end. The crucial question is a different one. Humanitarian intervention involves military action on behalf of oppressed people, and it requires that the intervening state enter, to some degree, into the purposes of those people. It need not set itself to achieve those purposes, but it also cannot stand in the way of their achievement. The people are oppressed, presumably, because they sought some end—religious toleration, national freedom, or whatever—unacceptable to their oppressors. One cannot intervene on their behalf and against their ends. I don't want to argue that the purposes of the oppressed are necessarily just or that one need accept them in their entirety. But it does seem that a greater attention is due them than the U.S. was prepared to pay in 1898.

This regard for the purposes of the oppressed directly parallels the respect for local autonomy that is a necessary feature of counter-intervention. The two revisionist principles reflect a common commitment: that intervention be as much like non-intervention as possible. In the one case, the goal is balance; in the other, it is rescue. In neither case, and certainly not in secessions and national liberation struggles, can the intervening state rightly claim any political prerogatives for itself. And whenever it makes such claims (as the U.S. did when it occupied Cuba and again when it imposed the Platt Amendment), we suspect that political power was its purpose from the start.

The Indian invasion of East Pakistan (Bangladesh) in 1971 is a better example of humanitarian intervention—not because of the singularity or purity of the government's motives, but because its various motives converged on a single course of action that was also the course of action called for by the Bengalis. This convergence explains why the Indians were in and out of the country so quickly, defeating the Pakistani army but not replacing it, and imposing no political controls on the emergent state of Bangladesh. No doubt, strategic as well as moral interests underlay this policy: Pakistan, India's old enemy, was significantly weakened, while India itself avoided becoming responsible for a desperately poor nation whose internal politics was likely to be unstable and volatile for a long time to come. But the intervention qualifies as humanitarian because it was a *rescue*, strictly and narrowly defined. So circumstances sometimes make saints of us all.

I shall not say very much about Pakistani oppression in Bengal. The tale is a terrible one and by now fairly well documented.[25] Faced with a movement for autonomy in what was then its eastern province, the government of Pakistan, in March 1971, literally turned an army loose on its own people— or rather, a Punjabi army loose on the Bengali people, for the unity of east and west was already a broken thing. The resulting massacre only completed the break and made it irreparable. The army was not entirely without direction; its officers carried "death lists" on which appeared the names of the political, cultural, and intellectual leaders of Bengal. There was also a systematic effort to slaughter the followers of these people: university students, political activists, and so on. Beyond these groups, the soldiers ranged freely, burning, raping, killing. Millions of Bengalis fled into India, and their arrival, destitute, hungry, and with incredible stories to tell, established the moral foundation of the later Indian attack. "It is idle to argue in such cases that the duty of the neighboring people is to look on quietly."[26] Months of diplomatic maneuvering followed, but during that time, the Indians were already assisting Bengali guerrillas and offering sanctuary not only to refugees but also to fighting men and women. The two-week war of December 1971 apparently began with a Pakistani air strike, but the Indian invasion required no such prior attack; it was justified on other grounds.

The strength of the Bengali guerrillas and their achievements between March and December are matters of some dispute; so is their role in the two-week war. Clearly, however, it was not the purpose of the Indian invasion to open the way for the Bengali struggle; nor does the strength or weakness of the guerrillas affect our view of the invasion. When a people are being massacred, we don't require that they pass the test of self-help before coming to their aid. It is their very incapacity that brings us in. The purpose of the Indian army, then, was to defeat the Pakistani forces and drive them out of Bangladesh, that is, to win the war. The purpose was different from that of a counter-intervention, and for an important moral reason. People who initiate massacres lose their right to participate in the normal (even in the normally violent) processes of domestic self-determination. Their military defeat is morally necessary.

Governments and armies engaged in massacres are readily identified as criminal governments and armies (they are guilty, under the Nuremberg code of "crimes against humanity"). Hence humanitarian intervention comes much closer than any other kind of intervention to what we commonly regard, in domestic society, as law enforcement and police work. At the same time, however, it requires the crossing of an international frontier, and such crossings are ruled out by the legalist paradigm—unless they are authorized, I suppose, by the society of nations. In the cases I have considered, the law is unilaterally enforced; the police are self-appointed. Now, unilateralism has always prevailed in the international arena, but we worry about it more when what is involved is a response to domestic violence rather than to foreign aggression. We worry that, under the cover of humanitarianism, states will come to coerce and dominate their neighbors; once again, it is not hard to find examples. Hence many lawyers prefer to stick to the paradigm. That doesn't require them, on their view, to deny the (occasional) need for intervention. They merely deny legal recognition to that need. Humanitarian intervention "belongs in the realm not of law but of moral choice, which nations, like individuals must sometimes make."[27] But that is only a plausible formulation if one doesn't stop with it, as lawyers are likely to do. For moral choices are not simply *made;* they are also judged, and so there must be criteria for judgment. If these are not provided by the law, or if legal provision runs out at some point, they are nevertheless contained in our common morality, which doesn't run out, and which still needs to be explicated after the lawyers have finished.

Morality, at least, is not a bar to unilateral action, so long as there is no immediate alternative available. There was none in the Bengali case. No doubt, the massacres were a matter of universal interest, but only India interested itself in them. The case was formally carried to the United Nations, but no action followed. Nor is it clear to me that action undertaken by the UN, or by a coalition of powers, would necessarily have had a moral quality superior to that of the Indian attack. What one looks for in numbers is detachment from particularist views and consensus on moral rules. And for that, there is at present no institutional appeal; one appeals to humanity as a whole. States don't lose their particularist character merely by acting together. If governments have mixed motives, so do coalitions of governments.

Some goals, perhaps, are cancelled out by the political bargaining that constitutes the coalition, but others are super-added; and the resulting mix is as accidental with reference to the moral issue as are the political interests and ideologies of a single state.

Humanitarian intervention is justified when it is a response (with reasonable expectations of success) to acts "that shock the moral conscience of mankind." The old-fashioned language seems to me exactly right. It is not the conscience of political leaders that one refers to in such cases. They have other things to worry about and may well be required to repress their normal feelings of indignation and outrage. The reference is to the moral convictions of ordinary men and women, acquired in the course of their everyday activities. And given that one can make a persuasive argument in terms of those convictions, I don't think that there is any moral reason to adopt that posture of passivity that might be called waiting for the UN (waiting for the universal state, waiting for the messiah . . .).

> Suppose . . . that a great power decided that the only way it could continue to control a satellite state was to wipe out the satellite's entire population and recolonize the area with "reliable" people. Suppose the satellite government agreed to this measure and established the necessary mass extermination apparatus. . . . Would the rest of the members of the U.N. be compelled to stand by and watch this operation merely because [the] requisite decision of U.N. organs was blocked and the operation did not involve an "armed attack" on any [member state]?[28]

The question is rhetorical. Any state capable of stopping the slaughter has a right, at least, to try to do so. The legalist paradigm indeed rules out such efforts, but that only suggests that the paradigm, unrevised, cannot account for the moral realities of military intervention.

The second, third, and fourth revisions of the paradigm have this form: states can be invaded and wars justly begun to assist secessionist movements (once they have demonstrated their representative character), to balance the prior interventions of other powers, and to rescue peoples threatened with massacre. In each of these cases we permit or, after the fact, we praise or don't condemn these violations of the formal rules of sovereignty, because they uphold the values of individual life and communal liberty of which sovereignty itself is merely an expression. The formula is, once again, permissive, but I have tried in my discussion of particular cases to indicate that the actual requirements of just interventions are constraining indeed. And the revisions must be understood to include the constraints. Since the constraints are often ignored, it is sometimes argued that it would be best to insist on an absolute rule of nonintervention (as it would be best to insist on an absolute rule of a nonanticipation). But the absolute rule will also be ignored, and we will then have no standards by which to judge what happens next. In fact, we do have standards, which I have tried to map out. They reflect deep and valuable, though in their applications difficult and problematic, commitments to human rights.

NOTES

1. "A Few Words on Non-Intervention" in J. S. Mill, *Dissertations and Discussions* (New York, 1873), III, 238–63.

2. See Irving Howe, ed., *The Basic Writings of Trotsky* (New York, 1963), p. 397.

3. John Norton Moore, "International Law and the United States' Role in Vietnam: A Reply," in R. Falk, ed., *The Vietnam War and International Law* (Princeton, 1968), p. 431. Moore addresses himself specifically to the argument of W. E. Hall, *International Law* (5th ed., Oxford, 1904), pp. 289–90, but Hall follows Mill closely.

4. For a brief survey, see Jean Sigmann, *1848: The Romantic and Democratic Revolutions in Europe*, trans. L. F. Edwards (New York, 1973), ch. 10.

5. Charles Sproxton, *Palmerston and the Hungarian Revolution* (Cambridge, 1919), p. 48.

6. "Non-Intervention," pp. 261–62.

7. See S. French and A. Gutman, "The Principle of National Self-determination," in Held, Morgenbesser, and Nagel, eds., *Philosophy, Morality, and International Affairs* (New York, 1974), pp. 138–53.

8. This is the general position of R. J. Vincent, *Nonintervention and World Order* (Princeton, 1974), esp. ch. 9.

9. Sproxton, p. 109.

10. See, for example, Hall, *International Law*, p. 293.

11. "On the Principle of Non-Intervention" (Oxford, 1860), p. 21.

12. See Hugh Thomas, *The Spanish Civil War* (New York, 1961), chs. 31, 40, 48, 58; Norman J. Padelford, *International Law and Diplomacy in the Spanish Civil Strife* (New York, 1939), is an incredibly naive defense of the nonintervention agreements.

13. A useful statement of this position can be found in the essay by John Norton Moore already cited; see note 3 above. For an example of the official view, see Leonard Meeker, "Vietnam and the International Law of Self-Defense" in the same volume, pp. 318–32.

14. I shall follow the account of G. M. Kahin and John W. Lewis, *The United States in Vietnam* (New York, 1967).

15. "On the Principle of Non-Intervention," p. 16.

16. See Gregory Henderson, *Korea: The Politics of the Vortex* (Cambridge, Mass., 1968), ch. 6.

17. Kahin and Lewis, p. 146.

18. Ellery C. Stowell suggests some possible examples in *Intervention in International Law* (Washington, D.C., 1921), ch. II. For contemporary legal views (and newer examples), see Richard Lillich, ed., *Humanitarian Intervention and the United Nations* (Charlottesville, Virginia, 1973).

19. Quoted in Philip S. Foner, *The Spanish-Cuban-American War and the Birth of American Imperialism* (New York, 1972), I, 111.

20. Quoted in Stowell, p. 122n.

21. See, for example, Julius W. Pratt, *Expansionists of 1898* (Baltimore, 1936), and Walter La Feber, *The New Empire: An Interpretation of American Expansion* (Ithaca, 1963); also Foner, I, ch. XIV.

22. Foner, I, ch. XIII.

23. F. E. Chadwick, *The Relations of the United States and Spain: Diplomacy* (New York, 1909), pp. 586–87. These lines are the epigraph to Walter Millis' account of the war: *The Martial Spirit* (n.p., 1931).

24. Millis, p. 404; it should be noted that Millis also writes of the American decision to go to war: "Seldom can history have recorded a plainer case of military aggression" (p. 160).

25. For a contemporary account by a British journalist, see David Loshak, *Pakistan Crisis* (London, 1971).

26. John Westlake, *International Law,* vol. I, *Peace* (2nd ed., Cambridge, 1910), pp. 319–20.

27. Thomas M. Franck and Nigel S. Rodley, "After Bangladesh: The Law of Humanitarian Intervention by Military Force," 67 *American Journal of International Law* 304 (1973).

28. Julius Stone, *Aggression and World Order,* p. 99.

10

The Reagan Doctrine in Nicaragua

CHARLES R. BEITZ

In this chapter, Charles Beitz argues, as did Michael Walzer, that intervention in the internal affairs of foreign nations is sometimes justified. Beitz attempts to lay down necessary and sufficient conditions under which a certain type of interference is permissible—namely, support for groups that are resisting established governments. But he also wants to show that the sort of intervention into the affairs of Nicaragua supported by President Ronald Reagan is impermissible.

According to Beitz, the following conditions are necessary and jointly sufficient for the permissibility of foreign intervention on behalf of movements against established regimes:

1. *The established regime grossly violates its citizens' basic human rights; for example, rights against torture, arbitrary arrest, and racial and religious persecution.*
2. *The insurgent movement is indigenous, committed to respect for human rights, and broadly supported by the local populace.*
3. *There is a reasonable prospect that the intervention can succeed in bringing the opposition movement to power under circumstances in which it will be able to govern effectively without repressive measures.*
4. *Intervention will not do significant harm elsewhere—for example, it will not cause disruptive instability in other countries.*

*Once he has offered this analysis, Beitz then assesses the so-called
Reagan Doctrine as it applies to Nicaragua, claiming that none of his
four conditions is met in the case of U.S. aid for the contras.*

My subject is the morality of U.S. intervention in Nicaragua. This is part
of the larger subject of the ethics of intervention in internal wars. In his
State of the Union Address in February 1985, President Ronald Reagan set
forth a distinctive view about this. "Our mission is to nourish and defend
freedom and democracy. . . . We must not break faith with those who are
risking their lives—on every continent, from Afghanistan to Nicaragua—to
defy Soviet-supported aggression and secure rights which have been ours
from birth."[1]

These words announce a policy of support for prodemocratic insurgent
movements directed against so-called Marxist-Leninist governments in the
Third World.[2] Although the president himself has resisted giving the policy
a label, both his supporters and critics alike—with some official encouragement—call it the Reagan Doctrine.

The president's words recall President John Kennedy's declaration, in his
inaugural address, that the United States would "pay any price, bear any
burden, meet any hardship . . . to assure the survival and the success of
liberty." Kennedy's appeal to the moral value of liberty was an attempt to
summon support for a policy of containment of Soviet power. A generation
earlier, similar aims moved President Harry Truman when he proclaimed
what became known as the Truman Doctrine. Today, a generation later, the
Reagan Doctrine needs to be understood in the same context; it is part of
an effort to portray the geopolitical competition between the United States
and the USSR, particularly in the Third World, in terms of a moral conflict
between democracy and tyranny.

Although it represents a continuation of the cold war strategy of containment, the Reagan Doctrine differs from its predecessors in two important
ways. First, it elevates the policy of containment to the position of a moral
duty. As Secretary Shultz said, "Our moral principles *compel* us to support
those struggling against the imposition of Communist tyranny."[3]

Second, the Reagan Doctrine states an offensive rather than a defensive
policy. As practiced by prior administrations, containment was applied mainly
to *support* governments that were threatened with communist insurrectionary
movements. In contrast, the Reagan Doctrine would have the United States
intervene on behalf of insurgent groups fighting *against* established governments. Reform intervention—that is, interference in the affairs of other
sovereign states in order to bring about democratic political change—is now,
for the first time since World War II, an officially acknowledged element of
U.S. foreign policy.[4]

Bipartisan majorities in the Congress have endorsed or initiated four key
applications of the Reagan Doctrine since the president proclaimed it in

early 1985. Congress authorized aid for the contra army in Nicaragua; for noncommunist rebel groups in Kampuchea (Cambodia); for the anti-Soviet rebels in Afghanistan; and for the South Africa–backed insurgents led by Jonas Savimbi in Angola. Recently, there has been conservative pressure within the administration for a fifth application of the Reagan Doctrine, this time in Mozambique.[5]

I will concentrate on the question of aid to the contras in Nicaragua. This question is controversial in several respects. First, many people regard the application of the Reagan Doctrine in Nicaragua as particularly dangerous to U.S. national strategic interests, owing largely to its disdain for negotiations, its radicalizing effects on the Sandinista regime, and the political instability it is engendering elsewhere in the region. Second, some think the use of improper and probably illegal means to sustain the contra war in the face of domestic opposition, rather than being merely accidental, is endemic to the kind of interventionary diplomacy required by the Reagan Doctrine and thus constitutes an independent basis for criticizing the policy.

Both of these are matters of concern. Important as they are, however, they can obscure a more fundamental reason why the administration's policy in Nicaragua is, or at least ought to be, controversial. This involves the validity of the moral argument on which the Reagan Doctrine rests. Let me try to say why I think the moral dimension is important.

Congress first authorized overt aid to the contras in 1985. But U.S. support for them was initiated several years earlier. The CIA began a program of covert action against the revolutionary Sandinista government soon after the overthrow of the Somoza dictatorship in 1979. At the time, the contras consisted of a few hundred disgruntled former members of Anastasio Somoza's hated National Guard. They were financed by ex-patriots who had transferred their wealth out of the country before the revolution, and they operated from Honduras. With this group as a nucleus, the CIA used secretly appropriated funds to build up an armed force of considerable size. U.S. funds were also used to induce other anti-Sandinista groups to place themselves under a common leadership. While publicly denying any involvement, the Reagan administration, as we now know, then moved to provide guns, ammunition, and advice to the contra army this administration had created.[6] The United States also provided logistical and even tactical support—for example, when the CIA oversaw the mining of Corinto harbor in 1984. That incident became the basis for the successful lawsuit brought by the Nicaraguan government against the United States at the International Court of Justice at the Hague.

At first, the administration claimed it had no intention of trying to overthrow the Sandinista regime and aimed only to discourage the Sandinistas from supplying the leftist rebels in neighboring El Salvador. However, it proved impossible to produce hard evidence to convince U.S. allies and a skeptical press, or even some of the administration's own supporters in Congress, that the Sandinistas were providing significant aid to the Salvadoran insurgents. Then, the administration argued that the destabilization of the

Nicaraguan government was necessary to prevent the Soviets from building military bases there that would threaten the sea-lanes in the Caribbean; but the Soviets gave no hint of having any such intentions, and the Sandinista government actually offered to promise not to allow foreign bases in return for an end to the U.S.-sponsored intervention. Finding neither argument persuasive, the Congress in 1984 cut off any further U.S. government support for the contras.

The Reagan Doctrine is the administration's third attempt to justify contra aid. Whereas the first two attempts failed, the third has succeeded, at least thus far. (The revelations of improper diversion of funds from the Iran arms sales to the contras, which are emerging as I write, may change this.) The first two attempts involved appeals to U.S. interests, but these appeals were not convincingly documented, and they did not demonstrate that in the absence of contra aid, the national security would be threatened. Under these circumstances, the failure to elicit public support was predictable. The third attempt, however, took a different tack, linking contra aid not to interests but to deeply held American values. This appeal drew on a history of sympathy and generosity toward those struggling for democratic institutions against oppressive governments. The moral element in the Reagan Doctrine plucked a familiar string. This is the source of its political appeal, and it is why the moral element needs to be examined.

ARGUMENTS AGAINST
FOREIGN INTERVENTION

The Reagan Doctrine holds that intervention in the affairs of another country is morally permissible, or perhaps even required, when the intervention supports forces fighting for democracy. I will try to answer three questions about this. First, is intervention *ever* permissible? Second, if so, under what conditions? Third, do these conditions exist in the Nicaraguan case?

Let me begin with the first question. I raise it because conventional opinion in both international law and morality holds that intervention in the internal affairs of other countries is almost always forbidden.[7] I say *almost;* there are exceptions, which mainly involve intervention to defend against aggression and to put a stop to "crimes against humanity" such as genocide. But these exceptions are fairly narrow and offer little comfort to advocates of Reagan Doctrine interventionism.

The administration tacitly accepted this when it refused to recognize the jurisdiction of the International Court in the case brought by Nicaragua. The U.S. defense was that the court was unlikely to render an impartial verdict. A more accurate statement of the administration's position would be that it thought the conventional prohibition of intervention unjustifiably restrictive.[8] Accordingly, the first question we should consider is this: From a moral rather than a legal point of view, is it really true, as conventional opinion holds, that intervention in internal wars is nearly always wrong?

Those who think it is advance two arguments. First, they say that intervention disrupts the internal political life of other societies. Intervention in international affairs is like crime in domestic society. States, like individuals, have a right to live their own lives in their own ways, and intervention, like crime, violates this right.[9] Second, they say that intervention threatens international stability. If one country does it, others will follow suit, and the mutual restraint necessary for international order will collapse.[10]

I am not persuaded by either of these arguments for the conventional ban on intervention. Each one is too simple to capture the complex reality of international politics. Consider first the argument that intervention is like crime because it violates a state's freedom to conduct its own affairs in its own way. The question that needs asking is, Why should we think that states have such a right? Most people would reply, I think, that the freedom of states rests on the freedom of their citizens; in fact, from a moral point of view, the most important fact about states is that they protect the freedom of their people to conduct their private lives, and their common life together, as they see fit. Or, at least, *some* states do; the problem is that some do not. It stretches language to say that tyrannies, whether of the right or of the left, protect the freedom of their people; certainly, it would come as a surprise to a black South African, or a Chilean, or a Pole, to be told that a state that devotes so much of its resources to repressing its own people is the protector of their freedom.

Missing from this argument is the distinction between individual freedom and national independence. When we speak of "free" states, we normally mean *independent* states, ones that are not bound to others in the manner of colonies and dependencies. But obviously, a state can be independent, and thus a free *state*, without respecting the freedom of its *people*. What does this imply about the argument against intervention? Remember that the argument holds intervention to be wrong because it involves a violation of a state's freedom, and the argument explains the moral value of a state's freedom by pointing out that free states defend the freedom of their citizens. In light of the distinction between (individual) freedom and (national) independence, this argument is overreaching. What the argument really shows is that states that respect the political freedom of their people enjoy a moral status not available to tyrannies. The argument against intervention applies to these states, but not to others.

In response to this, it has been said that some societies are not ready for democratic institutions; the histories and cultures of these societies may be better suited to authoritarian regimes. In those cases, refraining from intervention is the way we show our respect for cultures different from our own.[11] Perhaps there are such cases, in which the overwhelming majority of a population, conforming to its own inherited values, accepts authoritarian rule. For myself, I suspect that this is an unrealistically romantic conception of the social circumstances characteristic of most authoritarian regimes today. However, we need not decide what to say about such cases here.[12] For the cases we are concerned about—that is, those at which the Reagan Doctrine is officially addressed—are different. In these cases, an internal conflict has already broken out; domestic forces are fighting for freedom against a government intent on repressing them. At least when the forces fighting for freedom represent a significant part of the population, it cannot be that there is no basis for democratic values in the local political culture. Instead, the culture is divided. To say that refraining from sending help is a way of showing respect for cultures different from our own is to be blind to this fact.

I will come back to this point, but let us move on to the second traditional argument against intervention—that it upsets international order. This argument seems especially important if one accepts my criticism of the earlier argument. That criticism seems to open the door to intervention in unfree states, and this may evoke an image of unbridled international anarchy, with strong states competing to impose their own judgments about how other peoples should be governed. This is not an attractive image. But the anti-interventionist argument it suggests faces two powerful objections.

First, the world today is closer to the image of anarchic competition for influence than to the alternative image of orderly coexistence. We might be misled about this by thinking about Europe, where, in spite of their rhetoric, the great powers have been fairly scrupulous in respecting each other's spheres of influence as these emerged from World War II. But Europe is not the world, and outside of the agreed spheres of influence, particularly in the Third World, we have witnessed a pattern of recurring competition among the superpowers in which interference in the internal affairs of states is routine. In international law, nonintervention is the rule; in international politics, it has been the exception. Therefore, it cannot plausibly be argued that interventionary policies should be avoided because they would undermine a convention of respect for national boundaries whose widespread acceptance helps keep the peace.

The second objection is this: The argument that intervention is wrong because it causes instability rests on a distortion of both history and ethics. As a historical matter, it is plain that intervention can come in many forms and degrees and in many places, and that some interventions are more destabilizing than others. For example, when the United States encouraged, and then actually helped, Corazon Aquino to vanquish the Marcos regime in the Philippines, it was practicing a kind of intervention. But no one would claim that this caused international instability. Nor is this point limited to cases of nonmilitary interference; the invasion of Grenada by U.S. military forces does not appear to have been any more destabilizing internationally than was the nonmilitary interference in the Philippines. I do not mean that the potential for instability is never a matter of concern, but only that we should be cautious about generalizing. Here, as elsewhere in international morality, undiscriminating reliance on excessively general historical propositions distorts judgment. It is better to consider individual cases on their own merits.

The ethical distortion is the thought that dangers to stability, of whatever form and degree, are so much worse than the harms that intervention might alleviate that the latter could never outweigh them. But stability is no more the only value in international affairs than it is in domestic life. From a moral point of view, many things matter. The things that matter include peace and stability. They also include human rights and social justice. In international affairs, in view of the danger and costs of war, peace is always a paramount concern. But it is not the only concern. When the danger to peace is not great, other values may properly influence foreign policy, including the value of protecting basic human rights and of enabling people to participate in decisions about their own destiny. Taken together with the historical observation that the destabilizing effects of intervention can vary greatly, this suggests that interventionary policies cannot always be ruled out on the grounds that their costs are worse than their benefits.[13]

CONDITIONS FOR INTERVENTIONS
THAT BOLSTER INSURGENTS

If the foregoing is correct, then reform-oriented interventionary policies, including those of the kind contemplated by the Reagan Doctrine, ought not to be rejected simply on the grounds that they offend the conventional prohibition of intervention—that prohibition itself lacks convincing foundations. But it does not follow that the Reagan Doctrine has been vindicated, even as a matter of theory. The preceding criticisms suggest that any morally acceptable intervention ought to meet several conditions. In its public formulations of the Reagan Doctrine, the administration has been insufficiently attentive to these matters. Once the conditions are made explicit, however, it will be seen that in combination they are extremely restrictive.

In this space I can hardly offer a complete theory of intervention from which a comprehensive set of limiting conditions could be derived. Instead, I shall proceed more informally, listing several conditions that seem plausible in view of what I have already said and indicating briefly the range of considerations that support them. I will restrict myself to interventions on behalf of insurgent opposition movements that are fighting against an established regime. (This restriction is important. It is conceivable, although perhaps not likely, that reform intervention could be justified even where there is no insurgent opposition—a possible example would be Grenada. As these are not the sort of cases envisioned by the Reagan Doctrine, I leave them aside.)

1. *The established regime should be a tyranny.* By this I mean that it must be one that systematically engages in gross violations of the basic human rights of its citizens. Admittedly, this is somewhat vague because people disagree about what things count as human rights. In referring to "basic" human rights I mean to limit the condition to fairly clear cases— for example, the rights against torture, arbitrary arrest and detention, cruel and degrading treatment, and racial and religious persecution; the rights to freedom of speech and press; and the right to an adequate material minimum. In referring to "systematic" and "gross" violations, I mean to exclude cases in which there is a single instance, or only a few instances, of violations of

one or another particular right. Intervention is obviously a crude instrument, even under the best of circumstances; it is not wisely used as a means of redressing individual grievances or preventing adventitious violations, no matter how serious these may appear when viewed in isolation.

2. *The insurgents should be genuinely committed to respect for human rights and should represent a truly indigenous movement with substantial popular support.* If the opposition movement were not committed to protecting the human rights it accuses the regime of neglecting, intervention might simply replace one kind of tyranny with another. Of course, it may be difficult to say how genuine a movement's human rights commitments are; but it is not usually impossible. For example, there is good reason for skepticism about the public professions of democratic faith we have recently heard from Jonas Savimbi, the leader of the Angolan rebels. In previous incarnations he has claimed to be a Marxist and a Maoist; he is more fairly viewed as an opportunist tribal leader who was dealt out of power by the regime he is now fighting.

This condition also holds that the opposition movement must be truly indigenous and must represent a substantial body of domestic opinion. This guarantees that intervention will not involve the imposition of essentially foreign values on a culture that does not share them. Again, it may be hard to know exactly what the facts are; in a civil war it is usually unclear how many people support the insurgents. But normally it will be possible to say whether the movement draws its strength from local sentiment or whether it sustains itself instead primarily by outside support.

3. *There should be a reasonable prospect that the intervention can succeed in bringing the opposition movement to power under circumstances in which it will be able to govern effectively without repressive measures.* The rationale of the first element of this condition—that the intervention should be reasonably likely to succeed—seems obvious enough. But the victory would be Pyrrhic if it gave rise to social forces, either within the opposition movement or elsewhere in society, that confronted the new government with a choice between ineffectiveness and repression. Intervention improves the prospects for basic human rights only when carried out in a way that avoids such results.

4. *Intervention should not do significant harm elsewhere.* As I said earlier, some interventions are destabilizing, whereas others are not. It is impossible to generalize about this. U.S. interference in the Philippines and in Grenada did not do perceptible damage elsewhere. More typically, however, intervention will have disruptive effects beyond the society where it takes place. Those effects should be brought into the moral calculus.

I will not try to say more in defense of these conditions. They are an attempt to describe circumstances in which intervention would effectively advance important political values within the state without imposing unwarranted moral costs, either internally or internationally. A moment's reflection suggests that, taken together, the four conditions are likely to restrict the range of permissible interventions to a very small number of cases.

U.S. INTERVENTION IN NICARAGUA

Let me turn to the case of U.S. intervention in Nicaragua. A review of the evidence shows that the policy of aiding the contras does not satisfy any of the conditions listed.

First, although the Sandinista regime is certainly no liberal democracy, it is also not a regime that engages in a systematic pattern of gross violations of basic human rights. The reality is more ambiguous. Not even the Reagan administration claims that conditions there are worse now than under the Somoza dictatorship. For example, there are no credible reports of the use of torture or of disappearances as means of social control, and only a few of arbitrary arrests; there is more scope for political dissent within the Sandinista structure than there was in the Somoza dictatorship; at the local level, Sandinista institutions have provided people with a greater degree of leverage over the immediate conditions of life and work; and, for the first time, the basic material and health care needs of the population are being systematically addressed.[14] Most impartial observers, such as Amnesty International, say that the human rights record of the Sandinistas is actually better than that of many other Latin American regimes, including our allies the Salvadorans.[15]

On the other hand, the Sandinistas' record is far from admirable. Freedom of the press has been curbed with the closing of *La Prensa*—although in view of the fact that the newspaper supported the contras and received financial backing from the CIA at the time the agency was sponsoring a war against the Nicaraguan government, the censorship is perhaps not surprising;[16] political dissent has been chilled by the excessively broad powers granted to the popular tribunals; some opposition political parties have had difficulty staging public meetings and rallies; other non-Sandinista organizations have been harassed; there are reports of brutality in the prisons; and in the early days of the regime, it dealt harshly and insensitively with the Misquito Indians on Nicaragua's Atlantic coast. In a few respects the regime's record has improved; for example, the Sandinistas have admitted at least some of their mistakes in connection with the Misquito and tried to do better. In other respects things have grown substantially worse; in particular, as outside pressure on the regime has intensified, the more hard-line elements of the Sandinista front have gained in strength, and there has been more repression of political dissent.

One must bear in mind that Nicaragua is a country at war, and countries at war typically behave badly. During World War II, the U.S. government sequestered the ethnic Japanese, imprisoned draft resisters, and expelled foreigners who opposed the war effort. During the present war, the Nicaraguan government has adopted similar policies. This certainly does not excuse the excesses, but it does place them in context. Anyone who expects a country at war to live up to its peacetime ideals will be disappointed. Conversely, anyone who thinks that a country's wartime behavior accurately predicts its peacetime conduct probably will be misled.

The point of all this is that the Sandinista regime, for all its faults, is not, or at least not yet, a brutal tyranny. On the other hand, we must not delude ourselves; it is not now, and is not going to become, a liberal democracy either. There are two things one can say with some confidence. First, viewed in historical perspective, this is perhaps the least repressive regime Nicaragua has ever known. Second, for the duration the contra war will make matters worse rather than better.[17] I think we should conclude that the Nicaraguan case fails my first test for legitimate intervention.

There is room for dispute about this conclusion in view of the contradictory nature of some of the evidence about the political conduct of the Sandinistas and the difficulties in judging the extent to which the worsening human rights situation is due to the pressures of war. Therefore, it is important to reiterate that the first condition is only one of four, all of which should be satisfied before intervention can be counted as legitimate.

The second condition holds that the insurgent forces should be genuinely committed to respecting the human rights it accuses the regime of violating. I do not believe this can be said about the contras. The military leadership, including virtually all of the commanders in the field, are remnants of the Somoza era and come mainly from the ranks of noncommissioned officers of the brutal and hated National Guard. There is nothing in the pasts of these leaders to suggest concern for human rights or for democratic processes. Nor in the present—there have been recurring reports of serious human rights violations carried out against civilians by the contra forces.[18] In part, this reflects a military strategy that emphasizes strikes against civilian targets such as health care facilities, schools, and peasant farming cooperatives. But many of the reported violations have taken place outside the context of military operations and are more akin to the terror tactics adopted by right-wing paramilitary groups in some other Latin American countries.

It is true that some people associated with the contras—Arturo Cruz, for instance—have democratic credentials and that some significant figures in Nicaraguan domestic life—such as the archbishop, Cardinal Obando y Bravo—have expressed sympathy for the contra cause. The question, however, is whether there is any reason to believe that a contra victory would lead to a government substantially more likely to respect human rights than the Sandinista regime. The most likely scenario is that divisions between the military and political elements of the opposition would emerge very rapidly, with political figures such as Arturo Cruz and the church hierarchy finding themselves in increasing conflict with the military leadership of the contras. In that kind of situation, with the political elements demanding greater pluralism and the military elements pressing for greater repression, it is not hard to predict who would prevail. How many divisions has the archbishop?

Whether the contras represent a truly indigenous movement with substantial popular support is a more complicated question. They are certainly indigenous in the sense that the vast majority of them are Nicaraguans; and they have apparently attracted a large number of people to their ranks (although how many is unclear; the current consensus is twelve to fifteen thousand men, but as all involved have interests in overstating the number, there is really no reliable basis for estimating). However, it is a different matter to say that the contras represent a movement that enjoys the support of a substantial portion of domestic political opinion. In composition, the contras are a diverse aggregation of groups, with no discernable commonality of interest beyond their shared opposition to the Sandinistas. In addition to the nucleus of former national guardsmen who make up the military leadership, the contras include peasants and small farmers who are unhappy with the course of the rural economy, poor volunteers with no other source of employment or income, some who have been kidnapped from rural villages, and others.[19] Moreover, there is no evidence that the contras have produced a groundswell of popular support within Nicaragua itself. In fact, there is some indirect evidence to the contrary. For example, Nicaragua is the only country in the region with an armed popular militia. No government that had reason to fear that an insurgent movement enjoyed significant popular support would take such a risk. Beyond this, there have been surprisingly few reports of peasant villages providing support or shelter for contra brigades—a typical phenomenon in most guerrilla insurgencies and one that is routine, for example, in El Salvador. Indeed, after five years of civil war subsidized by U.S. covert, overt, and private aid, the contras have yet to gain control of any Nicaraguan territory and still seek refuge in sanctuaries in Honduras and Costa Rica.

These observations raise doubt about the third condition as well—that there should be a reasonable chance that outside aid will enable the insurgents to attain power under circumstances in which they can govern effectively without recourse to repression. The absence of significant civilian support makes it very unlikely that the contras could do so, assuming the nascent internal cleavages were somehow repaired. But it is not even clear that under current policy the contras can attain power at all. The Reagan administration itself has acknowledged that the funds appropriated so far will not be enough to ensure a contra victory, and more—probably much more—will eventually be needed. Prediction is hazardous, but in view of the Pentagon's reluctance to support direct U.S. military involvement and growing congressional resistance to higher military budgets, substantially higher levels of contra aid seem a dubious prospect at best. If that is right, then the present policy will succeed in prolonging the fighting and increasing the killing, but the policy will not succeed in defeating the Sandinistas. In view of this, as Michael Walzer wrote, the administration's policy "is an act of willful cruelty toward the Nicaraguans."[20]

Finally, what about the policy's effects on other countries in Central America? There is no time to discuss this question in the detail it deserves, but let me note how the contra war is causing political instability and impeding economic and social reform in the two critical countries that share borders with Nicaragua.

In Honduras, to the north, the Reagan administration already has made vast investments in military bases and has financed a large buildup in the

Honduran army. This is at least partly intended to put pressure on the Sandinistas and is certainly intended to prepare for the possibility of a Honduran-Nicaraguan war arising from Nicaraguan operations against contra bases in Honduras. As a result, the political power of a reactionary military establishment has been reinforced, and the prospects of social and economic reform, which looked promising as recently as 1981, have virtually disappeared.[21]

Costa Rica, to the south, is the only country in Central America with an enduring democratic tradition. Costa Rica is also the only country that has avoided the pattern of continuing military interference in politics that has plagued every other country in the region—largely because Costa Rica has had no army. The contra war could change all this. Costa Rica shares a border with Nicaragua, and in spite of government protests, the contras have been operating from bases on the border, which, predictably, has triggered Nicaraguan retaliation. Pro-contra, right-wing paramilitary groups have sprung up within Costa Rica. Costa Rica is already developing a military establishment in order to defend itself against both the Nicaraguan retaliatory raids on contra camps and its own right wing. As domestic politics becomes more polarized and the military establishment grows, Costa Rica's historic commitment to peaceful change and democratic institutions appears more and more precarious.[22]

There is more to be said about the effects of the contra war on other countries in the region, but this is enough to illustrate my point. Intervention in Nicaragua will do considerably more damage elsewhere in Central America than the good it can possibly do in Nicaragua—if, indeed, it can do any.

CONCLUSION

To conclude, if the principle underlying the Reagan Doctrine is understood to comprehend restrictive conditions like those I have discussed—a big "if"—then it cannot be faulted simply on the grounds that the interventions it contemplates are prohibited by some general moral principle requiring respect for established boundaries. The trouble with the Reagan Doctrine is in its application. The conditions that might justify intervention in theory do not often apply in practice. They certainly do not apply in the Nicaraguan case. The contra forces lack the power and the popular support they need to win the war and secure the peace; if, against the odds, the contras did win the war, they would be more likely to institute a tyranny of the right than to establish a pluralistic democracy; and the record thus far suggests that, win or lose, the contras are going to fight a bloody, dirty, and prolonged war. Elsewhere in Central America, U.S. support for the contras is likely to generate internal political instability and to reinforce antidemocratic military establishments at the expense of other groups pressing for critical economic and social reforms.

A long tradition in international thought, known today as political realism, cautions against efforts to found foreign policy on moral principle rather than on national interests. Philosophers[23] have made good sport of revealing the crude forms of moral skepticism that typically occur in presentations of the realist view. However, there is a truth in realism that ought not to be lost sight of: In the hands of public officials, moral principle is too easily transformed into crusading doctrine, which invites misperception, rhetorical manipulation, and public hypocrisy. As the case of contra aid illustrates, the Reagan Doctrine furnishes ample grounds for the realists' fears.

NOTES

An earlier version was presented in a lecture series on "Global Issues" at Trinity University, San Antonio, Texas, on November 5, 1986. I am grateful to the audience there, and especially to Steven Luper-Foy, for helpful comments. I would also like to thank Douglas Bennett and Michael Doyle for helpful comments on the earlier draft. I am much indebted to my Swarthmore colleague Kenneth Sharpe for a series of conversations over several years that have helped to inform my thinking about U.S. policy in Central America.

1. U.S. Congress, House, "Message from the President of the United States Transmitting a Report on the State of the Union," February 6, 1985 (House Doc. 99-25), pp. 7–8.

2. See Secretary of State George Shultz's gloss in "America and the Struggle for Freedom," speech before the Commonwealth Club of California, San Francisco, February 22, 1985 (Washington: Department of State, Bureau of Public Affairs, Current Policy, no. 659).

3. Ibid., p. 4 (emphasis added).

4. On these matters, see Robert H. Johnson, " 'Rollback' Revisited—A Reagan Doctrine for Insurgent Wars?" *Policy Focus 1986*, no. 1 (Washington, D.C.: Overseas Development Council); and Stephen S. Rosenfeld, "The Guns of July," *Foreign Affairs* 64, no. 4 (1986):698–714.

5. See *Philadelphia Inquirer*, October 26, 1986, p. 2-E.

6. For a summary and discussion, see Richard H. Ullman, "At War with Nicaragua," *Foreign Affairs* 62, no. 1 (1983):39–58. There is a revealing account of the U.S. role in organizing the contras in the series of articles by reporters Robert C. Toth and Doyle McManus published in the *Los Angeles Times*, March 3, 4, and 5, 1985.

7. See, for example, article 2(4) of the U.N. Charter, article 18 of the Charter of the Organization of American States, and the Declaration of Principles of International Law (approved by the U.N. General Assembly in 1970). All of these documents of international law were supported by the United States when they were adopted.

8. For such a view, see William Safire, "A Decent Respect," *New York Times*, February 4, 1985, p. A19.

9. This argument is most clearly and elegantly developed by Michael Walzer, *Just and Unjust Wars* (New York: Basic Books, 1977), Chs. 4 and 6; and in his subsequent article, "The Moral Standing of States," *Philosophy & Public Affairs* 9, no. 3 (1980):209–229.

10. A clear statement of this view is in R. J. Vincent, *Nonintervention and International Order* (Princeton, N.J.: Princeton University Press, 1974), Ch. 9. For this argument applied to the Reagan Doctrine, see Rosenfeld, "The Guns of July," p. 714.

11. The argument is made by Michael Walzer. See "The Moral Standing of States," p. 225.

12. I discussed such cases briefly in "Nonintervention and Communal Integrity: A Rejoinder to Walzer," *Philosophy & Public Affairs* 9, no. 4 (1980):385–391.

13. A similar argument is made by Charles Krauthammer in "Morality and the Reagan Doctrine," *The New Republic*, September 8, 1986, pp. 17–24. As my remarks below indicate, my conclusions about the implementation of the Reagan Doctrine differ sharply from Krauthammer's.

14. Amnesty International, *Report 1986* (London: Amnesty International Publishers, 1986), pp. 179–183; Americas Watch, *Human Rights in Nicaragua, 1985–1986* (Washington, D.C.: Americas Watch, 1986).

15. Compare, for example, the sections on El Salvador and Nicaragua in Amnesty International, *Report 1986*, pp. 152–156 and 179–183. One might object that comparisons—with a country's own past and with its neighbors—are insufficient to establish the noncomparative claim represented by condition 1. However, the interpretation of the operative element of this condition—that a regime *systematically* engage in *gross* violations—is inevitably a matter of judgment, and these comparative observations help give content to this judgment. They suggest that if the Sandinista regime is an appropriate target for reform intervention, then most other countries in the region would be even better targets, as would have been the Somoza regime that preceded the Sandinista regime.

16. See the report of an interview with *La Prensa* managing editor Horacio Ruiz in Michael C. Bagge's letter to the editor, *New York Times*, August 13, 1986.

17. For a further discussion, see Lars Schoultz, "Nicaragua: The United States Confronts a Revolution," *From Gunboats to Diplomacy*, ed. Richard Newfarmer (Baltimore, Md.: Johns Hopkins University Press, 1984), pp. 123–130.

18. Amnesty International, *Report 1986*, p. 183.

19. See Christopher Dickey, *With the Contras* (New York: Simon & Schuster, 1985); and Robert S. Leiken, "The Battle for Nicaragua," *New York Review of Books*, March 13, 1986, especially pp. 50–51.

20. "Bleeding Nicaragua," *The New Republic*, April 28, 1986, p. 15.

21. Philip L. Shepherd, "Honduras," in *Confronting Revolution: Security Through Diplomacy in Central America*, ed. Morris J. Blachman, William M. LeoGrande, and Kenneth E. Sharpe (New York: Pantheon, 1986), pp. 125–155.

22. Morris J. Blachman and Ronald G. Hellman, "Costa Rica," ibid., pp. 156–182.

23. Including myself; see *Political Theory and International Relations* (Princeton, N.J.: Princeton University Press, 1979), part 1.

11

Foreign Intervention

ALAN H. GOLDMAN

*Alan Goldman notes that if principles of international justice are to
help maintain peace, then they must be neutral among the various
existing conceptions of political justice advocated by the nations of the
world. Unfortunately, Goldman thinks, Charles Beitz's first and second
conditions (requiring, respectively, that a regime be a gross violator of
basic rights before its autonomy is violable by foreign powers and that
insurgents respect basic rights before these insurgents are supportable by
outsiders) will be biased once a list of basic rights is nailed down, for
nations disagree about what constitutes a basic right. In the opinion of
socialists, Western nations are constantly violating economic rights; in the
opinion of democrats, Eastern nations are in the habit of violating
political rights. The rights that matter, at any rate, are not the rights
endorsed by outside nations. To avoid subjecting itself to foreign
intervention, a regime must respect the rights broadly recognized by the
people it rules.*

*Goldman also questions Beitz's third condition and insists that the
probability of success is not a necessary condition for intervention.
Goldman says this restriction implies that the more brutal and thorough
the oppression, the less foreign powers can be justified in opposing it.
However, it is a necessary condition for intervention that it have the
probability of reducing the oppression of an established regime. As for*

*Beitz's fourth condition, Goldman accepts it, along with Beitz's claim
that U.S. intervention on behalf of the contras is unjustified.*

───────────────────────────────

When deriving acceptable rules to govern public policy, we must be wary
of generalizing from single concrete cases. We know from experience that
historical lessons tend not to be ignored, but learned too well. Too often
what results is policy that is excessive where earlier approaches were insufficient.
The problem lies in the temptation to generalize broadly from real cases
with many complex variables and to apply such simply derived rules to later
cases without requisite attention to morally relevant differences among them.
This tendency lends plausibility to the realists' complaint against basing
foreign policy on moral principle. Interpreted literally, the complaint lacks
clear sense because proper moral reasoning must determine what we ought
to do on the social level. But the complaint has force when directed against
simplistic moral rules derived from insufficient data.

To his credit, this generally is not Beitz's method in his discussion of
the interventionist policy of the Reagan administration and its application
in Nicaragua. His chapter may give the appearance of arguing only from
the single case because he follows his initial comments on the policy with
the derivation of necessary conditions for justified intervention that seem
plausible in light of that discussion. But, in fact, he simply states some
general reasons for the presumption against foreign intervention, notes that
these can be overridden, and then proposes some restrictions on interventions
in favor of insurgent movements at war with established governments.

The justification for the presumption against intervention is stated too
briefly. Understanding that justification helps us to understand its legitimate
exceptions, and so first I shall expand upon Beitz's allusion to it. Following
J. S. Mill and Michael Walzer,[1] he appeals to an analogy between states and
individuals; he contends that states, like individuals, have a right to live
their own lives in their own ways and that intervention, like crime, violates
this right.

In expanding upon this analogy, we must be careful not to attribute, as
Beitz's remark comes dangerously close to doing, personal properties to
states ("living their own lives" must be a metaphor). States are not autonomous
moral beings. If the analogy here is to be informative, then attributing rights
to governments must reduce entirely to appeal to the rights of their citizens.
But within this constraint, the comparison may serve to indicate both the
sources and limits of states' rights against intervention by others. To see
how, we need to examine both sides of the reduction more closely.

The value of individual autonomy derives from at least three sources.
Individuals value their freedom to make choices and enjoy its exercise.
Differing in values and preference orderings, individuals are more likely than

other people to realize their own most central values and highest preferences and even more likely to know or to learn the best or least costly means to do so. Others are as likely as not to impose alien values when they interfere. Finally, individuals develop the capacity to choose wisely only through the exercise of autonomous choice. Children, for example, who are not permitted this freedom where it can be exercised without harm are slow to develop the capacity to lead their own lives or to be productive members of the community. The right to choose for oneself is therefore instrumentally valuable in two distinct ways and valued for itself as well.

In avoiding the fallacy of personifying states, we may still find parallels for all three sources of value for individual autonomy. Citizens value their sense of community, their shared ideals and aspirations, and the freedom to express those ideals through indigenous social and political institutions. If anything tends to be resented as much as interference with an individual's autonomy, it is interference in a nation's political processes by another nation. Shared values differ as much or more across states than preferences differ across individuals. Thus states, like individuals, are likely to err when they paternalistically intervene in the affairs of other states. Finally, there is independent value in allowing states to develop their own political and social forms of interaction. Like individuals, states become more capable of self-government in this way. The variety of political forms so developed may in the long run increase the options available to individuals for political interaction and prevent that consolidation of power across national boundaries that could threaten individuals' political and other freedoms.

As Beitz indicates, we may add to this list of internal values of political self-determination another reason for the presumption against intervention or interventionism as a national policy. Foreign interventions may destabilize the international balance of power and threaten world peace. In order to preserve this balance and avoid this threat, we require a presumption or rule against intervention that does not depend upon or favor one set of controversial political norms. The rule must be neutral between competing political visions if it is to help maintain peace between their advocates. This is one criterion for an acceptable principle in this area, although it is ignored in Beitz's discussion of necessary conditions for justified intervention.

As he also notes, the justification of the presumption against foreign intervention does not create an absolute or exceptionless rule but rather, as I have been saying, a presumption that can be overridden. He points out that tyrannies, which violate the rights and freedoms of their subjects, cannot claim a right to self-determination based on those rights and freedoms. He therefore takes as one necessary condition for justified intervention that the established regime be a tyranny. But there is already a problem here in the definition of this emotively laden political category. Beitz defines a tyranny as a regime that systematically and grossly violates the basic human rights of its subjects. This definition is fine as far as it goes, but it simply transfers the potential controversy to the specification of basic human rights. Beitz claims to limit his list to "fairly clear cases," but he includes rights against arbitrary arrest and detention, rights against racial and religious persecution, rights to freedom of speech and freedom of the press, and rights to an adequate material minimum.

If a free press is included among the basic rights, then a country such as Israel probably would not qualify as having a right to self-determination or against foreign intervention on this score. If foreign intervention is permitted on grounds of religious and racial persecution, then the Soviet Union and the United States would be legitimately subject to it (the latter at least until recently). Certainly the United States, and many other seemingly respectable regimes as well, fail to guarantee an adequate material minimum to all their citizens, under any plausible construal of "adequate minimum." Even the right against arbitrary arrest and detention is subject to conflicting interpretations. A radical socialist who views private property as theft might view arrests for conventional thefts as morally arbitrary. To say the least, this aspect of the rule for just interventions suggested by Beitz fails to maintain neutrality among competing political ideologies.

In fairness to Beitz, he states his requirement that the established regime be viewed as a tyranny only as a necessary, not a sufficient, condition for justified intervention. But the lack of neutrality in this condition robs it of any real bite, making it doubtful that the condition imposes any real constraint. What appears tyrannical under one conception of rights will appear perfectly natural and proper under another. The socialist views Western nations as systematically violating economic rights, while the democrat views Eastern nations as violating political rights.

Although this condition therefore appears to be too weak, Beitz's second and third conditions may be too strong. They may not be genuinely necessary for the justification of foreign intervention. Concentrating exclusively on the case in which an armed insurgent group engages in civil war may again mislead. Beitz insists that such a faction must be likely to succeed in imposing a morally more acceptable regime before aid to it can be justified. But is probable military success a genuine moral requirement for foreign support? If certain sorts of oppression or gross violation of the rights of sizable segments of a population can justify intervention even in the absence of a faction with the means to mount military opposition to the oppressive regime, then why should the probable success of such a venture be a necessary condition for intervention? Making it so implies that the more brutal and thorough the oppression, the less foreign powers can be justified in opposing it. Looking only at the Nicaraguan situation, one might well conclude that aid to the contras will contribute only to needless bloodshed in the absence of a real chance for success in toppling the Sandinista regime. But, again, we must be wary of generalizing from the single case. In other contexts, foreign pressure might succeed in altering the oppressive policies of a regime in power or might convince it to share power more broadly, without ensuring the success of a military insurgency. If we simply thought of South Africa, for example, instead of Nicaragua, we would be likely to summon different intuitions in regard to this proposed condition.

In order to see better what conditions are necessary for the justification of foreign intervention, we should return to the case against (and for) paternalistic intervention in the affairs of individuals. That analogy can indicate not only the sources, but the limits of the presumption against intervention, the contexts in which that presumption can be overridden. The great danger from paternalism in the individual case is that the persons who interfere will succeed only in imposing their own values and preferences on the agent whose autonomy is denied. Unless there is good reason to think otherwise, the persons who interfere will not in all probability aid the agent in realizing his own values, but only will deny him the satisfaction of attempting to do so on his own. But this presumption can be overridden in contexts in which it is clear that an agent, through ignorance, carelessness, or incompetence, will otherwise act so as to frustrate the realization of his own highest preferences. In such circumstances we can say either that choice on the part of the agent is not truly autonomous (defining autonomy in terms of acting on one's true preferences) or that autonomous choice loses its net positive value for the agent, thus resulting in harm or frustration.

The parallel in the case of states should be clear. We saw that each source of value for individual autonomy has its counterpart in the sources of value for political self-determination. We saw also that a rule justifying exceptions to the presumption against intervention must in the interest of peace and international stability be neutral between competing foreign ideologies (and that Beitz's conditions fail in this respect). Fortunately, it turns out that the restriction implied by the analogy with justified paternalism toward individuals meets (at least partially) the condition of neutrality in regard to the perceptions of foreign powers. We cannot allow states to intervene in the affairs of other states whenever the former perceive systematic violations of rights by the latter. Such interventionism, especially if military, would be destabilizing and likely to violate rights to political self-determination. Neither can we construe the restriction on intervention as absolute. Political self-determination may be nonexistent in any case if a large segment of the population is disenfranchised. Furthermore, other rights violated by an established government may be more important than the right of even a majority to govern itself. The analogy with the requirement that individuals act consistently with their own values and preferences if they are not to be subject to paternalistic interference suggests that states must respect those rights that their subjects recognize as such if states are not to be subject to foreign intervention.

Utilizing this criterion, we do not rely solely on the moral perceptions of foreign powers. The constraint is real because foreign powers must rather agree in their judgments with the internal consensus of a state's inhabitants. But cannot a foreign power always find (or form) a faction within any nation that will agree with that power's political ideology and hence with its perceptions of rights violations? Perhaps, but any reasonable criterion in this area must insist that violations of the rights that it specifies be systematic and widespread. The difference between this and Beitz's first condition lies in the rights that will be specified as relevant in particular cases. There is no widespread perception in the United States that arrests for theft are morally perverse or in systematic violation of fundamental rights. Freedom of the press is not considered a fundamental right in many countries. The restriction on foreign intervention imposed by the proposed criterion is therefore stronger than that imposed by Beitz's first condition as he interprets it.

On the other hand, there remains a problem in applying the proposed criterion in practice. How do we verify the internal perception of systematic violations of fundamental rights in a foreign state? Here some of the conditions rejected previously might reappear in a new guise, as purported answers to this question. It might be claimed that only an insurgent faction with sufficient support to make military victory likely verifies widespread resistance to an established regime. But this is again implausible. If we were to accept it, why not insist, as Walzer does,[2] that such a faction must be capable of succeeding on its own, without foreign assistance, that only then does that faction reaffirm the self-determination of the state in question? Our deeper reason for rejecting this as a criterion of internal perception of the systematic violation of fundamental rights is the same as our reason for rejecting Beitz's third condition. The success of an established regime in preventing or stifling military opposition is not a measure of its willing acceptance by the indigenous population. Success may signal only the population's forced submission to the regime.

A Reaganite might suggest alternatively that only democratic elections can reliably indicate that a government enjoys popular support and is not perceived by its citizens as in violation of their fundamental rights. It might be argued that when a government does not enjoy power through majority support at the polls, we must presume that a majority would not support it and would perceive it as violating their rights. I agree with Beitz that this is far too strong a criterion. Its indirect support in this argument cannot succeed if the direct argument for democracy as a necessary condition of self-determination does not succeed. If the right to vote is not internally perceived as fundamental, then the criterion for justified foreign intervention that I have proposed so far will not equate with support for democratic factions wherever they exist. If this right is not internally perceived as fundamental, then its exercise cannot be the sole test of popular support for or dissent from an established regime.

Rather, in applying the criterion we must rely on a variety of factors. These will include whether force or brutality is required to prevent large segments of the population from exercising rights that we recognize; whether resistance to the denial of rights is expressed internally in any of a variety of ways, for example in the foreign press, through strikes or other forms of nonmilitary resistance; whether organized resistance movements exist (regardless of their military means); whether the rights that we perceive to be denied are universally perceived as fundamental (as in the case of genocide or enslavement). In practice I do not believe that it is impossible to identify internal resistance to oppressive regimes in the absence of free elections or internal military opposition that is likely to succeed.

The criterion so far proposed must be combined with several other conditions. As Beitz notes, the probable costs of intervention in terms of stable international relations, threats to peace elsewhere, and the stability of neighboring regimes must be worth the probable moral benefits. (This need not be a utilitarian calculation, but once more can be conceived in terms of the protection and probable violation of rights.) Of course, foreign intervention can take many forms. If it is covert, it may well have negative repercussions at home; if military, it is likely to represent serious threats of the kinds mentioned previously. In addition to threats against peace and stability, the probable loss of innocent lives must be weighed in the balance in contemplating military intervention or military support for factions, when such support is likely to initiate or prolong civil war.

Finally, although probable military success is not a prerequisite for moral intervention, even for intervention in the form of military aid to an insurgent group, probable success in reducing the oppression of an established regime in the long run is a necessary condition. Pressure for reform or compromise can succeed in conceivable circumstances when military victory is not possible or too costly. This additional condition is simply an extension of the moral cost/benefit analysis proposed previously. It is worth emphasizing again that this analysis is not to be of the usual utilitarian form, nor does it amount to a "utilitarianism of rights," as perceived by the foreign power. In contemplating intervention, the U.S. government is not to seek simply to minimize violations of fundamental rights in the long run, according to its own list of fundamental rights. Rather, our government is to support the development of political forms perceived as just by their indigenous populations.

It is an interesting question for ethical theory how, operating as we must from within our own moral framework, we can in good conscience support or acquiesce in the existence of foreign regimes that violate rights as we perceive them. Must it not be morally more important to us whether a regime is wrong in its practices from our point of view, according to our conception of right and wrong, than whether it is morally legitimate in the eyes of its subjects? After all, their moral perceptions may strike us as primitive or perverse. If, for example, a religiously fanatic regime regiments the lives of its subjects in totalitarian fashion, must we approve because those subjects have not reached the level of moral consciousness at which they would feel oppressed and disapprove? The answer, I believe, is that we need not approve, but ought not intervene on the basis of our disapproval. A sense of our own moral fallibility should be pertinent here, as well as attention to the likely global effects of a policy of intervention on grounds of moral disagreement alone. Given that the value of political self-determination mirrors that of individual autonomy, and that paternalistic interference in the lives of individuals that does not further their own values is illegitimate, we should expect that the disvalue from intervention in the affairs of states that enjoy broad popular support will outweigh any moral good that could come of it. Here, as elsewhere, the content of a moral decision is one thing; the right to decide or to govern is another. The two are sometimes, although not always, separable.

There is a possible problem nevertheless for the proposed analysis in the case of a regime with seemingly content but enslaved inhabitants. Given that this situation is conceivable (which I grant only for purposes of argument), must we really allow such a regime to exist without outside pressure for reform? Here we could perhaps make the case that slaves who do not believe that their fundamental rights are violated are simply irrational, according to some morally neutral understanding of rationality. We could argue that all rational agents who have other desires to fulfill must desire autonomy or free agency in the minimal sense violated by enslavement, that this minimal degree of autonomy must be viewed as a good by any consistent moral framework. Our criterion for justified intervention could be weakened in this way to allow for the protection of rights that must be rationally recognized, without violating the requirement for neutrality among competing political ideologies. Appeal to this clause would be far more implausible when it comes to such rights as freedom of the press or the right to have a government elected by majority vote. Barring uncontroversial cases of irrationality in attitudes toward fundamental rights, we must restrict intervention within the constraints of the main condition proposed.

The philosopher's job here, I take it, is to bring moral reasoning to bear on the development of acceptable general principles meant to govern international relations. As philosophers, we can leave the task of applying these principles to concrete situations to others. The absence of a professional duty to do so does not of course prevent a philosopher from engaging in that empirical research that renders him or her sufficiently expert to publish opinions on such matters. My own knowledge of the Nicaraguan situation, I confess, is that of a citizen informed soley by news reports and similar articles. I cannot therefore offer expert comments on that portion of Beitz's chapter that specifically evaluates that situation. It strikes me as a reasonable assessment of the circumstances at the time he wrote it. More recent developments, including the defection of one of the few contra leaders who seemed at all worthy of support and information regarding the lengths to which the U.S. government went in pursuit of its interventionist policy, make me confident that my conditions for justified intervention, like Beitz's conditions that I have rejected, prohibit further intervention in Nicaragua (at least until such time as we have evidence of more aggressive policies on the part of the Sandinistas). I will refrain from supporting this intuition in print; here I simply defer to Beitz's sensible summary.

NOTES

1. J. S. Mill, "A Few Words on Non-Intervention," *Dissertations and Discussions* (New York, 1873), pp. 238–263; Michael Walzer, *Just and Unjust Wars* (New York: Basic Books, 1977).

2. Michael Walzer, "The Moral Standing of States: A Response to Four Critics," *Philosophy & Public Affairs* 9, no. 3 (1980):209–229, especially p. 222.

12

War and Nuclear Deterrence

DAVID GAUTHIER

Not only is it prudent for the United States to combine a deterrence with a mutual disarmament policy, according to David Gauthier; it is also morally obligatory. His argument depends heavily on a view of morality derived from Thomas Hobbes that Gauthier spells out in his book Morals By Agreement (Oxford: Clarendon Press, 1986). Moral rules are those that it would be mutually advantageous for communities of people to follow. Whereas threat behavior such as the deterrence policy would not occur in a moral community, one bound by such rules, it might well be essential in bringing one about. To bring a moral community into existence, we must each tell the other, "I shall abide by mutually beneficial rules if you do, but not if you refuse. I shall not do so unilaterally because you would then have no reason to enter into a moral community with me but would instead find it profitable simply to take advantage of my restraint." Similarly, nuclear powers will become a moral community only if each entices the others into doing so by offering to disarm only if the others do and to retaliate if the others attack.

Gauthier gives these arguments toward the end of his chapter. The lion's share of his work is devoted to showing that disarmament and deterrence can be rational actions in spite of certain puzzles. The first puzzle is that nuclear powers such as the United States and Soviet Union are in a Prisoner's Dilemma situation vis-à-vis the retention of nuclear arms. In trying individually to do what is best for itself, each superpower seems poised to bring on a disastrous situation for both. Gauthier terms

*this the disarmament dilemma. Another dilemma for nuclear powers
arises when they try to decide whether to maintain a policy of deterrence.
This second problem, called the deterrence dilemma, is not a Prisoner's
Dilemma situation. Instead, to borrow an analogy from Douglas Lackey,
the deterrence dilemma consists in the fact that deterrence resembles a
game of chicken in which winning depends upon appearing more
irrational than one's opponent.*

Thinking about war in the nuclear age is difficult. One source of this
difficulty is the complexity of modern weaponry. Another is the unimagin-
ability of full-scale nuclear war. Were there such a war, the survivors, if any,
would not find it unimaginable, but for us, now, it falls too far beyond
anything we have experienced. Let us hope that it always remains so, but
let us not forget how our inability to imagine nuclear war limits our reactions.

A third source of difficulty in thinking about nuclear war involves analyzing
the strategic structure of interaction among nations with opposed interests
but similar nuclear capacities. One feature of this analysis is that it reveals,
almost immediately, some quite simple but deeply puzzling features of our
conception of practical rationality. This is my primary theme—to examine
what I shall call the rational dilemmas of deterrence and disarmament. But
there is at least one other source of difficulty in thinking about nuclear war,
which is that our ordinary moral ideas and rules have not been shaped as
guides for such an apocalyptic possibility. I shall not ignore the morality of
deterrence and disarmament, although what I shall say about them will
follow from what I shall first try to establish about their rationality.

THE RATIONAL DILEMMAS OF
DETERRENCE AND DISARMAMENT

Let us begin with the dilemmas, for it is here that philosophic thinking
can make a contribution that requires neither a technical understanding nor
an imaginative insight to which I, as a philosopher, could make no special
claim. These dilemmas, I must emphasize, need not arise whenever deterrence
or disarmament is an issue. Rather, they relate to extreme cases, in which
many of the usual characteristics of international interaction get stripped
away. But discussion of nuclear war has been unable to avoid these extreme
cases.[1] The deterrence dilemma threatens the credibility of deterrence policies;
the disarmament dilemma threatens the practicability of disarmament policies.
What, then, are these dilemmas?

The deterrence dilemma exhibits the seeming irrationality of threat behavior; I exhibit its structure in Figure 12.1. Party A chooses whether or
not to attack Party B, which then chooses whether or not to retaliate. The
dilemma arises for B, which seeks a strategy to deter A from attacking. For
deterrence to be a concern, B must believe that A prefers, or at least may

Figure 12.1 The deterrence dilemma

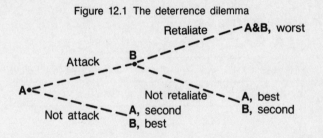

prefer, an unretaliated attack to no attack. Otherwise, B would have nothing to deter. Furthermore, B must believe that A would prefer no attack to an attack with retaliation. Otherwise, B would have nothing with which to deter. B wants to deter A from attacking by threatening to retaliate against an attack.

In itself, B's concern to deter does not create a dilemma. For B to have such a concern, it must prefer not to be attacked; if B prefers to retaliate if attacked rather than not to retaliate, then its only problem would be to get A to recognize B's preferences. But if B prefers not to retaliate if attacked, supposing that retaliation does it no good, or at least insufficient good to outweigh the harm of escalating conflict by retaliating, then B faces a dilemma. To deter A, B must credibly threaten to retaliate if attacked, although B prefers not to retaliate. Thus, a threat would be seemingly irrational. If A believes B to be rational, then A will reason that if attacked, B will not retaliate; thus, B's deterrent threat will lack credibility.

Successful deterrence would protect B from attack; thus, B acts rationally in seeking to deter A. But B can succeed, it seems, only if A believes that B is prepared to act irrationally and retaliate should its deterrent threat fail, and B may have no way of inducing A to believe this, short of actually being willing to retaliate.

The deterrence dilemma arises from a conflict between intention and possible action. It seems rational for B to intend retaliation if attacked because such an intention, communicated to A, minimizes B's risk of being attacked and so yields B its best outcome. But it does not seem rational for B actually to retaliate if attacked because such an action yields B's worst outcome. How can B rationally form an intention believing, even at the time of formation, that it would not be rational to carry the intention out?

The disarmament dilemma is structurally quite different from the deterrence dilemma and takes a form now familiar in the literature of rational choice and also moral philosophy—the form of a Prisoner's Dilemma. I exhibit the structure of the deterrence dilemma in Figure 12.2. Each party chooses whether or not to disarm and makes its choice independently of the other. Should the choices be fully interdependent, so that both parties must disarm together or not at all, then there is no dilemma; disarmament is straightforwardly best.

Each party has the same preferences for the four possible outcomes relative to its own position. Each party prefers most to be the sole armed power.

Figure 12.2 The disarmament dilemma

	B	
	Disarm	Not disarm
A Disarm	Mutual second best	A, worst; B, best
Not disarm	A, best; B, worst	Mutual third best

Each party has mutual disarmament as its second preference and mutual armament as its third. Each party least prefers to be the sole disarmed power. This ordering reflects the desire of each to be dominant and the fears, on the one hand, of war provoked by mutual armament and, on the other hand, of being dominated.[2] Given these preferences each party prefers not to disarm whatever the other does; remaining armed enables the party to avoid being dominanted if the other party remains armed, and to be dominant if the other party disarms. So it seems that each party acts rationally in not disarming. But the outcome, both parties agree, is less desirable than mutual disarmament. Hence the dilemma—rational behavior leads to a mutually undesirable outcome.

The disarmament dilemma arises from a conflict between action and possible outcome. There is an outcome—mutual disarmament—that both parties prefer to the one that by seemingly rational action they bring into being. More technically, the conflict is between choosing a dominant course of action and attaining an optimal outcome. A course of action is dominant if it is a party's best response whatever the other party chooses. Not disarming is dominant. An outcome is optimal if no alternative is preferred by all parties. The outcome if neither disarms is not optimal; both prefer mutual disarmament. It seems irrational for two parties to end up with an outcome that is not optimal; both are needlessly disadvantaged. But it seems irrational for any party not to choose a dominant course of action; the party is needlessly disadvantaged.

To think about war in the nuclear age we must think about these dilemmas. But when faced with a dilemma, we are not likely to know what to think. However sophisticated our understanding of the technology of nuclear weaponry, and however imaginative our conception of nuclear holocaust, we do not thereby resolve the dilemmas of deterrence and disarmament. We need more thought, more reflection about rationality.

But first, let us ask about the applicability of our discussion. I assume that it is plausible to think of such nations as the United States and the Soviet Union as facing these dilemmas. Now one very reasonable response, if one faces a dilemma, is to endeavor to restructure one's situation so that it disappears. Thus, one seeks a deterrent response that one can plausibly represent, to a potential attacker, as one's preferred choice in the face of attack. One also seeks a disarmament strategy that can be fully mutual—a lock-step procedure in which each party can link its actions with those of the other, so that each can be sure that it disarms if and only if the other does. In this way, the possibilities of being either dominant or dominated are removed.

One may go farther. The dilemmas arise out of certain perceptions that nations have of each other and that lead to the fear that one is in danger of being attacked by a power that seeks forcible dominance. These perceptions may be accurate. But they are dangerous. A nation will want to be sure that it does not mistakenly perceive others, or behave so that others misperceive it, in ways that give rise to fears that invite deterrence and preclude mutual disarmament.[3]

If I thought that by appropriate restructuring and reorientation, the United States and the Soviet Union could move beyond the impasses of the dilemmas, then I should think it unprofitable and even undesirable to continue discussing them. For we should not needlessly complicate thinking about war and the avoidance of war in the nuclear age. But I believe instead that the dilemmas frustrate our thinking about deterrence and disarmament policies. Therefore, as a philosopher I find myself concerned with problems about rationality that, as a citizen, seem to me to have serious practical implications.

PRACTICAL RATIONALITY

I return to my concern with rationality. I shall address these questions: Is deterrence rational? Is disarmament rational? In addressing them, I shall assume that deterrence and disarmament involve interactions that give rise to the dilemmas that I have sketched. However, I shall begin by setting the dilemmas to one side. Let us define a deterrence policy simply as "retaliate if attacked," and let us define a disarmament policy as "disarm if you expect the other party (or parties) to disarm." Now if we set the dilemmas aside, we may suppose that a nation can adopt, and make credible its adoption of, one or both of these policies. We ignore the fact that each seems to commit one to be conditionally prepared to perform a dispreferred action— to retaliate if attacked or to disarm if one expects others to disarm. Or perhaps we bypass this by adopting the fiction that in choosing a policy one ties one's hands, leaving no choice but to carry it out.

In the usual maximizing view of practical rationality, an agent, faced with a choice, explicitly or implicitly determines an expected value or utility for each alternative and selects one with the greatest expected value. Although the dilemmas raise problems for this view, it is, I believe, the only plausible account of practical rationality. This view simply requires fine-tuning to remove the dilemmas. Rationality is instrumental; the rational person is the one who acts to realize what she or he values to the fullest extent possible. Let us apply this view to answer our questions.

Is deterrence a rational policy? Compare it with acquiescence. An acquiescence policy is "do not retaliate if attacked." The benefit of a deterrence policy is that it reduces the probability of being attacked. The cost is that the policy increases the probability of retaliation. To evaluate deterrence in relation to acquiescence, we need to make some estimate of these probabilities.

We also need to make some estimate of the relative values, to the would-be deterrer, of the three possible outcomes—not being attacked, being attacked with no retaliation, and being attacked with retaliation.

Different estimates yield different results. Roughly speaking, we balance the expectation of success against the cost of failure. But as a philosopher my business is not to make such estimates, and in any event, sensible estimates will vary for differing circumstances. Hence, my conclusion is a simple one. A policy of deterrence may or may not have a greater expected value than a policy of acquiescence, depending on the particular context. That deterrence offers a better chance of the best outcome—no attack—is not enough to support this policy. That it may lead to the worst possible outcome—attack plus retaliation—whereas acquiescence avoids it, is not enough to condemn deterrence. What matters is its expected value, which may or may not be greater than that of any alternative, and so a deterrence policy may or may not be rational.

I shall argue that the deterrence dilemma does not affect this conclusion. Thus, it may be rational to threaten—and if necessary to carry out—retaliation against nuclear attack, even though such retaliation is not in itself preferred. But I am not therefore offering a blanket endorsement of any actual deterrence policies. They may have lesser expected values than the corresponding acquiescence policies or than other alternative policies. In any real case, one must consider how much one improves one's prospect of avoiding attack by adopting a deterrence policy and how undesirable retaliation to an attack would be in comparison with acquiescence. For all I know, the resulting calculations may tell against any actual deterrence policy.

Is disarmament a rational policy? Compare it with unconditional refusal to disarm. The benefit of a disarmament policy is that if there is some chance that the other party is also a conditional disarmer, then there is a genuine prospect that mutual disarmament will be achieved. The cost is that the policy creates the possibility of mistaken unilateral disarmament, on the erroneous expectation that the other party will disarm. Without some estimate of the probability that the other party actually is a conditional disarmer, as opposed to the probability that one mistakenly believes this, and of the relative values of the possible outcomes—mutual disarmament, no disarmament, unilateral disarmament—we cannot say whether a disarmament policy has greater expected value than unconditional refusal to disarm. But a disarmament policy may.

I shall argue that the disarmament dilemma does not affect this conclusion. But I am not therefore offering a blanket endorsement of any real-world disarmament proposals. Circumstances may be such that the risks inherent in adopting such proposals would outweigh their expected benefits. Let me emphasize that although a disarmament policy could result in mistaken unilateral disarmament, the policy aims at multilateral disarmament. Nothing in my argument supports a policy calling for unilateral disarmament.

Figure 12.3 Case in which my situation depends on you

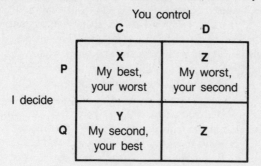

KAVKA'S CASE

Deterrence and disarmament may be the best policies. But that one's best policy may commit one to performing a dispreferred act leading to one's worst outcome may seem more than paradoxical. It may seem self-contradictory. For, it may be argued, consider any policy involving such a commitment. Replace the policy with one that is identical except that where the original policy calls for a dispreferred act, the new policy calls for the most preferred act—the one with greatest expected value. Surely the new policy must be equally as good as the original one where the two agree and better where they differ.

This argument is fallacious, and understanding precisely why will help us resolve the dilemmas of deterrence and disarmament. Let P and Q be two policies, identical in their prescriptions in all circumstances except C, where P calls for act x with greatest expected value, and Q for y with lesser expected value. Now if one's probability of being in C were unaffected by one's choice of policy, then it would of course be the case that P would be the better policy. But suppose that whether I am in C depends on what you do. You can act so that I am in C, or in some alternative circumstance D, in which both P and Q call for act z. I illustrate this in Figure 12.3. Suppose that although we both prefer y to z, you prefer z to x, whereas I prefer x to y. If you believe that I have adopted Q, calling for y in C, then you will act to ensure that I am in C. If you believe that I have adopted P, calling for x in C, then instead you will act to ensure that I am in D. My choice of policy thus affects the circumstances I find myself in, and because I would prefer the outcome of doing y in C to the outcome of doing z in D, policy Q has greater expected value for me than P, even though P and Q differ only in C, and there P calls for the act with greater expected value.

Some may object that what I have shown is that a person may benefit by adopting a policy that calls for her to perform a dispreferred act. In adopting such a policy, she presumably intends to act in accordance with it, and she benefits from having this intention. But she does not benefit from actually following the policy or carrying out her intention. When the time comes for her to act on her intention, either she has gained the benefit for which she hoped or she has not. Nothing she can now do can affect this. So when the time comes for her to act, then whatever policy she may have adopted, and whatever intention she may have formed, surely, from a rational perspective, she should perform her most preferred act.

Consider an example, which I owe to Gregory Kavka.[4] An eccentric millionaire offers to deposit $100,000 to your bank account at midnight tonight, provided that at that time he believes that you intend to, and actually will, take a pill tomorrow morning that will make you mildly ill for several hours. You are assured, on the best possible medical advice, that this is the only effect the pill will have; you will be nauseous and run a slight fever— nothing more. Let us suppose that it is worth $100,000 to you to be mildly ill tomorrow. So it is rational for you to form the intention to take the pill.

Tomorrow comes. Either the eccentric millionaire has deposited the money in your account or he has not. You will not find out until the bank opens, and you must take the pill, or refuse it, earlier in the morning. But what you do cannot affect whether or not the money is in your account. Surely you would be downright foolish to take the pill. Why endure a few hours sickness for nothing? If taking the pill could affect the millionaire's decision, then you would have good reason to take it, but taking it now can have no such effect. If someone in the same position were to ask you, "Shall I take the pill?" you would surely advise her or him not to do so. Therefore, you have no reason to take it yourself.

But now the same problem arises that I noted in introducing the deterrence dilemma; there is a conflict between intention and action. If you realize, when the millionaire makes the offer, that come tomorrow you will have no reason to take the pill, but instead good reason not to take it, then how can you, today, form the intention to take it? But you must form this intention if the millionaire is to expect you to take the pill and so deposit the money to your account.

It may be urged that frequently we intend to perform some action, or at least to try performing it, knowing that we may be unable or simply unwilling to do it when the time comes. I put off an unpleasant task, forming the intention to do it tomorrow, even though I have some doubt that I will then bring myself to do it. So can't you form the intention to take the pill, even though you doubt that you will carry it out? Such an intention might do you little good; the millionaire, sharing your doubt, might not put any money into your bank account. But this apart, can you form the intention? For it is not that you have some doubt that you will actually bring yourself to carry it out. It seems that you have no doubt at all that, come tomorrow, it would be positively unreasonable for you to take the pill. Surely, you have no doubt that you will not do something that, at the time, you will neither desire to do nor think reasonable to do. You might enlist the services of a professional hypnotist in the hope that you could bring yourself to take the pill as the result of posthypnotic suggestion, but this would not be, in any ordinary sense, to form an intention to take the pill, even if you bring it about that you have the intention.

Suppose then that you cannot form the intention to take the pill even though if you could, it would be advantageous for you to do so. Now apply this conclusion to our dilemmas. It seems that you cannot adopt a policy that may require you to choose a dispreferred action, for the same reason that you cannot form an intention to take the pill. Adopting the policy requires forming the intention to act in accordance with it, and this you cannot do. Granted that it would be beneficial for you to adopt the policy if you could; the fact is, or so it seems, that you cannot.

This may seem regrettable. But many inabilities are regrettable. One could frequently expect to benefit if one could perform actions that are beyond one's powers. But one's powers are limited, and one limitation, although perhaps not one of which we are usually aware, has to do with the capacity to form intentions. One cannot just form the intention to do anything at all. In particular, one cannot form the intention to do what one believes that one would neither desire nor have reason to do.

If we accept this argument, then we have resolved the dilemmas of deterrence and disarmament. Neither is a possible policy whenever its adoption would commit its holder, should certain conditions come about, to do something that he or she cannot do—in the case of deterrence, to retaliate when he or she would prefer to acquiesce; in the case of disarmament, to disarm when the holder would prefer to remain armed.

RETHINKING KAVKA'S CASE

But how strange that it is not possible for us to adopt policies that, could we but adopt them, would be in our interest, and that do not call for actions exceeding our physical or mental capacities. Let us reconsider the argument of the preceding section. So let us rethink Kavka's example. Perhaps it is not downright foolish for you to take the pill. Consider how you might respond to someone asking you why you were taking it. You might say that it had been to your advantage to commit yourself to taking the pill, that committing yourself and then carrying out your commitment were clearly better than not committing yourself at all, and now you are simply carrying out your commitment. You could point out that if you did not take the pill, then given that the circumstances are just what you anticipated in making the commitment, you could not really have committed yourself.

Could you say more? Suppose that when the eccentric millionaire offered you the opportunity, you realized that a bondage freak would have no problem arranging to take the pill the following morning. Before midnight, she (or he) would lock herself into her favorite chains, so arranging it that a time-release device would drop the pill into her mouth—wired open— the next morning, and only later would a further device drop the key into a position from which she could reach it to unlock her chains. Now you, unless you are a bondage freak, would no doubt find this unpleasant—but for $100,000? If the millionaire allowed you this method of committing yourself to take the pill, would it not be rational for you to adopt it in lieu of a better one?

But of course there is a better method (for those of us who are not bondage freaks). You can avoid the cost of being chained up all night with your mouth wired open. You can simply make up your mind to take the pill no matter what. If it would be rational for you to undergo some real unpleasantness to ensure your taking the pill, then is it not rational for you to adopt a procedure that leads to your taking the pill without incurring that cost? The least costly procedure is simply to commit yourself.

Resorting to bondage would be a way of denying yourself the choice between taking and not taking the pill. If you believe that, given the choice, you would not take the pill, then you would want to deny yourself the choice. But if you would want to deny yourself the choice rather than choose not to take the pill, then is it not rational for you to choose to take it, rather than either denying yourself the choice at some cost or choosing not to take it? If it is not downright foolish, but rather perfectly sensible, to force the pill on yourself at some cost, then is it not even more sensible, and not foolish at all, simply to choose to take the pill? Is it not an irrational inability to resist temptation that might lead you not to take it, rather than a determination to choose rationally? I think it is.

KEEPING PROMISES

Rational people can commit themselves to perform a dispreferred action and carry out their commitment. This is my claim. It may seem even more plausible if we consider a very different example. Consider one of our fundamental moral practices—promising.

One might treat promising as a device for coordinating the actions of different persons and for communicating intentions. But the obligatory character of a promise bespeaks something more. One is expected to keep one's promise even if doing so is not in one's interest—not one's preferred or utility-maximizing action. Of course, one's promise does not override all concern with one's interest. If I promise to meet you at the ballgame tomorrow, you would not expect me to endanger my life in order to show up, but you would expect me to decline some more attractive prospect should it present itself. One might then think of promising as a practice from which everyone expects to benefit given that one may expect to gain more on balance as promisee than one loses as promissor. But were this all, it would seem to be in one's interest to accept promises but not to make them. Rather, I suggest, promising is a practice whereby one commits oneself, where it is to one's advantage at the time of making the commitment, to be committed. It is then a device for denying oneself the right to act on some subsequent occasion on one's usual basis of choosing one's most preferred act.

Consider this example. Suppose that next week you will help me to harvest my crops, provided you can count on my assistance in harvesting your crops the following week. But at the end of the season I am giving up farming and retiring to Florida; I will have nothing to gain, in terms of future dealings with you or others in our community, by helping you. But it is worth my while to get your help in exchange for helping you. I need a device to commit myself, to give you the assurance that if you help me, I will help you even if, after receiving your assistance, I have nothing further to gain. Promising is just this device. In making a sincere promise, I commit myself to helping you—not, to be sure, no matter what, but despite the usual temptations that may arise. Absent such a device, I have no way of giving you the assurance you need so that I may gain your assistance next week.

Promising, we think, creates a moral obligation, and in this view it does, in the sense that it commits promise-makers to act without regard to their direct preferences. But promising does this because it is advantageous to us to have available a practice of commitment and to be able to put ourselves under obligation. We do not think it downright foolish to carry out our obligations, even if carrying them out runs counter to our interests.

This may seem a low view of promising and its attendant moral obligation. On the contrary, I think this view demystifies promising and its obligatory character. We can see clearly the point of having a practice, adherence to which requires that one be willing to override one's usual concern with fulfilling one's preferences. My analysis does not explain away the obligation, but rather makes it intelligible by placing it within the framework of rationality.

Understanding the existence of and rationale for practices by which we commit ourselves to act in ways that, absent such practices, we should deem irrational—ways that lead us to incur costs that do not themselves bring about greater benefits—enables us to understand the rationality and possibility of deterrence and disarmament policies. We resolve the dilemmas of rationality that seem to plague these policies by recognizing that each requires a commitment on the part of the agent to act, given certain conditions, in an otherwise irrational manner, and that the agent may have sufficient reason to undertake such a commitment. A nation faced with the need to deter, or the desire to disarm, does not want to be free to act in its ordinary way because such freedom would prevent it giving some other party the assurance needed to influence its behavior in the way that maximizes the nation's expectation of benefit.

In defending the rationality of deterrence and disarmament policies, in those contexts in which adopting the policies maximizes one's expectation of benefit, I am implicitly advocating a revision in our usual account of rationality. I am arguing that the rationality of a particular action or choice must be judged, not in isolation, but in an appropriate context. Intentions, plans, commitments, and dispositions are all tied to particular choices in ways that rule out certain combinations—one cannot sincerely commit oneself to do x if one is quite sure that one will actually do y. A person disposed to promise-keeping cannot consistently fail to ignore his or her particular promises. Thus, I suppose that although it is indeed rational to seek the greatest fulfillment of one's preferences, it is rational to do this at the level of one's overall set of dispositions, intentions, and particular choices.[5] Hence, one is not rationally prevented from adopting a policy because it calls for particular actions that in themselves run counter to one's preferences. The apparent dilemmas of deterrence and disarmament arise from an inadequate understanding of rationality. If agents expect to do best by adopting a deterrence or disarmament policy, then it is rational for them to do so, and it is within their capacity to form and to carry out any necessary commitments to particular dispreferred actions.

INTEGRATING DETERRENCE
WITH DISARMAMENT

Before turning explicitly to the morality of deterrence and disarmament policies, I want to examine some of their effects and the linkages among them. A successful deterrence policy is primarily redistributive, making the deterring party better off and the deterred party worse off than they would otherwise have been. An unsuccessul deterrence policy is mutually costly, leading to the outcome least preferred by both parties. Thus, there need be no possible net gain, but there must be a possible net loss, from a deterrence policy. A disarmament policy is productive and cooperative. If successful, it makes both parties better off than had they remained armed. If unsuccessful, a disarmament policy either preserves the status quo—not expecting the other to disarm, one remains armed oneself—or is redistributive—one party mistakenly disarms unilaterally, making it worse off and the other better off than they would otherwise have been. Therefore, there need be no possible net loss, but there must be a possible net gain, from a disarmament policy.

This difference between deterrence and disarmament policies suggests that we should evaluate the need for each very differently. To resort to deterrence must be unwelcome, whereas to participate in mutual disarmament should be welcome. Both policies may be rational, but the rationality of a policy in given circumstances is one thing; the desirability of the circumstances, and hence the rationality of seeking or continuing them, is quite another. It is obviously rational to avoid, prevent, or terminate the circumstances that would make deterrence rational, whereas it is equally rational to seek or maintain the circumstances in which disarmament is rational. A rational deterrence policy thus looks to its own supercession—to ending the danger of an attack against which the best defense is the threat to retaliate. That it would be costly to carry out the threat makes it an unwelcome mode of defense, even when rational. Thus, to suppose that a situation of mutual deterrence should be considered stable and desirable would be quite mistaken. On the other hand, a rational disarmament policy looks to its own realization— to converting a conditional willingness to disarm if others may be expected to do likewise into an actual willingness because others are equally willing.

The need to resort to a deterrence policy should be a strong spur to the adoption of a disarmament policy. Recognizing that in existing circumstances, one's best defense involves making a threat that one would clearly not want to carry out, one sees the need for transforming these circumstances. The surest transformation, if existing weaponry is such as to make deterrence rational, is to do away, multilaterally, with the weaponry. A nation that believes that because it can deter, it does not need to be willing to disarm, is pursuing a deeply irrational policy.

But if the need to resort to deterrence should lead to awareness of the rationality of mutual disarmament, the success of a rational disarmament policy may itself be furthered by the existence of a rational deterrence policy. The prospect of achieving mutual disarmament depends not only on saying, "I will disarm if I expect that you will," but also on reminding, "And I will not disarm if I expect that you will not." The most effective way of emphasizing this reminder may involve a firm policy of deterrence; thus, one says both "I will if you will" and "I will not, and what's more I'll surely retaliate, if you will not, and I will think then that you may attack." The need to deter thus creates an incentive for oneself to be willing to disarm, and the willingness to deter then creates an incentive for the other party to be willing to disarm. Neither of these incentives should be overlooked.

Thus, deterrence and disarmament can and should be viewed as linked policies, in precisely the way advocated four hundred years ago by Thomas Hobbes, when he said that "it is a precept, or generall rule of Reason, That every man, ought to endeavour Peace, as farre as he has hope of obtaining it; and when he cannot obtain it, that he may seek, and use, all helps, and advantages of Warre."[6] To seek peace is to be willing to disarm if others also are willing. To use all advantages of war is to be willing to retaliate if others attack. The costs of having to resort to the advantages of war should prevent one from being remiss in seeking peace. The willingness, nevertheless, to resort to those advantages should encourage others not to be remiss in seeking peace.

The lesson here is hard to learn and one that, in the real world, has yet to be learned sufficiently. There has been little serious attention given to the development of a policy that would integrate deterrence and disarmament. Such a policy would aim at bringing about a stable condition of multilateral disarmament in which the danger of nuclear warfare would be minimized in the long run and in which our present dependence on deterrence would be ended, not by abandoning deterrence unilaterally, but by using the commitment to deter in the absence of any better alternative as a means to motivate the agreement to provide such an alternative through disarming. We should deter in order to be able to disarm and then disarm so that we should no more need to deter.

MORALITY AND RATIONALITY

The link between deterrence and disarmament may help us understand their morality. This is my final theme, and I must be brief and, in one sense, dogmatic. For I shall have to appeal to a conception of morality that, given the scope of this chapter, I cannot defend here, although I do develop and defend it elsewhere.[7] I do not suppose that this conception, or its implications, will sit comfortably with everyone. Persons have radically different views, not only of the requirements and prohibitions of morality, but also of the appropriate way of grounding these requirements and prohibitions. Those who understand morality as based on divine command, or on natural rights, or on the greatest happiness of the greatest number, may all find my position unconvincing. But I cannot argue with these persons here. All that I can do is to sketch why I believe that a disarmament policy may be morally required and a deterrence policy morally acceptable when and insofar as each is rationally justifiable.

I have shown that there can be circumstances in which it is not only rational to commit onself to deterrence or to disarmament, but irrational not so to commit oneself because commitment would offer one a better prospect than any alternative. I now want to insist that whatever morality may require or prohibit, it does not contravene rationality. In principle, morality may extend beyond rationality in prohibiting actions that are rationally permissible and requiring actions whose omissions are not rationally forbidden. But morality may not require actions that are rationally forbidden or prohibit those that are rationally required. A morality that would do either of these latter things would be irrational and therefore mistaken.

How precisely does morality relate to rationality? I have shown that in some circumstances it is rational to dispose oneself to act in ways that need not be in one's interest. One such way, relevant to our present concern, is promise-keeping, and this offers us the appropriate clue. Moral requirements override the pursuit of one's interests or the endeavor to fulfill one's preferences. But not all cases in which the pursuit of one's own interest is overridden constitute moral requirements. It would be peculiar to suppose that, in Kavka's example, you would be morally required to take the pill. When the pursuit of one's own interests is overridden for the benefit of others, we speak naturally of moral requirements. Such requirements are endorsed by reason in just the way we have seen in our discussion of promising. Insofar as people may expect to benefit by a practice that requires them not to act directly to further their own particular interests, then where that practice benefits others, it is not only rational but also moral.

This gives us a test for correct moral practices. For we need not and should not suppose that all of the practices, with their sundry requirements and prohibitions, that we have come to accept as part of our everyday morality will in fact receive the necessary seconding of reason. The true morality, in my view, is constituted by the set of mutually advantageous constraints on individual preference-satisfaction.

It is now easy to see that a willingness to disarm, if others are also willing, may well be a requirement of morality. For to refuse is to reject a constraint that if accepted by everyone, benefits each. My willingness to disarm promotes your good, just as your willingness promotes mine. Thus, if I am unwilling, I am giving in to the temptation to be a free-rider, to take advantage of others if they disarm, and to refuse to cooperate with them in bringing about a mutually beneficial state of affairs.

I want to praise the morality of mutual disarmament. But I also want to allay concern about the morality of deterrence, in those circumstances in which a deterrence policy is rationally adopted. This should not be surprising, given the way in which the policies are related. But let me argue the point directly. In the view of the morality I espouse, we may think of a moral community as a group of persons linked to each other by the mutually advantageous constraints needed for cooperation and sociability to be gen- uinely possible. Within such a community, deterrence would have no place, for it is a form of threat behavior, and one of the constraints that would surely be operative would be a prohibition of threats. To be sure, such a ban would not operate alone. The point of a deterrent threat is to prevent attack; within a moral community each person or party would be constrained from attacking or more generally from seeking to dominate or to control other community members. A moral community embraces free and auton- omous individuals who respect and value each other's freedom and autonomy.

It is surely apparent that in the real world of nations, a moral community is in many cases limited or even absent. It would be foolish to suppose that the rules constraining behavior within such a community apply straight- forwardly outside it. We must make Hobbes's distinction between validity *in foro interno* and *in foro externo*. Although the rules of a moral community are *in foro interno* valid—they represent the possibility of mutually advan- tageous and rational cooperation and sociability among both individual persons and nations—yet these rules are not therefore *in foro externo* valid; people who put these rules into direct practice where they are not followed by others would simply worsen their own position[8] and would more likely be victims of those who do not comply.

If we now ask how we might best bring about a moral community, where none initially exists, then it is plausible to suppose that such a community requires not only a willingness to abide by mutually beneficial constraints, but also a clear refusal to do so unilaterally. For if I am willing to constrain myself whether or not you do, then you have no initial incentive to join in a moral community with me. Instead, I simply make it easier for you to dominate me and to survive without putting yourself under any constraints in the pursuit of your own interest.

This suggests a general defense that may be offered for policies that would rightly be condemned within a moral community as admissible and even necessary if one is to bring such a community into being. But there are more particular considerations to note about deterrence. It is tempting to suppose that given the horrific consequences of escalating nuclear war by retaliation, the cost is so great that the risk of deterrence failure can never outweigh the benefit of preventing attack. But although the failure of deterrence, given a commitment to retaliate, does escalate nuclear war, the willingness to acquiesce without retaliation is no guarantee that such war will be avoided.

Let us return, briefly and speculatively, to the real-world situation. Some talk as if, were the United States to renounce its nuclear arsenal, then the threat of nuclear war would vanish because the Soviet Union would not use nuclear weapons against a non-nuclear opponent. But even now, several other nations have the capacity to engage in large-scale nuclear warfare, and their number must be expected to increase. It is surely in the strong interest of the United States to try preventing any outbreak of nuclear conflict as well as to avoid participating in such conflict itself. To that end, it is in the strong interest of the United States to promote multilateral nuclear disarmament. But, I believe, the United States can do this effectively only if it does not unilaterally renounce its own nuclear weapons or commit itself never to use them. I return to the idea that a deterrence policy is an incentive to others to move beyond deterrence and more generally beyond the development of and reliance on a nuclear arsenal. The hard truth here is that only a power willing to use nuclear weapons in some circumstances may expect to play a significant role in moving the world away from those circumstances in which nuclear weapons might be used.

Hence, I have an operational test of both the rationality and the morality of a policy about nuclear weapons. Does it offer the best chance, all things considered, of moving the world away from those circumstances in which nuclear war might become a reality? That such a policy may involve short-run risks of the very war it would avoid, and that it may require us to embrace those risks in a way that, however rational, must be profoundly unwelcome, is one of the somber lessons that must be drawn from an analysis of the structure and relations of deterrence and disarmament policies.

CONCLUSION

In thinking about war in the nuclear age, we have found ourselves faced with fundamental questions about practical rationality. We also have found ourselves faced with fundamental questions about the grounds of morality. We should not be surprised to find that we must rethink our view of rationality and our understanding of morality in order to deal with the issues that nuclear war poses. Only after such rethinking can we expect to provide a framework within which a concrete and informed discussion of policies about war and weapons can proceed. That framework has been my concern, in endeavoring to show what tests we should employ to decide whether a deterrence policy or a disarmament policy is either rational or moral. I conclude with the reminder that nothing I have said can be applied directly to assess real-world policies. Without much more particular knowledge, we cannot say, for example, whether the United States has run undue risks in its deterrence postures or shown undue hesitation in its disarmament efforts. These are questions that must be addressed, not so much to praise or condemn what has been done, as to chart the future course that can best establish the moral community of humankind in the nuclear age.

NOTES

1. Indeed, even the U.S. secretary of defense focuses on the extreme: "The policy of deterrence is difficult for some to grasp because it is based on a paradox." Caspar Weinberger, letter of August 23, 1982, in *New York Review of Books*, November 4, 1982, p. 27.

2. If we remove the desire to dominate, so that each prefers mutual disarmament to being the sole armed power, then we transform the situation into a form of the Assurance Game. More attention should be paid to this structure in examining the problems of disarmament.

3. Misperception characteristically leads one party to perceive the other's preferences as they would be in a Prisoner's Dilemma rather than as in an Assurance Game (see note 2).

4. See Gregory S. Kavka, "The Toxin Puzzle," *Analysis* 43 (1983):33–36.

5. This scratches the surface of very complex and controversial issues about maximizing rationality that I cannot pursue here. For some first words on the issues, see my *Morals by Agreement* (Oxford: Clarendon Press, 1986), pp. 182–187.

6. Thomas Hobbes, *Leviathan* (London, 1651), Ch. 14.

7. See, especially, Gauthier, *Morals by Agreement*.

8. Hobbes, *Leviathan*, Ch. 15.

13

Prisoners and Chickens

DOUGLAS P. LACKEY

Douglas Lackey disagrees with David Gauthier on all counts. First, the United States is not playing Chicken with the USSR as far as deterrence policy is concerned. U.S. presidents seem to think that even after a strike, retaliation would be rational, and it is by no means clear that Soviet leaders prefer striking without any reprisal to not striking at all (to strike would be to destroy the things they might covet). Furthermore, it might well be in the U.S. interest to retaliate; perhaps by doing so the United States could prevent the Soviet Union from seizing U.S. territory. Hence, three of the assumptions that must be made if deterrence is to be a game of Chicken are false.

Second, the United States and Soviet Union are not in a Prisoner's Dilemma vis-à-vis disarmament. The NATO powers may well prefer mutual retention of nuclear weapons to mutual disarmament. Offsetting Soviet conventional power with nuclear weapons is cheaper than matching its conventional arsenal. Moreover, Lackey makes the surprising claim that unilateral disarmament would be better for the United States than would bilateral armament.

Lackey also claims that Gauthier has not shown that nuclear deterrence is morally obligatory and unilateral disarmament morally forbidden. Even if retaliatory threats are in the collective best interest, it does not follow that they are obligatory, and even if the threat of retaliation is obligatory, it does not follow that retaliation itself is.

David Gauthier has a longstanding interest in the theory of games and in decision theory, and it is only natural that he should try to apply the insights of these disciplines to problems of nuclear weapons policy. This he has attempted to do in two recent and interesting analyses, "Deterrence, Maximization, and Rationality," (DMR) *Ethics* (April 1984), and "War and Nuclear Deterrence," first published in this volume. Roughly speaking, the focus of the earlier analysis is on nuclear deterrence; the later analysis addresses both deterrence and the nuclear arms race. Gauthier's argument implies that in certain conditions, conditions that many responsible parties believe presently to exist, nuclear deterrence is a game of Chicken and the nuclear arms race is a Prisoner's Dilemma. Given what he believes about Chicken and the Prisoner's Dilemma, he concludes that it is rational and moral to continue practicing nuclear deterrence and irrational and immoral to engage in unilateral nuclear disarmament. Any analysis of Gauthier's views, then, must address three issues: Is nuclear deterrence really a game of Chicken, and are the nuclear superpowers really in a Prisoner's Dilemma as regards nuclear weapons possession? Second, if we are playing Chicken and if we are in a Prisoner's Dilemma, are Gauthier's instructions as to how we should behave in these situations rationally justifiable? Third, if we are playing Chicken and if we are in a Prisoner's Dilemma and if Gauthier's instructions as to how we should behave in these situations are rationally justifiable, can we infer that rational conduct in these situations is also morally acceptable conduct?

WHAT GAMES ARE WE PLAYING?

Is This Chicken?

The analysis of nuclear deterrence as Chicken goes back to Bertrand Russell's *Common Sense and Nuclear Warfare* (1959), in which Russell described Chicken as a game played by "elder statesmen and youthful degenerates."[1] Two cars deliberately speed toward each other head on. Each driver thinks that his best outcome is not swerving when the other swerves; his next best, swerving when the other swerves; his third best, swerving when the other does not; and his worst outcome, not swerving when the other does not. Russell noticed that this game was like mutual nuclear deterrence, in which each nation would prefer most to attack without being counterattacked; would prefer next to not attack if the other does not attack; would prefer next to be attacked without counterattacking; and would prefer least to be attacked and then to counterattack. (The reason why not counterattacking after a nuclear first strike is preferred to counterattacking is that such a counterattack is, according to Russell, "useless revenge.")

At the time, Thomas Schelling and others[2] noticed that this situation created a paradox as regards the rationality of threatening to counterattack. If your opponent, studying your own preference schedule, becomes confident that you will not counterattack when attacked, then your opponent, gunning for his or her best outcome, will attack, giving you your third best outcome. On the other hand, if you credibly threaten to counterattack when attacked, this will force your opponent to not attack, giving you your second best outcome. Given that your second best outcome beats your third, it seems ineluctably rational to threaten counterattacking when attacked. But now suppose that your opponent does not believe your threats and chooses to attack. If you stick by your threats, given what your opponent does, the result is your fourth best outcome, which is worse than your third.

If you are rational and free to choose what to do when the opponent attacks, you always will choose not to counterattack. Thus, your threats are never credible, and your opponent is free to attack if you are free to choose. Schelling's celebrated solution to this credibility problem was "the threat that leaves something to chance." If the decision to counterattack when attacked is automated, then the opponent cannot count on your free and rational choice not to respond. Because rationally you do not wish to respond when attacked and because it is not necessary to threaten an absolutely certain response in order to deter the opponent, Schelling's analysis suggests that the best strategy is not only automatic but randomized. One of the more exquisite results of decision-theoretic analysis in the late 1950s is that simple formulas determine the correct randomization ratios for "counterattack" and "do not counterattack" in this automated response, given what the opponent would hope to gain from attacking without being attacked and what the opponent would hope to lose by attacking and then suffering counterattack.[3]

Now what is historically relevant about Schelling's line of thought is that it was never incorporated into mainstream strategic thinking by those U.S. decisionmakers who could have chosen to implement it. Part of the reason for this lack of enthusiasm was that the notion of a threat that leaves something to chance was (perhaps unfairly) associated with the brinkmanship of John Foster Dulles, and, in the light of developing Soviet nuclear capacity, brinkmanship in the late 1950s was falling out of fashion. (It revived in October 1962.) The automated threat idea was also discredited by its Grand Guignol development into the doomsday machine described in Herman Kahn's *On Thermonuclear War* (Princeton, 1960); Kahn hypothesized that the perfect deterrent would be a credible device that would automatically blow up the world in the event of nuclear attack. But easily the strongest motive for not introducing automation and randomization into nuclear choices was the understandable reluctance of key decisionmakers to adopt policies that would put normally controllable actions beyond control at certain points in time. Presidents who precommit the nation to an automated and randomized chance of using nuclear weapons render themselves powerless to control events at the most crucial moment in U.S. history. Presumably persons who seek the presidency enjoy power. They are hardly likely to welcome or comprehend suggestions that in the deterrence game, impotence is bliss. Parallel psychological observations apply to the Soviet leadership.

I am not saying that Schelling's suggestions necessarily require the automation and randomization of Kahn's doomsday machine. On the contrary, it might be possible to develop a posture that gives the president the power to control the decision to use nuclear weapons, but that also acknowledges and publicizes the fact that in the radioactive fog of modern war there is a certain likelihood that U.S. nuclear weapons will be used even in the face of explicit presidential (or National Command Authority) orders to desist. The ineliminable chance of such unauthorized use might be high enough to provide a credible deterrent against Soviet or Warsaw Pact attack. But it does not seem that U.S. leaders around 1960 thought of "the threat that leaves something to chance" along these lines, nor did they design command and control systems to facilitate what came to be known as "the rationality of irrationality."

What John Kennedy, Robert McNamara, William Kaufmann, and Daniel Ellsberg sought to do when they replaced Massive Retaliation with Flexible Response was to design nuclear weapons policies that transcended the game of Chicken altogether. To do this, it was necessary to design nuclear second strikes whose launch would be rational in the event of a Soviet first strike. The single-massive-attack option provided to the president in the first single-integrated operational plan of 1960 was replaced by five attack options in the plan of 1962. In 1974, Secretary of Defense James R. Schlesinger broadened the scope of presidential choice by introducing a variety of limited nuclear options over and above the five big strikes of the 1962 plan.[4] On the European front, a succession of presidents repeatedly refused to endorse a pledge of "no first use" of tactical and intermediate-range nuclear weapons. From all this, we can infer that U.S. leaders have believed since 1962 and continue to believe that in the event of Soviet attacks of various types it would be rational to use nuclear weapons, *at that moment*, independently of all prior considerations of deterrence. Indeed, the situations in which U.S. leaders consider it rational to use nuclear weapons are the very situations in which U.S. leaders threaten to use them. If this is so, the United States is not playing Chicken with its nuclear threats. U.S. leaders believe that it is better to counterattack when attacked than to not counterattack when attacked.

This is not the only reason why Chicken is an inappropriate model for nuclear deterrence as it is currently practiced by the superpowers. In Chicken, each player prefers attacking if not counterattacked to not attacking at all. But if the attack in question is a nuclear attack, it is not clear that the Soviets would prefer to launch a nuclear attack, assuming no counterattack, over not launching a nuclear attack at all. Nuclear attacks on land destroy assets that one might seek to exploit, and even in the case of nuclear attacks at sea, it is possible to accomplish everything one might wish to achieve militarily with precision-guided conventional weapons in lieu of nuclear weapons. The Soviets have always presumed the superiority of their conventional forces, which is why they have always been prepared to endorse an agreement for "no first use." Why then would they prefer launching a nuclear attack to launching a conventional attack? Why, indeed, would they prefer any attack on the West at all, given their firsthand knowledge of the horrors of conventional war, and given their need to sell natural gas and maintain trade with freely and thereby eagerly cooperating Western states?

A person who maintains that Chicken correctly models the present superpower confrontation must maintain that, regardless of leadership beliefs, presently planned nuclear responses in fact are not rational, when assessed after a first strike and independently of prior considerations concerning deterrence. But current plans contain a wide variety of nuclear responses to a wide variety of Soviet provocations. What is the argument that *every one* of these responses is irrational? Clearly some of them are irrational, but some might not be. Among the clearly irrational I would include all responses that require a first use of tactical nuclear weapons when the Soviets have used none yet or a first use of strategic weapons when the Soviets have used none yet. But how about using tactical nuclear weapons after the Soviets have already used them and using strategic weapons after the Soviets have already used them? Is it so obvious that all types of these uses are irrational? Will every tit-for-tat response escalate the conflict, or will some tit-for-tat responses persuade the opponent to stop at that level?

Let us consider one of the grisliest first-strike scenarios, in which the USSR launches an all-out counterforce strike against the United States. After the strike, Soviet and Cuban troops, *Red Dawn*–style, prepare to occupy the United States. Assume that, despite everything, one U.S. nuclear submarine remains undestroyed at sea. Would it be irrational for the submarine commander, independently of prior considerations of deterrence, to launch a limited counterforce nuclear attack on the Soviet Union? Perhaps not, if such a strike could forestall the occupation of the United States.

My conclusion is that across a broad spectrum of situations, and independently of prior considerations of deterrence, it would not be irrational to execute nuclear threats. If so, the deterrence game is not a Chicken game. Such executions of nuclear threats in nearly all cases would be immoral, but that is another matter.

Is This a Prisoner's Dilemma?

Gauthier and nearly all authors who write about the nuclear arms race assume that the present situation as regards nuclear weapons acquisition and possession is a Prisoner's Dilemma. In this view, it is better for neither side to possess nuclear weapons than for both sides to possess them, but it is best for each to possess them when the other side does not, and it is worst for each to not possess nuclear weapons when the other side does. This preference pattern forms a Prisoner's Dilemma, and the usual grim results follow, in particular the result that it is better for each to possess nuclear weapons regardless of what the other side does. On the strength of this argument each side chooses to possess. Both sides end up with nuclear weapons, even though each side realizes it would be better off if neither possessed them.

Despite near unanimity on this subject, I do not believe that the Prisoner's Dilemma is the correct model for superpower weapons choices.[5] First, it is not obvious that the NATO countries believe that mutual nonpossession of nuclear weapons is better than mutual possession. When the NATO states decided to introduce tactical and intermediate-range nuclear weapons into NATO forces after the Lisbon meeting in 1953, they did so because they were not prepared, politically or financially, to field enough divisions to offset the strength of Soviet conventional forces. Nuclear weapons were billed as providing more bang for the buck, which made them congenial both to the budget-conscious Eisenhower administration and to Western European leaders, whose sense of the Red Menace was subsiding after the death of Joseph Stalin. It remains true today that NATO states are not prepared to bear the costs of achieving conventional parity in the European theater, even though the gap between NATO conventional strength and Warsaw Pact conventional strength, given recent developments in antitank weaponry, is perhaps smaller now than at any time since the Warsaw Pact was founded in 1955.

Second, although this is much tougher sledding, it is not clear to me that it is preferable for the United States to possess nuclear weapons when the other side possesses them, compared with not possessing them when the other side possesses them.[6] A full test of the rationality of U.S. nuclear possession in the face of Soviet nuclear arms must take into account the full range of costs of nuclear weapons possession for the United States, compared with unilateral nonpossession. These costs include (a) the possibility of involvement in a nuclear war that begins with a first strike or first use by the United States; (b) the possibility of involvement in an all-out, two-sided nuclear war that destroys life on most of the planet; (c) an increased chance of a Soviet first strike intended to preempt a presumed U.S. first strike; (d) the deterioration of U.S. conventional military capability due to a high-tech strategic emphasis focused around nuclear weapons and nuclear delivery systems; (e) the deterioration of the U.S. economy due to a monopoly of top scientific and engineering talent by the strategic weapons fraction of the national research budget; and (f) a decline in civil liberties and in democratic involvement in federal decisionmaking due to the secrecy within which nuclear weapons systems are necessarily enshrouded.

These costs must be carefully weighed against the costs of unilateral nuclear disarmament, of which the most frequently mentioned is a substantially increased chance of nuclear blackmail. A full assessment of the risks of nuclear blackmail cannot be given here,[7] but I must say that I think that these risks have been very much exaggerated. There are few genuine conflicts of interest between the United States and the Soviet Union, conflicts of the sort that would lead to a military confrontation that the Soviet Union would win if it held the nuclear cards. There are, of course, ideological conflicts between the superpowers—we would like to see the Soviet Union out of Afghanistan, off of Poland's back, less repressive toward its own dissidents, and so forth. (I call these "ideological" conflicts because their outcome does not affect U.S. domestic liberty or the U.S. standard of living.) But the current possession of nuclear weapons by the United States does not seem to have intimidated the Soviets into withdrawing from Afghanistan or accepting Solidarity, nor is it likely that there are many new repressive schemes that the Soviets would inflict on their own people in the face of unilateral U.S. nuclear disarmament. On the contrary, the presence of a palpable external nuclear threat only assists the Soviets in the business of domestic repression. Furthermore, one must recognize that what matters in nuclear blackmail is not whether it will be attempted but whether it will succeed, and it will not succeed if we are determined to resist it.

I recognize the heresy in this argument, and I am well aware of the fear that grips Americans at the prospect of unilateral nuclear disarmament. Why then, critics say, the Soviets could destroy the United States in the flicker of an eye. To which comes the obvious reply: They can do that now. If this argument is right, we are not forced into possession by the argument that possession dominates nonpossession, as the noncooperative choice dominates the cooperative choice in a Prisoner's Dilemma. If we acquire and retain nuclear weapons, we do so not on game-theoretic grounds but on the expectations of utility maximization that may well be empirically mistaken.

WHAT IS RATIONAL PLAY?

Chicken and the Deterrence Paradox

Suppose that the preceding arguments are unsound and that nuclear deterrence is indeed a Chicken game. In this view, it is irrational to carry out a threat to counterattack if attacked, assuming that we evaluate the counterattack independently of all prior considerations concerning deterrence. Then the critical problem for decision theory becomes whether or not it is rational to make such threats.

We can make such threats in four ways: We can threaten insincerely, intending not to counterattack when attacked and retaining full capacity to desist if attacked. We can threaten neutrally, not forming an intention to counterattack and not forming an intention not to counterattack. We can threaten sincerely, commiting ourselves to carrying out a counterattack and guaranteeing this commitment by rendering ourselves unable to not counterattack when attacked. Or we can threaten sincerely, forming an intention to counterattack when attacked.

The first sort of threat, essentially a bluff, is recommended by the National Council of Catholic Bishops.[8] Neutral threats were described and recommended by David Fisher in his book *Morality and the Bomb*.[9] The third sort of threat, sincere and helplessly committed, was recommended by Thomas Schelling, and its moral respectability has recently been defended by Daniel Farrell in the first issue of *Public Affairs Quarterly*.[10] The fourth sort, sincere and freely committed, is defended by David Gauthier. What Gauthier says is that if your threat to counterattack is utility maximizing, then it is rational to execute the threat, even though it is not utility maximizing to execute it and even if it is within your power to not execute it. What this means is that if it is utility maximizing for the United States to threaten a nuclear second strike of type A after experiencing a first strike of type B, then in the event of a first strike of type B it is rationally required to launch a second strike of type A, even though *at that time* it would not be utility maximizing to do so.

Despite the attraction of nuclear bluffs, it is exceedingly unlikely that the United States could maintain a policy in which threats of counterattack are completely insincere. The U.S. right wing would discover this policy and call it treason, and the United States would have a new administration in four years or less. Likewise, the option of neutral threats is a nonstarter if we are really playing Chicken; if we leave open the choice of responding or not responding, we will always, when the attack comes, choose not to respond because we have no reason to respond, not even the reason that we have made a prior commitment to do so. If the neutrality of our posture became known, our threats would fail to deter because the opponent would recognize that we would always decide not to carry them out. All real deterrent threats, in a Chicken game, must be sincere threats.

Among sincere threats, the most convincing sort require relinquishing the ability to not execute the threat. For reasons given previously, policies involving such threats have never been popular in Washington, although some strategies have suggested a semiautomated launch-on-warning system as a remedy for ICBM vulnerability. Given the stories that have leaked out during the years and throughout the 1980s about difficulties in the U.S. attack assessment system,[11] there is a justified fear that an automated system might turn sorcerer's apprentice and set off a nuclear attack in response to a nonexistent first strike. Once the disutility of mistaken and accidental launches is added in, it appears likely that automated deterrent threats do not maximize expected value and therefore should not even be made, much less executed.

What about the rationality of sincere threats that involve a commitment to a freely chosen second strike? Here we can reason in three ways. We could argue that because the execution of the threat is irrational, the making of the threat must be irrational, too. This is the standard view. Or we could argue that because the making of the threat is rational, the execution of the threat must be rational as well. The second view is Gauthier's in DMR. The third view is that the rationality of threat-making is logically independent of threat execution.

Because making a threat and executing a threat are distinct events, it would seem to follow that they must be logically independent of each other and that the third view is correct. But if by "making a threat" we mean making a sincere threat that includes forming the intention to execute the threat if conditions warrant, then threat-making and threat execution are logically related. The reason, explicated by Gregory Kavka,[12] is that it is logically impossible to form an intention to do X unless one feels that there will be good reasons to do X when the time comes to do it. One cannot form intentions at will, in the absence of reasons, no more than one can form beliefs at will, in the absence of what one takes to be evidence. For this sort of sincere threat, the threat-making and the threat execution must be both rational or both irrational. But which is it?

Why should we say that if executing such a threat is irrational, making the threat must be irrational as well? The main reason is that rational action is simply utility-maximizing action. If it is clear that executing the threat is not utility maximizing at the time of executing it, then it is not rational to execute the threat, and from this it follows that it is not rational to make the threat. Indeed, in Kavka's view, it is not even possible to make the threat because we cannot form an intention to perform an action that we know will be irrational at the time of performance.

The trouble with this argument is that it seems to work equally well in the opposite direction. If making the threat is utility maximizing, then it is rational to make it, and from this it follows that it would be rational to carry the threat out. Because it would be rational to carry the threat out, it is quite possible to form the intention to carry it out. So far, the result is stalemate.

When Kavka says that executing the threat is irrational and Gauthier says that executing the threat is rational, they are not in fact contradicting each other because they are using the word *rational* in different senses. When Kavka says that executing the threat is irrational, he means simply that executing the threat is not utility maximizing at the time of execution, and Gauthier certainly agrees that it is not utility maximizing *then* to execute the threat. Gauthier is arguing that it is rational to execute the threat because execution follows from a utility-maximizing policy, and Kavka certainly would agree that executing the threat proceeds from a utility-maximizing policy adopted at an earlier point in time. Which sense of rationality is true rationality, the sort that a rational person should follow when subjected to attack?

Gauthier believes that his sense of "rational" is clearly superior because "the fully rational actor is not one who assesses her actions from now but who subjects the largest, rather than the smallest, segments of her activity to primary rational scrutiny, proceeding from policies to performances, letting assessment of the latter be ruled by assessment of the former."[13] The background force of Gauthier's argument is Platonic: If we evaluate from the point of execution, we are bound up in time; if we evaluate from the stretch of time that includes both the threat-making and the threat execution, we are comparatively emancipated from time, looking at things sub specie aeternitatis, as philosophers should. If this is his argument, there are three ways in which it might be going wrong.

The first problem is that the argument assumes a continuity of self through the stretch of time that includes the threat-making and the threat execution. If we are Buddhists or Humeans and believe that things in the universe are loosely connected, then such continuity of self cannot be presumed. We have instead many selves at many points in time, each undertaking a rational evaluation from its own point of view. The same conclusion follows if we endorse a solipsism of the present moment, which seems to have led Aristippus to his view that the truly rational person seeks to maximize the pleasures of each present moment.

The second problem is that Gauthier's view might not be as temporally emancipated as he believes it is. Is it really the case that the person who evaluates the rationality of executing a threat from the time of execution is making the evaluation in a "small" stretch of time, while the person who evaluates the rationality of executing the threat from the standpoint of a policy regarding threat execution is making the evaluation in a "larger" stretch of time? Is it not rather the case that the policy of threat execution is adopted at a certain point in time, the point at which the threat is made, and that this point in time is no "larger" than the point of threat execution? If so, all that Gauthier is arguing is that the evaluation from the earlier point should prevail over the evaluation from the later point. Other things being equal, the preference for the earlier point is odd because at the later point we have more information relevant to the question of what we ought to do, especially the information that an attack has occurred. What, at the point of threat-making, is simply a probability of attack becomes, at the time of threat execution, a certainty of attack. (The wave packet of attack probability collapses at that point!) All that we are doing, at each point in time, is making choices that maximize utility in the future, and to assist us in making these choices we are rationally required to use all the information we can get.

The third and final problem is that it is not self-evident that philosophical wisdom consists in viewing matters sub specie aeternitatis. If time is unreal, then it is indeed wise to adopt this stance, but if time is real, then the stance is unwise.

Consider the following puzzle, suggested by Derek Parfit. You wake up and discover that you are in a hospital, with no memory of what happened the day before. You ask the nurse for information, and she says that her memory is bad but you are one of two persons: Person A, who had a terribly painful operation without anaesthetic the day before and then was hypnotized to forget the whole thing, or Person B, who is due to have a mildly painful operation tomorrow. Which person would you rather be? If you prefer the alternative that maximizes utility in your life, you prefer to be person B. If you prefer the alternative that maximizes utility in the stretch of life that remains before you, you prefer to be person A. Despite his affection, in other contexts, for non-utility-maximizing actions, Gauthier would clearly prefer to be person B. Most people, thinking that what matters are pains and pleasures yet to come, would prefer to be person A. Because such persons prefer lives in which there is more pain over other lives with less pain, ceteris paribus, Gauthier would dismiss the preferences of these persons as irrational.

Nevertheless, it seems to me that it is rational to prefer being person A, the person whose pain is over and done with. The reason is that our standards of rationality judge actions by their effects, and all the effects of an action come after the act. The "choice" in Parfit's example is confusing because it appears that you are given a choice as to what life you are to have, rather than a choice as to what action you will take in that life.

The choice of which person you would rather be instead of which action you would rather undertake is like the choice of a Leibnizian God who is choosing among possible worlds, each with their complete and inalterable histories. But in human life there are no such choices of lives, only choices within lives. If we chose lives before we lived them, who would be making the choice? Even if the philosopher should view things sub specie aeternitatis, the decision theorist should not.

Escaping Prisoner's Dilemmas

Gauthier's advice as regards the arms race is considerably less radical than is his advice regarding deterrence. He counsels that we should disarm if the other side disarms, but we should not disarm if we expect that the other side will not. Multilateral disarmament is wise; unilateral disarmanent is very unwise. This is simple advice, but there are problems with it.

To begin, Gauthier does not acknowledge that there is a relationship between deterrence and the arms race.. If you feel that it is necessary to play the deterrence game so long as your opponent has any nuclear weapons at all, then you will not be able to go through with a policy of multilateral disarmament. Suppose serendipitously the United States and the Soviet Union adopt a plan under which 10 percent of their nuclear arsenals, matched for strategic importance, will be scrapped each month. At the start, as the arsenals come down, each side will retain the ability to deter the other with threats of a second strike. Unfortunately, given the fact that each nuclear weapon when used can knock several opposing nuclear weapons out of commission, a time will come in the disarmament process when each side, if it attacks first, will be able to destroy enough of the strategic weapons of the other side that it may be utility maximizing to attempt a first strike. Furthermore, as soon as it begins to look possible and profitable for each side to launch a first strike, pressure increases on each side to launch a preemptive first strike, on the fear that the other side might succumb to temptation. If the preferences of nations are as Gauthier describes them (contrary to the account at the beginning of this chapter)—that nations prefer attack without retaliation to no attack—then the mutual disarmament process may well be doomed. To escape the armaments trap we must escape the deterrence trap first.

A second difficulty with Gauthier's "disarm mutually" program is that it provides no incentive for taking unilateral first steps. I may be prepared to disarm if and when my opponent disarms; my opponent may be prepared to disarm if and when I disarm. Even if we both prefer mutual disarmament to mutual armament, there is no way to move from mutual armament to mutual disarmament, unless one side is prepared to act first. If Gauthier's distrust of unilateral disarmament extends to distrust of such unilateral steps, then the mutually advantageous result will never be reached.

The fact that Gauthier analyzes the arms race in terms of conditional strategies such as "disarm if the other side does" shows that he is perhaps thinking of the arms race not as a simple Prisoner's Dilemma but as a repeated game in which previous moves are kept in account. Then the strategy he proposes is "disarm if the other side has chosen to disarm in the most recent play of the game." Many authors have suggested such repeated play routes out of the iterated Prisoner's Dilemma, and Robert Axelrod's computer tournaments have shown that if the world is a system in which different players play repeated Prisoner's Dilemmas against each other, round robin, you will probably be best off if you (a) cooperate after the other side does, (b) do not cooperate after the other side does not, and (c) never are first not to cooperate (this strategy is known as Tit For Tat).[14]

The problem for nations in the real world—not Axelrod's computer world—is this: If the superpowers are locked in a Prisoner's Dilemma, as Gauthier thinks they are, will Tit For Tat get them out of it? I think not, for two reasons.

First, many strategists exude confidence about Tit For Tat,[15] but the results of Axelrod's tournaments, fascinating in themselves, have little application to the current superpower confrontation. Tit For Tat "defeated" opposing strategies only in the sense that it scored highest in a round robin tournament. In pairwise confrontations, Tit For Tat never managed better than a tie. In short, Tit For Tat beat no one; the other strategies beat each other. Now, in the present historical situation, the superpowers play each other, while the other powers largely cheer from the sidelines. In such pairwise situations, there is no reason to think that Tit For Tat will do best in the long run.

Second, all repeated play escapes from the Prisoner's Dilemma require both sides to correctly identify the moves of the opponent and to remember those moves in succeeding plays of the game. But on the superpower scene there is little charity extended when interpreting the moves of the other side—does anyone on the U.S. side believe that the Krasnoyark radar might be, as the Soviets say, just a satellite tracking system?—and the ability of both sides to remember past moves seems to be sorely limited. The efforts of a generation toward mutual disarmament can be sabotaged in a week by a president with faulty memory, especially if he has at his side a legal staff prepared to interpret past agreements not in the light of what was agreed to then but in conformity with what is convenient now.

WHAT IS MORAL PLAY?

The Morality of Deterrence

The bulk of Gauthier's arguments intends to show that nuclear retaliation can be rational and that unilateral disarmament is irrational. Confident that these judgments are rational, he claims that they are morally obligatory as well. Certainly, in the moral system developed in his splendid book, *Morals*

By Agreement (Oxford: Clarendon Press, 1986), Gauthier repeatedly alleges that there is an intimate connection between the moral and the rational; morality, it turns out, is simply constrained maximization. To dispute Gauthier's conclusions, it seems, is to begin the descent into irrationalism and barbarism.

But of course the contractarian system developed in *Morals By Agreement* is not the only moral system that carries the torch for rationality. Jeremy Bentham considered himself to be establishing morality as an exact science, and Immanuel Kant felt that he had discovered the rules of conduct for all rational beings. Hence, the question we should address is not whether Gauthier is right in claiming a deep connection between rationality and morality but whether he has discovered the right connection.

Let us go back to Gauthier's argument for the rationality of nuclear retaliation. Let us assume that it really is utility maximizing to threaten nuclear second strikes, but that such threats are utility maximizing only if we form intentions to carry them out. Unfortunately, our threats fail and we suffer a first strike. In that event, says Gauthier, we are rationally bound to carry out a second strike. The parallel argument for morality, then, must be that it is morally obligatory to make second strike threats and that if it is morally obligatory to make such threats, it must be morally obligatory to carry them out when conditions warrant. This parallel claim, however, raises a host of problems.

First, where is Gauthier's argument that it is morally obligatory to make the threat? He suggests hesitantly that the threat is utility maximizing, but the fact that an act is utility maximizing for the agent is hardly sufficient, even in Gauthier's system, for demonstrating the moral obligatoriness of the act. Even if Gauthier believes, as I do not, that the second-strike nuclear threats of the United States are utility maximizing for humankind, I do not think that this constitutes a proof that it is morally obligatory to make these threats.

Second, even if we assume that making the threat is morally obligatory, where is the proof that the moral obligatoriness of making the threat carries over to the moral obligatoriness of executing the threat? Gauthier argues, you will recall, that the rationality of threat-making carried over into the rationality of threat execution because the rationality of threat-making involved a policy that covered a "larger stretch of time" than did the policy involved in threat execution. We found that there was reason to challenge this argument. But even if the argument goes through for the rationality of threat-making, what reason is there to think that it goes through for the morality of threat-making? Isn't making a moral decision a matter that involves the condition of one's soul at the time that the decision is made? Isn't one's character affected by what one imagines oneself doing if one adopts the policy? We are considering here a policy that requires a conditional commitment to killing millions of human beings, and the conditions that provoke such killing are not fully under our control. I cannot believe that people of good characters can morally commit themselves to this course of action, even conditionally. If I am right, it follows that the moral impermissibility of executing the threat spills backward into the moral impermissibility of making it.

Morality and Disarmament

Just as we are rationally obliged to forego maximizing utility when we execute our deterrent threats, we are rationally obliged to forego maximizing utility and meet moves toward disarmament by our opponents with disarmament moves of our own. But we are not obliged, and for Gauthier not permitted, to make disarmament moves that are not reciprocated. But suppose that unilateral disarmament by one party, although a disadvantage to that party, would be a great advantage to the world as a whole. For example, if one side gave up its nuclear weapons unilaterally, this would eliminate the chance of an all-out, two-sided nuclear war, the kind of nuclear war that at a minimum would throw the human race back to the Stone Age. If so, then utilitarianism would require that the United States make such a move and unilaterally give up its nuclear weapons. (Utilitarianism makes such a demand on the USSR as well, but the two demands are logically independent, and what the USSR does makes no difference as to what the United States should do.)

Now, it is one of the features of Gauthier's concept, not Bentham's, of the rational basis of morality that morality as a whole cannot require individuals to take such losses. Morality may constrain us from maximizing as much as we might, but it cannot constrain us so much that we are worse off, at least in terms of expected value, under the moral regime than we would be if there were no moral regime at all. Thus, Gauthier's system will not require any nation to make sacrifices for the welfare of humankind, unless humankind is prepared to make some sacrifices in return. This idea of confining morality to mutually advantageous sacrifices is appealing, but in such cases where the harm to the individual is relatively small and the gain to the human race is great, I think unilateral sacrifices are in fact moral duties. Rational cooperation, then, is not the ultimate moral standard; rather, insistence on rational cooperation is impermissible if the overall results of cooperation for the human race are markedly inferior to those obtainable by unilateral sacrifice.

The improvements in the human condition brought about by rational cooperation are so extensive and dramatic that one may be swept away into thinking that rational cooperation can do no harm and that every breach of the standards for cooperation can do no good. But now and then situations arise in which the threat to the common interest of humanity is so great and the obstacles to cooperation are so substantial that an insistence on a mutual approach to the difficulty may cause enough delay to ensure disaster. Perhaps the possession of nuclear weapons by antagonistic superpowers is just such a situation. For humanity's sake, then, unilateral sacrifices are morally required. But for those of us who consider nuclear weapons worse than useless for the nations that possess them, this is a sacrifice in name only.

NOTES

1. For Russell's priority, see Douglas P. Lackey, "Bertand Russell's Contribution to the Study of Nuclear Weapons Policy," *Russell* 4, no. 2 (Winter 1984–85).

2. The relevant papers from the late 1950s are collected in Thomas Schelling, *The Strategy of Conflict* (Cambridge, Mass.: Harvard University Press, 1960).

3. Daniel Ellsberg, "The Crude Analysis of Strategic Choice," *American Economic Review* (May 1961).

4. Desmond Ball, *Targeting for Strategic Deterrence* (London: Institute for Strategic Studies, 1983).

5. For an attack on the appropriateness of the Prisoner's Dilemma model, see D. Lackey, "Ethics and Nuclear Deterrence," in *Moral Problems*, edited by James Rachels (New York: Harper and Row, 1975).

6. This argument is presented in my "Missiles and Morals," *Philosophy and Public Affairs* 11 (Summer 1982):189–232.

7. The best assessment of nuclear blackmail known to me is Jeffrey McMahan's chapter, "Nuclear Blackmail," in *Dangers of Deterrence*, edited by Nigel Blake and Kay Pole (London: Routledge and Kegan Paul, 1983).

8. The National Council of Catholic Bishops, *The Challenge of Peace: God's Promise and Our Response* (Washington, D.C.: United States Catholic Conference, 1983), p. 17.

9. David Fisher, *Morality and the Bomb* (New York: St. Martin's Press, 1985), p. 76.

10. Daniel M. Farrell, "Strategic Planning and Moral Norms: The Case of Deterrent Nuclear Threats," *Public Affairs Quarterly* 1, no. 1 (January 1987):61–78.

11. For anecdotes that would make for comedy were they not all too real, see Daniel Ford, *The Button* (New York: Simon and Schuster, 1985).

12. Gregory Kavka, "The Toxin Puzzle," *Analysis* 43 (June 1983):33–36.

13. David Gauthier, "Deterrence, Maximization, and Rationality," *Ethics* (April 1984):488.

14. Robert Axelrod, *The Evolution of Cooperation* (New York: Basic Books, 1984).

15. One such is Bruce Russett, *The Prisoners of Insecurity* (San Francisco: W. H. Freeman, 1983).

14

Terrorism: A Critique of Excuses

MICHAEL WALZER

Michael Walzer characterizes terrorists as people who single out a large class of people and indiscriminately attack individuals within that group, thus terrifying the entire group; in this way terrorists hope to force their victims to make various political concessions. Because terrorism is an attack upon innocent bystanders, its practice is undefended and indefensible, according to Walzer. At best, advocates offer only unconvincing excuses for their crime: It is the last resort, everything else having failed; it is the only resort against powerful states; it is the only effective resort; or it is the universal resort, the one adopted in secrecy by all states, so that the terrorist is only fighting fire with fire.

Terrorism must be resisted, Walzer maintains, but its enemies must avoid stooping to terrorism. They must retaliate against the terrorists themselves, not those people the terrorists claim to represent. If terrorists are drawing attention to genuine oppression, their enemies must work to end the oppression, thus undermining the rationale for the terrorism. To do otherwise is to allow terrorism to be an excuse for doing nothing about oppression.

No one these days advocates terrorism, not even those who regularly practice it. The practice is indefensible now that it has been recognized, like rape and murder, as an attack upon the innocent. In a sense, indeed, terrorism is worse than rape and murder commonly are, for in the latter cases the victim has been chosen for a purpose; he or she is the direct object of attack, and the attack has some reason, however twisted or ugly it may be. The victims of a terrorist attack are third parties, innocent bystanders; there is no special reason for attacking them; anyone else within a large class of (unrelated) people will do as well. The attack is directed indiscriminately against the entire class. Terrorists are like killers on a rampage, except that their rampage is not just expressive of rage or madness; the rage is purposeful and programmatic. It aims at a general vulnerability: Kill these people in order to terrify those. A relatively small number of dead victims makes for a very large number of living and frightened hostages.

This, then, is the peculiar evil of terrorism—not only the killing of innocent people but also the intrusion of fear into everyday life, the violation of private purposes, the insecurity of public spaces, the endless coerciveness of precaution. A crime wave might, I suppose, produce similar effects, but no one plans a crime wave; it is the work of a thousand individual decisionmakers, each one independent of the others, brought together only by the invisible hand. Terrorism is the work of visible hands; it is an organizational project, a strategic choice, a conspiracy to murder and intimidate . . . you and me. No wonder the conspirators have difficulty defending, in public, the strategy they have chosen.

The moral difficulty is the same, obviously, when the conspiracy is directed not against you and me but against *them*—Protestants, say, not Catholics; Israelis, not Italians or Germans; blacks, not whites. These "limits" rarely hold for long; the logic of terrorism steadily expands the range of vulnerability. The more hostages they hold, the stronger the terrorists are. No one is safe once whole populations have been put at risk. Even if the risk were contained, however, the evil would be no different. So far as individual Protestants or Israelis or blacks are concerned, terrorism is random, degrading, and frightening. That is its hallmark, and that, again, is why it cannot be defended.

But when moral justification is ruled out, the way is opened for ideological excuse and apology. We live today in a political culture of excuses. This is far better than a political culture in which terrorism is openly defended and justified, for the excuse at least acknowledges the evil. But the improvement is precarious, hard won, and difficult to sustain. It is not the case, even in this better world, that terrorist organizations are without supporters. The support is indirect but by no means ineffective. It takes the form of apologetic descriptions and explanations, a litany of excuses that steadily undercuts our knowledge of the evil. Today that knowledge is insufficient unless it is supplemented and reinforced by a systematic critique of excuses. That is my purpose in this chapter. I take the principle for granted: that every act of terrorism is a wrongful act. The wrongfulness of the excuses, however, cannot be taken for granted; it has to be argued. The excuses themselves are familiar enough, the stuff of contemporary political debate. I shall state them in stereotypical form. There is no need to attribute them to this or that writer, publicist, or commentator; my readers can make their own attributions.[1]

THE EXCUSES FOR TERRORISM

The most common excuse for terrorism is that it is a last resort, chosen only when all else fails. The image is of people who have literally run out of options. One by one, they have tried every legitimate form of political and military action, exhausted every possibility, failed everywhere, until no alternative remains but the evil of terrorism. They must be terrorists or do nothing at all. The easy response is to insist that, given this description of their case, they should do nothing at all; they have indeed exhausted their possibilities. But this response simply reaffirms the principle, ignores the excuse; this response does not attend to the terrorists' desperation. Whatever the cause to which they are committed, we have to recognize that, given the commitment, the one thing they cannot do is "nothing at all."

But the case is badly described. It is not so easy to reach the "last resort." To get there, one must indeed try everything (which is a lot of things) and not just once, as if a political party might organize a single demonstration, fail to win immediate victory, and claim that it was now justified in moving on to murder. Politics is an art of repetition. Activists and citizens learn from experience, that is, by doing the same thing over and over again. It is by no means clear when they run out of options, but even under conditions of oppression and war, citizens have a good run short of that. The same argument applies to state officials who claim that they have tried "everything" and are now compelled to kill hostages or bomb peasant villages. Imagine such people called before a judicial tribunal and required to answer the question, What exactly did you try? Does anyone believe that they could come up with a plausible list? "Last resort" has only a notional finality; the resort to terror is ideologically last, not last in an actual series of actions, just last for the sake of the excuse. In fact, most state officials and movement militants who recommend a policy of terrorism recommend it as a first resort; they are for it from the beginning, although they may not get their way at the beginning. If they are honest, then, they must make other excuses and give up the pretense of the last resort.

The second excuse is designed for national liberation movements struggling against established and powerful states. Now the claim is that nothing else is possible, that no other strategy is available except terrorism. This is different from the first excuse because it does not require would-be terrorists to run through all the available options. Or, the second excuse requires terrorists to run through all the options in their heads, not in the world; notional finality is enough. Movement strategists consider their options and conclude that they have no alternative to terrorism. They think that they do not have the political strength to try anything else, and thus they do not try anything else. Weakness is their excuse.

But two very different kinds of weakness are commonly confused here: the weakness of the movement vis-à-vis the opposing state and the movement's weakness vis-à-vis its own people. This second kind of weakness, the inability of the movement to mobilize the nation, makes terrorism the "only" option because it effectively rules out all the others: nonviolent resistance, general strikes, mass demonstrations, unconventional warfare, and so on.

These options are only rarely ruled out by the sheer power of the state, by the pervasiveness and intensity of oppression. Totalitarian states may be immune to nonviolent or guerrilla resistance, but all the evidence suggests that they are also immune to terrorism. Or, more exactly, in totalitarian states state terror dominates every other sort. Where terrorism is a possible strategy for the oppositional movement (in liberal and democratic states, most obviously), other strategies are also possible if the movement has some significant degree of popular support. In the absence of popular support, terrorism may indeed be the one available strategy, but it is hard to see how its evils can then be excused. For it is not weakness alone that makes the excuse, but the claim of the terrorists to represent the weak; and the particular form of weakness that makes terrorism the only option calls that claim into question.

One might avoid this difficulty with a stronger insistence on the actual effectiveness of terrorism. The third excuse is simply that terrorism works (and nothing else does); it achieves the ends of the oppressed even without their participation. "When the act accuses, the result excuses."[2] This is a consequentialist argument, and given a strict understanding of consequentialism, this argument amounts to a justification rather than an excuse. In practice, however, the argument is rarely pushed so far. More often, the argument begins with an acknowledgment of the terrorists' wrongdoing. Their hands are dirty, but we must make a kind of peace with them because they have acted effectively for the sake of people who could not act for themselves. But, in fact, have the terrorists' actions been effective? I doubt that terrorism has ever achieved national liberation—no nation that I know of owes its freedom to a campaign of random murder—although terrorism undoubtedly increases the power of the terrorists within the national liberation movement. Perhaps terrorism is also conducive to the survival and notoriety (the two go together) of the movement, which is now dominated by terrorists. But even if we were to grant some means-end relationship between terror and national liberation, the third excuse does not work unless it can meet the further requirements of a consequentialist argument. It must be possible to say that the desired end could not have been achieved through any other, less wrongful, means. The third excuse depends, then, on the success of the first or second, and neither of these look likely to be successful.

The fourth excuse avoids this crippling dependency. This excuse does not require the apologist to defend either of the improbable claims that terrorism is the last resort or that it is the only possible resort. The fourth excuse is simply that terrorism is the universal resort. All politics is (really) terrorism. The appearance of innocence and decency is always a piece of deception, more or less convincing in accordance with the relative power of the deceivers. The terrorist who does not bother with appearances is only doing openly what everyone else does secretly.

This argument has the same form as the maxim "All's fair in love and war." Love is always fraudulent, war is always brutal, and political action is always terrorist in character. Political action works (as Thomas Hobbes long ago argued) only by generating fear in innocent men and women. Terrorism is the politics of state officials and movement militants alike. This argument does not justify either the officials or the militants, but it does excuse them all. We hardly can be harsh with people who act the way everyone else acts. Only saints are likely to act differently, and sainthood in politics is supererogatory, a matter of grace, not obligation.

But this fourth excuse relies too heavily on our cynicism about political life, and cynicism only sometimes answers well to experience. In fact, legitimate states do not need to terrorize their citizens, and strongly based movements do not need to terrorize their opponents. Officials and militants who live, as it were, on the margins of legitimacy and strength sometimes choose terrorism and sometimes do not. Living in terror is not a universal experience. The world the terrorists create has its entrances and exits.

If we want to understand the choice of terror, the choice that forces the rest of us through the door, we have to imagine what in fact always occurs, although we often have no satisfactory record of the occurrence: A group of men and women, officials or militants, sits around a table and argues about whether or not to adopt a terrorist strategy. Later on, the litany of excuses obscures the argument. But at the time, around the table, it would have been no use for defenders of terrorism to say, "Everybody does it," because there they would be face to face with people proposing to do something else. Nor is it historically the case that the members of this last group, the opponents of terrorism, always lose the argument. They can win, however, and still not be able to prevent a terrorist campaign; the would-be terrorists (it does not take very many) can always split the movement and go their own way. Or, they can split the bureaucracy or the police or officer corps and act in the shadow of state power. Indeed, terrorism often has its origin in such splits. The first victims are the terrorists' former comrades or colleagues. What reason can we possibly have, then, for equating the two? If we value the politics of the men and women who oppose terrorism, we must reject the excuses of their murderers. Cynicism at such a time is unfair to the victims.

The fourth excuse can also take, often does take, a more restricted form. Oppression, rather than political rule more generally, is always terroristic in character, and thus, we must always excuse the opponents of oppression. When they choose terrorism, they are only reacting to someone else's previous choice, repaying in kind the treatment they have long received. Of course, their terrorism repeats the evil—innocent people are killed, who were never themselves oppressors—but repetition is not the same as initiation. The oppressors set the terms of the struggle. But if the struggle is fought on the oppressors' terms, then the oppressors are likely to win. Or, at least, oppression is likely to win, even if it takes on a new face. The whole point of a liberation movement or a popular mobilization is to change the terms. We have no reason to excuse the terrorism reactively adopted by opponents of oppression unless we are confident of the sincerity of their opposition, the seriousness of their commitment to a nonoppressive politics. But the choice of terrorism undermines that confidence.

We are often asked to distinguish the terrorism of the oppressed from the terrorism of the oppressors. What is it, however, that makes the difference? The message of the terrorist is the same in both cases: a denial of the peoplehood and humanity of the groups among whom he or she finds victims. Terrorism anticipates, when it does not actually enforce, political domination. Does it matter if one dominated group is replaced by another? Imagine a slave revolt whose protagonists dream only of enslaving in their turn the children of their masters. The dream is understandable, but the fervent desire of the children that the revolt be repressed is equally understandable. In neither case does understanding make for excuse—not, at least, after a politics of universal freedom has become possible. Nor does an understanding of oppression excuse the terrorism of the oppressed, once we have grasped the meaning of "liberation."

These are the four general excuses for terror, and each of them fails. They depend upon statements about the world that are false, historical arguments for which there is no evidence, moral claims that turn out to be hollow or dishonest. This is not to say that there might not be more particular excuses that have greater plausibility, extenuating circumstances in particular cases that we would feel compelled to recognize. As with murder, we can tell a story (like the story that Richard Wright tells in *Native Son*, for example) that might lead us, not to justify terrorism, but to excuse this or that individual terrorist. We can provide a personal history, a psychological study, of compassion destroyed by fear, moral reason by hatred and rage, social inhibition by unending violence—the product, an individual driven to kill or readily set on a killing course by his or her political leaders.[3] But the force of this story will not depend on any of the four general excuses, all of which grant what the storyteller will have to deny: that terrorism is the deliberate choice of rational men and women. Whether they conceive it to be one option among others or the only one available, they nevertheless argue and choose. Whether they are acting or reacting, they have made a decision. The human instruments they subsequently find to plant the bomb or shoot the gun may act under some psychological compulsion, but the men and women who choose terror as a policy act "freely." They could not act in any other way, or accept any other description of their action, and still pretend to be the leaders of the movement or the state. We ought never to excuse such leaders.

THE RESPONSE TO TERRORISM

What follows from the critique of excuses? There is still a great deal of room for argument about the best way of responding to terrorism. Certainly, terrorists should be resisted, and it is not likely that a purely defensive resistance will ever be sufficient. In this sort of struggle, the offense is always ahead. The technology of terror is simple; the weapons are readily produced and easy to deliver. It is virtually impossible to protect people against random and indiscriminate attack. Thus, resistance will have to be supplemented by some combination of repression and retaliation. This is a dangerous business because repression and retaliation so often take terroristic forms and there are a host of apologists ready with excuses that sound remarkably like those of the terrorists themselves. It should be clear by now, however, that counterterrorism cannot be excused merely because it is reactive. Every new actor, terrorist or counterterrorist, claims to be reacting to someone else, standing in a circle and just passing the evil along. But the circle is ideological in character; in fact, every actor is a moral agent and makes an independent decision.

Therefore, repression and retaliation must not repeat the wrongs of terrorism, which is to say that repression and retaliation must be aimed systematically at the terrorists themselves, never at the people for whom the terrorists claim to be acting. That claim is in any case doubtful, even when it is honestly made. The people do not authorize the terrorists to act in their name. Only a tiny number actually participate in terrorist activities; they are far more likely to suffer than to benefit from the terrorist program. Even if they supported the program and hoped to benefit from it, however, they would still be immune from attack—exactly as civilians in time of war who support the war effort but are not themselves part of it are subject to the same immunity. Civilians may be put at risk by attacks on military targets, as by attacks on terrorist targets, but the risk must be kept to a minimum, even at some cost to the attackers. The refusal to make ordinary people into targets, whatever their nationality or even their politics, is the only way to say no to terrorism. Every act of repression and retaliation has to be measured by this standard.

But what if the "only way" to defeat the terrorists is to intimidate their actual or potential supporters? It is important to deny the premise of this question: that terrorism is a politics dependent on mass support. In fact, it is always the politics of an elite, whose members are dedicated and fanatical and more than ready to endure, or to watch others endure, the devastations of a counterterrorist campaign. Indeed, terrorists will welcome counterterrorism; it makes the terrorists' excuses more plausible and is sure to bring them, however many people are killed or wounded, however many are terrorized, the small number of recruits needed to sustain the terrorist activities.

Repression and retaliation are legitimate responses to terrorism only when they are constrained by the same moral principles that rule out terrorism itself. But there is an alternative response that seeks to avoid the violence that these two entail. The alternative is to address directly, ourselves, the oppression the terrorists claim to oppose. Oppression, they say, is the cause of terrorism. But that is merely one more excuse. The real cause of terrorism is the decision to launch a terrorist campaign, a decision made by that group of people sitting around a table whose deliberations I have already described. However, terrorists do exploit oppression, injustice, and human misery generally and look to these at least for their excuses. There can hardly be any doubt that oppression strengthens their hand. Is that a reason for us to come to the defense of the oppressed? It seems to me that we have our own reasons to do that, and do not need this one, or should not, to prod us into action. We might imitate those movement militants who argue against the adoption of a terrorist strategy—although not, as the terrorists say, because these militants are prepared to tolerate oppression. They already are opposed to oppression and now add to that opposition, perhaps for the same reasons, a refusal of terror. So should we have been opposed before, and we should now make the same addition.

But there is an argument, put with some insistence these days, that we should refuse to acknowledge any link at all between terrorism and oppression—as if any defense of oppressed men and women, once a terrorist campaign has been launched, would concede the effectiveness of the campaign. Or, at least, a defense of oppression would give terrorism the appearance of effectiveness and so increase the likelihood of terrorist campaigns in the future. Here we have the reverse side of the litany of excuses; we have turned over the record. First oppression is made into an excuse for terrorism, and then terrorism is made into an excuse for oppression. The first is the excuse of the far left; the second is the excuse of the neoconservative right.[4] I doubt that genuine conservatives would think it a good reason for defending the status quo that it is under terrorist attack; they would have independent reasons and would be prepared to defend the status quo against any attack. Similarly, those of us who think that the status quo urgently requires change have our own reasons for thinking so and need not be intimidated by terrorists or, for that matter, antiterrorists.

If one criticizes the first excuse, one should not neglect the second. But I need to state the second more precisely. It is not so much an excuse for oppression as an excuse for doing nothing (now) about oppression. The claim is that the campaign against terrorism has priority over every other political activity. If the people who take the lead in this campaign are the old oppressors, then we must make a kind of peace with them—temporarily, of course, until the terrorists have been beaten. This is a strategy that denies the possibility of a two-front war. So long as the men and women who pretend to lead the fight against oppression are terrorists, we can concede nothing to their demands. Nor can we oppose their opponents.

But why not? It is not likely in any case that terrorists would claim victory in the face of a serious effort to deal with the oppression of the people they claim to be defending. The effort would merely expose the hollowness of their claim, and the nearer it came to success, the more they would escalate their terrorism. They would still have to be defeated, for what they are after is not a solution to the problem but rather the power to impose their own solution. No decent end to the conflict in Ireland, say, or in Lebanon, or in the Middle East generally, is going to look like a victory for terrorism—if only because the different groups of terrorists are each committed, by the strategy they have adopted, to an indecent end.[5] By working for our own ends, we expose the indecency.

OPPRESSION AND TERRORISM

It is worth considering at greater length the link between oppression and terror. To pretend that there is no link at all is to ignore the historical record, but the record is more complex than any of the excuses acknowledge. The first thing to be read out of it, however, is simple enough: Oppression is not so much the cause of terrorism as terrorism is one of the primary means of oppression. This was true in ancient times, as Aristotle recognized, and it is still true today. Tyrants rule by terrorizing their subjects; unjust and illegitimate regimes are upheld through a combination of carefully aimed and random violence.[6] If this method works in the state, there is no reason to think that it will not work, or that it does not work, in the liberation movement. Wherever we see terrorism, we should look for tyranny and oppression. Authoritarian states, especially in the moment of their founding, need a terrorist apparatus—secret police with unlimited power, secret prisons into which citizens disappear, death squads in unmarked cars. Even democracies may use terror, not against their own citizens, but at the margins, in their colonies, for example, where colonizers also are likely to rule tyrannically. Oppression is sometimes maintained by a steady and discriminate pressure, sometimes by intermittent and random violence—what we might think of as terrorist melodrama—designed to render the subject population fearful and passive.

This latter policy, especially if it seems successful, invites imitation by opponents of the state. But terrorism does not spread only when it is imitated. If it can be invented by state officials, it can also be invented by movement militants. Neither one need take lessons from the other; the circle has no single or necessary starting point. Wherever it starts, terrorism in the movement is tyrannical and oppressive in exactly the same way as is terrorism in the state. The terrorists aim to rule, and murder is their method. They have their own internal police, death squads, disappearances. They begin by killing or intimidating those comrades who stand in their way, and they proceed to do the same, if they can, among the people they claim to represent. If terrorists are successful, they rule tyrannically, and their people bear, without consent, the costs of the terrorists' rule. (If the terrorists are only partly successful, the costs to the people may be even greater: What they have to bear now is a war between rival terrorist gangs.) But terrorists cannot win the ultimate victory they seek without challenging the established regime or colonial power and the people it claims to represent, and when terrorists do that, they themselves invite imitation. The regime may then respond with its own campaign of aimed and random violence. Terrorist tracks terrorist, each claiming the other as an excuse.

The same violence can also spread to countries where it has not yet been experienced; now terror is reproduced not through temporal succession but through ideological adaptation. State terrorists wage bloody wars against largely imaginary enemies: army colonels, say, hunting down the representatives of "international communism." Or movement terrorists wage bloody wars against enemies with whom, but for the ideology, they could readily negotiate and compromise: nationalist fanatics committed to a permanent irredentism. These wars, even if they are without precedents, are likely enough to become precedents, to start the circle of terror and counterterror, which is endlessly oppressive for the ordinary men and women whom the state calls its citizens and the movement its "people."

The only way to break out of the circle is to refuse to play the terrorist game. Terrorists in the state and the movement warn us, with equal vehemence, that any such refusal is a sign of softness and naiveté. The self-portrait of the terrorists is always the same. They are tough-minded and realistic; they know their enemies (or privately invent them for ideological purposes); and they are ready to do what must be done for victory. Why then do terrorists turn around and around in the same circle? It is true: Movement terrorists win support because they pretend to deal energetically and effectively with the brutality of the state. It also is true: State terrorists win support because they pretend to deal energetically and effectively with the brutality of the movement. Both feed on the fears of brutalized and oppressed people. But there is no way of overcoming brutality with terror. At most, the burden is shifted from these people to those; more likely, new burdens are added for everyone. Genuine liberation can come only through a politics that mobilizes the victims of brutality and takes careful aim at its agents, or by a politics that surrenders the hope of victory and domination and deliberately seeks a compromise settlement. In either case, once tyranny is repudiated, terrorism is no longer an option. For what lies behind all the excuses, of officials and militants alike, is the predilection for a tyrannical politics.

NOTES

1. I cannot resist a few examples: Edward Said, "The Terrorism Scam," *The Nation*, June 14, 1986; and (more intelligent and circumspect) Richard Falk, "Thinking About Terrorism," *The Nation*, June 28, 1986.

2. Machiavelli, *The Discourses* I:ix. As yet, however, there have been no results that would constitute a Machiavellian excuse.

3. See, for example, Daniel Goleman, "The Roots of Terrorism Are Found in Brutality of Shattered Childhood," *New York Times*, September 2, 1986, pp. C1, 8. Goleman discusses the psychic and social history of particular terrorists, not the roots of terrorism.

4. The neoconservative position is represented, although not as explicitly as I have stated it here, in Benjamin Netanyahu, ed., *Terrorism: How the West Can Win* (New York: Farrar, Straus & Giroux, 1986).

5. The reason the terrorist strategy, however indecent in itself, cannot be instrumental to some decent political purpose is because any decent purpose must somehow

accommodate the people against whom the terrorism is aimed, and what terrorism expresses is precisely the refusal of such an accommodation, the radical devaluing of the Other. See my argument in *Just and Unjust Wars* (New York: Basic Books, 1977), pp. 197–206, especially 203.

    6. Aristotle, *The Politics* 1313-1314a.

15

Understanding Terrorism

ROBERT K. FULLINWIDER

According to Robert Fullinwider, terrorists are often quite discriminating in their choices of targets, and they do not regard their victims as innocent. Therefore, either they are not terrorists, or else Michael Walzer's characterization of terrorists as indiscriminate killers of innocent bystanders will not do. To characterize terrorists as such is to ignore the work of showing that their actions are wrong and deliberately to refuse to understand them.

Once we take terrorism seriously, we will see that there are defenses, not just excuses, for it. Terrorists quite often defend their actions on moral grounds, especially on the grounds that it is up to terrorists to take the law into their own hands because the existing law is unjust. Terrorists also may take the attitude that the world is so corrupt that the lives of everyone are expendable. Likewise, terrorists may claim that the entire worth of individuals is derived from the groups of which they are part; given that certain groups are valueless, so are the lives of individual members.

I hold that a little rebellion now and then is a good thing, & as necessary in the political world as storms in the physical.

What signify a few lives lost in a century or two? The tree of liberty must be refreshed from time to time with the blood of patriots & tyrants. It is its natural manure.
　　　　　　　　　　　　　　　　　　　　　　　　　　—*Thomas Jefferson*

It belongs to men to judge the law at the risk of being judged by it.
—*Maurice Merleau-Ponty*

"No one these days advocates terrorism," writes Michael Walzer, "not even those who regularly practice it." This is because there is no moral defense available to the terrorist, no justification. Terrorism is worse than murder and rape, and no one can justify *them*. The only thing we can do with terrorists is excuse them. But the standard excuses we might offer are themselves lame and unpersuasive. So Walzer begins his analysis.

It is a puzzling analysis. First, there is no precise characterization of the terrorist. We do not know exactly who it is that is beyond justification, and so we remain unclear as to why. Second, and more puzzling, Walzer does not talk about excuses at all. The arguments he criticizes are all defenses of terrorism.

Consider the second point first. The avowed aim of the chapter is to examine excuses made for terrorism. According to Walzer, there are basically four of them: Terrorism is an act of last resort; terrorism is a tool of the weak; terrorism is the only effective tool the weak have; everybody practices terrorism. But these are not excuses, strictly speaking.

We excuse people by arguing that they acted in ignorance or under compulsion.[1] This is not what the apologists of terrorism say about terrorists. As Walzer himself points out, the four "excuses" he discusses acknowledge that terrorism is the deliberate choice of rational men and women. The apologists for terrorism do not offer an *apology* but an *apologia*. They put forward arguments that say the terrorist, all things considered, did not act wrongly.

So it is puzzling to find half of Walzer's chapter attacking defenses of terrorism when he begins by saying that no defense is available, that he will simply take for granted that every act of terrorism is a wrongful act. To reintroduce the first point: This puzzlement is compounded by the lack of a clear account in the chapter of who the terrorist is. Walzer pictures the terrorist as attacking "innocent bystanders," as killing or harming "indiscriminately." This is not a picture likely to enlist our sympathetic ear to the terrorist's case. We are going to take it for granted, too, that the terrorist is wrong. But some of Walzer's own later observations belie his initial description. Terrorists are often very discriminate in their targets.

I press these points because the outrage we feel for terrorist acts too easily prompts us to make and support blanket condemnations of terrorism by resort to equivocation or word play.[2] Therefore, it is important not to be vague about who the terrorist is and not to blur distinctions or relevant questions.

Who are terrorists? Here is a list: Basque separatists, factions of the PLO, the IRA, the Red Brigades, Croation nationalists, the Tupamaros, the Puerto Rican National Liberation Front, the Baader-Meinhof Gang, Black September, Shining Path, Posse Comitatus, South Moluccan nationalists, Armenian revanchists, the Symbionese Liberation Army. Why is there no defense for what they do? Why are they beyond justification? It must be because (1) they make no claims and arguments at all or in terms we can understand or (2) they make claims and arguments so flimsy that it is a waste of energy to go through the exercise of answering them.

Benzion Netanyahu takes the first path by diabolizing the terrorist. "The terrorist," he claims, "represents a new breed of man which takes humanity back to prehistoric times, to the times when morality was not yet born. Divested of any moral principle, he has no moral sense, no moral controls, and is therefore capable of committing any crime, like a killing machine, without shame or remorse."[3] If this is the terrorist, then he or she is so alien from our own moral experience that there is no ground for understanding him or her. There are no moral claims and arguments to answer.

Even Walzer's characterization of terrorists as indiscriminate killers of the innocent puts terrorists and their cause beyond the pale. What recognizable moral view could these killers possibly employ? What arguments could there be for us to take seriously? Walzer, in fact, uneasily straddles the line between the first and second paths. There *are* arguments, although Walzer puts them not in the mouths of terrorists—what could indiscriminate killers say?—but in the mouth of the apologist for terrorism. These arguments are "excuses" too incomplete or shallow to be taken very seriously.

The slaughter of Jewish worshippers in the Neve Shalom Synagogue in Istanbul last year exemplifies the mad and indiscriminate terrorism that Walzer obviously has in mind. During services, two terrorists entered the synagogue, barred the doors, and machine-gunned twenty-two people to death before exploding grenades to destroy themselves and all identity of who they were.[4] The worshippers in Istanbul met their deaths because they were Jews and because their attackers were willing to target Jews as such in the former's "war against Zionism." The slaughter was so horrible and revolting that it may strike us as too morally grotesque to understand, from their point of view, the goals and the values that animated the slaughterers.

But the Turkish synagogue episode is less typical of terrorism during the last one hundred years—or even the past twenty years—than is, for example, the kidnapping and murder of Aldo Moro in 1978. The Red Brigades abducted Moro, probably the most respected political leader in Italy, subjected him to a "trial" for his "crimes" (as representative and principal agent of the "rotten" and "repressive" Italian state), and "executed" him. The abduction had been planned over several months and followed a period of kidnappings and kneecappings of industrialists and lesser political figures. There was nothing indiscriminate about the taking of Aldo Moro.

Are the *brigatisti*, too, morally beyond the pale, subhuman throwbacks to a prehistoric time, divided from us by some moral chasm, their aims not worth a charitable understanding? It is, unfortunately, too easy to foreclose questions of justification here by definitional sleights of hand. Benjamin Netanyahu agrees with Walzer that "terrorism is always unjustifiable."[5] This seems to follow from Netanyahu's definition ("Terrorism is the deliberate and systematic murder, maiming, and menacing of the innocent to inspire fear for political ends"[6]) and from the fact that deliberately killing innocents is wrong. But Netanyahu gets the kidnappers of Aldo Moro under his proscription only by sliding over to a characterization of terrorists as attackers of *civilians*, implicitly equating "innocents" and "civilians."[7] According to the Netanyahu definition—and under Walzer's characterization—the Red Brigades' kidnapping of Aldo Moro does not qualify as terrorism unless we characterize Moro as an *innocent* civilian, but that just begs the question against the Red Brigades. They chose Moro because he was *not* innocent (by their lights).

Italy was convulsed by the Aldo Moro kidnapping not because the actions of the Red Brigades were incomprehensible but because the actions were fully comprehensible in moral terms. Everybody understands crime and punishment. The arguments of the Red Brigades were so understandable, in fact, that the Italian establishment feared they might even seduce many Italian citizens.

The political parties of Italy from the onset of the Moro crisis locked themselves into a rigid position: No negotiations for Moro's release. The parties did not take this position because they thought the arguments of the Red Brigades had no credibility. If the Red Brigades had defended their kidnapping of Moro on the grounds that he was guilty of secretly poisoning all the water in Italy with fluorides, or that he had betrayed the planet earth to galactic enemies, the Italian government would not have felt that negotiations for Moro's life risked giving the kidnappers widespread legitimacy among the populace. It was precisely because the Red Brigades' arguments had enough facial credibility to start with that the government saw any concessions as undermining its own legitimacy.[8] Its policy on Moro amounted to an argument-by-deed addressed to the Italian public that there was no truth to the charge that the state was rotten, repressive, and illegitimate.

Thus, not only were the arguments of the Red Brigades comprehensible; they had to be answered. The answers were not, and are not, transparent. They have to be worked at, especially if they are not to beg the central questions. Simply taking for granted that every act of terrorism is wrong may allow us to make short work of the Red Brigades, but not honest work. Pushing aside the question of justification as pointless is more likely to impede rather than advance our understanding of terrorism.

THE APPEAL TO MORALITY
VERSUS THE APPEAL TO LAW

Benzion Netanyahu gets the matter exactly backward: Terrorists are not throwbacks to a prehistoric time "when morality was not yet born." If anything, terrorists are throwbacks to a "time" when morality was not yet under control. What is often scary about terrorists is that they appeal to morality without appealing to the law. Let me explain.

Political theorists tell a story about the "state of nature" to explain and defend government. The state of nature proves to be intolerable for its inhabitants, whose lives are "solitary, poore, nasty, brutish, and short."[9]

Contrary to common impressions, however, the problem in the state of nature is not that people are so immoral—so selfish and rapacious that they persistently endanger each other. The problem is that people are so moral—so determined to vindicate rights or to uphold honor at any costs that they become a menace to one another.

The distinctive feature of the state of nature, as John Locke points out, is not the absence of morality but the absence of law. It is a circumstance in which "the law of nature"—the moral law—must be enforced by each person. Each is responsible for vindicating his or her own rights and the rights of others. All prosecution of crime and injustice in the state of nature is free-lance. Such a situation is the inevitable spawning ground of the neverending chain of retaliation and counter-retaliation of the blood feud. "For every one in that state being both Judge and Executioner of the Law of Nature, Men being partial to themselves, Passion and Revenge is very apt to carry them too far, and with too much heat, in their own Cases; as well as negligence, and unconcernedness, to make them too remiss, in other Mens."[10]

Even if persons were not biased in their own favor, the problems of enforcing justice in the state of nature would remain deadly. How would crime be defined? How would evidence for its commission be gathered? Who is to be punished, and in what manner? Nothing about the state of nature ensures any common understanding about these questions. The contrary is the case. Private understanding pitted against private understanding produces an escalation of response and counter-response that lets violence erupt and feed on itself.

The solution, of course, is "an establish'd, settled, known *Law*, received and allowed by common consent to be the Standard of Right and Wrong, and the common measure to decide all Controversies" and "a known and indifferent Judge, with Authority to determine all differences according to the established Law."[11] Conventions, established standards, and enforced rulings keep the peace, and when they exist by "common consent," they do justice as well.

"Consent of the governed" is the ideal that underlies democratic regimes, at least in Anglo-American cultures. It is an attractive ideal. When a regime of law is "chosen" by "free and rational persons," the "strains of commitment" will be minimal.[12] That is to say, there will be widespread willingness to obey the law and accept its rulings.

But in the real governments we live under—even the best of them—the strains of commitment often are severe. Impatience with the existing procedures of law can, and does, lead people to resort to "irregular justice," including political violence. Such "irregular justice," even when it is violent and rebellious, need not repudiate the existing rule of law. Irregular justice may be directed only at egregious failures of the law or at illegality tolerated as law.

Ordinary political violence can itself have all the earmarks of terrorism. The Molly Maguires—a secret band of Irish miners in mid-nineteenth century

Pennsylvania—carried on a decade-long labor "war" with mine owners and police. Emerging from violent resistance among Pennsylvania Irish to the Civil War draft, the Molly Maguires had their own way of dealing with the labor strife of the time. They resorted to arson, beatings, and murder, directed against mine foremen, superintendents, policemen, and others against whom the Molly Maguires had grievances. The violence was meant to intimidate (targeted foremen, for example, often left the community after receiving threats) for political ends.[13] The Molly Maguires resorted to war because they perceived both the law and its enforcers to be in the pockets of owners and bankers.

A less remote situation is the bombing and burning of scores of abortion facilities in the United States during the last decade. The aim of the attackers is to stop or impede abortions, and these attackers resort to "irregular justice" because the law fails to protect the unborn. They appeal to a "higher law," to morality itself.[14]

Our responses to political violence of this kind are ambivalent. In general we do not want free-lance justice; we do not want people arrogating to themselves decisions the law should make. But in particular cases, our sympathies often are enlisted on the side of the violent, even if we go through pro forma condemnations of their actions. We as often romanticize the Molly Maguires of our history as vilify them.

This is not surprising because it is a part of U.S. political tradition that we may be forced, in Merleau-Ponty's words, "to judge the law at the risk of being judged by it."[15] "I like a little rebellion now and then," wrote Thomas Jefferson to Abigail Adams. "The spirit of resistance to government is so valuable on certain occasions, that I wish it to be always kept alive. It will often be exercised when wrong, but better so than not to be exercised at all."[16] Political violence serves the useful function of shaking government out of its unresponsiveness to the rights and interests of some of its citizens.[17] The violence strains but does not rupture the rule of law because the appeal to morality made by the rebels draws from the same principles embodied in the law.

It is not Jeffersonian rebellions and outbreaks that truly frighten and disturb us, but revolutionary violence directed against a whole existing regime of law, including its underlying principles. The kidnapping and trial of Aldo Moro were an assault against the very idea of capitalist and bourgeois legality. They were acts of war on behalf of a new social order that would emerge from the ruins of "rotten" Italy.

Political violence that strikes against the very regime itself is doubly disturbing. For one thing, such violence is more frightening than ordinary dissidence or rebellion because the underlying common allegiance to the principles of the law that we expect to moderate or contain the violence of the dissident or rebel is absent. It is false to say that the revolutionary terrorist has no moral limits; but it is true that he or she repudiates the conventional boundaries that guide our own actions.

More importantly for our purposes, revolutionary violence is more frustrating because it is hard to answer the challenge of revolutionaries without begging the question against them. We can condemn ordinary political violence, including ordinary terrorism, by appealing to the "constitution," that is, the basic ideas of legality upon which our political, economic, and cultural institutions rest. Revolutionaries repudiate the "constitution." They do so in the name of recognizable moral ideas: creating a just or humane society, ending oppression and misery. But "just," "humane," and so on are abstractions that we typically fill in by reference to the principles and practices of our existing social order. If we cannot resort to this strategy in answering revolutionaries, then how do we convincingly repudiate their claims of justice? How do we show their violence to be condemned rather than supported by morality?

I do not mean we have to answer these questions for the satisfaction of revolutionaries. They have already pulled a gun. It is for our own satisfaction that we would like to give an intellectually honest answer to revolutionaries' rejectionism. We appeal to the law; they reject our law and appeal to morality. We claim morality, too, but then notice we have filled it up with our law.

ATTACKING THE INNOCENT

The ease with which we beg the question against revolutionaries is illustrated by Walzer's depiction of terrorists as killers of the innocent. How are we to understand "innocence"? Aldo Moro was clearly innocent in one sense: He had never been convicted of any wrong by a duly authorized judge or jury of any state or officially recognized international agency. But this sense of innocence is not terribly helpful for condemning the Red Brigades. Many instances of political violence that any of us would endorse are directed against innocents in this respect. Was Moro innocent in a deeper sense: not causally or morally responsible for the "crimes" of Italy, not an accessory, not complicit?

If we accept that the Italian state is a "criminal" enterprise, a repressive and unjust system, then it was clearly reasonable directly to connect Moro with it and its "crimes." Few other figures in Italy were so centrally involved in maintaining the rule of Christian democratic governments since World War II. Other targets of the Red Brigades were similarly connected in some important way to the political, military, or economic functioning of the state. If we *grant* the premises of the Red Brigades, then the charge that they killed innocent people is not so readily sustainable.

But aren't there some lines to be drawn that are independent of point of view, lines that everyone must acknowledge? Perhaps so, but finding an institutionally contextless conception of innocence will not be easy.[18] Consider the infamous massacre of the Israeli athletes at the 1972 Munich Olympics. Weren't they uncontroversially innocent? Yet a case can be made, from the point of view of their attackers, that these athletes were legitimate targets. They were willing and knowing representatives of their state to an international affair in which their presence and participation would lend yet further international credibility and legitimacy to Israel. Thus, from the point of view of their attackers, the athletes were active and informed accessories in a continuing "crime"—the support of the "criminal" state of Israel.

Of course, by international convention, unarmed athletes participating in the Olympics *are* "innocent." The willingness of terrorists to violate this convention burdens their defense. A great deal can be said in favor of such a convention; even terrorists are unlikely to prefer a world in which every "criminal" is an open target. Nevertheless, the circumstances, as the terrorists saw them, may have justified "irregular justice." Like the Molly Maguires, the terrorists saw themselves as attacking fair targets that current conventions protect. Such terrorists concede that they attack the "conventionally innocent," but not that they attack the "really innocent."

What about the victims of the slaughter at Neve Shalom Synagogue in Istanbul? Surely *they* cannot be connected to "crimes" of any sort. Their only connection to "Zionist imperialism" was that they were Jews; and if that is enough of a connection to make them fair targets, then "immunity of the innocent" is emptied as a moral notion and there will be no one who is "really innocent."

There is, doubtless, some point of view from which the slaughter in Istanbul makes sense, but it is a point of view that comes close to being too alien for us to comprehend or even credit as a moral point of view. Here the claims of Walzer and the rhetoric of Netanyahu seem appropriate. But I say "comes close" because the rationalization of the Istanbul massacre may be less alien than we expect.

Walzer's response to terrorism, or the terrorism I am describing now, flows from a conception of universal human rights.[19] Every human individual has an inviolability and dignity *just as a human being.* Independently of any feature of his or her social environment or historical circumstance, a person has a claim to our moral concern, a claim expressed in the possession of basic human rights. The "immunity thesis"—that innocent persons cannot be made the targets of violent assault—describes one of those rights.

An alternative view denies the moral individualism and universalism underlying the human rights approach. This view claims that the value of a person is wholly exhausted in his or her class or group membership. There is no transgroup or extraclass "humanity" that creates moral pull. Moral universalism is false.

Stated so starkly, perhaps this is a view not subscribed to by anyone. But there clearly are views that show considerable kinship. For example, at least some forms of Marxism imply, in present historical circumstances, that a person's rights and duties are wholly a function of his or her class.[20] Moreover, parochial moralities that see the universe from the point of view of God's, or history's, chosen people are not hard to imagine or even to find in history.

Another alternative conception sees the modern world as so dehumanized, so devoid of value, that it is perverse to agonize over the protection of innocents, to erect conventions, make law, and pass judgments as if current humanity itself had any value. Modern humans are deracinated and deformed, a mockery of what a fully realized humanity could be. That such beings are

incidentally slaughtered, maimed, and terrorized in the upheaval of a revolution for a transformed social order is of no importance. What will their
deaths signify in a century or two, from the perspective of a new order and
a new humanity?[21]

Thus, two basic ideas compete against the idea of universal human rights.
One measures the worth of people according to their group membership.
The other measures the worth of people against an ideal of humanity. These
measures are not alien and incomprehensible to us. In attenuated and confined
forms, they are a part of the moral armory of even those of us who, like
Walzer, subscribe to universal human rights. We value community and cherish
special relations of affinity and kinship. We hold ideals and strive for collective
reform and improvement.

We thus can comprehend the role of these ideas for those who acknowledge
no limits on their force. Even the maddest terrorism shows a familiar face.
Moreover, within our own philosophical culture, we cannot say with confidence
that the intellectual foundations of human rights are clear or that they are
universally acknowledged. The reigning fashions in the academy today include
various attacks on "liberal individualism." In contrast to the "atomistic"
individual supposedly subscribed to by liberalism, current critics offer pictures
of individuals "essentially connected" to others in community, individuals
whose identities are "constituted by community."[22]

The ideas of essence and constitution in these pictures are not made clear;
these ideas may turn out to be innocuous enough and hardly at odds with
anything except a caricature of individualism. But lurking within them are
possible interpretations that would make the grounds of moral universalism
obscure. To say that people are *essentially related* to community may mean
they have no value outside *some* community or other; or it may mean they
have no value outside their own community. "Community" may encompass
the loosest human associations and the most casual forms of sociability, or
it may mean a highly structured group bound by corporate values. Out of
these options there can emerge interpretations that render the view that
human beings have a worth and dignity independently of *any* of their relations
a proposition too abstract and empty to hold.

Perhaps other grounds of universalism are available; or perhaps a conception
of human rights can be erected on nonuniversalist views. But our intellectual
house is not in such good order that rationally irrefutable barriers are in
place against an extreme extension of the quest for community or the quest
for ideals—both of which can lead us to discount rather sharply the value
of some humans. Then the rationalization of Neve Shalom is not so far
away.

To understand terrorists and to take their self-justification seriously is not
to acquiesce in the terrorists' deeds or concede them any measure of right.
Rather, the point is to see the full spectrum of political violence realistically,
without demonization, for our *own* sake, not the sake of terrorists. Because
revolutionary terrorists repudiate so much of what is settled and in place,
we struggle to make sense of the meaning they give to the moral notions

they deploy. But they invite us to see how rotten the existing system is and to trust that in destroying it a new and morally preferable society will emerge. If terrorists war on us, we can war on them without compunction, but that does not answer their invitation. To do that, we have to say why the existing rule of law deserves allegiance.

Terrorists typically appeal to history for vindication. We can appeal to history, too, in defense of the conventions and practices terrorists revolt against or violate. Some terrorism we can condemn by appeal to those very conventions, some we can condemn by appeal to abstract principle, but most we must condemn because we judge the terrorists grotesquely mistaken in their understanding of historical possibilities. The Red Brigades deluded themselves into thinking the kidnapping of Aldo Moro would bring on the revolution. The Molly Maguires might have thought their violence was an effective—or the only—way to bring justice for the miners. Walzer's discussion of the four "excuses" eloquently shows the burden of proof that terrorism, ordinary or revolutionary, seldom meets. But this failure is contingent, not necessary. We cannot define terrorism into a moral corner where we do not have to worry any more about justification.

NOTES

I am grateful to Steven Luper-Foy and to my colleagues at the Center for Philosophy and Public Policy, especially Claudia Mills, for comments on an earlier draft of this chapter.

1. See J. L. Austin, "A Plea for Excuses," *Philosophical Papers*, 2nd ed. (London: Oxford University Press, 1970), p. 176: "In the one defence [i.e., justifying], briefly, we accept responsibility but deny [of the conduct] that it was bad. In the other [i.e., excusing], we admit [of the conduct] that it was bad but don't accept full, or any, responsibility." In subsequent correspondence, Michael Walzer writes that what he is talking about *are* excuses because they "have this construction: 'of course it is wrong to kill innocent people, but. . . . '" This construction, however, is ambiguous between "of course it is *ordinarily* wrong to kill innocent people, but there are special circumstances in this case to justify it," and "of course it is wrong to kill innocent people and *it was wrong in this case*, but there are special circumstances that excuse it," the special circumstances in this second construction being the presence of responsibility-relieving factors. Because Walzer acknowledges that the apologist for terrorism does not deny the terrorists' responsibility, I take the apologies to have the form of the first rather than the second construction and thus to be justificatory in nature. In any case, I do not want to make too much of the difference between excusing and justifying or of the way I draw the distinction.

2. I have benefited, on this point, from reading Judith Lichtenberg's unpublished essay, "Beneath the Rhetoric of Terrorism."

3. Benzion Netanyahu, "Terrorists and Freedom Fighters," in Benjamin Netanyahu, ed., *Terrorism: How the West Can Win* (New York: Farrar, Straus, Giroux, 1986), pp. 29–30.

4. See the account by Judith Miller, "The Istanbul Synagogue Massacre: An Investigation," *New York Times Magazine*, January 4, 1987, pp. 14–18.

5. "Defining Terrorism," in Netanyahu, *Terrorism*, p. 12.

6. Ibid., p. 9.

7. Ibid., p. 10. Netanyahu explicitly refers to the Red Brigades. Walzer's writings are usually rich with examples and cases but in the present case, we never meet any real examples of terrorism. Part of the initial puzzlement I express at the beginning of this chapter derived from uncertainty about whether Walzer's initial characterization of terrorists as indiscriminate killers was meant as a *description* of those individuals and groups most frequently referred to as terrorists (and this would include the Red Brigades) or was meant as a *stipulative definition,* marking off as terrorists only those who engage in indiscriminate murder. In subsequent correspondence, Walzer writes, "I do not believe that the kidnapping of Aldo Moro was a terrorist act . . . [and] I don't think that it unduly restricts the idea of terrorism to insist on its randomness: the carpet bombing of cities, the bomb in the pub, cafe, bus station, supermarket— all this is common enough, and awful enough, to deserve a name."

8. Nations also resist negotiating with terrorists in order not to encourage future terrorism. This was a secondary consideration in the present case. On the Italian policy of no-negotiations, and on the Moro kidnapping generally, see Robin Erica Wagner-Pacifici, *The Moro Morality Play: Terrorism as Social Drama* (Chicago: University of Chicago Press, 1986), pp. 47–163; and Robert Katz, *Days of Wrath: The Ordeal of Aldo Moro* (Garden City, N.Y.: Doubleday, 1980), p. 70ff.

9. Thomas Hobbes, *Leviathan* (Baltimore, Md.: Penguin Books, 1968), p. 186.

10. John Locke, *Two Treatises of Government* (New York: New American Library, 1965), pp. 395–396.

11. Ibid., p. 396.

12. John Rawls, *A Theory of Justice* (Cambridge, Mass.: Harvard University Press, 1971), pp. 175–183.

13. The Molly Maguires clearly count as terrorists on some definitions. See, for example, C.A.J. Coady, "The Morality of Terrorism," *Philosophy* 60 (January 1985):52.

14. "Perhaps it *is* terrorism to use violence to intimidate. But which is the greater terror: the destruction of two dozen buildings without loss of life in 1984, or the destruction of 1.5 million human beings because they were inconvenient to the mothers who carried them?" Patrick Buchanan, *Washington Times,* January 4, 1985, p. C1.

15. Maurice Merleau-Ponty, *Humanism and Terror* (Boston: Beacon Press, 1969), p. xxxix.

16. Thomas Jefferson, *Writings* (New York: Library of America, 1984), pp. 889–890. For the quotations at the beginning of this chapter, see p. 882 (letter to James Madison, January 1787), and p. 911 (letter to William Smith, November 1787).

17. Shay's Rebellion, which was the occasion for Jefferson's comments, is a case in point. To a certain extent we owe our Constitution to this insurrection of desperate farmers in western Massachusetts (but it apparently would have failed Walzer's strictures about last resort). A few lives were lost in the affair. See Marion L. Starkey, *A Little Rebellion* (New York: Knopf, 1955).

18. Less easy, perhaps, than I supposed in R. Fullinwider, "War and Innocence," *Philosophy & Public Affairs* 5 (Fall 1975):90–97.

19. See Michael Walzer, *Just and Unjust Wars* (New York: Basic Books, 1977), pp. 134–135. See also his *Spheres of Justice* (New York: Basic Books, 1983), p. xv.

20. "The correct basis for what is morally good, what one's duty is, what the right thing to do is, what is fair to do . . . is one's place in one's society. The correct basis is not the human person taken in isolation. Rather, the focus is on the groups in society to which a person belongs. . . . The right thing to do is determined by a consideration of what ultimately, in view of the primacy of class, advances the

realization of the tendencies of one's class." Milton Fisk, *Ethics and Society: A Marxist Interpretation of Value* (New York: New York University Press, 1980), pp. xiii, xvi.

"Whoever does not care to return to Moses, Christ, or Mohammed; whoever is not satisfied with eclectic *hodge-podges* must acknowledge that morality is a product of social development; that there is nothing immutable about it; that it serves social interests; that these interests are contradictory; that morality more than any other form of ideology has a class character.

"But do not elementary moral precepts exist, worked out in the development of humanity as a whole and indispensable for the existence of every collective body? Undoubtedly such precepts exist but the extent of their action is extremely limited and unstable. Norms 'obligatory upon all' become the less forceful the sharper the character assumed by the class struggle. The highest form of the class struggle is civil war, which explodes into midair all moral ties between the hostile classes." Leon Trotsky, *Their Morals and Ours* (New York: Pathfinder Press, 1973), p. 21.

21. For a discussion of views that find the modern world generally worthless, see Bernard Yack, *The Longing for Total Revolution: Philosophic Sources of Social Discontent from Rousseau to Marx and Nietzsche* (Princeton, N.J.: Princeton University Press, 1986).

22. For a typical recent attack on "liberal individualism," see Suzanna Sherry, "Civic Virtue and the Feminine Voice in Constitutional Adjudication," *Virginia Law Review* 72 (April 1986):546ff, and her citations of Alasdair MacIntyre, Michael Sandel, Carol Gilligan, and so forth.

PART THREE

Justice and World Government

16

World Government, Security, and Global Justice

KAI NIELSEN

Kai Nielsen defends the desirability of establishing a world government conceived of as a single court of final appeal for the adjudication of international disputes, with the authority to enforce its decisions through complete control over the legitimate means of violence. The cultural diversity of distinct political communities is extremely important because through our memberships in these groups we have the personal identities we do; hence, it is important for a world government to protect the integrity and limited power of self-determination of political communities.

To ensure this, the world government should be a constitutional democracy and take a federalist form. To be legitimate, a world government must also institute world justice. Such a conception should be identified using something like John Rawls's original position, Nielsen says. The conception of world justice Nielsen advocates requires the achievement of basic human rights and an equality of condition for everyone in the world, at least as far as this is compatible with individual autonomy, and the flourishing of human life to the greatest extent possible. To bring about a world government of the sort Nielsen calls for would be extremely difficult, however, so much so that he believes that we should not place it high on our political agendas.

World government to many, if not most, will sound like a thoroughly Quixotic idea, crazily impractical if not actually dangerous. We live in a world of entrenched and often fiercely antagonistic nation-states, large and small. These states frequently are jingoistic, almost invariably possess a sense of being a particular people with determinate traditions, and are quite unwilling to cede authority in any very fundamental sense, if possible, to larger units.

Even within nation-states, there are broadly ethnic or class conflicts where one group has hegemony (although sometimes an unstable hegemony) rooted in sheer power over another. We have, that is, both interstate and intrastate conflict. There will be struggles (sometimes violent struggles) for a new nation-state or at least a new government where there is interstate conflict and where there is an uneasy balance of power in which the extant hegemony can be feasibly challenged or one group sees the balance of power tipping toward it and moves into the breach. All these situations make for oppression of one sort or another and for strife and conflict, and such situations are very pervasive in our world.

However, throughout the world the sense of being a people runs very deep. Although we live, or so it is said, in a world of *Gesellschaften,* there is a sense, if only an ersatz sense, of *Gemeinschaft.* This sense, in concept although seldom in name, is very pervasive and persistent. (Hitler, after all, made *Gemeinschaft* a dirty word.) Even highly educated, politically sophisticated, well-travelled people are not citizens of the world. They tend to have a firm sense of their being a particular people and sometimes, although increasingly less often, a half-conviction of their superiority. But even with the ethnocentricism gone, there remains a particularist identity. "We" comes trippingly to the tongue. We have a longing for *Gemeinschaft.*

But hegemonic nation-states, such as the United States and the USSR, hate each other and are set on a firmly conflicting course that only an elementary sense of prudence keeps from breaking into war. Similar things obtain for smaller states such as Syria and Israel, Mozambique and South Africa, South Korea and North Korea. With such conflicts there is little likelihood of a movement toward world government. If by some miracle it could be achieved, for a time it would be inherently unstable, thereby threatening repeatedly, given the different national and cultural identities, to break out into civil war. Given the realities of the situation, it is dangerous, foolish, and irresponsible to speak of the desirability of establishing a world government.

I want, running against the stream, in what is perhaps an utterly utopian way, to defend the very idea of a world government as a single final authority, a court of last appeal. I will articulate and defend a conception of world government, with constrained authority, and without the savagery of a Hobbesian sovereign, in a fraternal, worldwide, cantonal system of diverse peoples. But before I face the challenge that this is cloud cuckooland, I must face the quite different challenge that, even if world government were possible, it would be undesirable.

THE DESIRABILITY
OF WORLD GOVERNMENT

We live in a world of diverse peoples with different prized traditions and partially distinct conceptions of self; the world's peoples have different conceptions of how one is to live and of how the affairs of state are to be arranged. A respect for persons and a belief in *moral* equality (the belief that the life of everyone matters and matters equally) require (or at least seem to require) a respect for these different traditions even when they conflict with our own. This may even be extended, although it need not be, to embrace the relativistic claim that all these ways of living and believing have equal validity.

There is, with such a Herder-like way of viewing things, a stress on sustaining the values of cultural independence and sovereignty and a commitment to distinct political communities. Without them, life will be flattened to a dull gray in which people will lose their sense of being a distinct people, which is something, nonrational or not, to which people, even reflective, informed people, attach a considerable importance. Some claim we cannot find our personal identities in an identification with humanity— in the great ideals of the Enlightenment—but in being a particular people: a Swede, an American, a Frenchman, a Catholic, a Jew, an Irish working man, a Wasp professional, an athlete, a communist, a fascist, a liberal intellectual, a lawyer, an architect, and the like.[1] We find our identities in distinct communities that sometimes are real and less frequently are imagined or ascribed.

Many of us firmly believe that nation-states exist to protect the integrity of at least the larger of these communities, these cultural entities, that constitute distinct peoples. (A state protects our identities as Swedes but not necessarily as architects, although we also expect a civilized state to protect our rights.) To protect this cherished cultural identity, without which we will experience a very deep estrangement indeed, these nation-states claim, against other states, rights of territorial integrity and political legitimacy over distinct territories. It is a claim to have, and to have legitimately as well, the sole right to sovereign power over a territory and the persons in that territory.

Within its boundaries the state claims to have the sole right to the legitimate means of violence. All use of force not sanctioned by state authorities is deemed by them illegitimate. To have the sovereignty they claim, they must be able to enforce this. Recognizing this and recognizing the value of these prized ways of life, Michael Walzer claims, we must have respect "for communal integrity and for different patterns of culture and political development."[2] What we have, and valuably have, is a community of *nations.* But we are not within a good country mile of getting a community of *humanity.* The relevant "we" is not humankind as a whole but a distinct community in which we come to find ourselves, in which we discover and sustain our identity. Morality, most centrally, is a morality of *Sittlichkeit.*

By attaching fundamental political sovereignty to a distinct nation-state protecting a distinctive *Sittlichkeit,* we are most likely to secure our distinct identities and for ourselves, whoever we are, viewed now collectively as the "we" of humanity, a richness of life not establishable and sustainable if there were simply to be a single humanity with a single way of life. We do not want a world government to flatten all this out into a single cultural unit under a single sovereign power. Just as, the argument goes, we do not want a single language in the world, so we do not want to have a single culture. There is richness, vigor, and beauty in diversity, and it keeps open human options as well.[3]

Moreover, as Michael Walzer argues, such a world government would give us not only cultural drabness but is dangerous as well. Peter Bauer's remarks about totalitarianism may be an exaggeration, but we still should not try to transcend distinct political communities with their distinct and not infrequently conflicting nation-states.[4] Walzer, who argues this, gives two arguments for believing it to be so.[5] First, he appeals to considerations of tolerably elementary prudence. The outcome of political processes in particular communal arenas, he reminds us, is not infrequently brutal. This is a well-known fact of political life. Given that, it is reasonable to expect that "outcomes in the global arena will often be brutal too."[6] But such brutality in a world government will be "far more effective and therefore a far more dangerous brutality, for there will be no place left for political refuge and no examples left of political alternatives."[7]

This first argument seems to me unpersuasive. I am not advocating just any world government; I am advocating a government that would be assented to by fairminded, informed and through and through rational moral agents if they were to set out the design of their lives together under conditions of undistorted discourse. I speak here of a world government that is democratic and federalist with something like a cantonal system that provides a place in a constitutional democracy for diverse peoples. That is to say, we would have the loose federalism of a cantonal system, which would protect the distinctive ways of life of different cultures. That federalist constitutional democracy would protect the traditions of its discrete components and the rights of individuals under a system that cedes ultimate sovereign authority to a democratically controlled world government that is committed to respecting the traditions of its discrete parts. Just as in some nation-states there are distinct parties and distinct conceptions of alternative socioeconomic orders—for example, laissez-faire capitalism, welfare-state capitalism, state socialism, libertarian socialism and the like—so there would be such alternatives with a world government. Moreover, just as in nation-states rebellion, revolution, and secession are possible, the same thing could obtain with the establishment of a world state. There is here, as well as in our present situation, a place for political refuge. There is no reason to believe that a world government must be authoritarian, let alone (*pace* Bauer) totalitarian.

Let us turn now to Walzer's second argument against the very possibility of a world government being a desirable state of affairs. A world government,

Walzer claims, would undermine the very possibility of a political life, something already threatened by great modern nation-states. "Politics," he tells us, "depends upon shared history, communal sentiment, accepted conventions."[8] But these things are hardly conceivable in a global state. "Communal life and liberty requires the existence of relatively self-enclosed arenas of political development."[9] But, or so Walzer has it, world government would break "into the enclosures" and "destroy the communities."[10] Individuals in such an eventuality would clearly lose something that they value and to which they have a right—"namely their participation in the 'development' that goes on and can only go on within the enclosure, where, as against foreigners, individuals have a right to a state of their own."[11]

Again Walzer's argument seems to me unpersuasive. Analogously to nation-states with distinct peoples, located in distinct provinces or cantons in a federal system, the loose federalism of a world government would also give, in important areas of their lives, autonomy to the different groups while (a) protecting them more adequately from war and (b) enhancing more mutually beneficial cooperation among them than could a nation-state system. Some modern nation-states today do respect autonomy and the local attachments of distinct peoples while still providing a single control of the legitimate means of violence. The world state can do exactly the same thing. Once Italy, Yugoslavia, and Germany were not states but many frequently warring principalities. Now these regions, although unified into their respective nation-states, still have (particularly in Yugoslavia, less so in Germany) distinct traditions cooperating without losing their distinctness in a unified state. Although Yugoslavia has its ethnic frictions, there still is the general acceptance of a single nation-state, and the various ethnically diverse sections of the country work together fruitfully in extensive mutually beneficial cooperation. We have, to put the matter more generally, nation-states with very divergent populations, and while there is not infrequently friction (for example, Belgium), they, that notwithstanding, continue to cooperate in mutually beneficial ways with a common army, currency, taxation powers, and the like. On the one hand, we have both relative self-enclosure and respect for distinct traditions and peoples, and, on the other hand, these distinct peoples, proud of their distinctiveness, can still regard themselves as brothers and sisters in a common state. Canada is perhaps a good example of this and Switzerland as well. People in Switzerland traditionally have considered themselves members of a particular canton, but they also see themselves as Swiss. People from Cape Breton or Saskatchewan have a definite sense of local identity, and yet they also firmly see themselves as Canadians and all this without any ambivalence or conflict.

As the universalistic values of the Enlightenment deepen, there is a natural extension of this. We can see ourselves as members of particular nations and also as citizens of a common world. We can have distinct local identities and attachments, as J. G. Herder stressed, without feelings of cultural superiority. A person can be proud of being a Dane without thinking the Danes are God's chosen people. Americans and New Zealanders will be to the world state what British Columbians and Newfoundlanders are presently to being Canadian. Different peoples can protect their identities without a nation-state of their own charged with representing in some exclusive or dominating way that identity. They can protect their identities while living in and being committed to such a world state. Within that world state, there will be distinct areas with considerable autonomy that still cede, without losing that autonomy, ultimate sovereign power to a global state, thereby radically lessening the possibilities of war and enhancing possibilities for mutually advantageous cooperation.

It is here where we can, *pace* Walzer, have our cake and eat it, too. A commitment to basic human rights—something universal that we have simply in virtue of being human—commits us to such a mixed view as does a belief in moral equality. The vital thing is that we can have both universalistic commitments and local attachments and the right to distinct ways of doing some important things as well. Certain regions of the world, for example, can and indeed should have rights to linguistic choice in public education, as in the region around Belzano, while in other regions, say around Perth, there will be no such right. At the same time, other rights, say sexual equality, are human rights and should be quite universal. We can have universalist humanitarian politics and with that a universal sense of sisterhood and brotherhood and still have a prized sense of being a particular kind of person with valued local attachments. A cosmopolitan vision of humanity need not be a philosopher's conceit, and it is not incompatible, as Isaiah Berlin shows, with a Herderian acknowledgment of the immense value of distinct and perhaps incommensurable ways of life.[12] Herder's stress and Marquis de Condorcet's need not be in conflict.

National sovereignty should not be seen as our most important entitlement, such that without this sovereignty, we lose our centers of gravity or what makes us a people. We do not need such national sovereignty to be a people, and we should see ourselves, to put the matter moralistically, as members of the human community first and as Italians, Americans, Greeks, Germans, or Canadians second. We should come to recognize that the socially necessary rights of security and subsistence, rights that no one can do without if he or she is even to approximate living a tolerable life, are universal. Moreover, because no one can do without these rights, they should be accorded to all people and should not be subverted by nationalist considerations. This moral stance follows from a respect for persons.

In the contemporary world—and this is becoming truer everyday—nations are not self-enclosed. As modernization runs apace, we are becoming increasingly more and more interdependent economically, culturally, and politically. The metaphor of a global village is a truistic exaggeration by now but, where recognized as such, hardly inaccurate for all of that. The nationalism that would see the only global community as a community of sovereign states and not of humanity is backward looking. Such nationalism fails to see a steadily growing cosmopolitanism emerging, albeit not without its setbacks, from the Enlightenment and growing with our economic interdependence, increased education, and enlarged understanding. Indeed, with these beings, these children of the Enlightenment, there emerges an increasing sense of the right of self-determination for a people: the right to choose the political forms by which they wish to be ruled. But this need not continue to lead to the hegemony of the nation-state. People, as their sense of universalism develops (with a corresponding loss of ethnocentric chauvinism), and their recognition of the need for secure peace in a nonviolent world grows, can come to accept a world government voluntarily and in a democratic manner. I do not speak here of being forced to accept a world state. I rather argue for the desirability of its acceptance where it has the character suggested in this section.

ADVOCATING WORLD GOVERNMENT

On the assumption that I have made at least plausible the belief that a world government of a certain determinate sort would be a good thing if we could get it, I now want to face the challenge that to advocate it is irresponsible, given the way the world is and reasonably can be expected to be. (Think, for example, of the deep hatreds between Arabs and Jews and between Irish Protestants and Irish Catholics.) Given national chauvinism, given national intransigence—consider just the USSR and the United States— there just is no possibility of moving in that direction. If our aim is to achieve a world with more justice and more humanity in it than there are in the world now, we, if we are serious, waste our time in directing our political and moral energies into trying to achieve world government rather than something more practical. Assuming, the argument goes, that nation-states are here to stay (at least for anything like the foreseeable future) the thing to do is, either, on the one hand, to aim for the expansion or the refinement of the welfare state—say to push our societies somewhat more in the direction of Sweden—or, on the other, to aim at social revolution and the transformation of our societies into democratic socialist societies. It is a dangerous dispersal of our political energies to put them into Quixotic efforts for world government.

I want to say both yes and no to that. Yes, in the sense that what I shall call nonideal theory should say yes to the foregoing and should not concern itself with the issue of the establishment of world government. Rather, nonideal theory should concern itself instead with social issues and social struggles, with the here and now, with how we can transform our existing societies more in the direction of decency, both in the sense of being better, more caring societies for those within their respective borders, and for being more caring and responsible to those beyond their borders. (In speaking of nonideal theory I am speaking of theory that is very much concerned with mechanisms, with how to get from here to there.)

The struggle here may concern small communities, and often it will be, in the first instance, about particular social issues (better hospital care, better education, greater equality between men and women, better and less expensive day care facilities, and the like), although I hope a larger agenda would be firmly in the background as well. Let me say here what I have argued for elsewhere: The struggle, in addition to such particular issues, should also be concerned with whether we should pursue a feasible socialism and if so, how. These issues, which often are avoided in our societies, should be put on the agenda.

All this is part of nonideal theory as I conceive it. But there is also ideal theory, which does not ask how we get from here to there but asks what it is, ideally and generally, we would like to see achieved, forgetting, for the moment, about how we would achieve it. What, we ask—as if we were gods, all wise, all good, all powerful, and could just bring it about like that—is what kind of world we would like for human beings everywhere such that this world would provide people with security and meet their needs, would be just and humane, and would be a place where human flourishing could be maximized. One feature of such a world, I shall argue, is that it will have a world government.

Why should this world have a world government? Because a secure, just, and humane society would be a society ordered by the rule of law, and that would require, among other things, something like a sovereign authority with the procedures to settle conflicts between different ethnic groups and cultures in an equitable, authoritative way. These procedures would settle conflicts without resort to war or to fighting where might prevails. A world government would have only one supreme authority to settle such questions, not unlike many present-day supreme courts and/or diverse executive authorities have within their respective territories in the various nation-states. No world of independent nation-states could provide people with that security.

Perhaps, to shift for a moment back to nonideal theory again, such a world would be unstable. A people (a nation) who did not like the decision rendered by the supreme authority might very well revolt, and we, with a kind of civil war within the global state, would be faced with the same old thing all over again. But if we could postulate (as in ideal theory we could) that people would not revolt, we would, with full compliance, have with a world government a single mechanism to settle conflicts of interest peacefully and equitably.

However, it remains the case that we could have a world government that turned out to be as authoritarian and tyrannical as any government we find among nation-states. However, in the case of world government there would be no possibility of an external power breaking that tyranny, although of course there could be a civil war or a coup d'état. Thus, it is not just a world government that is desirable but a certain kind of world government— namely, a cantonal-type democratic federation where considerable autonomy devolves to distinct cultural entities within this global federation.

In adjudicating conflicts there would be the supreme authority of the world government. It is the place where the buck stops. Here it is not difficult to share Mikhail Bakunin's anarchist concerns. Nevertheless, the world government we are discussing would be a democratically elected government with the usual democratic controls of a federal system. Thus, there would be democratic mechanisms for appointing a supreme court, and there would be a constitutional world democracy with a specified system of rights, some of which devolved to the cantons and some to the central government. This provides the protection of a constitutional democracy for a world government.

SQUARING WITH
OUR CONSIDERED JUDGMENTS

Federal systems such as Switzerland and Canada are hardly paradigms of just societies, however. What more do we need in order to secure a just world order? We need a coherent and feasible conception of global justice that would square with our considered judgments in wide reflective equilibrium—a conception that would square, that is, in a coherentist model of justification, with all we know or can reasonably believe and with those moral judgments to which on careful reflection we are most firmly committed in light of this knowledge or reasonable belief.[13] It, as well, must be a conception of global justice that we must be able to make a good start at showing could have a reasonable chance at a stable institutional exemplification in a feasibly possible world order. (That does not mean that it must be feasible tomorrow.)

Let us start characterizing it with the abstract conception of social justice first and move to a consideration of whether we can specify a possible institutional home for it. (Ideal and nonideal theory tend to meet in this last issue.) To get a start at this let us begin with a general considered judgment that, in modernizing contemporary societies, has a very firm acceptance at least in theory—namely, the belief in moral equality, the belief that the life of everyone matters and matters equally.[14] This indeed gets different readings and different phrasings, but it is accepted in some form across the political and moral spectrum in modern societies. Among current social philosophers, moral equality is accepted as much by Robert Nozick, F. A. Hayek, and Milton Friedman as it is by John Rawls, Michael Walzer, and Alasdair MacIntyre.

If we start with the considered judgment that the life of everyone matters and matters equally, then (if we are thinking clearly) we will want a world, as far as this is achievable, in which there is an equal protection of rights for everyone; an equal societal concern for the well-being of everyone; a concern with achieving, as far as it is reasonably possible, an equality of condition for everyone alike in a way that is compatible with individual autonomy and the possibility for human flourishing; and, finally, a concern for the fullest satisfaction of needs compatible with a fair treatment of people and with an equal respect and societal concern for their autonomy as interdependent individuals.[15]

This is, of course, a tall order, and it is not unreasonable to believe that the components of the package are incompatible to the extent that not all these values can be satisfied together. In particular, equality of condition and autonomy might not both be achievable.[16] It was the burden of my *Equality and Liberty* to show that a commitment to the most extensive possible autonomy for everyone requires a commitment to achieving or as fully as possible approximating an equality of condition. Without some reasonable success here, differential power relations will develop among people that will undermine the autonomy of some and thus will conflict with a commitment to moral equality. Perhaps neither extensive human equality nor autonomy is achievable in the modern world, but without their achievement there can be nothing like moral equality, and without that there can be no global justice. If both approximate equality of condition and autonomy are really impossible, then moral equality is a chimera. Whether, given human differences, anything like an equal satisfaction of needs or equal well-being is possible, is through and through questionable, particularly where this stress on equal well-being at the highest possible level of well-being for each is linked to a commitment to the fullest human flourishing possible for individuals whose needs will in certain respects be different. In being committed to moral equality we will be committed to as full an approximation as possible and to the fullest satisfaction of needs possible for everyone, taking into consideration that the needs of people will not be identical. To be committed to the fullest satisfaction of needs possible also is to be committed to achieving, as far as possible, the fullest human flourishing possible for all human beings.

We would only get global justice if we got something approximating the satisfaction of these conditions or, at least, if we had a world in which there were no institutional blocks to the achievement of these conditions. A world government with a legitimate authority would be a government that was committed to securing the conditions that would enable the achievement of global justice.

SO-CALLED INTRACTIBLE CASES

Nevertheless, questions generated by nonideal theory keep returning. People, when we look at them in their variety and across cultures, are rather different, their belief systems are different, and they have different perceived interests and some different genuine interests as well. A world government that tried to represent these different people in some equitable way could fail because there are just too many conflicts for an equitable adjudication of them. Consider, for example, a sparsely populated, tolerably well-off part of the world such as New Zealand and then a crowded impoverished part of the world such as Bangladesh. People from Bangladesh might wish to come to New Zealand, but New Zealanders, even when they had overcome social and ethnic prejudices, might still reasonably wish to preserve their world with its small population, uncrowded beaches, and mountain tracks. Thus, it is in the New Zealanders' interests to keep New Zealand as it is and not take on an extensive increase in population, and it is in the interests of many Bangladeshians to emigrate to New Zealand. Here interests, plainly rational interests, clash. Global justice with its commitment to moral equality would be committed to favoring the more extensive satisfaction of interest and the more basic interests. Thus, considerations of global justice would lead to a further opening of immigration in New Zealand so that there can be both a more extensive well-being and a greater equality of life conditions in the world. But this may, as John Rawls would put it, strain the strands of commitment to the breaking point.[17] Of course, there will be conflicts of genuine interests, but what needs to be shown for this to be devastating to the case I wish to make here is that there are no principles and practices of global justice that, together with a good knowledge of the world, can give us definite guidance here as to what is to be done.

There can be no doubt that conflicts like the one just discussed are very real, and it is understandable and not unreasonable to believe that it is just asking too much to expect New Zealanders, for example, to give up a prized way of life to equitably meet pressing population problems rooted in the needs of often desperate human beings. Yet fairness, rooted in moral equality, seems at least to require it. A prized way of life notwithstanding, if a people's lives are miserable and they can only be made nonmiserable by such population redistribution, then justice requires the population redistribution, where doing so would not make the general situation worse, particularly when the present inhabitants (in our case the New Zealanders) will not be made miserable by such a redistribution. Yet to insist on this would put a terrible strain on the strands of commitment. It is, without question, asking a lot of people.

The edge of this is taken off by the fact (indeed a convenient fact) that in actual life other measures can be taken such that there need not be this pressure to emigrate. Generally speaking, in statistically relevant numbers people will not want to emigrate to a faraway place with a radically different culture and language if the condition of life at home is not desperate. If the security and subsistence needs are firmly met and the condition of life improves with a development of the productive forces, people will not want to uproot themselves and move. Their identification with being a particular people is too strong for that.

With the development of the productive forces, with an intelligently and socially committed use of resources (world resources), and with a firm commitment to the conceptions of global justice I have outlined, Third World peoples for the most part can come to find a tolerable life without emigrating. The lives of many may not have the abundance of the New Zealanders' resources, to say nothing of the Swiss. But such a use of resources will allow them to flourish, and it will be a better answer to their needs, given their cultural commitments, than will emigration. Given some time and given a world government committed to policies designed to achieve moral equality, we will not have to make the hard choices discussed previously, choices that put a very considerable strain on what we can expect most people to do. But where we do, if we ever do, we still can see what justice requires.

Now one robin does not make a spring or one fine day. When we look at the diverse conflicts of interests among different peoples, we may come to the conclusion that often, indeed too often for the achievement of social justice, there can be no equitable resolution of conflicts of interest. But at least in the case discussed previously, the conflict appears to be intractable, and there plainly is justice on both sides. But to characterize the conflict as intractable is a superficial view. When we look at the conflict squarely, what justice would require, everything considered, is also evident. Justice here requires siding with (if you will) a utilitarianism of rights that requires the protection of the more extensive interests where the interests of everyone cannot be satisfied. Better a lesser harming of interests than a greater when it is unavoidable that some interests be harmed. However, it is also the case that there in fact need be no such conflict. The problem, if treated rationally and morally, would admit a morally accepted political and economic solution that would not require a redistribution of people. What is lacking, to achieve an equitable resolution, is political will and the resolute use of human intelligence. The lack of political will results from the entrenched interests of some and from the mystification of others—very many others—about what their interests are. (I believe the interests in question here are largely class interests on both sides, but I need not assume that here.)

I believe that this tough case is paradigmatic of a whole range of cases that involve issues of global justice and that they are rationally resolvable in a way similar to the way my paradigm case was. In nearly all non-desert-island moral conflicts, a thorough knowledge of the facts in the case plus a steadfast awareness and acceptance of a few moral truisms are sufficient to settle in a rational and morally acceptable manner what is to be done. It is a truism that people are different in certain respects, but it is also a truism that people are the same in certain respects. There are enough common needs and interests among people to give us a basis for some common policies and some commonly justifiable moral judgments (including judgments of global justice) on which a world government could act in accordance with the pervasive interests of its citizens. In such assessments, some of the differences among human beings can be accepted as tolerable differences, and others—where interests do clash—can be adjudicated, as we did in the foregoing example, by principles of global justice that, starting from widely shared considered moral convictions and a good knowledge of certain general facts, would be acceptable by reasonable people after careful deliberation in something like the original position.

SOCIALLY BASIC RIGHTS

Although I would not defend a rights-based ethical theory, I think the general point made in the last section can be strengthened when put in terms of human rights and when some suggestions developed by Henry Shue and David Luban are utilized.[18] In speaking of human rights I am speaking of demands of all humanity on all humanity. Among these human rights some are socially basic human rights and some are not. By a socially basic right I mean "a right whose satisfaction is necessary to the enjoyment of any other rights."[19] As Shue puts it, "Socially basic human rights are everyone's minimum reasonable demands upon the rest of humanity."[20] Some of these rights are what Shue calls *security rights*, such as the right not to be subject to killing, torture, assault, and the like. There are also *subsistence rights*, such as rights to healthy air, water, adequate food, clothing, and shelter where these can be had. There are, of course, other human rights such as our civil rights, but these socially basic rights are strategically central for they are the means for satisfying all other rights. A world government committed to global justice would be committed to the most extensive satisfaction of those rights for everyone. Moreover, these rights must first be secured before other rights are secured.

In conditions of moderate affluence and extensive security these rights can more or less be taken for granted, but ours is not yet even nearly that kind of world. A central aim of a good world government is to secure these socially basic human rights for everyone, and with the continued development of the productive forces it will become increasingly possible to do so. If we develop production relations that will optimally develop those productive forces and if we remain committed to global justice, it will become increasingly possible for a good world government to secure those socially basic rights for all and in an equitable manner (starting from the baseline that every person has an equal claim on them). With those rights secure, it will be possible to secure other human rights as well as many more of the interests of human beings than were previously secured. These latter interests can be increasingly met as the productive forces continue to develop.[21] Where we have conflicts of interests, the interests that answer to these socially basic interests will normally take pride of place. Socially basic interests will plainly override lesser interests, which could not count as human rights, and this provides the rationale for my judgment in the New Zealand example. But these socially necessary human rights will normally trump other rights as well because the former provides the causal foundation for the latter's very existence. With these, we would have a basis in rights for global justice, which for its achievement would require a world government.

SUMMING UP

I have set aside questions concerning the mechanism by which a unified global state with a world government would be achievable, although I have argued that it is not so fanciful as to be impossible in more propitious circumstances. I have also argued that in envisioning an acceptable global state we are looking at constitutional democracies on the model of a cantonal federation. This provides our model for what a good global state would look like—namely, a just and a humane cantonal federation writ large on a global scale with extensive cantonal autonomy for each canton. Surely nothing like that federation is even remotely in the offing. But it is neither conceptually nor morally anomalous or untoward, and under certain conditions it could be put on a realistic political agenda.

However, I also argued that a global state is not something we should presently put high on our political agenda. Indeed, perhaps when a global state is practically achievable it will not be needed. A world of democratic socialist nation-states would stand in fraternal peaceful relations with each other and would surely mutually cooperate. Perhaps in such a world of socialist democracies a global state would not be needed.

We surely could not answer that one way or another with any confidence ahead of the social experiment. A world government and a world state, as any state and government, have instrumental value only. Such institutions are valuable only if they, more than any alternative human arrangements, answer more adequately and more equitably to human needs. The anarchists are surely right in thinking that it would be a good thing if we could get along without a state, any state at all, and perhaps some day in some sense of that ambiguous notion we can.[22] There is nothing very nice about any group of people, no matter how moral, just, and well informed, having a monopoly on the means of violence. Such a thing is desirable only if it could prevent still more violence. We have no reason to love the state per se, but it may well be something that we will continue to have to live with and, in some of its forms, welcome as the lesser evil.

My argument has been that in answering our need for security (in making a relatively stable peace possible), a world state of the sort I have characterized is our best bet. I have also argued that a global state, by its very firm commitment to human rights and to furthering the good of humanity as a whole, would be a more just and a more humane social order than any of its alternatives. Moreover, by giving us an international law with sanctions, it would provide conditions, better than any alternative social arrangements, for furthering mutual cooperation, cooperation that could be materially advantageous.

If it turned out that none of these things were likely to be so, then there would be no reason to wish for a world government. Without such advantages, the value of a more complete autonomy for discrete peoples would tip the scales against a world government. But that, or so I have argued, is not how things stand.

FURTHER DOUBTS
ABOUT WORLD GOVERNMENT

Someone might argue that we do not need a global state to secure global justice and, in particular, to best secure socially basic human rights. There is something called international law, which obtains without a world state, and we could implement the rule of international law without a world state and without sanctions.[23] There indeed is law without the threat of effective sanctions, but it is also the case that there is likely to be little effective *rule* in the rule of law if there are no effective sanctions against noncompliance.

In a world of independent nation-states, there would be no such device to enforce compliance; in such a world there could be no international law with teeth and thus no rule of international law by which that law could enforce its verdicts. For security, if for nothing else, we need a world state with international law capable of enforcing its verdicts. Justice and a more humane order aside, a peace, secure from the alarms of war, most particularly nuclear war, makes a world state, as an institution capable of securing that, very desirable indeed. International law without teeth—our present state of affairs—cannot ensure that. Even if great warlike nation-states, such as the United States and the USSR, take it as a matter of elementary prudence to avoid a nuclear war (something it is reasonable to believe they would attempt), nevertheless, given their chauvinism, mutual dislike and distrust, and extensive nuclear stockpiles, the likelihood of an accidental nuclear war of (to put it minimally) devastating proportions is very real indeed and is a growing threat as these nations continue to build up their war machines. A world state would afford us significant protection from this situation, and that alone is worth the price of admission.

Some might counter that a world state would not really protect us more adequately from the ravages of war and the unthinkable consequences of nuclear destruction. With such conflicting, disparate elements as we have in the world, rebellions and revolutions would repeatedly break out. Consider, to see what is at issue, such entities as the USSR and the United States in the status of bloated, ungainly cantons.[24] They, to make a world state possible, have given up their claim to sovereignty, but they could, it is not unreasonable to argue, never be relied on to accept the dictates of international law when it worked against what they perceived to be important sectional interests.

Although I have set aside causal questions concerning how we could get these erstwhile states into a cantonal status, if somehow we could, then we would have set some additional impediments, moral and legal, to naked aggression and the pressing of their own perceived (and sometimes misperceived) interests in such a way that it would lead to global war. After all, we have an army, a world state executive, a world parliament, and a judicial system, all not creatures of any individual canton or clique of cantons, representing wider interests. Nevertheless, given the depth of cultural differences, the radically different economic position of different states, their dependency/domination relations, and the like, there are bound to be hatreds and struggles, attempts at secession, rebellions, revolutions, coup d'états, shifting hostile alliances, mean-spirited and destructive stratagems, and the like. Even with nuclear matters, there still could be trouble. Suppose a world government, with general consent, abolished nuclear arsenals; such a government hardly could abolish nuclear knowledge. Cantons that did not like the way things were going in the federation could, although it would not be easy, secretly develop weapons systems, and, particularly where several did this at once, something very similar to the same old nuclear standoff might occur again; some might even say, predictably would occur again, given the not inconsiderable economic disparities and the radically different ideologies that obtain across the planet. No world state, it is natural to think, even in a loose federation, could adequately answer such disparate interests or adjudicate the conflicts among them.

If we tried to form a world state, even the federation I spoke of, it would be inherently unstable and would either break up or lead in time, in trying to hold these disparate and hostile elements together, to a repressive dictatorship. There are not enough common bonds to make such a federation possible. We would end up with an authoritarian regime.

Here I first want to bite the bullet and accept for a moment the near-worst-case scenario by assuming that the world federation would be unstable and generate in time a repressive authoritarian government that would be prone to domination, to civil wars, and to a situation in which some of the cantons in the struggle for power within that system would develop nuclear weapons systems again. Even if this dreadful scenario were the more likely one and indeed became the one that transpired, we would still be better off than we are now; even with such an oppressive world government, the threat of nuclear devastation would still not be as great as it is at present.

It is also the case that there is something relevant here that those of us who live in North America are particularly prone to forget or even to never have adequately noticed or taken to heart. I refer to the fact that we have plenty of oppressive governments about now. Sometimes they are only internally oppressive, sometimes they are principally externally oppressive (for example, the United States), and sometimes they are both. Moreover, since the end of World War II, we have constantly had wars, sometimes civil and sometimes between states, and, war or not, we have had widespread massive exploitation, starvation, and impoverishment. We live in a world where some have an overabundance while others at best just barely survive. Thus, even if the world government were oppressive, it is not clear that it would be a worse state of affairs than we have now. If we read Hans Magnus Enzensberger and Noam Chomsky and not just F. A. Hayek and Peter Bauer we will get a vivid sense of that.

In fact, I think as bad as it would be, even an authoritarian and oppressive world state, unless (as is highly unlikely) on a world scale it became like the Nazis, would still be the lesser evil to the evil of the world order we have now. (Remember that ten thousand people starve to death each day mostly unnecessarily, that we now have a frightening nuclear insecurity, and that there is a considerable number of hostile, oppressive, and authoritarian states that from time to time engage in wars.) For our purposes, it is perhaps most important to note that the nuclear threat would be less, even with such a bad world state, than what we face now. It would be much harder with a world government, even an oppressive world government, to recapitulate the present war machines that obtain in nation-states. Even as aggressive oversized cantons, they would not be quite as dangerous as they presently are in the world system of nation-states, and it would take time, and there would be resistance, to their transformation back into nation-states again.

That aside, once the very idea of a world federation had come firmly into being in the minds of the great masses of people and had had a brief, even though unstable, institutionalization, of which the authoritarian world government was a perversion, there would be an effort to recapture a world state in its federated form. People would be motivated, as they are now, to struggle to regain democracy. When this happens, there is, as happened in Greece, Argentina, Spain, Portugal, Brazil, and Uruguay, and is happening in Chile, an attempt, which eventually is successful, to reconstitute a democratic order. In most of these cases, the society that succeeded the oppressive regime became more democratic than the society that preceded it.

If we start with the idea of a world federation, and with the underlying idea of a humanity that goes with it, and then move, under difficult political circumstances, to a world dictatorship in order to contain rebellious elements, we can expect that after a few years of that dictatorship there will be a struggle to regain the federation and, in time, a move on the part of the conflicting elements to find some mutual accommodation with each other as they engage in a common struggle against the oppressive regime. It is also reasonable to hope that these cantons would choose to avoid a replay of the situation that gave rise to a new dominating power and instead would find it in their respective interests to make mutual accommodations.

This, of course, as with all political encounters among different cultures and classes contending for a place in the sun, is fraught with difficulties but no more so than is our present situation, and, unlike our present situation, there would be a greater chance for world peace, more of a hope for global justice, more of a protection of human rights, and more of an extension of the bonds of sisterhood and brotherhood, where everyone, in commitment at least, comes under the net and with equal status. This is much easier for someone—or at least an educated someone—in the Third World than in the First to appreciate and take to heart.

I also think this near-worst-case scenario is not nearly as likely as some far more benign scenarios. I only accepted it provisionally for the sake of argument. World conquest, particularly given the nuclear situation, by any one power is rather unlikely, and the only kind of world government that would stand much chance of being accepted (if any would at all) by these different powers would be one that had something like the democratic and federalist structure of the world government I have described. But that structure surely could not come into being until an extension of the idea of democracy to all humankind went much further, as a popular ideology, than it has yet gone and until the various nationalisms, at least in idea, had been considerably weakened.

With the emergence of states from imperialist and racist domination, nationalism has grown, but so, too, paradoxically, has internationalism. The idea of democracy, once introduced, is very catching indeed. It goes readily with an increase in de facto interdependence, the extension of communications and knowledge, the continued development of the productive forces, and relentless modernization. There is no steady development here; there are blips and downturns, such as we are now experiencing in some parts of the world, but if we look at longer time spans, it is evident that all of these forces are developing, carrying forth what one might call the logic of the Enlightenment.

With these Enlightenment ideas of democracy and the fellowship of humankind, with a firm sense of prudence about mutual nuclear destruction (and the like), and with the continued development of the forces of production, we have before us the conditions that, with luck, could generate the impulse necessary to make world government a live option.

CONCLUSION

I have defended the utopian possibility, in coherently statable circumstances, of a world government of a distinct democratic sort, and I also have defended the desirability of having such a government when we can get it in a reasonably tolerable way. I do not see anything like a movement toward it presently, although I do believe the unfoldment of the dialectic of the Enlightenment and the development of the forces of production, with congruent developments in the relations of production, will eventually make such a world, provided in the interim we do not blow ourselves up, a feasible nonutopian possibility. But I do not deny that there are staggering difficulties along the way, only some of which I have alluded to here. Surely, as a very central issue, there is the problem of whether, as long as capitalism survives, there is much chance of a world government of the sort I have characterized. I do not believe, although this claim is surely tendentious and needs arguing, world government has much chance as long as capitalism remains a major element in the world order. I think, however, that the same forces that push us toward a world government, even more evidently and more immediately, push us toward democratic socialism, which is an extension of the idea of democracy from the political to the economic realm. If we are well informed and morally reflective, we should want industrial democracy, workers' control of their workplace, and ownership by the public of the means of production, as well as political democracy, and we should want these things principally because they extend both human autonomy and human well-being.[25] Indeed, without industrial democracy, political democracy is not very likely to be effective. However, it is also the case that without political democracy, economic democracy will not flourish. All that notwithstanding, the crucial consideration for our argument is that the idea of democracy, like the related idea of moral equality, is an idea that once brought to people becomes irresistible. In the longer view of things, unless our social fabric is utterly destroyed, there is no turning back from democracy—a democracy that will continue to be extended.

NOTES

1. Richard Rorty's "Solidarity and Objectivity," in J. Rajchman and C. West (editors), *Post-Analytic Philosophy* (New York: Columbia University Press, 1985), pp.

19; and Richard Rorty, "Postmodern Bourgeois Liberalism," *Journal of Philosophy* 80 (1983):583–589. Michael Walzer, *Just and Unjust Wars* (New York: Basic Books, 1977), pp. 51–63, 86–101, 106–108, 339–342. Michael Walzer, "The Rights of Political Communities" in Charles R. Beitz et al. (editors), *International Ethics* (Princeton, N.J.: Princeton University Press, 1985), pp. 165–194. See in the same volume, David Luban, "Just War and Human Rights," pp. 195–216; Michael Walzer, "The Moral Standing of States: A Response to Four Critics," pp. 217–237; and David Luban, "The Romance of the Nation-State," pp. 238–243. See, as well, G. A. Cohen, "Reconsidering Historical Materialism" in J. R. Pennock and J. W. Chapman (editors), *Marxism* (New York: New York University Press, 1983), pp. 227–254; and Isaiah Berlin, *Against the Current* (New York: Viking Press, 1979), pp. 333–355.

2. Walzer, "The Moral Standing of States," p. 224.

3. Johann Gottfried Herder, among the classical writers, and Isaiah Berlin, among our contemporaries, have the best sense of that. See J. G. Herder, *Herders Werke* (Berlin und Weimar: Aufbau-Verlag, 1964). Isaiah Berlin, *Vico and Herder* (London: Hogarth Press, 1976); Isaiah Berlin, *Four Essays on Liberty* (London: Oxford University Press, 1969); and Isaiah Berlin, *Fathers and Children* (Oxford: Clarendon Press, 1972).

4. P. T. Bauer, *Equality, The Third World and Economic Delusion* (Cambridge, Mass.: Harvard University Press, 1981), p. 19.

5. Walzer, "The Rights of Political Communities," pp. 165–194.

6. Walzer, "The Moral Standing of States," p. 236.

7. Ibid.

8. Ibid.

9. Ibid.

10. Ibid.

11. Ibid.

12. Berlin, *Vico and Herder*, pp. 145–216.

13. John Rawls, *A Theory of Justice* (Cambridge, Mass.: Harvard University Press, 1971), pp. 19–21, 48–51, 577–587. John Rawls, "The Independence of Moral Theory," *Proceedings and Addresses of the American Philosophical Association* 47 (1974/5):7–10; Norman Daniels, "Wide Reflective Equilibrium and Theory Acceptance in Ethics," *The Journal of Philosophy* 76 (1979); "Moral Theory and Plasticity of Persons," *The Monist* 62 (July 1979); "Some Methods of Ethics and Linguistics," *Philosophical Studies* 37 (1980); "Reflective Equilibrium and Archimedean Points," *Canadian Journal of Philosophy* 10 (March 1980); and "Two Approaches to Theory Acceptance in Ethics" in David Copp and David Zimmerman (editors), *Morality, Reason and Truth* (Totowa, N.J.: Rowman and Allanheld, 1985); Jane English, "Ethics and Science," *Proceedings of the XVI Congress of Philosophy*; Kai Nielsen, "On Needing a Moral Theory: Rationality, Considered Judgements and the Grounding of Morality," *Metaphilosophy* 13 (April 1982); "Considered Judgements Again," *Human Studies* 5 (April-June 1982); *Equality and Liberty* (Totowa, N.J.: Rowman and Allanheld, 1985), Chapter 2; and "Searching for an Emancipatory Perspective: Wide Reflective Equilibrium and the Hermeneutical Circle" in Evan Simpson (editor), *Anti-Foundationalism and Practical Reasoning* (Edmonton, Alberta: Academia Press, 1987).

14. Thomas Nagel, *Mortal Questions* (New York: Cambridge University Press, 1979), pp. 106–127.

15. I have extensively argued for those views in my *Equality and Liberty: A Defense of Radical Egalitarianism* (Totowa, N.J.: Rowman and Allanheld, 1985); my "Capitalism, Socialism and Justice" in T. Regan and D. VanDeVeer (editors), *And

Justice for All (Totowa, N.J.: Rowman and Littlefield, 1982), pp. 264–286; and my "On Liberty and Equality: A Case for Radical Egalitarianism," *The Windsor Yearbook of Access to Justice* 4 (1984):121–142.

16. Friedrich A. Hayek, *The Constitution of Liberty* (Chicago: University of Chicago Press, 1960). For a perceptive criticism of Hayek's views, see Richard Norman, "Does Equality Destroy Liberty?" in Keith Graham (editor), *Contemporary Political Philosophy* (Cambridge: Cambridge University Press, 1982), pp. 83–109.

17. Rawls, *A Theory of Justice*, pp. 145, 176, and 423.

18. Henry Shue, *Basic Rights: Subsistence, Affluence and U.S. Foreign Policy*, (Princeton, N.J.: Princeton University Press, 1980), Chapter 1; and David Luban, "Just War and Human Rights," pp. 195–216. In this general context, see Marshall Cohen, "Moral Skepticism and International Relations" and Charles R. Beitz, "Justice and International Relations" both in Beitz et al., *International Ethics.*

19. Luban, ibid., p. 209.

20. Shue, "Foundations for a Balanced U.S. Policy on Human Rights: The Significance of Subsistence Rights," Working Paper HRFP-1 (College Park, Md.: Center for Philosophy and Public Policy, 1977), p. 3.

21. G. A. Cohen, *Karl Marx's Theory of History: A Defense* (Oxford: Clarendon Press, 1978).

22. For a perceptive discussion of that complex issue, see Andrew Levine, *The Withering Away of the State* (London: Verso, 1987).

23. H.L.A. Hart, *The Concept of Law* (Oxford: Oxford University Press, 1961). See his discussion of international law.

24. They are surely too large and, particularly the USSR, have too diversified populations to be cantons. In working toward a global federation of cantons, a rigid adherence to an old notion of nation-states as the basis for cantonal units would not be the optimal solution. It would be important to look for significant cultural units.

25. Andrew Levine, *Arguing for Socialism* (London: Routledge and Kegan Paul, 1984).

17

Moral Progress

THOMAS POGGE

Thomas Pogge rejects Kai Nielsen's claim that ideally there ought to be a central world authority with ultimate sovereign power. Instead, we should rest content with something that in rudimentary form we already have: international law and some central governmental organs with limited powers of adjudication and enforcement.

The notion of a world government with ultimate sovereign power appeals to those who, working in the Hobbesian framework, see nations as mutually disinterested rational egoists; that is, as each concerned only to do the best it can for itself alone. Pogge calls international relations that are based in this way solely on prudential grounds a modus vivendi. The present world order is a modus vivendi, although not one in which a Hobbesian sovereign power dominates. Powerful nations will not allow the existence of a sovereign global power because it would put them and their values in grave peril. Nevertheless, the modus vivendi that now exists is, according to Pogge, one in which the survival of each nation and its citizens' values are in constant danger. That is why the international order is not as peaceful and as just as are the institutions within various particular nations. To bring about a more just international order, what is required is an international order based on moral values shared by all and identified by an international dialogue among experts in law and social and political philosophy.

Kai Nielsen writes about the global order we would design "if we were gods, all wise, all good, all powerful, and could just bring it about like that." I must confess to being not nearly wise and good enough to validate such claims. Allow me then to oppose Nielsen's vision by engaging in a somewhat more worldly sort of ideal theory. I would like to aim for an institutional ideal for our world, one that takes account of our history and of the powers that be and that allows gradual implementation from where we are.

Working out the details of such an avenue of moral progress would evidently require much more than an abstract sketch. Nevertheless, the philosophical ideas I will explain and defend should make the general features of my proposal sufficiently clear to decide whether it is plausible enough to even bother thinking about the details.

WORLD GOVERNMENT

Nielsen's central assertion is that we should want a global state, ruled by a world government that has ultimate sovereign power and authority, constitutes a court of last appeal, and, through its army, has a monopoly on the means of violence.[1] In response, I will hypothesize that the absence of world government is *not* the central problem with our current global order, which is so lacking in peace and justice.

The standard question of whether or not there should be a world government is misleading. Presenting the issue in stark either/or terms reflects a deep and historically very influential mistake. The traditional form of this mistake might be called the dogma of absolute sovereignty—the belief that a juridical state (as distinct from a lawless state of nature) presupposes an authority of last resort. This view arises (in Thomas Hobbes and Immanuel Kant, for example) roughly as follows: A juridical state, by definition, involves a recognized decision mechanism that uniquely resolves any dispute. This mechanism requires some active authority because a mere written or unwritten code (a holy scripture, set of legal documents, or whatever) cannot settle disputes about its own interpretation. A limited or divided authority would not do, however, as conflicts might arise over the precise location of the limit or division. There then must exist one ultimate and supreme universal authority if civil peace is to be possible at all.[2]

This dazzling reasoning is now safely buried beneath the historical facts of the last two hundred years, which show conclusively that what cannot work in theory works quite well in practice. Law-governed societies are possible without a supreme authority or court of last appeal. To be sure, this means that there is a possibility of *ultimate* conflicts, of disputes regarding which even the legally correct method of resolution is contested. To see this, one need only imagine how a constitutional democracy's three branches of government might engage in an all-out power struggle, each going to the very brink of what it is constitutionally authorized to do. From a theoretical point of view, this possibility shows that we are not ensured against, and thus live in permanent danger of, constitutional crises. But this no longer undermines our confidence in a genuine division of powers; we have learned that such crises need not be frequent and can be resolved even when they do occur. From a practical point of view, we know that constitutional democracies can be stable, can ensure a robust juridical state.

Now all this is hardly seriously in dispute. What is perhaps not generally understood is that the same point applies on the "vertical" axis as well. Just as it is nonsense to suppose that in a juridical state sovereignty must rest with one of the branches of government, it is similarly nonsensical to think that in a federalist scheme sovereignty "must" rest either on the federal level or with the member states. Making this assumption, one is bound to conclude, as Nielsen does, that sovereignty must rest on the federal level because, if it rested with the states, then there would not be a federalist scheme at all. However, the assumption is philosophically unsound, descriptively inaccurate of existing federalist constitutions,[3] and, as I will show, politically disastrous for the prospects for peace and justice.

Once we dispense with the traditional concept of sovereignty and leave behind all-or-nothing debates about world government, there emerges a clear preference for an intermediate solution that provides for some central organs of world government without, however, investing them with "ultimate sovereign power and authority." Of course, such an intermediate solution is what we have now, in the form of some international law with some mechanisms of adjudication and enforcement (the International Court of Justice and the U.N. Security Council). To be sure, these existing institutions are not exactly successful. One might well claim that their failure, even in their own terms, is to be explained by the weakness of existing mechanisms of adjudication and enforcement—that the violence and injustice pervading our world are due to there being *not enough* world government.

Proponents of this view can use the weakness of international adjudication mechanisms to explain the pervasive ambiguity and vagueness of international law. So long as only a small fraction of intergovernmental disputes are ever impartially resolved, there will be a dearth of authoritative precedents, and major disagreements about the interpretation of international laws and treaties will persist unresolved. Moreover, so long as governments can presume that in all likelihood they will be able to avoid an authoritative rebuke, they will be tempted to put forward surprising (and even ludicrous) interpretations of international laws and treaties in justification of governmental conduct.

Similarly, one can—as Nielsen does[4]—use the weakness of international enforcement mechanisms to explain disregard of (and cynicism about) international law. So long as international laws and treaties are rarely enforced for their own sake, governments will be tempted to violate, abrogate, or reinterpret these laws and treaties if the net benefit of doing so is considerable. This tendency will affect even governments strongly committed to the ideal of a law-governed world order. Without assurances that other governments will fulfill their international obligations, the former governments cannot find it either responsible or morally required that they alone should make major unilateral sacrifices for the sake of law.

Although there is some truth in such (essentially Hobbesian) accounts, I do not think they get to the heart of the problem. Our global institutional order (international laws and treaties, the United Nations, and so on) is shaped by intergovernmental agreements and (more importantly) by government practice and acquiescence, all of which are based on prudential deliberations informed by the current distribution of power. This leaves politicians (and citizens) without a *moral* reason for wanting their state to support this order, which they see as merely the crystallization of the momentary balance of power. I would like to explore the possibility that this fact about international institutions, if it animates the dominant attitude toward them, could be the cardinal obstacle blocking moral progress in international affairs. In offering this hypothesis as an alternative to Hobbesian accounts, I do not mean to imply that stronger prudential restraints would not be a good thing—only that there is little chance of getting these stronger prudential restraints without changing that dominant attitude. The analysis in the next section seeks to offer a deeper understanding of our predicament, which includes an explanation of why progress toward more effective central mechanisms of adjudication and enforcement has been so elusive.

FROM MODUS VIVENDI
TO VALUE OVERLAP

In the Hobbesian dimension of progress, a first step beyond unlimited and universal war is an element of coordinated self-restraint. Here two parties (persons, tribes, states, or whatever) understand that each is restraining itself in some way in order to elicit some reciprocal self-restraint from the other side. Such a mutual understanding need not be explicit, nor does it require any value commitments. Mutual assurance can rest entirely upon each party's appreciation that the other party—given its interests, capabilities, and situation—would be foolish to destroy the arrangement.[5]

The Hobbesian ideal is an extension of this model. Peace is to be achieved by inaugurating a mode of coexistence that, once in place, perpetuates itself by ensuring that each party has sufficient incentives to participate so long as most others are participating as well. Presumably, large-scale arrangements of this sort are too complex to be tacit. But no matter how complex, the model is supposed to work without shared values; each party's continued participation is to be assured by the plain fact that it would be foolish to quit.

When the relations among parties center around (tacit or explicit) agreements along this Hobbesian axis—from the most narrow, fragile, and transitory bilateral understandings to the most comprehensive, robust, and enduring universal accord—I will characterize their coexistence as a modus vivendi. The participants in a modus vivendi are motivated primarily by their own self-defined interests and do not much care about one another's interests as such. Yet each has reason to support a shared institutional scheme—a system of rules and conventions, practices and procedures, organs and offices—that accommodates the interests of other parties to the point where they find it in their best interest to participate as well. This model contrasts, on the one hand, with the total absence of restraints, as in a state of unlimited violence (although a modus vivendi is compatible with limited violence, excluding certain times, targets, or methods, in warfare).

My focus here is on how the modus vivendi model contrasts, on the other hand, with the model of an institutional scheme based upon some value commitments that are genuinely shared.[6] For this it is not enough that all participants seek security, or that each wants its religion (or form of regime) to survive or to prevail in the end, as they may still differ about whose security or which religion (form of regime) they care for. Nor can we speak of shared values when the parties have a common interest—peace— that is instrumental to their disparate deeper commitments and projects; they are then not committed to peace as such. They merely, each for its own reasons, prefer peace *under current conditions.* Thus, their coexistence is still a modus vivendi because they do not share each other's ultimate values, which, in a different context, might lead them to war. An institutional scheme is value-based only if its participants hold in common some important *ultimate* values (including some principles for balancing or ordering them) that are significantly embodied in the institutions regulating their interactions.

My central hypotheses are (1) that current international relations are in essence a modus vivendi and (2) that the crucial reason why international institutions are so much less successful than are the institutions of well-governed national societies is that the latter enshrine shared values (not that they include more central government). These two hypotheses suggest the program: through international ethical dialogue to initiate institutional reforms toward a world order that reflects some shared ultimate values.

In discussing international relations, I will presuppose that, apart from the competition over power, there is lasting international disagreement about values and especially about acceptable forms of national (political and economic) organization. I also will take for granted a global background convention: The land of the world is divided up into clearly demarcated territories. Each territory has one government—the person or group wielding overwhelming power (and ultimately controlling irresistible means of coercion) within the territory. Each government is recognized (by others) as having full jurisdiction over all persons and resources within its domain. Given this background convention, the actors shaping international institutions are, first and foremost, governments, and my hypothesis then postulates an inter-governmental modus vivendi.

Let me begin, however, with some remarks about the modus vivendi model in general. On the surface, a modus vivendi is an agreement among a plurality of parties to restrain their competitive behavior in certain ways. Because the scheme must be designed so that continued participation is in each party's best interest, the terms of the scheme must satisfy the condition of prudential stability—that is, the terms must be such that all parties have reason to participate on the going terms. However, whether a given party,

P, views the going terms as acceptable depends upon a number of variables, such as P's self-defined interests and (most importantly) the general distribution of power (which affects P's vulnerabilities and opportunity costs of participation). Which terms satisfy the prudential stability condition is then subject to fluctuation. Suppose, for example, that P's power has increased, so that P now has more to gain and less to lose from a (partial) breakdown of orderly relations. It may then be prudent for P to press for more favorable terms and prudent for the others to accede to P's demand—at the expense of weakened participants, who are obliged to accept less favorable terms due to their increased vulnerability or decreased threat advantage.

For a modus vivendi to endure, the distribution of benefits and burdens may then have to be adjusted so that participation continues to be each party's preferred option. This possibility generates, below the surface, a competition over the terms of the modus vivendi; and *this* competition is not restrained at all. There is no limit to how weak a party may become through shifts in the distribution of power (compounded by shifts in the terms of the modus vivendi). There also is no limit to what a weak party may prudently acquiesce in within a modus vivendi, in preference to quitting.

Contrary to this conclusion, some might think that there *is* a limit to such shifts, that the terms of a modus vivendi must at least be mutually advantageous in the sense that each party derives a net benefit from participation as compared to total isolation. But this is not so. How well off a party would be in splendid isolation is irrelevant to the bargaining equilibrium, if this party cannot secure such isolation for itself. Even when accepting tributary status in a modus vivendi is clearly less attractive than isolation, it may still be the prudent thing to do—when the expected alternative is not exclusion but attack and enslavement, for example.

The great virtue of a modus vivendi is that it can work, can prevent all-out war, even among parties who have no faith in each other and believe they have nothing in common by way of shared values. In order to be assured of each other's continued compliance, the parties need only ensure that continued participation is each party's preferred option. In a non-zero-sum world, orderly coexistence is possible even in the absence of shared values and mutual trust.

However, precisely this virtue, which makes the modus vivendi model so wonderful a remedy against full-scale war, renders it unsuitable for achieving peace and justice. On the one hand, the indefinite malleability of its terms is needful to a modus vivendi's endurance through changes in the power, interests, and situation of its participants. Yet, on the other hand, this malleability is a source of instability and great danger. A modus vivendi can persist through such changes only if its participants can, at each time, agree on terms appropriately reflecting the current distribution of power. Moreover, the long-term malleability of a modus vivendi engenders short-term instability, as each participant must be afraid of getting into a vicious cycle in which its decline in power reinforces and is reinforced by a deterioration in the terms of its participation. If a participant anticipates such a trend, it may prefer to fight now rather than await a further decline in its power. If others suspect that this is such a participant's intention, then they in prudence may preempt by attacking it first. Such disturbances can lead to a partial or complete breakdown of ordered relations. But even if the modus vivendi survives, some of its participants may not (or may see their freedom and values destroyed). There is no lasting protection against even the very worst outcomes.

This explains why values, however deeply held, will have only a marginal impact upon the participants' conduct and (through this) upon the terms of the modus vivendi. Because the parties are fearful of one another, each will give precedence to the long-term security of its values over their short-term instantiation. No party is likely to impose ethical handicaps upon its pursuit of power through which alone it can hope to survive and (ultimately) prevail. And each will want to prevail so as to eradicate the threat from others, who presumably want to prevail for just this reason.

The following train of thought may illustrate this point: "Others may be seeking to shift the balance of power against us, which, in the long run, might enable them to eradicate our values altogether. We cannot eliminate this danger for the time being; thus, our best counterstrategy for now consists in trying, within a modus vivendi framework, to stem any advances on their part and to weaken their position. Because the very survival of our values is at stake, we must not constrain these efforts by our values. For if we do, we will be competing at a decided disadvantage—they will certainly not constrain their conduct by our values, and, because they are fearful (and perhaps bent upon prevailing), they are unlikely to constrain their conduct even by their own values. In this situation, we must not endanger the survival of our values by allowing these values to hamper our efforts to block and neutralize the threat from others."

I conclude that relations within a modus vivendi will be neither peaceful nor just. A modus vivendi is a state of persistent and extreme danger for its participants, demanding their permanent and utmost vigilance; the competition over the distribution of power and over the terms of association will be ferocious. Even if the parties to a modus vivendi have deep and sincere value commitments, it is likely that their values will not have a significant impact upon their (external) conduct—that is, their values will not figure prominently in their decisions about compliance or in their efforts to shape the terms of the scheme. Given that each participant cares primarily for its relative position, the terms of a modus vivendi will essentially reflect a dynamic bargaining equilibrium that is based upon the participants' power and strategic interests and is largely independent of what the participants' particular values may be. The inconstant terms of a modus vivendi are likely (at least over time) to violate *any* ethical conception—except possibly a belief in "the right of the stronger."

Interestingly, these difficulties are not susceptible to a Hobbesian solution through central mechanisms of adjudication and enforcement. To see this, consider first a modus vivendi whose five strongest participants are authorized to adjudicate any dispute by simple majority vote,[7] and suppose that the distribution of power is such that any three are actually strong enough to enforce their judgment even against a coalition including the other two. Here each of the five must fear that any three of the others will unite against it to reduce its power, especially because they must fear that *it* might join such a coalition against any one of them. Far from offering long-term security, this sort of arrangement is merely another version of the ferocious competition to the death, with the five principals bargaining over one another's support in the attempt to be part of a winning coalition.

This leaves the Hobbesian solution in its purest form: a modus vivendi whose most powerful participant is strong enough to control all the others. (This is still a modus vivendi insofar as the strongest party moderates its demands in exchange for more willing compliance by the weak.) As I will argue, this solution, while practicable in principle, is not attainable in the international arena. Short of global war, we cannot get there from where we are.

The alternative to the modus vivendi model is another conception of mutual accommodation—envisaging another way for a shared institutional scheme to emerge and be sustained even while its participants have divergent interests and values. The central idea is to base institutions upon a firm core of shared ultimate values rather than (as in the modus vivendi conception) upon free bargaining informed by the changeable distribution of power.[8]

Now one might have thought that reliance on shared values presupposes a shared value system, such as Catholicism in the Middle Ages, and that in a world of diverse fundamental outlooks appeal to values can only be divisive. But this objection appeals to a false dichotomy. We need not envision for the world what is lacking in every national society, namely, a *comprehensive* agreement on values. Instead, we can start from what we already have—a world in which *some* values are shared. Genuine international discussion of values could identify and perhaps expand existing value overlap. In the latter vein, a better understanding of each other's values is bound to broaden and deepen a commitment to the value of tolerance and of tolerance of alternative forms of national organization in particular.

Moreover, shared values need not be all-pervasive. In a national society, resources may be allocated to the highest bidder, and many legislative issues may be decided by self-interested bargaining (logrolling and so on). Nevertheless, in a well-governed society some matters are non-negotiable—for example, that none will be slaves, be left to starve, or be disenfranchised. These matters are protected not by a stable majority preference, but by the citizens' sense of justice, which here supercedes their particular interests. In the international arena, by contrast, the dominant assumption, and well-grounded fear, is that everything is negotiable and that any law, treaty, charter, or declaration may be "reinterpreted," violated, renegotiated, abrogated, abandoned, or simply forgotten.

The progress I envision begins then from some consensus on values, however narrow, which allows the establishment of institutional fixed points that stand above ordinary negotiation and bargaining and thus are immune to shifts in the power, interests, and opportunities of the major parties. The foremost prerequisite of such a transformation is that societies should accept—*morally* rather than only prudentially (as a vexing necessity imposed by the present distribution of power)—the continued existence of each other and of the values central to their domestic social contracts. Beyond this, the prospects for a value-based institutional scheme will depend upon what, concretely, the values and attitudes of the societies involved are and upon the following three conditions: First, the parties are convinced that there ought to be such a scheme that, through a fair distribution of benefits and burdens, accommodates all of them to the point where each can make a sincere and reliable commitment that will withstand tempting opportunities as well as shifts in relative power and self-defined interests. Second, the parties can identify, and perhaps extend, some common values—a shared rudimentary conception of justice or humanity, for example. Third, the parties are willing—for the sake of what is itself a valued goal—to modify their values to some extent. Here the pivotal question is whether the parties can see their way to embracing an institutional scheme that is more tolerant of some broader range of diverse values than each would have liked and tolerant enough to guarantee that the (similarly modified) values of others can, in their essentials, survive forever.

If such a transition succeeds, the typical participant may well come to value the resulting order in its own right rather than continue to wish for less tolerant institutions built upon the participant's own values alone. The commitment to a mutually acceptable scheme would then deepen further as a consequence of the transition itself (through the experience of mutual trust and cooperation), while the overlap of genuinely shared values would expand. This, at least, would be the favored outcome of the transition.

The hope that people should come to prefer a heterogeneous world, including capitalist and socialist societies, over the global imposition of their own form of regime may sound utopian. That it *can* happen is shown, however, by our historical experience—for example, the relation among the Christian faiths after the Protestant Reformation. From decades of bloody warfare emerged a modus vivendi. Although neither side gave up its goal to reunify the church on its own terms, both sides realized that for now they were unable to impose such a reunification and thus accepted a fragile bargain in preference to continued warfare. Because power was held by autocratic princes on both sides, the bargain struck, not surprisingly, reflected their *common* interests: *Cuius regio eius religio*—each lord may force his religion upon his subjects without outside interference. This temporary convenience was gradually transformed into a genuinely shared value commitment with quite a different content: liberty of conscience, freedom of thought, and religious toleration. No authority whatever may enforce religious beliefs. This *moral* conviction is now at the very core of Western political thought, whether academic or popular, and is widely taken for granted among members of the relevant denominations.

INTERNATIONAL PLURALISM

The *decisive* condition for an analogous transformation in our current world is, I believe, widespread acceptance of what I call international pluralism, of the idea that *knowledgeable and intelligent persons of good will may reasonably favor different forms of social organization*. There are two main grounds for wanting this idea as a shared basis from which to work toward a better world.

The first is realism. Contrary to Nielsen,[9] it is a minimal demand upon political ideal theory that it develop an ideal of a *future* world, of a world that is connectible to the status quo by a morally admissible route (one that does not pass through World War III, for example). This demand is not met by an ideal that envisions the dismemberment of existing superpowers[10] or by one that involves the abolition of capitalist states or socialist states or both. Of course, I have no right to demand that others should accept this constraint. They may be interested in designing a morally ideal world regardless of whether it describes a possible future for us. If so, they can make valuable contributions to science fiction or theodicy. But a useful contribution to the political task at hand, to overcoming violence and starvation, just *cannot* consist in arguing that all national societies must conform to the writer's favored social ideal.[11]

In fact, such arguments contribute to our predicament (our imprisonment in an intergovernmental modus vivendi). Today, each of several major societies is committed to the belief that its form of regime is plainly superior to that of some opposing societies and that it would not be wrong in principle to destroy the opponents' domestic institutions by force (so as to liberate the people they oppress). There is, in fact, some eagerness to "turn around" regimes on the other side because they, too, may recognize no ultimate restraints against "liberating" a system of our type, and they are liable to do so when they can in order to remove threats to *their* long-term survival. However, given the present distribution of power, neither side can be confident that it will survive an all-out attempt to liberate the societies on the other side. This military stalemate between East and West is, and is widely understood to be, the vital condition for continued coexistence. Neither side is convinced that, were it significantly weaker, its values would be allowed to survive. Rather, each side must assume, and will take its opponents to assume, that the other side stands ready to use any means at all, including global war, even for the secondary goal of prevailing, so long as the preeminent goal of survival is not significantly endangered thereby.[12]

The essential fragility of this status quo is clear from its complex preconditions. At least the great powers (know each other to) care much more for their own regime's survival than for the eradication of opposing regimes. The great powers are risk-averse—in part because the status quo is, for now, quite satisfying to them. Moreover, these governments have, and know each other to have, rational prudence and a cool appreciation of the current distribution of power. Finally, the dominant governments also are, and know each other to be, convinced that this distribution (the bargaining equilibrium) is not about to shift dramatically against any one of them in the medium term (which would make that power a likely aggressor and a likely target for preemption). We have no right or reason to hope that these fortunate conditions will last forever. Although there is every reason to welcome the existing intergovernmental mode of coexistence insofar as it postpones global war, we must then use the time to work for institutional reforms that will bring peace.

Widespread acceptance of the idea of international pluralism would make possible a world in which certain value clusters, with their coordinate national forms of regime, are *morally* accepted and permanently protected against violent extinction. Once societies know of each other that they sincerely accept the continued existence of one another's national constitutions, then it becomes reasonable to order one's preferences concerning a shared global institutional scheme by considering how well various alternatives reflect one's values, rather than by how these alternatives affect the capacity of one's society and values to survive and prevail in a ferocious competition.[13] This enables a shared institutional scheme based not upon a fickle power equilibrium but upon a firm core of values. If such a scheme can be agreed upon, then it is much more reasonable to comply with its terms, even when noncompliance would yield a net benefit, because the scheme better reflects one's own values and because the long-term survival of one's society and form of regime is no longer at stake.

The realist argument for accepting international pluralism has then, at bottom, a moral character; it appeals to those who reject the option of fighting it out and are concerned about the long-term danger of global war. The realist argument appeals to those who prefer to revise their vision of a just global order to the point where it can be implemented, rather than insist on an "ideal" vision that will exist only on paper in a world pervaded by violence and injustice. In the realist argument, it is then *for the sake of our values themselves* that we should modify these values in the direction of greater tolerance.

Am I then suggesting that because we cannot realistically hope for what Nielsen calls a through and through just and humane world, we must make do with whatever paltry optimum might still be attainable from where a bungled history dropped us off? Not at all! The second ground for accepting the idea of pluralism is its plausibility. In fact, the idea is robustly plausible, in that it can be accepted for various and even incompatible reasons: It accommodates those who, although convinced they know what a just and humane society would look like, realize that they cannot prove the superiority of their ideal from shared premises. It accommodates those who doubt that they can now (or that anyone can ever) be reasonably certain to have found *the* best way of organizing a human society. It accommodates those who believe that the best social world would contain a variety of forms of national organization. It accommodates those who are convinced that different in-stitutional ideals may be appropriate to societies that differ in natural

environment and level of development. And it accommodates those who
think that each national community must be left free (within broad limits)
to work out its own constitution in light of its history and culture, which
it alone is able and entitled to interpret and to extend into the future. No
doubt, some of these reasons can be combined, and new ones could be
added to the list. But perhaps the five kinds of reasons I have outlined are
enough to show that international pluralism is plausible and more plausible
than its opposite—the claim that someone is in possession of a blueprint
for a just and humane society whose superior merits could be denied only
by the morally corrupt and the dim-witted.

I am not claiming that one may reasonably favor *any* form of social
organization. In fact, the opposite is true; it does *not* seem reasonable to
advocate, say, slavery, colonialism, or autocracy. Hence, the idea of pluralism
that should be widely shared is by no means tantamount to a general
agnosticism with regard to the justice of national institutions. What is needed
is the concession that knowledgeable and intelligent persons of good will
may reasonably disagree about the fundamental issues dividing the world
today—for example, should the means of production be controlled by the
workers operating them, by the government, or by private owners? Is the
best forum for democratic discussion and decisionmaking afforded by a
single-party, two-party, or multiparty system? In appraising and reforming
social institutions, is it more important to focus upon civil liberties or upon
basic social and economic needs? If only we could understand our disagreement
about such matters as *reasonable* disagreement, then we could jointly work
toward a world in which alternative answers to these questions can coexist
in a peaceful, friendly, and supportive international environment. Insofar as
we see attempts to realize national institutional ideals different from our
own as neither evil nor deluded (and need not fear from them violence
against our domestic values and institutions), we have no good reason to
resist such attempts. We could come to respect, and even learn from, the
variety of national regimes existing beyond our borders. At least the mere
fact that people of another society live under social institutions that are
different from those we favor gives us no right at all to interfere in their
affairs.

AN OBJECTION

It will certainly be said against my plea for international pluralism that
there is very good reason for finding the opponents' values intolerable and
for denying that any intelligent and knowledgeable person of good will
could possibly advocate these values. The reason is our historical experience
with the adherents of those values, which features an abundance of horrendous
crimes committed by the other side. Even a cursory look at our opponents'
record of political repression or economic exploitation should convince any
reasonable person that we must not compromise our values to the point of
accepting our opponents' right to exist, as this would amount to a wholesale
betrayal of our most elementary commitments to humanity and decency.

But the fact that such a case could be made (and I will not deny this) against one or both main forms of regime does not show that any acceptable global order would have to exclude regimes of this sort. What our historical experience shows is how capitalist and socialist governments design global institutions and how these governments behave (within and outside their borders) *in the context of a modus vivendi framework*. But this may teach us very little about how capitalist and socialist governments would design global institutions and how these governments would behave if surviving and prevailing were no longer at issue. Let us at least entertain the thought that the horrors of this world are not, or at least not primarily, the horrors of capitalism or socialism per se, but are the horrors of an inconstant modus vivendi among deeply hostile governments, each fearing the eventual destruction of its values.

Whether a value-based global order is attainable, and what it might look like, is then, in my view, still an open question. Such a global order has never yet been tried, as existing agreements are essentially based upon strategic bargaining. Although the parties in a modus vivendi often *use* appeal to values (in order to justify their own conduct to those committed to the same or similar values, or in order to discredit and condemn the conduct of opponents), these parties do not engage each other in a serious ethical discourse about the institutions that ideally *ought* to regulate their interactions.

Obviously, the attempt to devise value-based global institutions through such an international ethical discourse cannot be made monologically. Hence, I cannot prove that this attempt would succeed. What can be shown is purely negative; namely, the extent to which the absence of peace and justice in the world today might be explainable merely in terms of tendencies endemic to an intergovernmental modus vivendi framework, without reference to the *content* of the competing value clusters. In this chapter, I cannot provide the detailed political analysis that might show this, but must settle for a brief, illustrative outline.

The modus vivendi analysis of the status quo explains the absence of genuine peace by viewing us as trapped within a vicious cycle. The very fact that governments fear and distrust each other gives them very good reason for such fear and distrust. This is bad news because it is quite difficult to break out of such a circle. But the point can also be recast in an optimistic light. Just as a climate of mutual fear and distrust makes it more rational to fear others and distrust them, so a climate of mutual trust and confidence makes it more rational to have trust and confidence in others. Small increases in the mutual assurance afforded by firm value-based institutional fixed points will lead to much greater increases in overall mutual assurance.[14] Being caught in a circle of fear and distrust does not then show that the parties are inherently untrustworthy or that their values are intrinsically so irreconcilably opposed that institutions based on value overlap are out of the question. Rather, untrustworthiness is engendered, quite predictably, by the situation the participants perceive themselves to be in (and therefore really *are* in), a situation in which each participant is preoccupied with ensuring that its values shall survive and prevail.

Before addressing the problem of justice more at length, let me recapitulate the relevant hypothesis: Governments are engaged in a competition that is regulated by whatever institutions the main adversaries find it advantageous to agree upon, or to acquiesce in, from time to time. Yet governments also see their rivalry, on a deeper level, as *unlimited.* No society's values, institutions, or form of life is beyond the threat of violent subversion by existing enemies outside the national territory. At bottom, international relations are a struggle to the death.

1. There are no realistic prospects for a world state. No national government can come to rule the world without a global war. The strongest governments will not allow the creation of independent effective mechanisms of adjudication and enforcement. Given the aversion of strong governments to risk (their greater concern for surviving than for prevailing), it would be irrational to accept powerful organs of world government, which, although certain to decrease each government's power, could affect each government's security in either direction. This is true in a world of competing interests. But it is even more true in a world of disparate values, in which each government must fear that its central organs might come to be dominated by those who believe that its domestic institutions and national form of life *ought* to be eradicated.[15]

To be sure, weaker governments may want central mechanisms of adjudication and enforcement—and may be forced to submit unilaterally to such mechanisms. But the strongest ones cannot be forced and will not submit. Of course, they may agree to dependent central mechanisms, which require unanimity or lack enforcement power of their own or both. But such mechanisms will not be effective because they are impotent in regard to the principal problem: They cannot bring the competition among the major powers firmly under the rule of law.

2. Governments will generally not honor individual provisions of an ongoing modus vivendi when the net benefit of noncompliance is substantial; and they understand and expect as much from one another. As there is no mutual trust and no other assurance of future compliance (for example, through effective mechanisms of adjudication and enforcement), each government must assume that others may "reinterpret," violate, renegotiate, or abrogate international laws and treaties when this is in their best interest (taking account of propaganda and credibility costs, and so on). Given this assumption about others, each government will itself act in this fashion. This seems permissible because international laws and treaties reflect only self-interested bargaining (have no inherent ethical standing) and because most other governments take the same attitude and surely do not rely on one another's good faith. In addition, being a scofflaw also seems *necessary* because governments that allow themselves to be seriously hampered by imprudent respect for the official rules of the game run a grave risk of being taken advantage of by others and of endangering the long-term survival of

themselves and their values. International laws and treaties can therefore furnish only a weak prudential restraint upon government conduct, and their infringement or abrogation is then much more likely than violations of domestic laws, which are backed by shared ultimate values (and more effective sanctions).[16]

The prevalent scofflaw attitude engenders wars, as governments take advantage of perceived opportunities to gain through (illegal) aggression, preempt perceived threats of (illegal) aggression, and punish perceived violations of international laws or treaties. This attitude also fosters a permanent climate of tension and insecurity, as governments must always reckon with noncompliance by others and thus can never fully take advantage of the freedom of action they might have, if adherence to international laws and treaties could be taken for granted. No declaration of neutrality, peace treaty, or nonaggression pact, for example, can relieve a government of the fear of foreign military attack.

3. The enduring climate of insecurity and hostility is aggravated by two additional tendencies. The (bargaining) power of governments within a modus vivendi framework is mainly a function of the distribution of military strength (the comparative unacceptability of war), with economic strength playing an important—partly subsidiary, partly independent—role. Any government whose military strength is greater than its economic strength (each relative to other governments) will enjoy increased bargaining power during periods of heightened tension, due to the greater importance of military (in comparison to economic) strength. A period of crisis, for example, will make it easier for a military giant to exact concessions from an economically strong but militarily weak ally. Of course, governments whose relative economic strength is greater than their relative military strength may much prefer a more relaxed global environment; but this preference is of little moment insofar as it is very much easier to fuel than to reduce international tension.

The tendency toward tension is further strengthened by each government's interest in increasing its support from its own population, which will enhance the government's international bargaining power. Vilifying opponents and staging crises are methods of increasing domestic support by exploiting the predictable tendency of populations "to rally around the flag" in response to a heightened sense of insecurity. Obviously, a government may be tempted to employ such methods in the interest of less patriotic purposes as well— for example, to improve its chances for reelection or to consolidate its position at home. Although the motives for fueling such crises arise domestically, the opportunity to do so depends on the hostility endemic to current international relations.

4. In a modus vivendi among hostile powers, the pressures toward strategic (amoral) government conduct are overwhelming. Even if politicians are racing *for* a value system, they cannot allow themselves to be hampered by these values during the race. Politicians must leave their values behind when they enter the political arena, where surviving and prevailing ("national security")

take precedence over all else. Thus, values are unlikely to play much of a genuine (as opposed to a propagandistic) role in the conduct of foreign policy and in the emergence of international institutions (through explicit or tacit bargaining).[17]

Instead, the terms of an intergovernmental modus vivendi will tend toward two analogues of the *cuius regio eius religio* settlement. First, these terms will embody little concern for how persons are treated within their own society. Each government's interest in controlling some particular matter within its own territory normally vastly outweighs its interest in influencing how the same matter is dealt with abroad.[18] Perhaps the value commitments on both sides would favor clear, internationally supervised rules against government abuse. But because it is unpredictable how such rules would affect the balance of power, risk-averse players are unlikely to create effective, independent mechanisms for determining human rights violations in an authoritative way. Nor will risk-averse players make unilateral sacrifices for human rights. Given the exigencies of the competition, each government must be extremely concerned with its own and its allies' international (bargaining) power, which depends to a significant extent upon the government's strength at home. The government may then have to use, and support its allies when they use, repressive measures (such as secrecy, disinformation, surveillance, infiltration, intimidation, and worse) to stifle domestic dissent and to maximize domestic control.[19]

Second, the terms of an intergovernmental modus vivendi are likely to include an understanding that great powers have a special claim to regions that for geographic or economic reasons are more important to their security than to that of any other great power. Within its sphere of influence, a great power may force weak states to change their government or political system, to accept (or "request") foreign military advisers and bases, to "open up" economically (to allow imports, private borrowing abroad, foreign appropriation of resources and productive facilities), and so forth—and all this without serious interference from other powers. Such an understanding is again mutually advantageous for risk-averse players.

The nationalist self-concern prevalent in a modus vivendi among governments preoccupied with their competition for power will also engender disregard for the poorest and strategically least significant societies and regions. No government will show much unilateral concern for foreigners, as this would tend to weaken its own bargaining position. And governments are unlikely to agree to incorporate such concern into the shared institutional scheme; being risk-averse, each will be reluctant to accept even a distribution of burdens that seems to weaken itself no more than it weakens its relevant competitors.

This concludes my outline of how some of the less appealing facts of our contemporary world might be explainable, in part, in terms of tendencies endemic to an intergovernmental modus vivendi framework. Even if not all these tendencies will always be strong or dominant, they do add up to a firm expectation regarding a global order that primarily reflects the common interests of, and bargains among, deeply hostile governments. So long as this order persists, our world will be pervaded by violence (and the threat and danger of violence), political repression, and extreme poverty of strategically worthless populations. This is not to deny that values sometimes do have a real impact upon foreign policy and upon international institutions (over and above the propagandistic employment of values to justify self-interested conduct). It is enough that the systemic explanation is approximately true, that the current mode of coexistence is *essentially* a modus vivendi, that it engenders *roughly* the tendencies I have outlined, and that these tendencies account for a good deal of current human misery.

In holding this view, I am unimpressed by all the documents that governments have produced and signed since the end of World War II. I see good reasons for holding governments to such documents by insisting on their prescriptive force, on their status as international law. It is important to raise the costs of noncompliance. But it would be a mistake, within the context of a purely descriptive inquiry into the actual terms of international relations, to take these documents as unassailable evidence. Governments violate their international obligations all the time and expect such violations from one another. To be sure, governments protest and "deplore" their opponents' violations, but continue business as usual and especially continue signing agreements with governments who have violated other agreements. This supports the modus vivendi explanation. Governments see their agreements as reciprocal exchanges of prudential restraints backed by (for example, propagandistic) sanctions, to which governments expose themselves in the event of noncompliance. It is fully understood that any government will break any agreement when the net benefit of doing so is substantial. But such agreements have great merit nevertheless; they serve to coordinate expectations and to make certain future events less likely or less frequent or both. In this capacity, international instruments play an important stabilizing role within an ongoing modus vivendi.

This view of international instruments is supported by the fact that the considerations determining a government's acceptance of some treaty or convention tend to be overwhelmingly prudential. Whether the United States will sign the Genocide Convention or the USSR the Final Act of the CSCE has little to do with whether they agree with the documents' content and much more to do with whether each thinks it can thereby strengthen its relative position.

But the most convincing evidence in favor of the modus vivendi account lies beyond the pompous solemnity of international documents in what the world is really like. Millions perish annually in the struggle over the distribution of power: in wars, civil wars, and campaigns of repression and insurrection, often supported from abroad and involving organized massacres, disappearances, and torture. Countless children die every year from malnutrition and easily curable diseases, while roughly a trillion dollars are spent on "defense" worldwide. Up to one-fifth of humankind spend their entire lives in poverty and on the edge of starvation—politically impotent, malnourished, and without reserves in the event of even a minor natural or social misfortune. Given their pervasiveness, such horrors cannot be blamed upon a few powerful actors who have perverse values or none at all. Rather, I submit, these horrors are engendered in large part by the reigning modus vivendi framework, within which the fear for one's security and that of one's values is paramount.

CONCLUSION

To the extent that my analysis of current international relations as an intergovernmental modus vivendi is successful, it will provide a systemic explanation of the sordid realities just sketched. Now one might have thought that such an explanation tends to condone prevalent government conduct and thus lets politicians off the hook too easily. But this is not so. The account I have sketched would merely reconceive our political task and responsibilities. Even if violence and injustice cannot be much alleviated within the ongoing modus vivendi, that framework itself can, and ought to be, transcended in the direction of a global order based upon some shared ultimate values.

So on my view as well, governments and politicians bear a special responsibility for the injustice and (actual and potential) violence that permeate our social world today. But I see politicians as primarily responsible not toward an existing global order, which they all too often violate, but toward a possible future order, which they lack the will and vision to help bring into existence. This is the ultimate crime against peace and justice because it perpetuates the modus vivendi character of international relations, which is incompatible with genuine peace and justice, however conceived.

This crime is especially serious, given that it would be so very easy to make progress. I am not raising extravagant demands of the kind Nielsen presents. What I envision is the gradual establishment, one by one, of firm value-based institutional fixed points that stand above ordinary negotiation and bargaining and are immune to shifts in the power, interests, and opportunities of governments. Even institutions that once began as negotiated bargains could slowly and undramatically develop into such fixed points. This could happen through the gradually escalating willingness on the part of different governments to make genuine sacrifices: to honor a law or agreement even when this goes against the government's interests when all things are considered. However, over and over again, governments create the opposite precedent: ignore laws, charters, treaties, and declarations that they had once inaugurated with great shows of commitment and thereby reinforce the dominant conception of international relations as amoral. A case in point might be the condemnation of war crimes, which, at Nuremberg, were said to shock the conscience of humankind. The relevant powers have since been willing, for the sake of trivial gains (if any), to ignore the war-crimes statutes the same powers formulated in situations where their own military actions or those of their allies were at stake. Through such conduct, politicians subvert the very idea that international documents couched in the language of fundamental law and supreme morality could ever be anything more than temporary bargains reinforced by propaganda penalties.

Value-based institutional fixed points might also develop, more formally, through an international ethical dialogue specifically set up for the purpose of identifying and extending shared value commitments that might guide the appraisal and gradual reform of the present global order. Just as teams of nuclear-weapons experts are asked to negotiate a draft agreement on arms control, so teams of outstanding political philosophers and international lawyers might be asked to develop mutually acceptable ideas toward a just world order. At least in the beginning (before much mutual confidence has been built up), the agreements emerging from such a high-level ethical dialogue will have to affect the participant states roughly equally, so as to minimize the strains of commitment. However, this does not mean that the discourse must aim for agreements that are mutually advantageous (as negotiations of the arms-control type do). Rather, they might (and perhaps better) be mutually *dis*advantageous, imposing, for the sake of a shared ethical concern, roughly equal burdens upon the participant states (so as to avoid significant risks to either side's bargaining position). An example might be the creation and funding of an independent organization whose mandate is to promote the economic development of the world's poorest countries and regions (by combating malnutrition, illiteracy, disease, and economic dependence). Such tangible concern for the world's most disadvantaged populations could accommodate central values of the world's states while also demonstrating their willingness to give increasing weight to values at the expense of concern for the preservation and expansion of national power.[20]

No, I am not proposing that philosophers should be kings. The preeminent task is, on the contrary, to devise (a gradual transition toward) just global institutions that will maintain a stable peace even among societies whose political leaders are *not* philosophers. What I propose is only that politicians should involve philosophers and international lawyers in the design of such a value-based global order (and in the transition to it), which in any case would have to be ratified through the political process of each participant state.

NOTES

Many thanks to Bruce Ackerman and to my colleagues at the University of Maryland Center for Philosophy and Public Policy for valuable suggestions and criticisms.

1. His ideal of a global state would, Nielsen thinks, require the withering away of capitalism and perhaps the worldwide spread of democratic socialism. Nevertheless, persons would still be allowed to have and advocate distinct conceptions of alternative socioeconomic orders—for example, laissez-faire capitalism, welfare-state capitalism, state socialism, and libertarian socialism.

2. This dogma—prefigured in Aquinas, Dante, Marsilius, and Bodin—is most fully stated in Thomas Hobbes, *Leviathan* (Harmondsworth: Penguin, 1981/1651), especially in Chapters 14, 26, and 29. For Immanuel Kant's statements of the point,

see *Theory and Practice* 291&299, and *Metaphysics of Morals* 319 (in volumes 8 and 6 of the Prussian Academy Edition). The dogma maintained its hold well into the twentieth century, when the dogma declined together with the Austinian conception of jurisprudence. Cp. Geoffrey Marshall, *Parliamentary Sovereignty and the Commonwealth* (Oxford: Oxford University Press, 1957), Part 1; S. I. Benn and R. S. Peters, *Social Principles and the Democratic State* (London: Allen and Unwin, 1959), Chapters 3 and 12; and H.L.A. Hart, *The Concept of Law* (Oxford: Oxford University Press, 1961).

Quite apart from the (anachronistic) historical objection offered in the text, I also believe that this reasoning is theoretically flawed and should never have been taken so seriously. Even the most unified scheme of supreme authority, involving a monarchical sovereign, does not provide a complete decision mechanism. It is still possible for disputes to arise about whether this is the king or an impostor, whether yesterday's king has transferred authority, or is dead (or insane); or, if he is dead, who his successor is. A "logically" complete decision mechanism is a mirage. If that were what it takes, then in principle we could not transcend the state of nature.

3. The U.S. Supreme Court, for example, is *not* empowered to review the application of state law.

4. Nielsen's complaint about current international law is, in standard Hobbesian fashion, that it is "without teeth."

5. Cf. Hobbes, *Leviathan*, Chapters 13 and 17, for the relevant passages.

6. In employing this contrast, I draw inspiration and support from the two latest articles by John Rawls: "Justice as Fairness: Political not Metaphysical," *Philosophy and Public Affairs* 14, no. 3 (Summer 1985):223–251; and, in particular: "The Idea of an Overlapping Consensus," *Oxford Journal of Legal Studies* 7 (1987):1–25. However, Rawls may well disagree with how I develop the contrast between the two institutional models and especially with my use of this contrast in response to international (rather than domestic) diversity of interests and values.

7. Consider here a strengthened version of the U.N. Security Council.

8. In a sense, Nielsen also wants to forge an international political consensus from shared values (although he seeks to do this monologically). His conception of (global) justice starts from a shared value—supposedly accepted by almost everyone, including Nozick, Hayek, Friedman, Rawls, Walzer, and MacIntyre—namely, the belief in *moral equality*—that the life of everyone matters and matters equally. From this uncontroversial premise we can, "if we are thinking clearly," derive that there ought to be "an equality of condition for everyone alike," "the fullest satisfaction of needs," "the most extensive autonomy for everyone," and "the fullest human flourishing possible for all human beings." The problems with this proposal are, I trust, obvious.

9. It is unclear whether—in Nielsen's religiously inspired conception of it—ideal theory is subject to any constraints at all. In ideal theory Nielsen can, for example, simply "postulate . . . that people would not revolt" within his preferred world state. Having helped himself to such powers of stipulation, Nielsen is naturally driven to wonder whether a world state with teeth is ideal enough; after all, a "world of democratic socialist nation-states" might be even better, if they "would stand in fraternal peaceful relations with each other and would surely mutually cooperate." But then, "if we were gods," we might do better still, for "the anarchists are surely right in thinking that it would be a good thing if we could get along without a state, any state at all." Indeed, why not paradise?

10. Yes, Nielsen demands this, too. Within his cantonal world state, "such entities as the USSR and the United States," rather than have "the status of bloated, ungainly cantons," are to be broken up into "significant cultural units."

11. Nielsen, with his demand for worldwide democratic socialism, does not stand alone in this regard: Michael Doyle, "Kant, Liberal Legacies, and Foreign Affairs," *Philosophy and Public Affairs* 12 (1983), advocates a world of liberal states, defined as democracies with "market and private property economies" (212, cp. 208). Although Nielsen does not worry about how his ideal might come about, Doyle invokes the increasing number of capitalist democracies during the past two centuries, from which he extrapolates that all states will be "liberal" by the year 2113 (p. 352). The worthy political scientist neglects to calculate an analogous projection based on the proliferation of *socialist* states, which, by the same argument, are similarly destined to cover the world.

12. Given this assumption, it is not surprising that the *terms* of the current intergovernmental modus vivendi trace a dynamic equilibrium of "free" (explicit and tacit) bargaining that is informed by each government's quest to maximize its power and thus is largely insensitive to ethical considerations of any kind. I will expand upon this point in the next section.

13. This is the next best thing to a piece of "perfect technology of justice" that would make it permanently impossible for values to be altered or extinguished by force (cf. Bruce Ackerman, *Justice and the Liberal State* [New Haven, Conn.: Yale University Press, 1980], especially p. 82). Note that such an analogue to a perfect technology of justice would not only make it impossible to destroy the values others hold—it would also cancel the most important reason for wanting to do so in the first place: the fear that *they* may seek to destroy *our* values.

14. This multiplier effect can be illustrated as follows:

A thinks that B is less inclined to seek to destroy A's values;
hence A has less reason to fear that B may try to destroy A's values;
hence A has less reason to seek to destroy B's values;
hence B has less reason to fear that A may try to destroy B's values;
hence B has less reason to seek to destroy A's values;
hence A has even less reason to fear that B may try to destroy A's values.

And so forth.

15. Hobbes clearly appreciated how disparity of values, even more than competing material interests, may block acceptance of a central supreme authority. Vast stretches of the *Leviathan* (in Parts III and IV) are devoted to showing, through scriptural exegesis, that good Christians ought to accept and obey the sovereign even when he commands acts and observances Christians consider blasphemous.

16. The dominant attitude toward international laws and treaties is then like the prevalent domestic attitude toward contracts with penalty clauses or perhaps like that toward parking regulations. Many accept that decisions about compliance may be made on the basis of a self-interested calculation of (probability-weighted) costs and benefits. This claim is evidently compatible with the fact that some treaties (covering copyrights, patents, postal cooperation, and such) are rarely or never violated. In these matters, the strains of commitment are minimal, and weak prudential restraints therefore are fully sufficient.

Note also that my concern here is with the current *global* institutional framework. In some local contexts, such as Western Europe, international relations may begin to acquire a value-based character.

17. Evidently, I am not urging a unilaterally "moralistic" foreign policy, as opposed to a "realistic" one (in Morgenthau's sense). Rather, my point is this: Within a modus vivendi framework, foreign policy will always be realistic in substance (although it also may be moralistic in rhetoric). If we want to see our values embedded in

international institutions and in our government's conduct of foreign affairs, then we must transcend the modus vivendi framework within which concern with the survival and prevailing of national constitutions is paramount. In the absence of perfect technologies, this requires a shared sense of mutual tolerance and an effort to base global institutions upon an overlap in ultimate values rather than upon the shifting balance of bargaining power among parties that consider themselves ultimately to have nothing in common.

As will be discussed in the next section, achieving such a transition requires states to take moral steps that certainly in the beginning must be acceptable from a prudential standpoint. Here a state might, for example, unilaterally signal its willingness to contribute to the transition to a value-based order by designing foreign policies that (without endangering its own survival and security) demonstrate its willingness to forego advantages that would be incompatible with a just global order.

18. This reinforces the global background convention mentioned previously.

19. Again, governments will be tempted to employ these methods in the interest of less patriotic, purely domestic purposes, and the opportunity to do so depends on the hostility and insecurity endemic to current international relations.

20. The transition to value-based institutional fixed points might be stabilized through agreement to create arbitration mechanisms that are independent of any of the participants and firmly committed to the transformation process itself, and thus can counterbalance the strains of the transition. As the strength of independent forces increases, they would add weight to the reasons in favor of continued compliance and thus would tend to allay fears of noncompliance on the part of others. On the other hand, creation of such independent forces may also appear risky to the protagonists, and thus it is of some importance that progress is possible without them.

About the Editor and Contributors

William Aiken, associate professor of philosophy at Chatham College, is the co-editor, with Hugh La Follette, of *World Hunger and Moral Obligation* (1977).

Charles R. Beitz is associate professor of political science at Swarthmore College. In addition to numerous essays, he wrote *Political Theory and International Relations* (1979) and is one of the editors of *Philosophy and Public Affairs.*

Norman Bowie is professor of philosophy and director of the Center for the Study of Values at the University of Delaware. He is the author or editor of numerous books and articles, including *Equal Opportunity* (Westview, 1988) and (with Tom L. Beauchamp) *Ethical Theory and Business,* 3d ed. (1988).

Peter French is Lennox Professor of Humanities at Trinity University. In addition to being co-editor of *Midwest Studies in Philosophy,* he has written or edited many books and articles, including *Collective and Corporate Responsibility* (1984).

Robert K. Fullinwider, research associate at the Center for Philosophy and Public Policy, University of Maryland, has written numerous essays and the book *The Reverse Discrimination Controversy: A Moral and Legal Analysis* (1980).

David Gauthier is professor of philosophy at the University of Pittsburgh. His works include *The Logic of Leviathan* (1969) and *Morals by Agreement* (1987).

Alan H. Goldman, professor of philosophy at the University of Miami, has written extensively in the area of social and political philosophy. He is the author of *The Moral Foundations of Professional Ethics* (1980).

Douglas P. Lackey is professor of philosophy at Baruch College and the Graduate Center, City University of New York. His book *Moral Principles and Nuclear Weapons* (1984) is part of his extensive work on the ethics of deterrence.

Steven Luper-Foy is associate professor and chair of the Department of Philosophy at Trinity University. He is editor of *The Possibility of Knowledge* (1987) and guest editor of an issue of *Synthese* covering the internalism/externalism controversy in epistemology.

Eric Mack is associate professor of philosophy, Newcomb College, and fellow at the Murphy Institute for Political Economy, Tulane University. He has published many essays in social and political philosophy and edited Herbert Spencer's *The Man Versus the State.*

Arne Naess is professor emeritus of philosophy and member of the Council for Environmental Studies at the University of Oslo. He has written extensively on environmental ethics.

Kai Nielsen, professor of philosophy at the University of Calgary, is an editor of *The Canadian Journal of Philosophy* and author of several books, including *Ethics Without God* (1973) and *Marxism and the Moral Point of View* (forthcoming, 1988).

Onora O'Neill, professor of philosophy at the University of Essex, is the author of *Acting on Principle* (1975) and *Faces of Hunger* (1987).

Thomas Pogge is assistant professor of philosophy at Columbia University and Rockefeller Resident Fellow at the Center for Philosophy and Public Policy, University of Maryland. He has written essays in the area of social and political philosophy.

Bernard E. Rollin is professor of philosophy and director of Bioethical Planning at Colorado State University. He has written extensively in the area of animal ethics.

Michael Walzer, professor of social science at the Institute for Advanced Study, has written several books, including *Just and Unjust Wars* (1977), and *Spheres of Justice* (1983).

Index

International Monetary Fund, 133
International pluralism, 292ff.
International Telephone and Telegraph (ITT), 98
International Union for the Conservation of Nature and Natural Resources, 147–148
Intervention, humanitarian, 174–179
Intervention, foreign. *See* Counterintervention, Walzer on; Nonintervention; *under* United Nations
Ireland, 103, 244
Israel, 105, 128, 152, 238, 254, 264
Italy, 251ff., 267
ITT. *See* International Telephone and Telegraph

Jackson, Tony, 82(n1)
Japan, 103, 110, 139
and innovation, 164
Jefferson, Thomas, 248, 253
Jesus, 90
Johnson, Robert H., 194(n4)
Jus in bello, 31

Kahin, G. M., 180(n14), 180(n17)
Kahn, Herman, 224
Kant, Immanuel, ix, 1, 84, 234
and absolute sovereignty, 284
and animals, 142
and benevolence, 85–88
and boundaries, 12
and egalitarianism, 12–13
and equity of resources, 21
and exchange, 108–109
and global tyranny, 5
and ideal theory, 53(n63)
on international justice, 31, 35
and intrinsic value, 127
on justice, 10–14, 95
and large sets of liberties, 83(n3)
and universalizability, 79, 118
on using people as a mere means, 13–14, 17
and utilitarianism, 15
Katangan controversy, 168n
Katz, Robert, 258(n8)
Katzenstein, Peter J., 51(n35)
Kaufmann, William, 225
Kavka, Gregory S., 211–214, 229

Kavka's Case, 211–214, 218
Kelman, Herbert, 53(n66)
Kennedy, John, 173, 183, 225
Keohane, Robert O., 52(n37), 52(n44)
Korea, 172, 264
Korean War, 159, 173
Kossuth, Lajos, 166
Krauthammer, Charles, 195(n13)

Lackey, Douglas P., 206, 222, 236(n1), 236(n5), 236(n6), 305
La Feber, Walter, 180(n21)
Lappe, Frances Moore, 96(n15)
Latin America, 35, 190
Law of nations, 7, 30, 51(n17), 37, 276, 285, 296ff.
Leahey, T., 142(n5)
Lebanon, 244
Legalist paradigm, 157–161, 165
defined, 160–161
revised, 151, 166, 179
Legitimate interference, 2–3, 6, 8, 19, 21–22
Leibniz, Gottfried, 232
Leiken, Robert S., 195(n19)
Lenin, Nikolai, 159, 183
Leopold, Aldo, 142(n2), 142(n7)
Levine, Andrew, 282(n22), 282(n25)
Lewis, John W., 180(n14), 180(n17)
Libertarianism, 1, 3, 10
and egalitarianism, 17, 20
and justice, 17–20
and legitimate cooperation, 19, 20, 21, 71–77, 81
and rights, 71–75, 76–77, 80–81, 85, 94–95
and socialism, 301(n1)
and universal obligations, 80
Liberty principle, 7, 8, 15, 29, 83(n3)
Libya, 105
Locke, John, 18, 22(n8), 60, 252
Lockean proviso, 18, 19, 33, 60
Lockheed, 98
Lodge, Henry C., 175
Loshak, David, 181(n25)
Louis XIV, 155
Luban, David, 274, 280(n1), 282(n19)
Luper-Foy, Steven, 24(n39), 112, 304
Lyons, David, 24(n48)

Machiavelli, Niccolò, ix, 1, 240